DESIGN
ELEMENTS

First published in the United States of America by
Rockport Publishers, a member of
Quayside Publishing Group
100 Cummings Center
Suite 406-L
Beverly, Massachusetts 01915-6101
Telephone: (978) 282-9590
Fax: (978) 283-2742
www.rockpub.com
Visit RockPaperInk.com to share your opinions,
creations, and passion for design.

Originally found under the following Cataloging
Samara, Timothy.
    Design elements : a graphic style manual :
understanding the rules and knowing when to
 break them / Timothy Samara.
         p. cm.
    ISBN-13: 978-1-59253-261-2 (flexibind)
    ISBN-10: 1-59253-261-6 (flexibind)
    1. Graphic design (Typography) 2. Layout
(Printing) I. Title.
  Z246 .S225
  686.2'2—dc22
  2006019038
                                        CIP

ISBN: 978-1-59253-927-7
Digital edition published in 2014
eISBN: 978-1-62788-057-2

10 9 8 7 6 5 4 3 2 1

Cover and text design
Timothy Samara, New York

Printed in China

Rockport Publishers
100 Cummings Center, Suite 406L
Beverly, MA 01915

rockpub.com • rockpaperink.com

TIMOTHY SAMARA

DESIGN ELEMENTS

Understanding the rules and knowing when to break them

SECOND EDITION
UPDATED + EXPANDED

A graphic designer is a communicator: someone who takes ideas and gives them visual form so that others can understand them.

WHAT IS GRAPHIC DESIGN?

Logo for a financial services company
LSD SPAIN

Logo for a food bank
NAROSKA DESIGN
GERMANY

Branding and wayfinding for a wine merchant **PARALLAX** AUSTRALIA

Book cover with transparent jacket
LABORATÓRIO SECRETO BRAZIL

The designer uses imagery, symbols, type, color, and materials—whether printed or on-screen—to represent the ideas that must be conveyed; and to organize them into a unified experience that is intended to evoke a particular response.

While more or less confined to the creation of typefaces and books from the Middle Ages until the Industrial Revolution of the late 1700s and early 1800s, design expanded into advertising, periodicals, signage, posters, and ephemera with the appearance of a new, consumer marketplace. The term "graphic design" itself appeared more recently (attributed to W. A. Dwiggins, an American illustrator and book designer, in 1922, to describe his particular activities). The formal study of design as an independent discipline didn't come about until the 1920s, and the term entered into wide usage only after World War II.

In contrast to other disciplines in the visual arts, graphic design's purpose is typically defined by a client—it's a service paid for by a company or other organization—rather than generated from within the designer. Although artistic creation historically had been commissioned by patrons, it wasn't until the 1830s that the mystique of the bohemian painter as "expresser of self" arose and, consequently, a marked distinction between fine and commercial art. Designers encouraged this distinction for philosophical, as well as strategic, reasons, especially as they began to seek recognition for design as a profession that could add tremendous value to corporate endeavors.

In the fifty-odd years since, the graphic designer has been touted as everything from visual strategist to cultural arbiter—and, since the mid 1970s, as an "author" as well—shaping not only the corporate

Invitation to a marketing event
STUDIO NEWWORK UNITED STATES

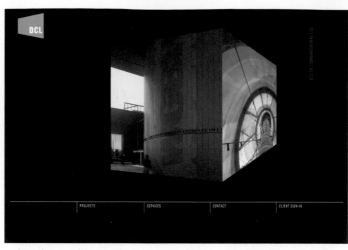

Website for an architecture firm POULIN+MORRIS UNITED STATES

bottom line through clever visual manipulation of a brand-hungry public, but also the larger visual language of the postmodern environment. All these functions are important to graphic design ... but, lest we forget the simplicity of the designer's true nature, let us return to what a graphic designer does. A graphic designer assimilates verbal concepts and gives them form.

This "giving form" is a discipline that integrates an enormous amount of knowledge and skill with intuition, creatively applied in different ways as the designer confronts the variables of each new project.

A designer must understand semiotics—the processes and relationships inherent in perception and interpretation of meaning through visual and verbal material. He or she must have expertise in the flow of information—instructional strategies, data representation, legibility and usability, cognitive ordering, and hierarchic problem solving—extending into typography, the mechanics of alphabet design, and reading. To design requires analytical and technical mastery of image making—how shapes, colors, and textures work to depict ideas, achieve aesthetic cohesion and dynamism and signify higher-order concepts while evoking a strong emotional response.

Further, a designer must be more than casually familiar with psychology and history, both with respect to cultural narratives, symbolism, and ritualized experiences, as well as to more commercial, consumer-based impulses and responses (what is often referred to as *marketing*). Last, but certainly not least, a designer must have great facility with—and more often, in-depth, specialized knowledge of—multiple technologies needed to implement the designed solution: printing media and techniques, film and video, digital programming, industrial processes, architectural fabrication, and so on.

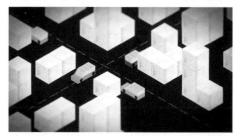

Animated motion sequence ONLAB GERMANY

To understand the meaning of design is … to understand the part form and content play … and to realize that design is also commentary, opinion, a point of view, and social responsibility. To design is much more than simply to assemble, to order, or even to edit; it is to add value and meaning, to illuminate, to simplify, to clarify, to modify, to dignify, to dramatize, to persuade, and perhaps even to amuse.

Design is both a verb and a noun. It is the beginning as well as the end, the process and product of imagination.

PAUL RAND/GRAPHIC DESIGNER/*From his book* Design, Form, and Chaos. *Yale University Press: New Haven, 1993*

But graphic design is greater than just the various aspects that comprise it. Together, they establish a totality of tangible, and often intangible, experiences. A designer is responsible for the intellectual and emotional vitality of the experience he or she visits upon the audience, and his or her task is to elevate it above the banality of literal transmission or the confusing self-indulgent egoism of mere eye candy. And yet, beauty is a function, after all, of any relevant visual message. Just as prose can be dull or straightforward or well edited and lyrical, so too can a utilitarian object be designed to be more than just simply what it is. "If function is important to the intellect," writes respected Swiss designer Willi Kunz, in his book, *Typography: Macro- and Micro-Aesthetics*, "then form is important to the emotions… Our day-to-day life is enriched or degraded by our environment."

The focus of this book is on these formal, or visual, aspects of graphic design and, implicitly, their relevance for the messages to be created using them. It's a kind of user manual for creating what is understood to be strong design, and empowering readers to effectively—and skillfully—harness their creativity to meet the challenges that a designer must meet every day.

Brochure page spread for an energy company COBRA NORWAY

TWENTY RULES FOR MAKING GOOD DESIGN

Event poster SANG ZHANG/PARSONS SCHOOL OF DESIGN UNITED STATES

Rules can be broken— but never ignored.

DAVID JURY/TYPOGRAPHER/
From his book About Face: Reviving the Rules of Typography *RotoVision, London, 1996.*

When people talk about "good" or "bad" design, they're referring to notions of quality that they've picked up from education and experience, and often from the experience of thousands of designers and critics before them. Sometimes, these notions are aesthetic—"asymmetry is more beautiful than symmetry," for example, or "a neutral typeface is all you need"— and sometimes strictly functional—for example, "don't reverse a serif typeface from a solid background if it's less than 10 points in size, because it'll fill in." Both kinds of observation are helpful in avoiding pitfalls and striving to achieve design solutions that aren't hampered by irritating difficulties—to make every design be all that it can be. Every time an attempt is made to cite rules governing what constitutes quality, however, people are bound to get their underwear in a knot: "That's so limiting!" To those people, I'll say this: get over it. Rules exist—especially the ones set forth here—as guidelines, based on accumulated experience from many sources. As such, rules always come with exceptions and can be broken at any time, but not without a consequence. The consequence of breaking one rule might mean reinforcing another, and it might mean true innovation, in the right context—a context in which a revelation occurs that, oddly enough, will establish yet another rule. This is how human creativity works. The importance of knowing which rules are considered important (at least historically), and why, is understanding the possible consequences of breaking them so that something unfortunate doesn't happen out of ignorance. In addition, rules act as guides in helping to build a communal discussion about interpreting and evaluating creative work. If everything is "good," then nothing really can be. Relativism is great, to a point, and then it just gets in the way of honest judgment; the result is a celebration of ubiquitous mediocrity. By no means should any rule, including those that follow, be taken as cosmic law. If you're unconvinced, simply turn to page 296, where breaking every rule in this book is advocated wholeheartedly. But these rules are a starting point, an excellent list of issues to consider while you work. In the end, you will decide how and when to apply the rules, or not, as well as understand the results of either course of action.

HAVE A CONCEPT.

If there's no message, no story, no idea, no narrative, or no useful experience to be had, it's not graphic design. It doesn't matter how amazing the thing is to look at; without a clear message, it's an empty, although beautiful, shell. That's about as complicated as this rule can get. Let's move on.

Zippered plastic bags with evidence stickers package the books in a series of detective novels. The books themselves become artifacts of the crime novels. THOMAS CSANO CANADA

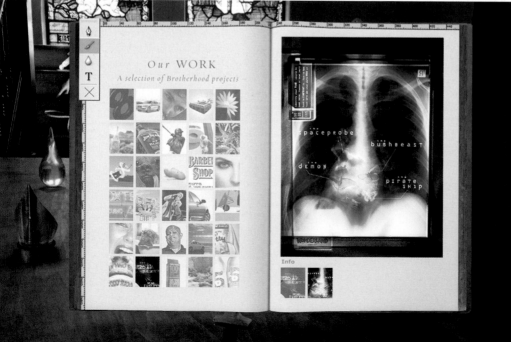

This website for a digital illustration studio foregoes conventional presentation in favor of an appropriately image-based environment designed to evoke the work-space of a medieval scribe— tasked with illuminating manuscripts. The studio's work is presented within the pages of an open book, with navigation appearing as a set of software-program tools at upper left. DISTURBANCE SOUTH AFRICA

COMMUNICATE—
DON'T DECORATE.

Oooh … Neat! But what exactly is it? Form carries meaning, no matter how simple or abstract, and form that's not right for a given message junks it up and confuses. It's great to experiment with images and effects, but anything that doesn't contribute to the composition or meaning is simply eye candy that no longer qualifies as design. Know what each visual element does and why, or choose another with purpose.

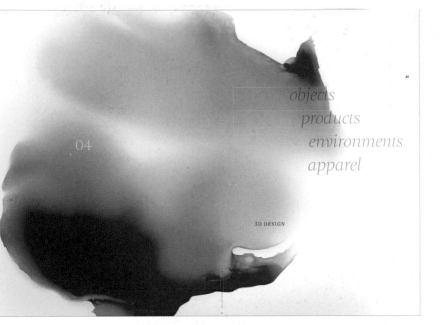

The notion of "blooming" underpins a publication of graduating students' design work; unique abstract ink washes create the sense of unfurling flower petals without being literal. TIMOTHY SAMARA UNITED STATES

BE UNIVERSAL.

A very large audience, not a few people who are "in the know," must interpet what you mean with those shapes, colors, and images. Sure, you get it, and other designers will get it, but ultimately it's the public who must do so. Speak to the world at large; draw upon humanity's shared narratives of form and metaphor and make connections, not boundaries. If you're unsure whether your ideas make sense, show them to someone on the street and find out.

One of the reasons you like this poster so much is that it speaks to our common knowledge so clearly; it feels almost as if it hasn't been designed. A hot-colored circle floating over a cool blue horizon and punctuated by a refreshing yellow field pretty much explains itself. ADAMSMORIOKA UNITED STATES

SPEAK WITH ONE VISUAL VOICE.

Make sure all the elements "talk" to each other. Good design assumes the visual language of a piece—its internal logic—is resolved so that its parts all reinforce each other, not only in shape or weight or placement, but conceptually as well. When one element seems out of place or unrelated, it disconnects from the totality and the message is weakened.

In this set of exhibition collateral, a specific visual language of silhouetted images—all similarly geometric in their shapes, monochromatically colored, and transparent—responds to the type's symmetrical axis with a rhythmic left-to-right positioning. Stroke contrast and graphic details in the serif type unify with the imagery's ornate internal details, while contrasting with its planar quality. GOLDEN COSMOS GERMANY

IF YOU CAN DO IT WITH LESS, THEN DO IT.

This is a riff on the "less is more" theory, not so much an aesthetic dogma now as it is a bit of common sense: the more stuff jammed into a given space, the harder it is to see what needs to be seen. There's a big difference between "complicated" and "complex." True power lies in creativity applied to very little—without sacrificing a rich experience. Adding more than needed is just "gilding the lily."

Exquisite, decisive control of the minimal elements, alignments, and the spaces around and between them creates a dynamic, almost architectural space that is active and three-dimensional ... which is all you really need for a brochure for a contemporary architecture firm. LSD SPAIN

CREATE SPACE— DON'T FILL IT.

Negative (or white) space is critical to good design. It calls attention to content and gives the eyes a resting place. Negative space is just as much a shape in a layout as any other thing. Carve it out and relate it to other elements. A lack of negative space overwhelms an audience, and the result is an oppressive presentation that no one will want to deal with.

From within a confined space enclosed by the visual angles creatd by headline and body text, hands stretch outward to release a symbolic butterfly; the image's message is restated subtly by the compositional space with which it interacts.
LOEWY UNITED KINGDOM

As one of the UK's leading providers of first aid training for the workplace, we offer courses running every week in convenient locations throughout the UK.

Courses include: first aid at work; first aid at work refresher (both HSE approved); basic first aid for the appointed person; on-site training.

To book, call **0870 170 9110** or email ctmarketing@redcross.org.uk
www.redcross.org.uk/faw
Quote ref: 0000000

07

GIVE 'EM THE ONE-TWO PUNCH.

Focus viewers' attention on one important thing first—a big shape, a startling image or type treatment, or a daring color—and then lead them to the less important items in a logical way. This is establishing a "hierarchy"—the order in which you want them to look at the material—and it is essential for access and understanding. Without it, you've already lost the battle.

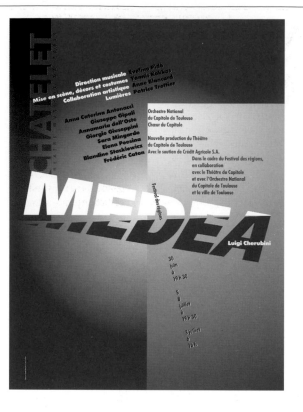

Viewers are likely to see this theater poster's title treatment from thirty strides away, followed by the theater's name and, in a sequence of decreasing contrast, weight, and size, the rest of the information. These type treatments, along with the movement creatd by the title and the supporting shapes, help move the viewer's eyes from most important item to least important. DESIGN RUDI MEYER
FRANCE

08

BEWARE OF SYMMETRY.

As in nature, symmetry can be quite effective, but approach it with extreme caution. Symmetrical layouts easily become static and flat, and they severely limit flexibility in arranging content that doesn't quite fit the symmetrical mold. Symmetry also is often perceived as traditional (not always relevant) and may suggest the designer is lazy and uninventive—as though the format has directed how the material will be arranged.

While the designers of this book, which organizes text and headings relative to both the vertical and horizontal center axes of the pages, retained the appropriate gravitas needed for its academic subject, they nonetheless also counteracted its potentially static quality through the use of extreme scale contrast, transparency, and rotation of text elements.
STUDIO BLUE UNITED STATES

FIGHT THE FLATNESS.

People make a weird assumption about two-dimensional visual stuff, and that is: it's flat! Go figure. Layouts that fail to impart a sense of depth or movement—those in which everything is the same size, weight, color, and perceived distance from everything else—are dull and lifeless. "Without contrast," Paul Rand once said, "you're dead." Fool the viewer into seeing deep space by exploiting changes in size and transparency. Create differences in density and openness by clustering some elements and pushing others apart. Apply color to forms such that some appear to advance and others recede. Convince the viewer that the surface is a window into a bigger, engaging world.

A strong progression of spatial divisions across this page spread (from wide to narrow), together with carefully arranged diagonal relationships among forms and continual contrast in the sizes, values, and proximities of the elements achieves dramatic optical movement and contributes to the perception of varied spatial depths.
STAYNICE NETHERLANDS

PICK COLORS ON PURPOSE.

Don't just grab some colors from out of the air. Know what the colors will do when you combine them and, more important, what they might mean to the audience. Color carries an abundance of psychological and emotional meaning, and this meaning can vary tremendously between cultural groups and even individuals. Color affects visual hierarchy, the legibility of type, and how people make connections between disparate items—sometimes called "color coding"—so choose wisely. Never assume that a certain color, or a combination of colors, is right for a particular job because of convention, either. Blue for financial services, for example, is the standout color cliché of the past fifty years. Choose the right colors, not those that are expected.

The muted rose tones in this fragrance packaging are feminine without being girlish; a slight shift toward brown in the typography creates a subtle, yet rich, interaction. The complementary green-gold—almost a direct complement, but again, slightly off—presents rich contrast and hints at complexity and allure. A10 DESIGN BRAZIL

11
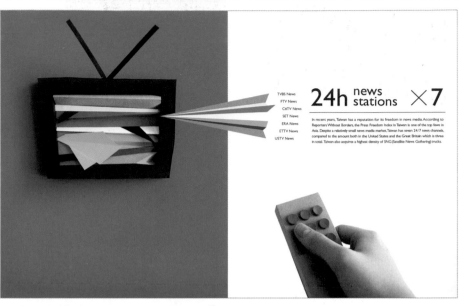

LESS COLOR IS MORE.

Color is exciting but, much like a circus, too many things happening at once with hue, value, and intensity prevents viewers from getting a memorable color idea. Stick to a simple palette and create rich relationships. A lot can be accomplished with black alone, for instance; and using a single dramatic color, rather than black, is a sure way of making a big impact.

The designer of this brochure spread, despite incorporating full-color photographic images, constrained the color palette to a set of closely related, cool greens, blues, and violets, with warm tones used only for supporting elements.
TIEN-MIN LIAO UNITED STATES

MASTER THE DARK AND THE LIGHT.

Tonal value is a powerful design tool. Make sure you're using a range of dark and light. Furthermore, don't spread out the tonal range all over the place. Use tone like firecrackers and the rising Sun: Concentrate areas of extreme dark and light; create explosions of luminosity and undercurrents of darkness. Counter these with subtler transitions between related values. Make distinctions in value noticeable and clear.

Soft, rippling transitions from deep black to luminous blue provide a sensuous backdrop for the bright, sparkling typography in this poster. By changing the sizes of type clusters, as well as the spaces between them, the designer also is able to introduce transitions in value that correspond to similar transitions in the image.
PAONE DESIGN ASSOCIATES
UNITED STATES

TYPE IS ONLY TYPE WHEN IT'S FRIENDLY.

It should go without saying that type that can't be read has no purpose, but, unfortunately, it bears repeating. Yes, typography should be expressive, visually inventive, and conceptually resonant. It must still transmit information. Choose typefaces that aid legibility, watch out for weird color contrasts, set text in a size that your grandmother can read, and you should be good to go.

Well-drawn, neutral typefaces that distinguish navigational levels from content through clear size, weight, and organizational relationships guarantee ease of use for visitors to this website. MANUEL ESTRADA SPAIN

USE TWO TYPEFACE FAMILIES, MAXIMUM.

OK, maybe three. Choose typefaces for specific purposes; you'll often find there are only two or three kinds of text in a project. Because a change in typeface usually signals a change in function—restrain yourself! A single type family with a variety of weights and italics can be enough; a second is nice for contrast, but don't overdo it. Too many typefaces are distracting and self-conscious and might confuse or tire the viewer.

Even the use of a single typeface family—here, a sans serif with a variety of weights—is enough to create dynamic textural vitality. The strategy boils down to decisive choices for the sizes of text elements and the combination of weights to maximize contrasts of dark and light, while ensuring overall stylistic unity. CONOR & DAVID IRELAND

TREAT TYPE AS YOU WOULD IMAGE.

A great deal of typography often fails in this regard: it's either blandly separated from images or insensitively slapped across them, under the assumption that this alone will integrate it as part of a layout. Type is visual material—made up of lines and dots and shapes and textures—that must relate compositionally to everything else included in the design, no matter how different they seem to be.

Both the style—bold, all uppercase sans serif—and placement of the type help complete the composition of this poster. The title does double duty as landing strip and identifier; the logo itself appears as an airplane (with the bowl of the numeral 5 creating its propeller); the angular quality of the numerals is placed in direct contrast with the curves of the cloud forms; and the small text at the top draws the diagonal motion of the other elements upward and activates the space at the top of the poster. C+G PARTNERS UNITED STATES

AVOID REDUNDANT REDUNDANCIES.

Be conscious of how much information is conveyed by a project's text. When you introduce imagery, you need not show the same information. Instead, consider what the text isn't telling the viewer and show that (and, conversely, text should tell what the images *don't* show). The image and text, working in concert, should not only complete each other but contribute to a new, deeper understanding. In closing the gaps and making such leaps, the viewer becomes more intensely engaged.

Rather than represent the subject of this exhibition poster—photography of birds—by showing the exhibition's work or by depicting the subject literally, the designer instead chose a more conceptual approach. Given that the subject was explicit in both the exhibition's title and subtitle, the designer was free to develop a visual idea that leapt beyond the expected and introduced a deeper, more conceptual message. The type forms, cut from paper and scanned, create not only a photographic dimensionality, but a visual association with legs, wings, feathers, tree branches, and wires—the environment that birds and people share. LESLEY MOORE NETHERLANDS

CREATE IMAGES—DON'T SCAVENGE.

Make what you need, and make it the best you can—or pay someone to do it for you and art-direct them. And remember: Not every idea benefits from a full-color photographic depiction. Very often, a more original, and meaningful solution is no further away than a couple of dots and lines, a simple, funky icon, or (gasp!) an abstract pattern or a scribble. Your options are limitless; consider them all. Try not to rely on what already exists, even though it might be cheaper or easier. Inventing images from scratch—in whatever medium—will help better differentiate your client's message and connect powerfully with the audience. Plus, you can say, quite proudly, that you did it all yourself.

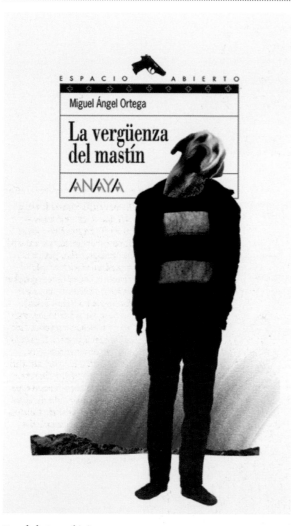

Found photographic images are reinvented in this collage, cut and pasted together and then drawn into with colored pencil.
MANUEL ESTRADA SPAIN

No photography or illustration available? Can't draw? No sweat. A designer with a strong understanding of how abstract form communicates—and what simple means (here, drawing software and a blur filter)—can transform uncomplicated visual elements into strikingly original and conceptually appropriate images.
CLEMENS THÉOBERT SCHEDLER AUSTRIA

All it takes to make an image new and original—even a bad one provided by a client—is a little manipulation. Whatever the source of this portrait, it's been given a new, specific life with a color change and a little texture. MUTABOR GERMANY

LOOK TO HISTORY, BUT DON'T REPEAT IT.

It's important to explore past approaches and aesthetics and to understand one's own work in context. More useful is the realization that another designer faced a similar problem—and solved it. Go ahead, be inspired! But, to slavishly reproduce a particular period style because it's cool hovers between plagiarism and laziness—not cool. Learn from the work of others, but do your own work.

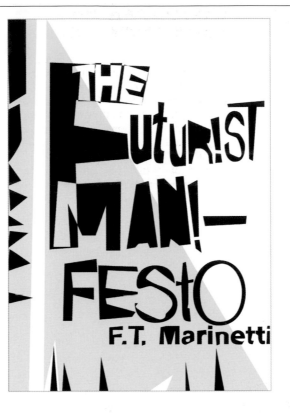

This cover for a reissued version of a significant art-movement text represents the energy and irreverence of the period and its style without mimicking it; instead of repetition and over-lap, hallmarks of the source style, this type is distorted and deformed. MAREK OKON CANADA

IGNORE FASHION. SERIOUSLY.

People in the present respond to what looks cool and "now." Many designers get significant attention for trendy work. Forget that. If you design around meaning, not current stylistic conceits, your projects will resonate more deeply, not get dated, and have impact far longer. Nobody looks at the Pantheon, designed almost 2,000 years ago, and says, "Ewww, that's like, so first century."

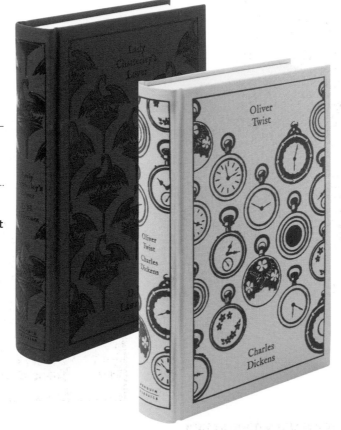

In the covers of these literary classics—part of a series—carefully crafted illustrative icons are arranged in symmetri-cal, wallpaperlike patterns and adorned with simple, small-scale serif type—graphic gestures that aren't in vogue (at the time of this edition). And yet, this visual language seems somehow modern while being appropriate to the subject matters and contexts of the books. By focusing on authentic messages and delivering them with sound, well-formed type style and images, the designer ensures an exquisitely timeless quality that transcends the fads of the moment. CORALIE BICKFORD-SMITH UNITED KINGDOM

BE DECISIVE: DO IT ON PURPOSE, OR NOT AT ALL.

Place visual material with confidence, and make clear decisions using your eyes—don't measure. Make things look the way you intend. Form elements often play tricks on the eyes. For instance, a circle and a square of the same mathematical size will not appear so. Which is bigger? Do they touch or not? Which is darker? If you align two items by measuring and they don't look like they do, it doesn't matter that they're really lined up. All the viewer will see is two items that look like they should have aligned—but don't. Decisiveness makes for a convincing impression; ambiguity or insecurity in the composition does the opposite. Convincing the audience that what you're showing them is true is the most important goal of all.

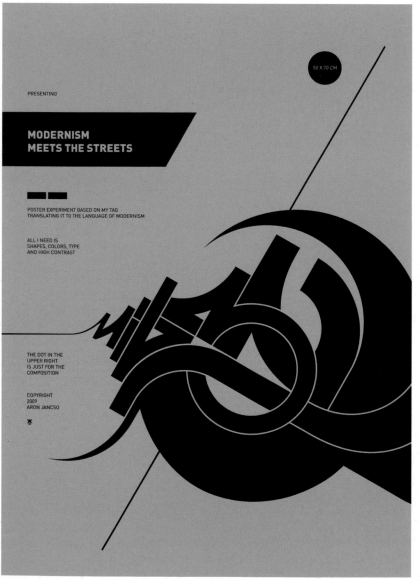

At a quick glance, the bold, confident, compositional dynamism of the graphical forms and type in this poster appears effortless and spontaenous—almost as though it happened naturally without forethought. Closer inspection, however, reveals intricate compositional relationships and decisive, carefully considered contrasts among the poster's parts.

The explicit diagonal axis of the main image cluster's thin line, for example, is more subtly restated by the angle of the shape enclosing the poster's title in relation to the lengths of the text lines below it; the dot at upper right is symmetrically positioned over a vertical axis defined optically by tension points created in the shapes below it; the progression from smaller, more linear forms to larger, more massive ones is optically seamless, despite their varied sizes, shapes and orientations; subtle adjustments in the leading, or interline spaces, between type elements of differing mass optically create the impression of equal spaces between them; the weights of the negative, reversed lines that intersect the heavier, planar forms correspond visually to those of the type elements; and a staggering variety of intervals and contour shapes among forms create continuous differentiation of positive and negative throughout the format.

ARON JANCSO HUNGARY

FORM SPACE

CHAPTER 01

> "There is no longer agreement anywhere about art itself, and under these circumstances we must go back to the beginning, to concern ourselves with dots and lines and circles and the rest of it.

ARMIN HOFFMANN / *Graphic designer and former director, Basel School of Design: 1946–1986*

BILLY BEN+ANNA HAAS SWITZERLAND

DAS BURO BRAND IDENTITY NETHERLANDS

First Things First All graphic design—all image making, *regardless of medium* or intent—centers on manipulating form. It's a question of making stuff to look at and organizing it so that it looks good and helps people understand not just what they're seeing, but what seeing it means for them. "Form" is that stuff: shapes, lines, textures, words, and pictures. The form that is chosen or made, for whatever purpose, should be considered as carefully as possible, because every form, no matter how abstract or seemingly simple, carries meaning. Our brains use the forms of things to identify them; the form is a message. When we see a circle, for example, our minds try to identify it: Sun? Moon? Earth? Coin? Pearl? No one form is any better at communicating than any other, but the choice of form is critical if it's to communicate the right message. In addition, making that form as beautiful as possible is what elevates designing above just plopping stuff in front of an audience and letting them pick through it, like hyenas mulling over a dismembered carcass. The term "beautiful" has a host of meanings, depending on context; here, we're not talking about beauty to mean "pretty" or "serene and delicate" or even "sensuous" in an academic, Beaux-Arts, home-furnishings-catalog way. Aggressive, ripped, collaged illustrations are beautiful; chunky

Form is stuff—including all kinds of imagery and type.

The idea of formal beauty is—highly subjective. Both these images can be considered beautiful, despite the fact that one is sensuous and "clean" and that the other is aggressive and "dirty."

People often overlook the potential of abstract form—or, for that matter, the abstract visual qualities of images such as photographs. This form study uses paper to investigate that very idea in a highly abstract way. What could this be? Who cares? It's about curl in relation to angle, negative space to positive strip. To understand how form works, the form must first be seen. JROSS DESIGN UNITED STATES

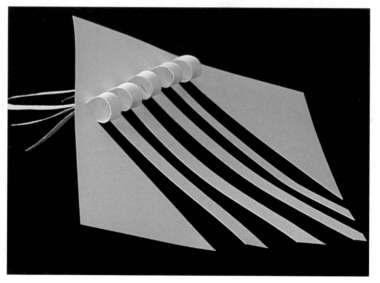

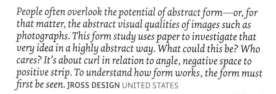

In this business card, the very basic form of dots, ordered as lines that become letterforms, become a dramatically simple and extremely clever symbolic gesture that communicates the identity of the cardholder's business. PARALLAX AUSTRALIA

Languages of the Pen

Line, mass, and texture communicate before words or a recogniz-able image. On this invitation for a calligraphy exhibit, the sense of pen gesture, flowing of marks, and the desertlike environment of high-contrast shadow and texture are all evident in a highly abstract composition. VCU QATAR

Inventive use of a die-cut in this poster creates a surprising, inventive message about structure and organic design. The spiraling strip that carries green type becomes a plant tendril and a structural object in support of the poster's message. The dimensional spiral, along with its shadows, shares a linear quality with the printed type, but contrasts its horizontal and diagonal flatness.
STUDIO WORKS UNITED STATES

woodcut type is beautiful; all sorts of rough images can be called beautiful. Here, the term "beautiful" as a descriptor might be better replaced by the term "resolved,"— meaning that the form's parts are all related to each other and no part of it seems un-considered or alien to any other part— and the term "decisive"—meaning that the form feels confident, credible, and on purpose. That's a lot to consider up front, so more attention will be given to these latter ideas shortly. Form does what it does somewhere, and that somewhere is called, simply, "space." This term, which describes something three-dimensional, applies to something that is, most often, a two-dimensional surface. That surface can be a business card, a poster, a Web page, a television screen, the side of a box, or a plate-glass window in front of a store. Regardless of what the surface is, it is a two-dimensional space that will be acted upon, with form, to become an apparent three-dimensional space. In painting, this space is called the *picture plane*, which painters have historically imagined as a strange, membrane-like window between the physical world and the illusory depth of the painted environment. Coincidentally, this sense of illusory depth behind or below the picture plane applies consistently to both figurative and abstract imagery.

The Shape of Space Also called the "format," the proportional dimensions of the space where form is going to do its thing is something to think about. The size of the format space, compared to the form within it, will change the perceived presence of the form. A smaller form within a larger spatial format—which will have a relatively restrained presence—will be perceived differently from a large form in the same format—which will be perceived as confrontational. The perception of this difference in presence is, intrinsically, a message to be controlled.

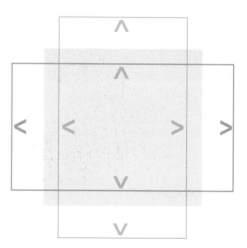

A small format enhances the presence, or apparent mass, of an element; a larger format decreases the presence of an element with the same physical size.

Each typographic element in this page spread subdivides the format's overall proportion to create new, smaller shapes and proportions of space.
VOICE DESIGN AUSTRALIA

The shape of a space produces overall visual effects that will have a profound impact on the perception of form interaction within it. A square format is neutral in emphasis—no side exerts any more influence than any other. A vertical format is confrontational, creating an upward and a downward thrust. A horizontal format produces a calmer, lateral movement that is relatively inert compared to that of a vertical format.

The shape of the format is also an important consideration. A square format is neutral; because all its sides are of equal length, there's no thrust or emphasis in any one direction, and a viewer will be able to concentrate on the interaction of forms without having to pay attention to the format at all. A vertical format, however, is highly confrontational. Its shape produces a simultaneously upward and downward thrust that a viewer will optically traverse over and over again, as though sizing it up; somewhere in the dim, ancient hardwiring of the brain, a vertical object is catalogued as potentially being another person—its verticality mirrors that of the upright body. Horizontal formats are generally passive; they produce a calming sensation and imply lateral motion, deriving from an equally ancient perception that they are related to the horizon. If you need convincing, note the root of the word itself. Not incidentally, the perception of these qualities relative to a format's proportion also are attributable to form elements.

The vertical format of this annual report intensifies the human element as well as the vertical movement of flowers upward; the sense of growth is shown literally by the image but expressed viscerally by the upward thrust of the format. COBRA NORWAY

The horizontal shape of this book's format echoes the horizon that is prevalent in the photographs of the urban landscape that it documents. The horizontal frame becomes the camera eye and it is relatively restful and contemplative. BRETT YASKO UNITED STATES

The square CD-ROM case is an appropriately neutral— and modular—format, considering the subject matter, pioneering Modernist architect Ludwig Mies van der Rohe. The circular CD-ROM obscures portions of the image in the tray but also adds its own layer. THOMAS CSANO CANADA

Positive and Negative Form is considered a positive element, a solid thing or object. Space is considered negative—not in a bad way, but as the absence, or opposite, of form. Space is the "ground" in which form becomes a "figure." The relationship between form and space, or figure and ground, is complementary and mutually dependent; it's impossible to alter one and not the other. The confrontation between figure and ground defines the kind of visual activity, movement, and sense of three-dimensionality perceived by the viewer. All these qualities are inherently communicative—resolving the relationships between figure and ground is the first step in creating a simple, overarching message about the content of the designed work, before the viewer registers the identity of an image or the content of any text that is present. Organizing figure—the positive—in relation to the ground—or negative—is therefore one of the most important visual aspects of design because it affects so many other aspects, from general emotional response to informational hierarchy. The figure/ground relationship must be understandable and present some kind of logic to the viewer; it must also be composed in such a way that the feeling this compositional, or visual, logic generates is perceived as appropriate to the message the designer

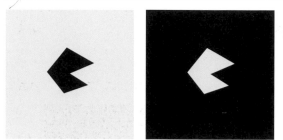

A positive (black) form on a negative (white) ground, and the reverse, retains its identity as positive if there is no other form or spatial break to define it as anything else. Note also how the white form on the black background appears larger than its same-sized black counterpart on the white field.

Darker and lighter fields of color are used interchangeably for light and shadow to define a three-dimensional space. LSD SPAIN

As a black (positive) form becomes larger within a negative (white) field, the leftover negative spaces become smaller and, eventually, might appear to be positive (white forms) in the context of a black field.

Comparison of an active figure/ground relationship (left) with an inactive figure/ground relationship (right) hints at the potential for meaning to be perceived even in such a fundamentally simple, abstract environment. Compare these pairs of simple, opposing ideas between the two examples: loud/quiet; aggressive/passive; nervous/sedate; complex/simple; energetic/weak; and living/dead.

The figure in this brochure page that promotes a dance company is the primary positive element, but the white type establishes an ambiguous relationship that sometimes casts the image as negative space. SURFACE GERMANY

is trying to convey. The logic of composition—the visual order and relationships of the figure and ground—is entirely abstract, but depends greatly on how the brain interprets the information that the viewer sees. Visual logic, all by itself, can also carry meaning. An extremely active relationship between figure and ground might be appropriate for one kind of communication, conveying energy, growth, and aggression; a static relationship, communicating messages such as quietness, restraint, or contemplation, might be equally appropriate in another context. The degree of activity might depend on how many forms are interacting in a given space, the size of the forms relative to the space, or how intricate the alternation between positive and negative appears to be. However, a composition might have relatively simple structural qualities—meaning only one or two forms in a relatively restrained

Dynamic, angular negative spaces contrast with the solidity of the letterforms' strokes and enhance the sharpness of the narrow channels of space that join them together. RESEARCH STUDIOS UNITED KINGDOM

The black, lightweight letter P in this logo, a positive form, encloses a negative space around a smaller version of itself; but that smaller version becomes the counterspace of a white, outlined P. Note the solid white "stem" in between the two. APELOIG DESIGN FRANCE

Varied contrasts in positive and negative areas—such as those between the angular, linear beak; the round dot; the curved shoulders; and the sharp claws in this griffon image—spark interest and engage the viewer's mind. VICKI LI/IOWA STATE UNIVERSITY UNITED STATES

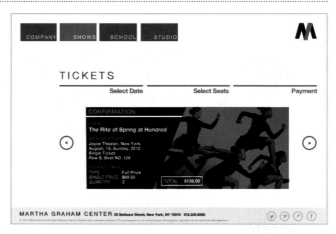

Each element in this web page—by virtue of its particular proportion and position—carves the background into shifting horizontal spaces of varied depth and contributes to a rhythmic lateral movement. YOUJIN CHOI/SCHOOL OF VISUAL ARTS UNITED STATES

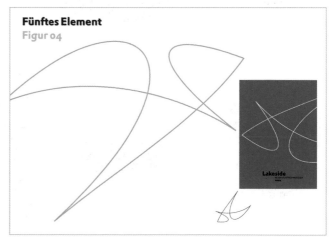

As the lines of this graphic form cross each other, the distinction between what is positive and what is negative becomes ambiguous. Some areas that appear to be negative at one glance become positive in the next. CLEMENS THÉOBERT SCHEDLER AUSTRIA

interaction—but unusual relationships that appear more active or more complex, despite the composition's apparent simplicity. In some compositions, the figure/ground relationship can become quite complex, to the extent that each might appear optically to be the other at the same time. This effect, in which what appears positive one minute appears negative the next, is called "figure/ground reversal." This rich visual experience is

extremely engaging; the brain gets to play a little game, and, as a result, the viewer is enticed to stay within the composition a little longer and investigate other aspects to see what other fun he or she can find. If you can recall one of artist M.C. Escher's drawings—in which white birds, flying in a pattern, reveal black birds made up of the spaces between them as they get closer together—you're looking at a classic example of figure/ground reversal in action.

The apparent reversal of foreground and background is also a complex visual effect that might be delivered through very simple figure/ground relationships, by overlapping two forms of different sizes, for example, or allowing a negative element to cross in front of a positive element unexpectedly. Changes among forms' relative opacity or value (lightness or darkness) may create a third space—a "middle ground" as discussed later (see *Near and Far*, page 66).

The negative arrows become positive against the large angled form. JOHN JENSEN/IOWA STATE UNIVERSITY UNITED STATES

The two mushroom shapes appear to be positive elements, but they are actually the negative counterspaces of a lumpy letter M, which, incidentally, bears a resemblance to a mound of dirt. FROST DESIGN AUSTRALIA

Despite the fact that most of the elements in this symbol are linear—and appear to occupy the same, flat spatial plane— the small figures toward the bottom appear to be in the foreground because one of them connects to the negative space outside the mark, and the line contours around these figures are heavier than those of the larger, crowned figure. SUNYOUNG PARK/IOWA STATE UNIVERSITY UNITED STATES

The flurry of birds in this poster transitions from being positive elements against a dark ground to the opposite; groupings of typographic elements perform the same trick. PAONE DESIGN ASSOCIATES UNITED STATES

Applying color changes to the intersections of larger forms on this brochure cover creates the perception that they are transparent. As a result, the viewer remains aware of the basic figure/ground distinction between the blue areas and the warmer orange and red tones, but also will perceive a series of layered spaces in which figure and ground continually change place.
MANUEL ESTRADA SPAIN

Vertical and horizontal divisions between tonal areas create the illusion of openings in the surface of this poster; the illusion is supported by the circular forms that cross over these divisions and appear to exist in front of the surface. The diagonally oriented title, on the other hand, defies this illusion by crossing under the white divisions between tonal areas—it appears to pass from the surface, at the lower edge of the poster, into the space of the "openings" as it moves upward.
LESLEY MOORE NETHERLANDS

The back side of a business card makes dramatic use of transparency and color value to create the perception of an extremely deep illusory space. In general, the brighter elements advance into the foreground while darker ones appear to recede; but sometimes—as is the case with the capital letter R—parts of some forms alternately appear both as foreground, middle-ground, and background elements, depending on their interaction with other forms.
UMBRELLA DESIGN INDIA

Clarity and Decisiveness Resolved and refined compositions create clear, accessible visual messages. Resolving and refining a composition means understanding what kind of message is being carried by a given form, what it does in space, and what effect the combination of these aspects has on the viewer. First, some more definitions. To say that a composition is "resolved" means that the reasons for where everything is, how big the things are, and what they're doing with each other in and around space—the visual logic—is clear, and that all the parts seem considered relative to each other. "Refined" is a quirky term when used to describe form or composition; in this context, it means that the form or composition has been made to be more like itself—more clearly, more simply, more indisputably communicating one specific kind of quality. Like the term "beautiful," the quality of "refinement" can apply to rough, organic, and aggressive forms, as well as sensuous, elegant, and clean ones. It's not a term of value so much as an indicator of whether the form is as clear as possible.

Look carefully at the small geometric and typographic elements on this magazine cover: Note how they travel at angles in response to axes within the photograph, as well as how their left and right edges correspond in vertical or horizontal alignment with each other, clearly overlap, or point to other elements.
STUDIO NEWWORK UNITED STATES

It is what it appears to be: Form is optically deceptive and so must be judged according to what it looks like. In this example, the three shapes are first shown being mathematically the same height (top). You'll notice that the square appears larger than both the circle and the triangle. So, for all intents and purposes, it is. This optical illusion is a function of how our brains interpret rounded, angular, and square images relative to each other (see **Geometric Form,** page 50). If the goal here is to make all three shapes appear to be the same size, the circle and the triangle must be adjusted in size until they do (bottom). Only when all three shapes appear to be the same size are they really the same size—as far as the viewer is concerned.

The delicate diagonal line, the medium-weight type at the right, and the bold, deconstructed geometric numeral— all of radically different shape and size—seem somehow uniformly distributed top to bottom and left to right around the vertical and horizontal axes of this bottle. The designer has optically adjusted the sizes, weights, and positions of all the elements to achieve the appearance of this balance.
DESIGNERS UNITED GREECE

This, of course, brings up the issue of "clarity," which has to do with whether a composition and the forms within it are readily understandable. Some of this understandability depends on the refinement of the forms, and some of it depends on the resolution of the relationships between form and space and whether these are "decisive," appearing to be on purpose and indisputable. A form or a spatial relationship can be called "decisive" if it is clearly one thing and not the other: for example, is one form larger or smaller than the one next to it, or are they both the same size? If the answer to this question is quick and nobody can argue with it—"The thing on the left is larger" or "Both things are the same size"—then the formal or spatial relationship is decisive. Being decisive with the visual qualities of a layout is important in design because the credibility of the message being conveyed depends on the confidence with which the forms and composition have been resolved. A weak composition, one that is indecisive, evokes uneasiness in a viewer, not just boredom. Uneasiness is not a good platform on which to build a complicated message that might involve persuasion.

Consider each element in this abstract page spread. Which form is descending? Which form is most in the background? Which form descends from right to left? Which form counteracts that movement? Which form moves from top to bottom? Which angles align and which do not? What effect does texture appear to have on the relative flatness or depth of the overall background color? Being able to describe what forms appear to be doing is crucial to understanding how they do it— and how to make them do it when you want to.

ANDREAS ORTAG AUSTRIA

An image's degree of refinement refers to how much it is like itself, how clear and undisturbed by distracting or conflicting elements— rather than how "clean" or "finished" it might appear. Shown here, first, is a form that is not yet refined; its internal relationships are unclear, somewhat awkward or unresolved. Slight adjustments refine its inherent characteristics so that they are more pronounced. An overlay of the original (gray) and refined forms provides comparison of these alterations.

Each of These Things Is Unlike the Other

There are several kinds of basic form, and each does something different. Rather, the eye and the brain perceive each kind of form as doing something different, as having its own kind of identity. The perception of these differences and how they affect the form's interaction with space and other forms around it, of differing identities, is what constitutes their perceived meaning. The context in which a given form appears—the space or ground it occupies and its relationship to adjacent forms—will change its perceived meaning, but its intrinsic identity and optical effect always remains an underlying truth. The most basic types of form are the dot, the line, and the plane. Of these, the line and the plane also can be categorized as geometric or organic; the plane can be either flat, textured, or appear to have three-dimensional volume or mass.

It's true that this book spread is a photograph of what appears to be a desktop. But it's actually a composition of dots, lines, rectangles, and negative spaces—all of different sizes and orientation, relative to each other.
FINEST MAGMA GERMANY

Although the jazz figures are recognizable images, they behave nonetheless as a system of angled lines, interacting with a secondary system of hard- and soft-edged planes. In addition to considering the back-and-forth rhythm created by the geometry of all these angles, the designer has also carefully considered the forms' alternation between positive and negative to enhance their rhythmic quality and create a sense of changing position from foreground to background.
NIKLAUS TROXLER DESIGN SWITZERLAND

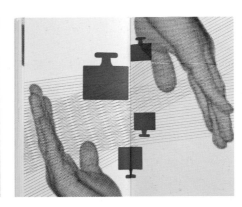

No matter how complex a representational form may seem, a designer must analyze and distill its true formal essence so as to understand how to work with the form in compositional space. The fish in the spread at far left is not a fish—it is a triangle. The leaves in that spread are not leaves—they are ellipses or, more fundamentally, diagonal lines, as are the hands in the spread at near left.
BRUKETA+ZINIC CROATIA

Line contrasts with texture, organic cluster contrasts with geometric text, and large elements contrast with small in this promotional poster. MUNDA GRAPHICS
AUSTRALIA

The dot pattern embodies ideas related to financial investing, given context by the typography: graphlike organization, growth, merging and separating, networking, and so on. UNA (AMSTERDAM) DESIGNERS
NETHERLANDS

The Dot The identity of a dot is that of a point of focused attention; the dot simultaneously contracts inward and radiates outward. A dot anchors itself in any space into which it is introduced and provides a reference point for the eye relative to other forms surrounding it, including other dots and its proximity to the edges of a format's space. As seemingly simple a form as it might appear, however, a dot is a complex object, the fundamental building block of all other forms. As a dot increases in size to cover a larger area and its outer contour becomes noticeable, even differentiated, it still remains a dot. Every shape or mass with a recognizable center—a square, a trapezoid, a triangle, a blob—is a dot, no matter how big it is. True, such a shape's outer contour will interact with the space around it more dramatically when it becomes bigger, but the shape is still essentially a dot. Even replacing a flat graphic shape with a photographic object, such as a silhouetted picture of a clock, will not change its fundamental identity as a dot. Recognizing this essential quality of the dot form, regardless of what other characteristics it takes on incidentally in specific occurrences, is crucial to understanding its visual effect in space and its relationship to adjacent forms.

Most of the visual elements in this brochure are dots; some are more clearly dots, such as the circular blobs and splotches, and some are less so, such as the letterforms and the little logo at the top. Despite not physically being dots, these elements exert the same kind of focused or radiating quality that dots do, and they react to each other in space like dots. In terms of a message, these dots are about gesture, primal thumping, and spontaneity . . . and, more concretely, about music. VOICE AUSTRALIA

When a dot enters a space, it establishes an immediate relationship with the space; the proportion of the dot to its surrounding area is the most important consideration; second is its relative position to the edges of the space.

The dot breaks the space in a neutral way, being weightless and internally balanced, but it might already create noticeable differences in spatial areas if it is placed off center. The centrally located dot is settled, comfortable, and static, but it dominates

the space around it; as it moves from the center, there is a shift in dominance—the background asserts itself and tension arises.

Introducing a second dot shifts attention away from the relationship of the space to the interaction of the two dots. They refer to each other and imply a structure—an invisible, connecting path that splits space apart.

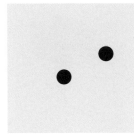

As dots approach each other, the tension between them increases. If the space between dots is just about zero, its presence assumes more importance than the dots themselves, and even more importance relative to any other

spatial interval. If the dots overlap, especially if they are different sizes, the tension created by their closeness is somewhat relieved. However, a new tension arises—the dichotomy of flat, graphic form and the appearance

of three-dimensional depth as one dot seemingly inhabits a foreground, and the other, a background position. The closer the dots are to each other, the more powerful the sense of their unique identity as objects; the further

apart, the more pronounced the sense of structure, induced by the invisible path between them.

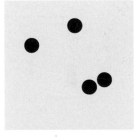

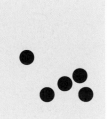

Additional dots in close proximity to the pair, however, reduce the focus on identity and increase attention to their reciprocal relationship and, thus, a sense of structure or meaning. How far are the dots from each other?

Is each dot the same distance from its counterparts? What is their configuration, and what outer shape does it make? What does this shape signify?

The flat dot and photographic images are all still dots.

Not all dots are circular! Barring a few elements that are clearly lines, many of the dots on the gatefold pages of this brochure are something other than circular. However, they are still treated as dots for the purpose of composition, judging size change, proximity, tension, and negative spaces between as though they were flat, black, abstract dots. Note how the type's linear quality contrasts with the dots on the pages.
C+G PARTNERS UNITED STATES

Working together, dots create an endless variety of arrangements and increasing complexity—a single vertical or horizontal row, rotated rows, an isolated dot in contrast to a group, progressions in interval, ordered rows in a grid structure, angles and geometric patterns, curves, and so on.

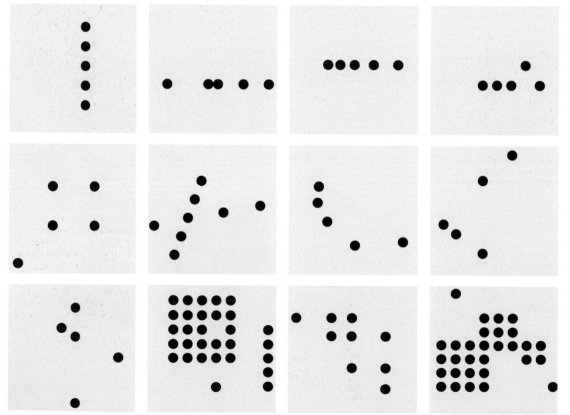

The negative dot is created in reverse from the convergence of other forms.

Clustering dots of different sizes creates a more varied contour, but overall the cluster retains its identity as a dot.

The perception of spatial depth occurs among dots that are different sizes; a larger dot advances in front of a smaller one. Changing the relative tonal values of the dots, however, can create an ambiguous spatial tension among the dots, even though their relative sizes remain the same.

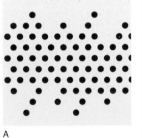

A

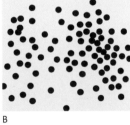

B

A tremendous number of small dots create (A) a regularized pattern or (B) a randomized texture.

The darkness or lightness of these dots depends on density—how close the dots are to each other.

The cluster of dots creates a kind of undulating mass. The outer contour of the cluster is very active, with differing proximity and tension to the format edges. The initial b offers a complement to the cluster and contrast in scale. The compositional logic is clear and decisive. LEONARDO SONNOLI ITALY

Basic form elements such as dots, however, often are not only simply fun to use as design elements, but help communicate. The dots in this logo and brand identity study for a city park become balls, balloons, freckles, and clouds, depending on their context. HEESEUNG LEE/SCHOOL OF VISUAL ARTS UNITED STATES

The Line A line's essential character is one of connection; it unites areas within a composition. This connection may be invisible, defined by the pulling effect on space between two dots, or it may take on visible form as a concrete object, traveling back and forth between a starting point and an ending point. Unlike a dot, therefore, the quality of linearity is one of movement and direction; a line is inherently dynamic, rather than static.

The line might appear to start somewhere and continue indefinitely or it might travel a finite distance. While dots create points of focus, lines perform other functions; they may separate spaces, join spaces or objects, create protective barriers, enclose or constrain, or intersect. Changing the size—the thickness—of a line relative to its length has a much greater impact on its quality as a line than does changing the size of a dot. As a line becomes thicker or

heavier in weight, it gradually becomes perceived as a plane surface or mass; to maintain the line's identity, it must be proportionally lengthened.

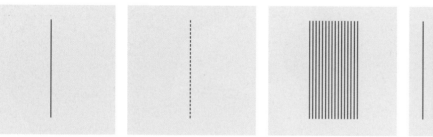

A thin, single line has no center and no mass, expressing only direction and an effect on the space surrounding it.

Breaking the line increases its surface activity without distracting from its movement and direction.

Several thin lines together create a texture, similar to that created by a dense grouping of similar-sized dots.

Separating the lines increases attention to their individual identities. It also calls attention to the intervals between them and what, if any, variation there might be.

 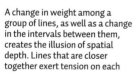 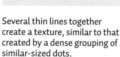 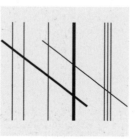 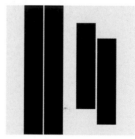

A change in weight among a group of lines, as well as a change in the intervals between them, creates the illusion of spatial depth. Lines that are closer together exert tension on each

other and advance in space, while those further apart recede. If any of the lines are rotated to cross their counterparts, the perception of spatial depth is enhanced—and even more so if their weights also are differentiated. Although

a thin line generally will appear to recede against a thicker line, the mind is capable of being convinced that the thin line is crossing in front of the thick line.

Two heavy lines that are very close together create a third—negative—line between them. The optical effect of the negative white line is that of a positive element on top of a single black element, even if the negative line joins open spaces at either end.

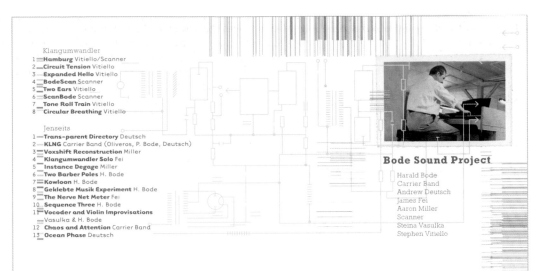

Klangumwandler
1 **Hamburg** Vitiello/Scanner
2 **Circuit Tension** Vitiello
3 **Expanded Hello** Vitiello
4 **BodeScan** Scanner
5 **Two Ears** Vitiello
6 **ScanBode** Scanner
7 **Tone Roll Train** Vitiello
8 **Circular Breathing** Vitiello

Jenseits
1 **Trans-parent Directory** Deutsch
2 **KLNG Carrier Band** (Oliveros, P. Bode, Deutsch)
3 **Voxshift Reconstruction** Miller
4 **Klangumwandler Solo** Fei
5 **Instance Degage** Miller
6 **Two Barber Poles** H. Bode
7 **Kowloon** H. Bode
8 **Geklebte Musik Experiment** H. Bode
9 **The Nerve Net Meter** Fei
10 **Sequence Three** H. Bode
11 **Vocoder and Violin Improvisations** Vasulka & H. Bode
12 **Chaos and Attention** Carrier Band
13 **Ocean Phase** Deutsch

Bode Sound Project

Harald Bode
Carrier Band
Andrew Deutsch
James Fei
Aaron Miller
Scanner
Steina Vasulka
Stephen Vitiello

Lines play a dual role on this CD-ROM insert. First, they create movement around the perimeter of the format, in contrast to the rectangular photograph. Other lines are more pictorial and represent musical scoring and circuitry. **JROSS DESIGN** UNITED STATES

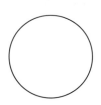

A line traveling around a fixed, invisible point at an unchanging distance becomes a circle. Note that a circle is a line, not a dot. If the line's weight is increased dramatically, a dot appears in the center of the circle, and eventually the form is perceived as a white (negative) dot on top of a larger, positive dot.

A spiraling line appears to move simultaneously inward and outward, re-creating the visual forces inherent in a single dot.

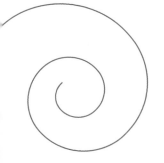

THEMA

**EINFACHER VERSUCH
ÜBER DEN BACKSTEIN**
EIN MATERIAL UND SEINE
VERWENDUNG IN DER
ARCHITEKTUR
Bettina Held

Er (Wies) vergaß nie seine frühen Lektionen bei seinem Vater, dem Steinmetz. Von ihm habe ich alles über den Stein gelernt' 'Und ich erinnere mich, daß er gern erzählte, wie er sich als junger Mann – kaum dem Knabenalter entwachsen – als reisender Maurer qualifizierte. 'Also ein Backstein', pflegte er zu sagen, 'das ist wirklich etwas! Wie vernünftig ist diese kleine handliche Form, so nützlich für jeden Zweck! Welche Logik im Verband, in Muster und Textur! Welcher Reichtum in der einfachen Mauerfläche! Aber wieviel Disziplin verlangt dieses Material!'[1]

Typography, as we'll see in chapter 3, is made up fundamentally of lines. On the right-hand page of the above page spread, therefore, are five lines—can you identify them? Once you do, also note the presence of the important line in the photograph on the left-hand page— the bright white line of the wooden palette on the worker's shoulder—and how it relates compositionally to the heavy red line on the right-hand page. **NAROSKA DESIGN** GERMANY

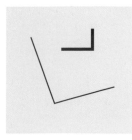 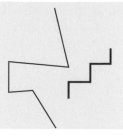  

  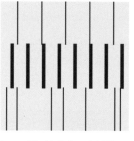  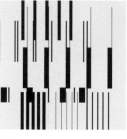

Two lines joining create an angle. The joint between two lines becomes a starting point for two directional movements; multiple joints between lines create a sense of altered direction in one

movement. An extremely acute angle might also be perceived as a rapid movement from one direction to another.

Lines that both enter and leave a format reinforce the sense of their movement along the direction in which they do so. If the beginning or ending points of the lines are contained within the format, their directional movement is changed

from continuous to specific; the result is that their tension with surrounding space or forms is increased greatly as the eye is able to focus on the point at which they start or stop.

White (negative) lines crossing in front of (and behind) black (positive) lines create increasingly complex spatial relationships.

Lines together produce rhythm. Equally spaced, a set of lines produces an even, relatively static tempo; differences in space produce a dynamic, syncopated

tempo. The kind of spatial difference introduced between lines affects the perceived rhythm and might create meaning: progres-

sion, sequence, repetition, or system. Such rhythmic changes in interval create directional movement; the more complex the changes and the more variation

in line weights, the more complex the rhythm becomes.

On this page spread from a concert program, lines of different weights are used to separate horizontal channels of information. Varying the weights of the lines, along with the degree to which their values contrast with the background, not only adds visual interest but also enhances the informational hierarchy.
E-TYPES DENMARK

On this brochure spread, less-distinct blue lines form a channel around images at the left while sharper yellow lines draw attention to the text at the right and help to join the two pages into one composition. The staggered lines created by the text at the lower left, as well as the thin vertical lines used as dividers in the headline, bring type and image together with corresponding visual language. C. HARVEY GRAPHIC DESIGN UNITED STATES

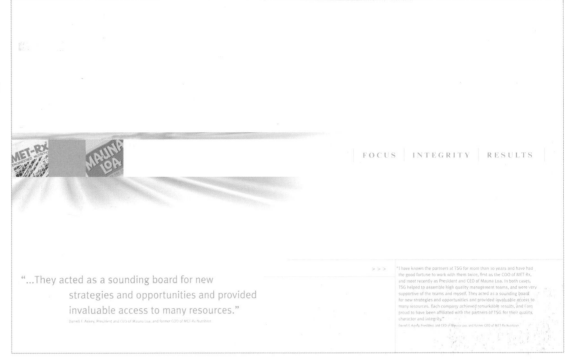

FOCUS | INTEGRITY | RESULTS

"...They acted as a sounding board for new strategies and opportunities and provided invaluable access to many resources."

Darrell F. Askey, President and CEO of Mauna Loa, and former COO of MET-Rx Nutrition

> > >

"I have known the partners at TSG for more than 10 years and have had the good fortune to work with them twice, first as the COO of MET-Rx, and most recently as President and CEO of Mauna Loa. In both cases, TSG helped to assemble high quality management teams, and were very supportive of the teams and myself. They acted as a sounding board for new strategies and opportunities and provided invaluable access to many resources. Each company achieved remarkable results, and I am proud to have been affiliated with the partners of TSG for their quality, character and integrity."

Darrell F. Askey, President and CEO of Mauna Loa, and former COO of MET-Rx Nutrition

A

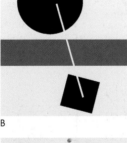

B

C

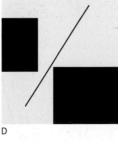

D

Lines might break or join spaces within a format. In breaking or joining these spaces, lines might perform additional functions relative to other forms within the same format.

(A) The line protects the circular form. (B) The white line joins both forms across a barrier. (C) The line offers contrast to the form, but supports it. (D) The line joins two spaces.

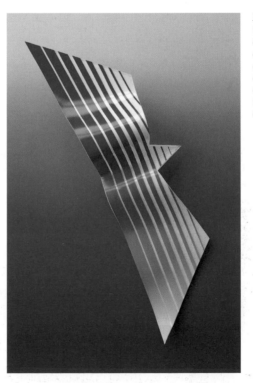

Because lines are rhythmic, they can be used to create or enhance meaning in images or compositions. Here, the idea of movement is imparted to the abstract bird by the progression of line weights from tail end to front. STUDIO INTERNATIONAL CROATIA

Plane and Mass A plane is simply just a big dot whose outer contour—the sense of its shape—becomes an important attribute: for example, that it may be angular rather than round. Its dotlike quality becomes secondary as the plane object becomes larger. This change depends on the size of the plane relative to the space in which it exists; in a large poster, even a relatively large plane object—a square or a triangle, for example—will still act as a dot if the volume of space surrounding it is much larger than the plane object itself. At the point where a plane object enlarges within a format so that its actual shape begins to affect the shapes of the negative space around it, the character of its outer contour, as well as its surface texture, come into question. All such shapes appear first as flat surfaces; their external contour must be defined by the mind to identify it as being one kind of shape or another and, subsequently, what meaning that shape might have. The more active the plane's contour—and more so if the contour becomes concave, allowing surrounding negative space to enter into the dimensional surface defined by the shape—the more dynamic the shape will appear, and the less it will radiate and focus in the way a dot, with a simple, undifferentiated contour, does.

As a dot increases in size, its outer contour becomes noticeable as an important aspect of its form; eventually, appreciation of this contour supersedes that of its dotlike focal power, and it becomes a shape or plane. Compare the sequences of forms, each increasing in size from left to right. At what point does each form become less a dot and more a plane?

A plane surface will be more or less definable as a dot, depending on the volume of space surrounding it. The plane's angular shape in the first example is unimportant because its shape is overwhelmed by the larger space and, thus, it remains a dot. In the second example, the form's increase in size causes its shape to become more important and, thus, is no longer simply a dot.

Rotating rectangular planes create movement—and mass as their densities build up toward the bottom—and an asymmetrical arrangement on this media kit folder. The planes in this case reflect a specific shape in the brand mark as well as refer to the idea of a screen.
FORM UNITED KINGDOM

The relative size and simplicity of the shape has an impact on its perceived mass or weight. A large form with a simple contour retains its dotlike quality and presents a heavy optical weight; a form with a complex contour, and a great deal of interaction between internal and external positive and negative areas, becomes weaker, more line-like, and exhibits a lighter mass. As soon as texture appears on the surface of a plane, its mass decreases and it becomes flatter—unless the texture emulates the effect of light and shade, creating a perceived three-dimensionality or volume. Even though apparently three-dimensional, the plane or volume still retains its original identity as a dot.

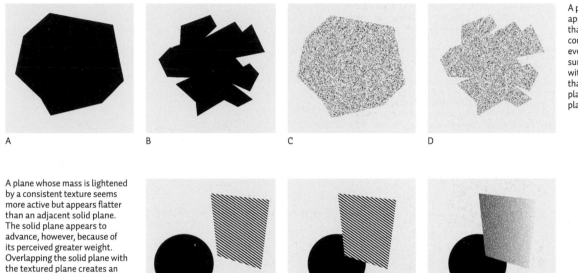

A | B | C | D

A plane with a simple contour (A) appears heavier (has more mass) than a plane with a complicated contour (B). Both planes appear even lighter when they take on surface texture. The simple plane with texture (C) appears lighter than the solid, more complicated plane; the textured, complicated plane (D) appears lighter still.

A plane whose mass is lightened by a consistent texture seems more active but appears flatter than an adjacent solid plane. The solid plane appears to advance, however, because of its perceived greater weight. Overlapping the solid plane with the textured plane creates an ambiguous tension between foreground and background. A plane whose texture emulates the effect of light and shade appears to have volume.

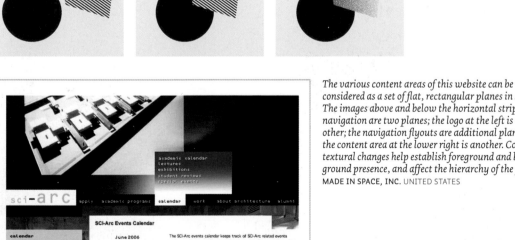

The various content areas of this website can be considered as a set of flat, rectangular planes in space. The images above and below the horizontal strip of navigation are two planes; the logo at the left is another; the navigation flyouts are additional planes; and the content area at the lower right is another. Color and textural changes help establish foreground and background presence, and affect the hierarchy of the page.
MADE IN SPACE, INC. UNITED STATES

Geometric Form As they do with all kinds of form, our brains try to establish meaning by identifying a shape's outer contour. There are two general categories of shape, each with its own formal and communicative characteristics that have an immediate effect on messaging: geometric form and organic form. A shape is considered geometric in nature if its contour is regularized (if its external measurements are mathematically similar in multiple directions) and, very generally, if it appears angular or hard edged. It is essentially an ancient, ingrained expectation that anything irregular, soft, or textured is akin to things experienced in nature.

Similarly, our expectation of geometry as unnatural is the result of learning that humans create it; hence, geometry must not be organic. The weird exception to this idea is the circle or dot, which, because of its elemental quality, might be recognized as either geometric or natural: Earth, Sun, Moon, or pearl. Lines, too, might have a geometric or organic quality, depending on their specific qualities. Geometric forms might be arranged in extremely organic

There are three essential types of geometric form: circle, polygon, and line. For polygons, the simplest are the square and the triangle, having four sides and three sides, respectively. The square is the most stable and presents the most mass; the triangle is the least stable polygon and induces a great deal of optical movement around its contour. The circle is nearly as stable as the square although its continuous curve hints at rotation; its curvy quality is completely opposite to that of the square. Lines that are straight, stepped, or configured as angles are also geometric.

The blocks on this poster are purely geometric. The lighting that is used to change their color also affects their apparent dimensionality; the blue areas at the upper left sometimes appear to be flat.
STUDIO INTERNATIONAL CROATIA

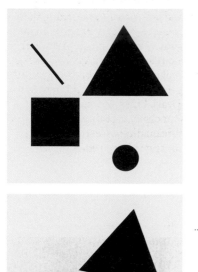

ways, creating tension between their mathematical qualities and the irregularity of movement. Although geometric shapes and relationships clearly occur in nature, the message a geometric shape conveys is typically that of something artificial, contrived, or synthetic. Organizing any kind of form elements (whether literally geometric, or otherwise) in a geometric relationship will similarly impose a sense of artificiality or contrivance, or possibly one of precision or analysis. In such a case, the geometry of the compositional structure will dominate any perception of organicism within the form elements themselves; such geometric arrangement becomes, in a sense, another kind of geometric form language.

An arrangement of geometric forms in geometric, or mathematical, spatial relationships (top) is contrasted by the irregular, organic quality of their arrangement in irregular relationships (bottom).

Basic geometric forms— the rectangular plane of the photographs, the circle of the teacup, and the triangle of the potting marker—provide a simple counterpoint to the organic leaves and the scenes in the photographs themselves.
RED CANOE UNITED STATES

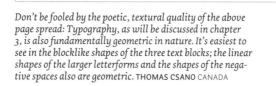

The hot pink-red area printed on this die-cut cover creates the sense of two trapezoidal planes intersecting within an ambiguous space in this brochure cover.
344 DESIGN UNITED STATES

Don't be fooled by the poetic, textural quality of the above page spread: Typography, as will be discussed in chapter 3, is also fundamentally geometric in nature. It's easiest to see in the blocklike shapes of the three text blocks; the linear shapes of the larger letterforms and the shapes of the negative spaces also are geometric. THOMAS CSANO CANADA

Organic Form Shapes that are irregular, complex, and highly differentiated are considered organic—this is what our brains tell us after millennia of seeing organic forms all around us in nature. As noted earlier, geometry exists in nature, but its occurrence happens in such a subtle way that it is generally overshadowed by our perception of overall irregularity. The structure of most branching plants, for example, is triangular and symmetric.

In the context of the whole plant, whose branches may grow at different rates and at irregular intervals, this intrinsic geometry is obscured. Conveying an organic message, therefore, means reinforcing these irregular aspects in a form, despite the underlying truth of geometry that actually might exist. Nature presents itself in terms of variation on essential structure, so a shape might appear organic if its outer contour is varied along a simple logic—many changing varieties of curve, for example. Nature also appears highly irregular or unexpected (again, the plant analogy is useful) so irregularity in measurement or interval similarly conveys an organic identity. Nature is unrefined, unstudied, textural, and complicated. Thus, shapes that exhibit these traits will also carry an organic message.

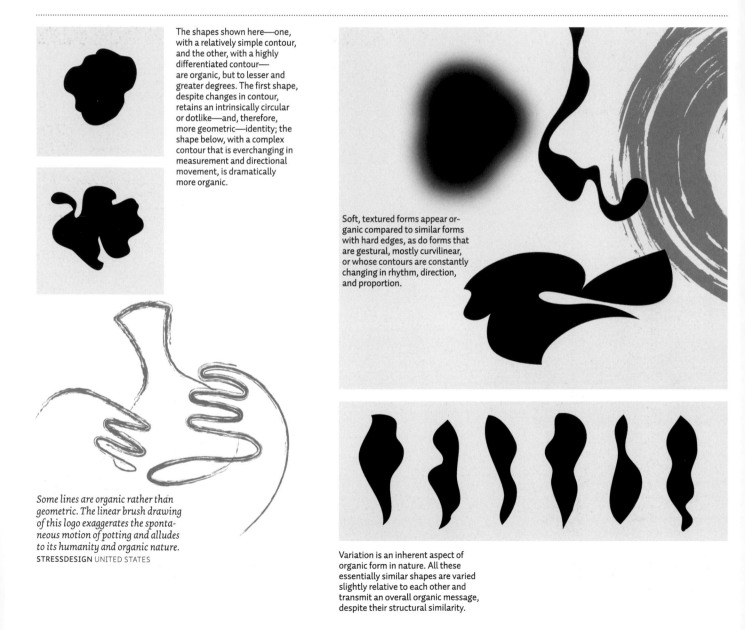

The shapes shown here—one, with a relatively simple contour, and the other, with a highly differentiated contour— are organic, but to lesser and greater degrees. The first shape, despite changes in contour, retains an intrinsically circular or dotlike—and, therefore, more geometric—identity; the shape below, with a complex contour that is everchanging in measurement and directional movement, is dramatically more organic.

Some lines are organic rather than geometric. The linear brush drawing of this logo exaggerates the spontaneous motion of potting and alludes to its humanity and organic nature.
STRESSDESIGN UNITED STATES

Soft, textured forms appear organic compared to similar forms with hard edges, as do forms that are gestural, mostly curvilinear, or whose contours are constantly changing in rhythm, direction, and proportion.

Variation is an inherent aspect of organic form in nature. All these essentially similar shapes are varied slightly relative to each other and transmit an overall organic message, despite their structural similarity.

Geometry exists as a building block of natural, organic forms. In the photograph of the leaf (A), lines and dots—the leaf's veins and holes from insect activity or fungal degradation—are clearly apparent. The outer contour of the leaf also presents a symmetrical structure. Distilled and stylized (B), this form retains its pictorial identity but loses its organic quality. Enforcing differentiated measurements between internal components (C) enhances its organic quality, while retaining its stylization.

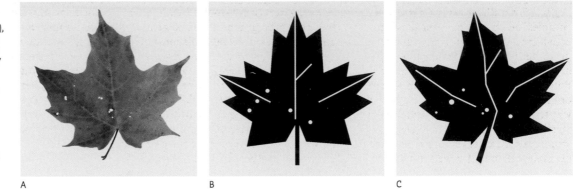

A   B   C

The irregular, unstudied, constantly changing outer contour of flowers is a hallmark of organic form. These qualities contrast dynamically with the linear elements—including type, both sans serif and script—and create striking negative forms. PAMELA ROUZER/ LAGUNA COLLEGE OF ART UNITED STATES

The drawings and textures that support the images of the dresses in this fashion catalog create a sense of the handmade, the delicate, and the personal. SAGMEISTER+WALSH UNITED STATES

A curling, organic wave form integrates with the curved, yet geometric, letterform in this logo. LSD SPAIN

Surface Activity The quality of surface activity helps in differentiating forms from each other, just as the identifiable contours of form itself does. Again, the dot is the building block of this formal quality. Groupings of dots, of varying sizes, shapes, and densities, create the perception of surface activity. There are two basic categories of surface activity: texture and pattern. The term "texture" applies to surfaces having irregular activity without apparent repetition. The sizes of the elements creating surface activity might change; the distance between the components might change; the relative number of components might change from one part of the surface to another. Because of this inherent randomness, texture generally is perceived as organic or natural. Clusters and overlaps of lines—dots in specific alignments—are also textural, but only if they are relatively random, that is, they are not running parallel, or appearing with varying intervals between, or in random, crisscrossing directions. "Pattern," however, has a geometric quality—it is a specific kind of texture in which the components are arranged on a recognizable and repeated structure—for example, a grid of dots. The existence of a planned structure within patterns means they are understood to be something that is not organic: they are something synthetic, mechanical,

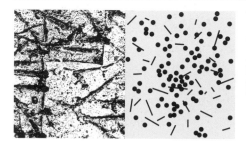

Visual activity on a plane surface is categorized as a texture if it appears random or if it changes in quality from one location to another. While most often organic in source (left), such textures may also be created from dot-based or linear form (right).

Visual activity on a plane surface should be categorized as pattern if it exhibits some repeated, consistent relationship, such as a grid structure, between its component elements. At left is a simple, linear herringbone pattern, while at right, a photographic image shows a complex grid pattern.

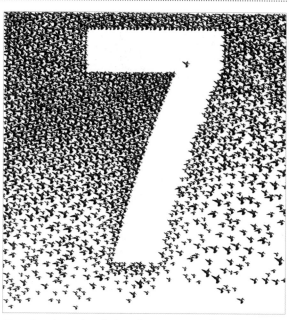

Upon closer inspection, the irregular texture around the numeral is revealed to be a flock of hummingbirds. Oddly enough, their apparently random placement is carefully studied to control the change in density.
STUDIO WORKS UNITED STATES

Both scale and value (light/dark) contrast affect the presence, or optical activity, of patterns and textures, as seen in these two related book cover designs. On the left, the smaller size and lesser contrast within the pattern element renders it a background or field; on the right, the pattern's much larger scale and strong contrast between dark and light values cause its elements to seem more like clusters of forms that appear to come to the surface. CORALIE BICKFORD-SMITH UNITED KINGDOM

mathematical, or mass produced. The scale of the texture or pattern, relative to the format, will establish different qualities. A pattern or texture made up of very small elements will present itself as a field or background. If the elements are very large, they will act as a grouping of foreground elements, competing for attention with other kinds of material in the space.

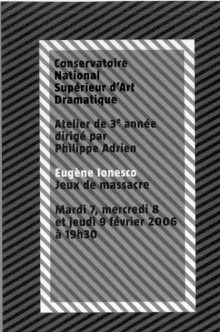

Rather than appearing to flatten out a compositional space, as patterns often do, the fields of diagonal lines in this poster create the perception of layered space—because of their varied transparency and color relationships—and of movement, because of their alternating directions.
APELOIG DESIGN FRANCE

Warping the proportions of a dot grid creates a dramatically three-dimensional pattern. This quality refers to the activity of the client, a medical imaging and networking organization.
LSD SPAIN

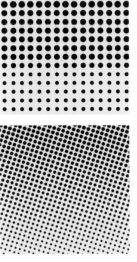

Increasing the density of a pattern's components creates a change in darkness or value. Changes in pattern density may be stepped, as in the example at top, or continuous, as in the example below it. While the continous transition from lighter to darker values in the bottom example is smooth, and less geometric in appearance, the pattern still retains its mechanical quality in contrast to texture.

In a patterned surface, creating the perception of three dimensionality and the play of light is also possible, but the geometric quality of the pattern presents a highly stylized version of volumetric appearance. Compare the patterned volume at top with the textured volume at bottom.

The more regular a texture's density is within a given area, the more two dimensional it will appear—and the less organic or natural. Conversely, strong contrast in density increases the texture's dimensional quality as well as its inherent organic quality. An evenly continuous transition from lighter to darker value will often be perceived as the play of light across a volume.

Pattern is considered decorative and man-made, and too much usually is a bad thing. In the case of this book on a trend in design called Maximalism, however, its use as an allover background treatment enhances the communication of excess. LOEWY UNITED KINGDOM

Surface activity can be an exceptionally useful element in digital, screen-based projects, like websites. One complaint designers sometimes make about screen-based work is its lack of tactility, compared to that of printed work, like books. That's not to say that a web page should be designed to look like a book—it's not a book. But there is a kind of flatness inherent to the screen, and the light it gives off tires the eyes more quickly and is sometimes perceived as cold. Even a subtle, monochromatic, texture or pattern, used as a background or within a navigational header, can enhance perceived dimensionality and warm up a site's feeling. Physical textures or patterns also may be used for conceptual reasons—to suggest a connection with real-world experience.

In the context of printed projects or packaging, always consider the selection and manipulation of paper stock—this, too, creates surface activity in a layout. A coated paper might be glossy and reflective, or matte and relatively nonreflective. Coated stocks are excellent for reproducing color and detail because they keep ink up on the surface. The relative slickness of coated sheets, however, might come across as cold or impersonal but also as refined, luxuri-

A photograpic image of a paper surface adds warmth and depth to this web page. ATIPUS SPAIN

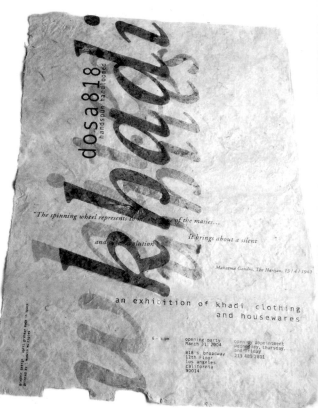

A translucent, handmade paper stock exaggerates this poster's typographic texture and adds a distintly organic quality.
MADE IN SPACE, INC. UNITED STATES

The delicate gloss varnish on the surface of this invitation is subtle and elegant.
THERE AUSTRALIA

ous, or modern. Uncoated stocks, on the other hand, show a range of textural qualities, from relatively smooth to very rough. Sometimes, flecks of other materials, such as wood chips, threads, or other fibers, are included for added effect. Uncoated stocks tend to feel organic, more personal, handmade, and warmer. The weight or transparency of a paper also will influence the overall feel of a project.

Exploiting a paper's physical properties through folding, cutting, short sheeting, embossing, and tearing creates surface activity in a three-dimensional way. Special printing techniques, such as varnishes, metallic and opaque inks, or foil stamping, increase surface activity by changing the tactile qualities of a paper stock's surface. Opaque inks, for example, will appear matte and viscous on a gloss-coated stock, creating surface contrast between printed and unprinted areas. Metallic ink printed on a rough, uncoated stock will add an appreciable amount of sheen, but not as much as would occur if printed on a smooth stock. Foil stamping, available in matte, metallic, pearlescent, and iridescent patterns, produces a slick surface whether used on coated or uncoated stock and has a slightly raised texture.

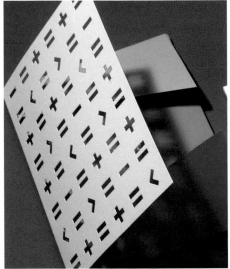

Diecuts of mathematical symbols on this folder cover allow the interior colors to show through.
C+G PARTNERS UNITED STATES

Embossed type adds a tactile quality to this brochure cover; colored stickers introduce random variation on each copy and allude to the subject matter.
MUTABOR GERMANY

A pearlescent foil stamp on these invitations refracts light and appears to change color at different viewing angles.
FORM UNITED KINGDOM

Bright white flecks within the craft paper stock of this pretzel packaging suggests salt crystals.
TRIBORO DESIGN UNITED STATES

A leather-bound box contrasts texture and subdued, neutral color with smooth, vibrantly-colored ribbons.
ROYCROFT DESIGN UNITED STATES

Complex diecuts help create a surprising pop-up image in this book spread.
VOICE AUSTRALIA

Breaking into It Space—the ground or field of a composition—is neutral and inactive until it is broken by form. But how does the designer break the space, and what happens as a result? Thoughtfully considering these fundamental questions gives the designer a powerful opportunity not only to engage a viewer but also to begin transmitting important messages, both literal and conceptual, before the viewer even gets the chance to assimilate the content.

Space is defined and given meaning the instant a form appears within it, no matter how simple. The resulting breach of emptiness creates new space—the areas surrounding the form. Each element brought into the space adds complexity but also decreases the literal amount of space—even as it creates new kinds of space, forcing it into distinct shapes that fit around the forms like the pieces of a puzzle. These spaces shouldn't be considered empty or leftover; they are integral to achieving flow around the form elements, as well as a sense of order throughout the composition. When the shapes, sizes, proportions, and directional thrusts of these spaces exhibit clear relationships with the form elements they surround, they become resolved with the form and with the composition as a whole.

As soon as a form enters a given space, the space is changed and structure appears—simple as this might be. There are now two spaces created by the form's location in the center of the format—each similar in quality, shape, and volume.

Without changing the form—except for a minor repositioning—the volumes, shapes, and qualities inherent in the spaces surrounding the form are made different from each other.

Changing any aspect of a form in space—its relative size, its shape, its orientation to horizontal or vertical—or adding an additional form, creates differentiated spaces with new, more complex relationships to each other.

udin.

Arti Grafiche
Friulane 80°
Dedicato a Udine
CODEsign

Tempio-Ossario (1925-30)
arch. P. Veleri-A. Limongelli
statue di S. Olivo (1936-39)

The forms on this poster break the space decisively—meaning that the proportions of negative space have clear relationships to each other—and the locations of elements help to connect them optically across those spaces. The accompanying diagram notes these important aspects of the layout.
LEONARDO SONNOLI ITALY

Static and Dynamic The proportions of positive and negative might be generally static or generally dynamic. Because the picture plane is already a flat environment where movement and depth must be created as an illusion, fighting the tendency of two-dimensional form to feel static is important. The spaces within a composition will generally appear static—in a state of rest or inertia—when they are optically equal to each other. Spaces need not be physically the same shape to appear equal in presence or "weight." The surest way of avoiding a static composition is to force the proportions of the spaces between forms (as well as between forms and the format edges) to be as different as possible.

Multiple forms situated around similar spatial intervals create static interaction. This composition—the arrangement of forms within space—seems restful, comfortable, and quiet, and exhibits a kind of stasis despite the irregularity and rotation of the forms.

Altering the intervals between form elements, or between elements and format edges, creates a dynamic composition. The movement of the eye is enhanced as these intervals exhibit more contrast with each other. Note the areas where the negative spaces become compressed or exhibit a directional thrust.

In this book spread, the designer rotates type elements, as well as crosses image boundaries with them to enhance the compositional movement already created by decisive spatial breaks of differing interval. MICHELLE LIV/PARSONS SCHOOL OF DESIGN UNITED STATES

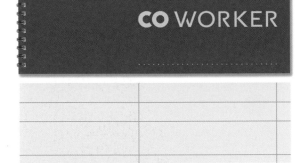

Decisively broken space can be restrained yet still have a visual richness to it. The placement of the type element and the dotted line create four horizontal channels of space and two vertical channels of space. ADAMSMORIOKA UNITED STATES

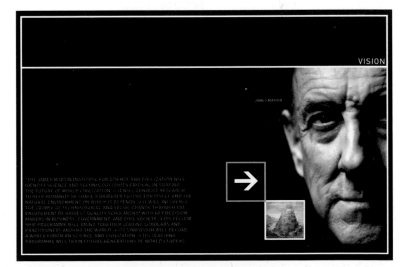

The differences in proportion between the various spaces surrounding the elements in this page spread—as well as the inward/outward contour of text and images—activate a tremendous amount of space without filling it. LOEWY UNITED KINGDOM

Arranging Form A designer must first consider two distinctly different options for distributing material within a format—symmetry and asymmetry—that will govern more specific kinds of arrangements. Just as the identities of selected forms, in dialogue, establish a set of visual opportunities and necessities for resolution, the organization of form adds an intrinsic dimension to a layout's visual logic.

Symmetry and Asymmetry The first kind of overall compositional logic is that of symmetry, in which forms respond positionally to a central axis of the format (horizontal, vertical, or diagonal). A composition may be structured very simply around a single axis or, for greater complexity, two or three axes. The relationship of forms to the format's axis is likewise open to variation; they may be mirrored, reflecting across the axis (bilateral symmetry), or they may

Symmetrical arrangements are indicative of more historical aesthetics. In this poster for a performance event, the designer exploits this gesture to refer to Old-World exotic circuses, supported by typeface and illustration styles from earlier times. Well-considered alternation between light and dark colors, large elements and sharper details, and lateral movement inward and outward from the box's center axis all help ensure a lively presentation. THOMAS CSANO CANADA

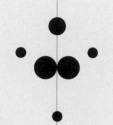

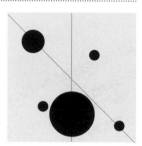

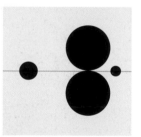

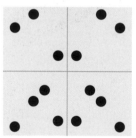

Arranging forms symmetrically around two axes creates greater complexity.

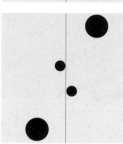

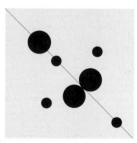

Within a symmetrical composition, elements (or groups thereof) may respond to a format's vertical, horizontal, or diagonal axis (shown top to bottom, respectively).

Symmetry is described as bilateral (top) if form elements' centers align with the axis, straddling it, as well as mirror each other across the axis. In rotational symmetry (bottom), elements invert in their orientation relative to the axis.

invert in orientation across the axis (rotational symmetry). Asymmetry, on the other hand, is a structural logic in which the relationships among the axes and contours of subject forms do not respond to a single axis. In contrast to the condition established by symmetrical logic, this means, generally, that no set of spaces, nor the contours of any forms, will correspond with each other in a direct, one-to-one repetition.

Symmetry and asymmetry rarely integrate well with each other. Symmetry imposes a strict order on arrangement that usually creates formal disconnect among elements that violate it. Asymmetrical arrangements, in contrast, require continual differentiation in structure to achieve resolution. Another potential concern deriving from symmetry is its inherently static quality. Overcoming such obstacles is possible, of course, even if challenging, and—if resolved

successfully by the designer—rewards the viewer with greater complexity and dramatic differentiation among parts.

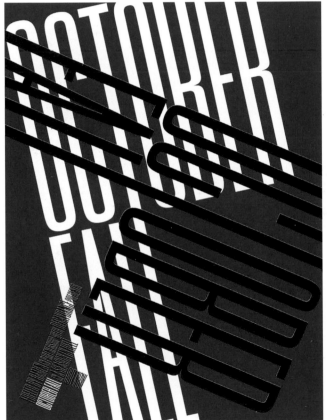

Asymmetry is inherently dynamic. The movement of the type, created by its repetition and rotation, creates strong diagonals and wildly varied triangular negative shapes. The movement is enhanced greatly by the rhythmic linearity of the ultracondensed sans serif type. STEREOTYPE DESIGN UNITED STATES

Department Store on Broadway

Twentieth-century design cognoscente Dorian LaPadura has lived in architectural gems by Frank Lloyd Wright, Frank Gehry, and Gregory Ain since selling his mural business in 1995 and moving west from New York City. He was feeling the itch to move again in the late '90s when a friend told him about a loft with lots of space, reasonable rent, and an intriguing location.

When he saw the 1919 five-story Kress Building on Broadway in the Historic Theater District, LaPadura was as excited by the neighborhood as by the space. His fourth-floor loft, shared with Museum of Contemporary Art store manager Fran Vincent, overlooks the 1911 Orpheum Theater (now the Palace) and directly abuts the 1931 Los Angeles Theater. Iconic Clifton's Cafeteria, also established in 1931, is across the street. St. Vincent's Court, a colorful back alley lined with

Content is always different and always changing, and an asymmetrical approach allows a designer to be flexible, to address the spatial needs of the content, and to create visual relationships between different items based on their spatial qualities. The horizon line in the room, the vertical column, the red headline, the text on the page, and the smaller inset photograph all respond to each other's sizes, color, and location; the negative spaces around them all talk to each other. THINK STUDIO UNITED STATES

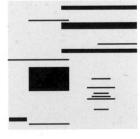

Reconciling these two overall kinds of logic to create unity is difficult, but the complexity and contrast that results can be very useful. It's important to ensure that the composition's overall logic is very clearly defined as one or the other, so that form elements or groups opposing it

don't create confusion. In the first example (left) an overall symmetrical composition is violated by asymmetrical elements; in the second example (right), a symmetrically arranged grouping takes on a remarkable specificity within an overall asymmetrical composition.

Structure Arranging forms in space, whether responding symmetrically to the format or asymmetrically, defines a kind of skeleton of visual interconnections that the designer must consider to create a totality within perceptual space. This totality is structure. A viewer recognizes structure unconsciously through the way a designer sets up visual relationships between a form elements' contour (the shape of its outer boundary) and axis (an imaginary line that separates its halves), and those of other forms. Most forms express two primary axes: horizontal and vertical. Forms that are composed of several elements present a dominant axis as a whole, as well as secondary axes. At the macro level, even before perception of contours intervenes, the axes create an underlying framework of interconnections across space. These are the broad strokes: vertical, horizontal, or diagonal orientation, relative to the parallel axes established by the edges of the format; position high or low, left or right; axis lengths, and their corresponding relationships to each other, their parallelism or divergence and, ultimately, the rhythm of proportional breaks around the format. Both within forms, as well as between forms, the contours and axes may be aligned or grouped in an almost limitless number of ways. The most basic compositional structures tend to be diagonal or

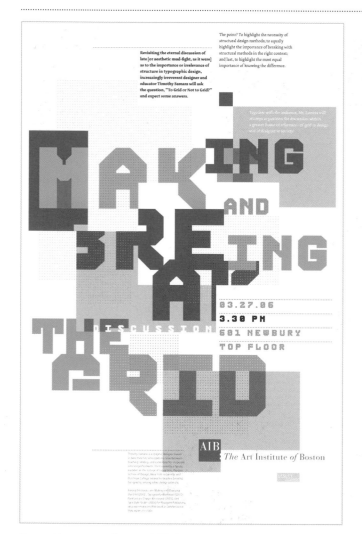

Type, grid patterns, and geometric blocks—some white—exhibit mostly clustering, aligning, and overlapping strategies. TIMOTHY SAMARA UNITED STATES

Aligning

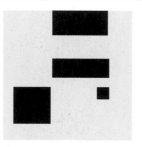

Staggering

Rotational

Chaining

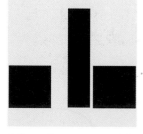

Orthogonal

Diagonal

orthogonal, meaning defined by vertical/ horizontal axes. Orthogonal and diagonal structures may be freely combined, of course (an orthogonal structure implies diagonal axes by virtue of the implied connections between nodes, or junctures between vertical and horizontal axes). But structures may be more complex than simply diagonal or orthogonal, even organic, and within the superstructure of the composition, individual elements may be arranged using secondary structures that correspond to the relationships in the superstructure, add to or evolve them, or contradict them entirely. Furthermore, structures may be very rigid and repetitive in interval or very fluid and irregular; each of these qualities will impart extremely different impressions that influence a viewer's overall perception of content and, therefore, of its meaning.

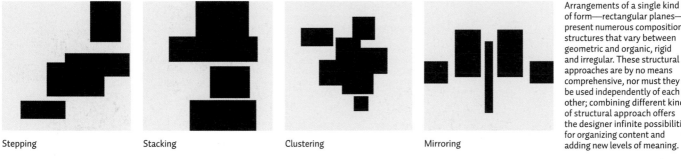

Stepping Stacking Clustering Mirroring

Arrangements of a single kind of form—rectangular planes— present numerous compositional structures that vary between geometric and organic, rigid and irregular. These structural approaches are by no means comprehensive, nor must they be used independently of each other; combining different kinds of structural approach offers the designer infinite possibilities for organizing content and adding new levels of meaning.

  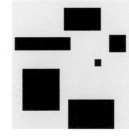

Radial Concentric Spiraling Waving

  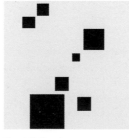 

Grid-Based Branching Constellational Networked

Proportional Spatial Relationships
Controlling the eye's movement through form elements and their structural relationships—which can become quite complicated—can be accomplished by establishing recognizable, repeated intervals to which both positive and negative elements adhere. A designer might develop these proportions in an intuitive way—moving material around within the space of the format or changing their relative sizes—to see at what point the spaces between elements and their widths or heights suddenly correspond or refer to each other. After this discovery, analyzing the proportions might yield a system of repeated intervals that the designer can apply, as needed. Alternatively, the designer might begin with a mathematical, intellectualized approach that forces the material into particularly desirable relationships. The danger in this approach lies in the potential for some material to not fit so well—making it appear indecisive or disconnected from the remainder of the compositional logic—or, worse, creating static, rigid intervals between positive and negative that are stiff, awkward, confining, or too restful.

The Law of Thirds A simplified mathematical approach divides any format into thirds—left to right and top to bottom—under the assumption that the intersection of these axes will be points of visual focus. As a format's proportions become more exaggerated relative to each other, so too do those of the thirds produced. While dividing a format into thirds presents an intrinsically symmetrical structure, the two axes that define the symmetry also provide a very asymmetrical proportional system of one-third relative to two-thirds.

Musical Logic The intervals between musical notes or chords—the octave established by the seven unique tonal pitches in Western music—have been used by book designers to create page divisions since the Middle Ages. Similarly to pitch intervals, the rhythmic or thematic structure attributed to structure musical compositions can be applied to the distances between elements in a layout: ABA, for example, or ABAC, in which **A** is one measurement, **B** another, and so on.

Mathematical Logic Any numeric progression or fractional relationship can be a starting point for creating spatial divisions—odd-number ratios (1:3:5:7), for example, or perhaps a system of halves (1:2:4:8:16), as shown in the first example. The second example shows a grid system based on a common prime number, 3. A thirteenth-century Italian mathematician, Leonardo Fibonacci, discovered a natural progression of numbers in which each number is the sum of the preceding two—for example, 1:1:2:3:5:8:13:21:34, and so on. Coincidentally, this same proportional relationship is what drives the golden section.

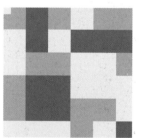

The Golden Section First implemented in a design context by Greek sculptors and architects, the golden section focuses on the relationship of a square and the rectangle that will be defined from it by using a line drawn from the square's corner to the midpoint of its bottom edge. Dividing this new rectangular area by the width of its short side creates a new square and rectangle in the same proportions as the originals; and this division may be repeated over and over again in decreasing size. By connecting the corners of the squares with circular arcs, the spiral that is present in the formation of nautilus shells is magically revealed.

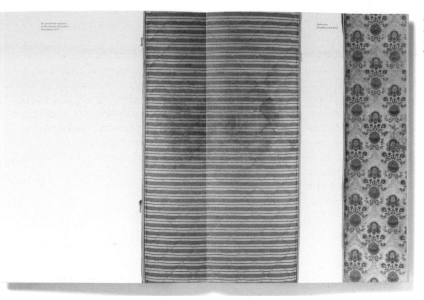

Patterned textiles create a system of mathematical proportions on this brochure spread.
VOICE AUSTRALIA

The break between the photograph and colored field at the right defines the right-hand third, but the first two-thirds are a square, indicating that the golden section might be playing a role in defining the proportions. **ADAMSMORIOKA** UNITED STATES

The bottom line of the colored type occurs at the lower third of the format in this ad. The white tag line, at the bottom, occurs at the lower third of that third.
PEOPLE DESIGN UNITED STATES

Near and Far In addition to side-by-side, or lateral, arrangements at the picture plane, a designer may also arrange form in illusory dimensional space—that is, by defining elements as existing in the foreground, in the background, or somewhere in between. Usually, the field or ground is considered to be a background and forms automatically appear in the foreground—but placing forms that are reversed (made negative, or the same value as the field or format space) on top of positive forms, will move them into the foreground. The relative size of forms encountered in the perceptual field is usually the quickest determination the brain can make and then interpret; larger objects are interpreted as being closer and smaller objects as farther away. Hence, the first strategy for introducing depth in an image is to enforce differences in size. Overlapping forms also optically positions them nearer or farther away from the viewer. The designer may increase this sense of depth by changing the forms' relative values (their lightness or darkness), and by making them transparent. The seeming nearness or distance of each form will also contribute to the viewer's sense of its importance and, therefore, its meaning relative to other forms presented within the same space.

Perception of a space will either acknowledge it as a field or a singularity—what can be called the space's "spread." The essence of a field is that its space appears to extend outward beyond the edges of the format. The perceptual space of a singularity—that of an independent form element— is cognitively finite, or self-contained, distinct from the space around it. This space is reflexive, meaning that its illusory depth continually refers inward, rather than outward.

The "amplitude," or apparent depth, of a space may be deep or compressed. Spaces of deep amplitude correspond directly to our physical perception of space in the natural world. Spaces of a compressed, or flattened, amplitude are more intellectual than experiential. Planar geometry, presented in an arrangement of static intervals and detached from each other, most typically presents a compressed amplitude.

VISIONS/ARTIFACTS

ARTIS ARCHITECTS

The tremendous amount of negative space enhances the illusion of deep space achieved by dramatic differences in the sizes and weights of the forms in this brochure cover. The large diagonal line appears closest—but this directness is thrown into question by the clever overlap of the small text element which, if positioned freely, would appear unquestionably to recede. TIMOTHY SAMARA UNITED STATES

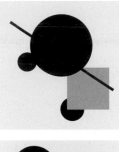

A difference in the relative size of form elements will immediately introduce the perception of depth into a composition. Larger forms typically appear to advance, while smaller ones appear to recede. Changing the relative values of forms will similarly contribute to the perception that they are closer or further away.

Allowing one form to cross in front of another, even if both are the same color, will create the illusion of foreground and background. Introducing size changes among forms that overlap, as well as changes in their relative values—or, for that matter, placing negative forms on top of positive—will greatly enhance the illusion that the forms exist within three dimensional space.

The use of transparency in a cluster enhances the illusion of their apparent existence in three-dimensional space. Carefully considering which elements appear solidly positive or negative— and which appear transparent— can result in startling conflicts in apparent spatial position.

When forms within the compositional space appear to bleed the format—that is, are cropped off by the edge of the format—they imply a much bigger composition extending outward into the real world.

In these panels that form part of an exhibition space, the designers make startling use of opacity, transparency, and scale change to exaggerate the space's physical dimensionality and, at the same time, create an ambiguously flattened space in which type elements that are farther away appear to sit on the same surface as others that are physically closer.
NAROSKA DESIGN GERMANY

Movement Creating a sense of movement within a composition is considered desirable because, like the illusion of spatial depth, it helps deny the inherent flatness of the format and so further engages the viewer. Given that one's assumed area of focus within a format will initially be its center, simply positioning a form elsewhere will instigate the perception of motion—that the form has moved from where it "should" have been. Overlapping and bleeding, as

well as the rotation of elements compared to others, may induce a feeling of kinetic movement. Juxtaposing a static form, such as a horizontal line, with a more active counterpart, such as a diagonal line, invites comparison and, oddly, the assumption that one is standing still while the other is moving. Creating sequential alternation or progression in the relative sizes or values of form elements—a series of squares ordered from light to dark and back again, for

example, or from smaller to larger—will suggest more complex spatial animation.

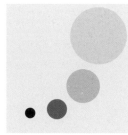

Even shifting a single element off center will cause it to be perceived as having moved.

Any element that is rotated away from orthogonal orientation will be perceived as moving, or kinetic, especially if it can be compared to any orthogonally oriented forms.

Forms that bleed the format, or overlap each other, are usually perceived as moving.

The sense of a sequence of animation occurs when forms change size, proportion, value, and/or orientation, either alternating between states or progressing from one state to another—especially along a consistent axis.

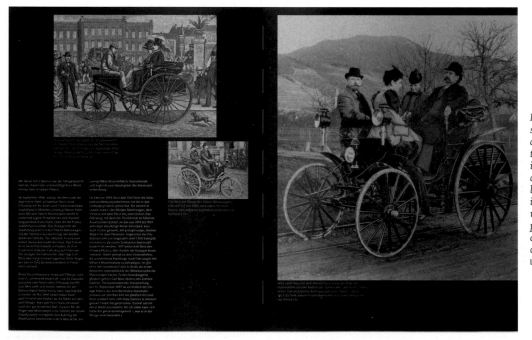

In this book spread, differently sized images appear at optically different depths to create the perception of movement inward and outward. More compelling, however, is the lateral movement the designer introduces by staggering the vertical edges of the cropped photographs and type columns, and by bleeding the large image off the right-hand page.
L2M3 GERMANY

Compositional rhythm may follow such laterally emphasized logic as alternation, where positive/negative proportions flip between compressed and open states in repetition, sometimes at differing overall scale.

Rhythmic progressions are those in which the interval differences between positive and negative components transition from one state to another (for example, from tight or compressed to open or expansive).

Another possibility, opposition, where one general area expresses a singular, specific rhythm in contrast to that expressed by another area.

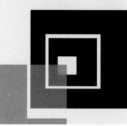

Figure/ground reversal may create the same alternation, progression, or opposition, not only laterally, but also with the appearance of moving "backward" or "forward." Value changes among elements in foreground, middle ground, and background may accomplish a similar effect.

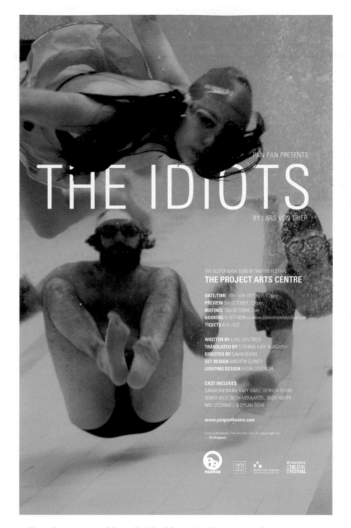

Follow the contours of the individual forms in this poster—those of the figures and of the typographic elements—and take note of two different rhythmic movements: one in which the outer contours push inward toward the center and then outward to the edges at changing intervals; and another in which major horizontal spatial breaks progress from more tightly compressed at the top to more open toward the bottom. CONOR & DAVID IRELAND

Rhythm Changing the intervals between elements or, more simply, placing some closer together and others farther apart, also invites comparison and, again, the odd conclusion that the changing spaces mean the forms are moving in relation to each other. The quality and degree of perceived movement thus created should establish a recognizable and decisive visual tempo across the format—a perceived rhythm in how much, and how often, the optical sensations of compression, or squeezing, and expansion, or opening, occur among the composition's positive and negative parts. As with structure, the nature of a particular rhythm in a layout contributes to the totality of its logic, and will evoke varying degrees of energy or restfulness. A clear, dramatic rhythm is important not only for visual interest, but also for delivering emotional or conceptual messages. Compositional rhythm alone may account for the majority of an audience's immediate interpretation of a message: the understanding of stability or uncertainty, for instance, or of frenzy or restfulness, precision or disorganization, growth or decline.

Activating Space During the process of composing form within a given space, portions of space might become disconnected from other portions. A section might be separated physically or blocked off by a larger element that crosses from one edge of the format to the other; or, it might be optically separated because of a set of forms aligning in such a way that the eye is discouraged from traveling past the alignment and entering into the space beyond.

Focusing the majority of visual activity into one area of a composition—for example, by clustering—is an excellent way of creating emphasis and a contrasting area for rest. But this strategy might also result in spaces that feel empty or isolated from this activity. In all such cases, the space can be called "inert" or "inactive." An inert or inactive space will call attention to itself for this very reason: It doesn't communicate with the other spaces in the composition.

To activate these spaces means to cause them to enter back into their dialogue with the other spaces in the composition.

The space that would have been most in danger of becoming inactive is that at the bottom of this collage, defined by the baseline of the text block and the barcode; the hand, crossing that boundary, easily solved that problem. Also note the vertical column of space to the far right; it too has been made active by allowing the small numeral to break into it.
KENICHI TENAKA JAPAN

Although the gigantic pink exclamation point—created by the line and the letter K—is strong, it is surrounded by relatively static spaces of the same interval, value, and color. This static quality is broken by the brass ball, a dot, which very decisively is not centered and activates the space defined by the floor.
MUTABOR GERMANY

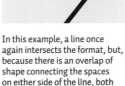

The diagonal line in the upper composition separates a triangular space from the remainder of the format; this space disconnects from the composition and is deactivated. By ending the line short of the format edge, even minimally, the eye is encouraged to travel optically around its ending point and join the two spaces together, activating and relating them to each other.

In this example, a line once again intersects the format, but, because there is an overlap of shape connecting the spaces on either side of the line, both spaces are activated.

Because the arrangement of these forms creates an optical alignment that, while open to the space at the top of the composition, stops the movement of the eye begun in the lower part, this same space now appears inert. In contrast, a simple shift of one element to violate this invisible alignment helps invigorate the formerly inactive space.

The degree of spatial activation in various parts of this composition differs because of the changing proximity and tension between forms … as well as from differences in how the various forms confront each other—some overlapping and decreasing tension, some aggressively opposing each other in direction or contrasting curve and angle.

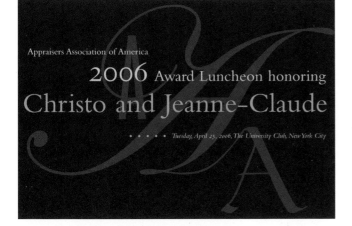

As the lines of type in the foreground shift left and right, they create movement, but they also create a separation of dead horizontal spaces above and below. The irregular contour of the background letterforms, however, breaks past the outer lines of type, activating both the upper and lower spaces.
C. HARVEY GRAPHIC DESIGN UNITED STATES

On the text side of this business card, the spaces are all activated with content. On the image side, the light, transparent blue wave shape activates the space above the purple wave; the line of white type activates the spaces within the purple wave area.
MONIGLE ASSOCIATES UNITED STATES

Building Strong Compositions The cornerstone of every effective visual communication—after a compelling concept or narrative—is a dynamic presentation of the content, accomplished through decisive control of the relationships among form elements. The importance of creating a strong composition can't be understated. The clarity, confidence, and rich interrelationship of elements that define a composition as successful contribute, first and foremost, to attracting—and then holding—the audience's attention, which is critical for ensuring the content is explored long enough to be understood and internalized. If the viewer loses interest because the visual presentation of the design isn't challenging enough, the viewer is unlikely to fully comprehend the message. A lack of visual, and thus cognitive, investigation is also likely to become difficult to recall later on. Second, the strong resolution of a composition contributes to persuasion; appreciating its totality effectively removes our wariness of being manipulated; similar to what happens when watching a film, we suspend our disbelief and the message becomes incontestable.

Active contours created by elements moving inward and outward from the centers of these images create movement and diminish the static quality inherent in their centered configurations.
MEDIA INVIA/DIEGO MORALES
BRAZIL

Nearly devoid of people and activity, these three photographic ads rely on compositional contrast (OK, and a little mystery!) to generate interest.
CHK DESIGN UNITED KINGDOM

Having become conscious of form's basic qualities and the spatial interactions in which they may be made to participate, a designer must then address these individual aspects in combination—understanding them in relation to more complex, overarching goals. Successful compositions exhibit contrast among its parts, even while establishing visual continuity in these parts' behavior; they always create synergy between these behaviors and the identities of the form elements that make them up. And all these strategies, together, serve to order the material in an understandable sequence or hierarchy—so that the viewer knows where and how to enter the communication and then proceed through it in a logical and intuitive way. Last, but certainly not least, a successful composition, in all its aspects, contributes to the more important goal a designer hopes to achieve—the creation of meaning.

Dramatic scale change is instantly engaging because the optical effect is one of perceiving deep space; the brain wants to know why one item is so small and the other is so large. In this particular ad, the foreground-to-background tension is intensified by making the figure and the chicken bleed out of the format. PEOPLE **DESIGN** UNITED STATES

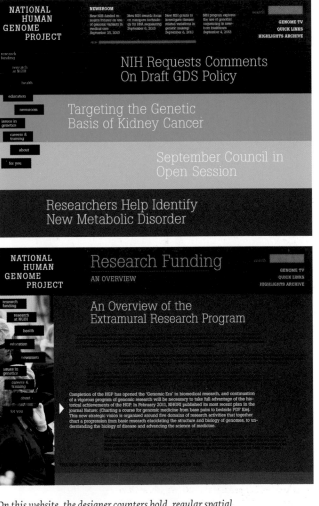

On this website, the designer counters bold, regular spatial breaks—used to separate fields of information—with irregular, side-to-side movement. This gesture derives from the helical quality of the navigation buttons at the left, creating an abstract metaphor for DNA and genetics. JUNE KIM/PARSONS SCHOOL OF **DESIGN** UNITED STATES

Compositional Contrast Creating areas of differing presence or quality—what is known as "contrast"—is crucial for the making of a successful composition. The difference between opposing visual states is what imparts vitality (underpinning the depth and movement discussed previously) and ensures that viewers remain engaged as they analyze the varieties of visual opposition with which the designer confronts them. While there are perhaps hundreds of individual kinds of contrasting relationships a designer may integrate within a single format space, from that of form identity (line versus plane) to organization (elements ordered geometrically versus those randomly scattered), the contrasts typically used the most, and that offer the most immediate impact, are those of scale (large versus small) and spacing or density (compressed versus open)—and their mutual effects on the perception of value: how overall light or dark the compositional space appears, in different areas, as a totality. Enforcing these contrasts first, whether to extremes or more subtly, sets up all the others.

The sensual pleasures of warmth and cleanliness seem to bring out the best in people: the Japanese respond with happy chatter and contented sighs. The smooth floors and walls of tile magnify the din of spirited conversation punctuated by splashes and the high-pitched laughter of children. The sounds of the bathhouse change with the shifting cycle of the daily clock, beginning relatively quietly in the midafternoon, when the doors open to the first customers — generally, elderly

PLEASURES OF THE JAPANESE BATH

retired folk eager for the company of other senior citizens. Later in the afternoon, the decibel level rises as the bathhouse fills up with children home from school and young mothers bathing babies before going home to begin preparing the evening meal. The noise reaches its highest pitch during the evening hours when older children come for their baths, along with fathers and young single men and women, many of whom may have thrown back a drink or two on their way to the bathhouse. By ten-thirty or eleven at night, quiet begins to fall on the bathhouse again as weary shopkeepers or late-returning office workers enjoy a relaxing soak before drifting home to bed. The last sounds of the day are the gurgle of drains, the splashing of water, and the swishing of soapy brushes as the proprietors and staff scrub the floors and tubs and rinse away the aftermath of one long day and prepare the bathhouse for the next.

A black line dividing the spread contrasts with the loose texture of the type; the white type in the line creates spatial tension as one word breaks out of the line and another appears to recede into it. The two photographs have very different edge relationships to the format.
CHENG DESIGN UNITED STATES

Contrast may be achieved using forms of opposing identity—as seen in the poster at far left, which confronts bold, vertical, linear shapes with irregularly clustered dots. But contrast also may be achieved in the interaction of forms with very similar identities: In the poster on the right, all of the elements are lines; the contrasts are in their relative weights, conflicting directional movement, and positive/negative inversions. The poster at the left benefits from the conflicting form contrasts, being a political message; the poster at right appears more harmonious, given that the form language is so specific.

STUDIO INTERNATIONAL [LEFT]
CROATIA
DESIGN RUDI MEYER [RIGHT]
FRANCE

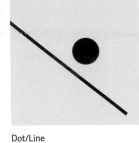

Dot/Line

Curve/Angle

Light/Dark

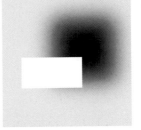

Thin/Thick

Opaque/Transparent

Flat/Textural

Planar/Volumetric

Geometric/Organic

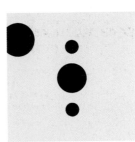

Hard/Soft

Large/Small

Orthogonal/Diagonal

Grouped/Separated

Active/Restful

Simple/Complex

Symmetrical/Asymmetrical

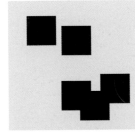

Adjacent/Overlapping

Inset/Bleeding

Parallel/Divergent

Ordered/Disordered

Continuous/Interrupted

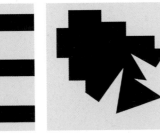

Compressed/Expanded

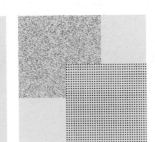

Uniform/Differentiated

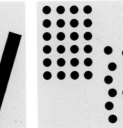

Textured/Patterned

Solid/Fragmented

Regular/Irregular

In this composition, the edge relationships offer one kind of tension within the space, some more aggressive and others less so. At the same time, the edge relationships of angular forms create tension relative to the open, sweeping forms of the curved elements; a similar change in tension occurs between the line elements—which are themselves angular, but in the foreground—and the angular plane surface—which appears as a background element. Both angled plane and lines contrast with each other in identity and apparent spatial position but complement each other's sharp, geometric qualities. This attribute is yet another type of tension.

Tension While the term *contrast* applies to relationships between specific elements, it also applies to the presence of different states of contrasting relationships among forms and spaces interacting within a format together. The confluence of varied states of contrast is sometimes referred to as "tension." A composition with strong contrast between round and sharp, angular forms in one area, opposed by another area where all the forms are similarly angular, could exhibit a tension in angularity; a composition that contrasts areas of dense, active line rhythms with areas that are generally more open and regular might be characterized as creating tension in rhythm. The term *tension* can be substituted for contrast when describing individual forms or areas that focus on particular kinds of contrast—for example, in a situation in which the corner of an angular plane comes into close contact with a format edge at one location but is relatively free of the edge in another; the first location could exhibit more tension than that of the second location.

Contrast in Symmetry Asymmetrical arrangements intrinsically involve a variety of contrasts that provoke rigorous optical and intellectual involvement; in so doing, they may improve the ability to differentiate, catalog, and recall content because the viewer's investigation of visual (especially spatial) is simultaneously tied to the ordering, or cognition, of the content itself. The restfulness and overall uniformity inherent in symmetry can be problematic relative to the goals of designed communication. Without an exaggerated degree of contrast to consider, the viewer is likely to gloss over material and come to an intellectual rest quickly, rather than investigate a work more intently. Exaggerating contrasts in scale (or proportion) and spacing (density and rhythm) when working with symmetrical compositions is advisable, even more so than with asymmetry.

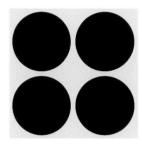

When symmetrically organized forms become so large that they are clearly bigger than any remaining symmetrical spaces, their confrontation with the format becomes very tense, reducing the composition's overall static quality.

Radical changes in size among elements, or in their relative lightness and darkness, helps enhance the illusion of deep space and, therefore, reorders the lateral movement typical of symmetrical arrangements dimensionally—that is, movement becomes perceived as occurring from near to far.

When attempting to ensure adequate contrast in a symmetrical configuration, it's important to exaggerate the differences in relative width of elements toward the axis and away from it (as well as clearly define a logic of progres-sions or alternations); of equal importance is the distance between forms as they travel along the axis from beginning to end.

Another strategy for introducing contrast is to juxtapose dramatically different emphases in proportion, among form elements themselves or the spaces that separate them—or both.

Changes in various elements' weights and sizes, and alternating distribution of material across the center axis, add vitality to these symmetrical page layouts. VRUCHTVLEES NETHERLANDS

The Flip-Side: Enforcing Unity Whether complex or simple, the various compositional relationships within a work must correspond with each other; to achieve this condition, a designer must enforce part-to-whole relationships throughout the work, even among elements and relationships that contrast each other. One can conceive of the primary part-to-whole relationship as the "big picture" that creates the basic compositional gesture in relation to the

format. For instance, all of the material may be organized in a series of horizontal bands from top to bottom, in which each is readily appreciated as deeper or more shallow, denser or more open. This basic relationship may then be restated—at a smaller scale, perhaps or in a different proportion—by the form elements and their behaviors within the main structure. One can refer to the whole as the macrolevel of composition, and to the secondary,

or detailed parts, as the micro level. The idea of unity, therefore, may be understood in two ways: first, in which the macro level lends its qualities to, or influences, compositional relationships downward in greater specificity or variation on the micro level; or second, as a set of microcompositions that influence each other to create the macrocomposition. This idea is similar in concept to that of a fractal.

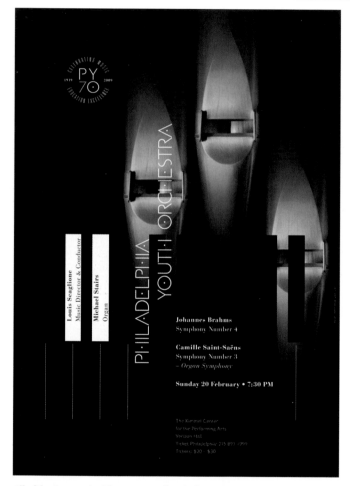

All of the elements in this poster are of vertical proportion; their dimensions change, as do their relative positions high and low, along with their alignment relationships and the intervals between them. PAONE DESIGN ASSOCIATES UNITED STATES

Although some elements in this web page are images, others, blocks of color, and yet others, purely typographic, all align vertically in columns that depend from a horizontal alignment, ending at varied depths. The page detail at bottom shows how this structure is restated by the shaping of the type, but in horizontal orientation. STUDIO BLUE UNITED STATES

Parts within the whole may, as noted, more simply restate each other, but they may also contrast each other simultaneously—and often do so, or must, to prevent a viewer from experiencing visual monotony as they transition from the appreciation of one level to the next. Following the example of the horizontal band composition just described, it might be that the compression and expansion of the bands' depths may be reflected in spatial breaks between elements left to right across the bands, establishing vertical connectivity between spaces or forms; or perhaps the majority of the form elements are horizontal in proportion themselves (even linear), but details are emphasized with dots that mark both horizontal, as well as vertical, alignments. Designers may look to the intrinsic properties of the form elements themselves as a source for both micro- and macro-level compositional unity and, as a result, create direct synergy between formal qualities and compositional qualities. The directionality and parallelism of lines governs the compositional strategy of the example given; if the forms to be used happened to have been dots, or irregularly contoured planar forms, perhaps the composition would have been better organized using a radial or clustering structure.

The individual layouts on each of the pages of this magazine spread are quite different: one creates an inward-focused cluster with a stepped outer contour; the other creates a horizontal band shape with irregular contours along the bottom. Unifying their compositions is their response to the respective pages' center axes. BUREAU MIRKO BORSCHE + ANNA MEYER GERMANY

Visual Hierarchy All the aspects of compositional structure, movement, depth, and contrast ultimately must create a pattern that viewers can dissect and follow—a hierarchy. Upon confronting a composition, a viewer must immediately be able to rapidly categorize the material and determine which element is the most important. The designer helps the viewer discover this element—the primary level, or "top" of the hierarchy—essentially by causing its

qualities to be differentiated from those of the remaining elements as a group. A particular relationship must be made different enough from the others—the secondary level—so that the viewer is able to focus on it. For instance, it could be that the majority of material is relatively small—and the primary focal element is remarkably larger in size, regardless of other formal relationships. The contrasts among all of the secondary material, while still dynamic,

must be overcome by the degree of contrast between these items and the one that is emphasized. Given, as previously discussed, that creating contrast in a variety of ways is important, the designer must be extremely judicious with the contrasts he or she applies to whatever is intended not to be seen first. The clearest hierarchies are those of two levels—one thing is very important, and all else more or less equally less important.

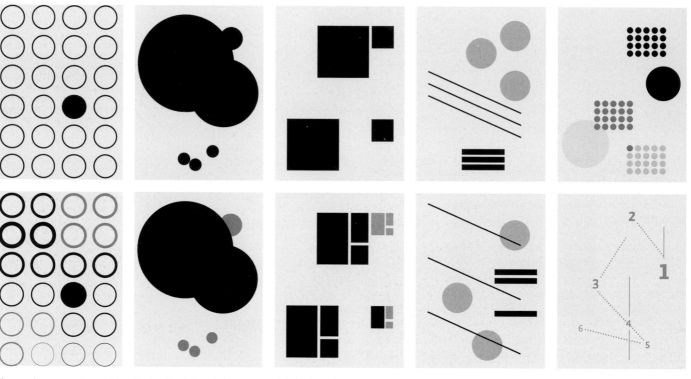

When an element in a visual field disconnects from the others, it becomes a focal point and, therefore, assumes the greatest level of importance. Although there are other kinds of contrast evident in the secondary material, the extreme degree to which the primary element disconnects diminishes the effect of these contrasts.

Contrast in relative size (large versus small) and relative spacing (or density and openness) account for the most effective ways to establish a clear hierarchy. These two contrasts, as expressions of purely positive/negative interaction, affect our sense of the format being divided into darker and lighter areas. This effect is enhanced through the use of actual value change—changing elements from solid positives to middle tones of gray.

Relationships of proximity can help separate—and so distinguish—or join, and thereby relate, elements. In separating the main levels of this hierarchy, the radical distinction among levels by large spaces allows for the creation of similar, but smaller-scale, hierarchies within each level.

Repetition assigns relative meaning to elements that will be understood as related no matter where they occur within the visual field—even if separated by material that is clearly different. Hierarchy, in addition to being strictly about level of importance, is also about relation or establishing which elements are alike in meaning (whether they are important or not).

Compositional flow, sometimes called "eye path," occurs as a viewer compares each hierarchic level's degree of contrast from the others and senses the difference as a decrease in optical resistance (another way of thinking about contrast, incidentally). The eye will move from area of greatest overall contrast to less, following a predetermined direction that the designer can support by positioning axes to help direct or by using graphical forms to point.

A hierarchy may be divided into more than two levels, of course; groupings of similarly emphasized forms and structures can be distinguished from each other, the designer using clear kinds of visual separation to alert the viewer to the presence of each level. Further, each grouping or level must disconnect in decreasing degrees: the first level must stand out the most, or contrast the entirety most severely; the second level must stand out a bit less (or in a different way), but more than the third level, and so on. The changes between each level that act to differentiate also then create a kind of path, or flow. The designer can further use directional axes or movement as "pointers" or guideposts to help the viewer confirm this flow from level to level.

Visual hierarchy has profound implications when working with typography (see *Type as Information*, p.170), as one might guess. And, this basic distinction between elements—that of importance, compared to relative nonimportance—is the very beginning of creating messages.

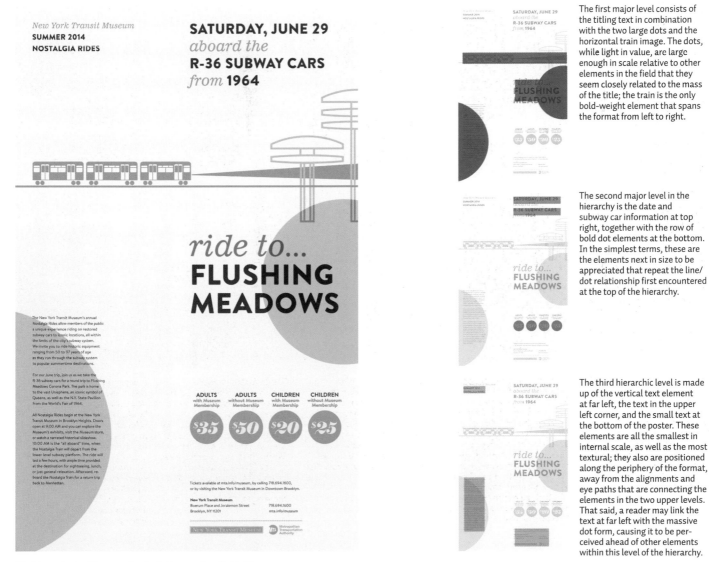

The first major level consists of the titling text in combination with the two large dots and the horizontal train image. The dots, while light in value, are large enough in scale relative to other elements in the field that they seem closely related to the mass of the title; the train is the only bold-weight element that spans the format from left to right.

The second major level in the hierarchy is the date and subway car information at top right, together with the row of bold dot elements at the bottom. In the simplest terms, these are the elements next in size to be appreciated that repeat the line/dot relationship first encountered at the top of the hierarchy.

The third hierarchic level is made up of the vertical text element at far left, the text in the upper left corner, and the small text at the bottom of the poster. These elements are all the smallest in internal scale, as well as the most textural; they also are positioned along the periphery of the format, away from the alignments and eye paths that are connecting the elements in the two upper levels. That said, a reader may link the text at far left with the massive dot form, causing it to be perceived ahead of other elements within this level of the hierarchy.

The hierarchy in this poster is relatively complex, divided into three major levels, as diagrammed at right. ROBERT MCCONNELL/ PARSONS SCHOOL OF DESIGN UNITED STATES

Composition as Foundation for Meaning

Seeing, then understanding, and finally choosing which compositional aspects are best for a designed communication is to initiate the understanding of meaning at the most fundamental level. Abstract forms carry meaning because they are recognizably different from each other; the abstract formal qualities of pictorial images (their very shapes, linearity, and so on) carry meaning by suggesting parity in, or distinction between, the subjects they depict; and the positioning of forms, and the optical superstructures they create, set up a general context and frame of reference that will influence the perceived meaning of every content element encountered, no matter how literal it happens to be. That is, the designer must also strategically develop the composition (in concert with all other considerations noted thus far) to be a relevant message.

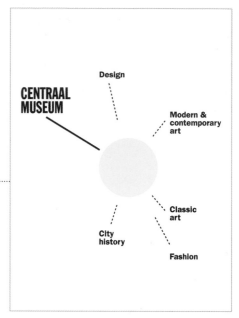

Clustered and constellational arrangements evoke the molecular or scientific; their components will be understood as interrelated, interactive, or interdependent.
LESLEY MOORE NETHERLANDS

Symmetrical compositions evoke formality, authority, or the classical; asymmetry connotes modernity, complexity and, sometimes, organicism.
STUDIO ASTRID STAVRO SPAIN [LEFT] / TRIBORO DESIGN UNITED STATES [RIGHT]

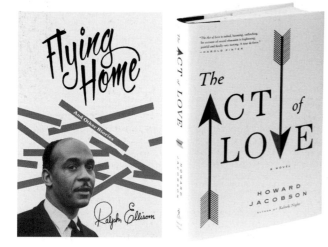

Compositions of elements that are arranged in conflicting directions or that exhibit multiple axes that are not parallel, suggest complexity, conflict, and opposition between ideas or protagonists. CARDON WEBB [LEFT], CATHERINE CASALINO [RIGHT] UNITED STATES

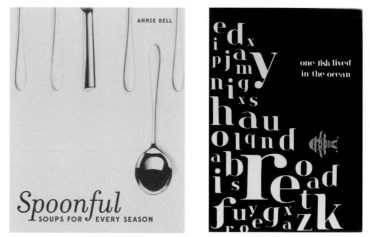

A visual form that is separated from a grouping acquires tremendous importance; this kind of differentiation may evoke specific kinds of interpretation, such as isolation, confrontation, or difference of identity or quality. The grouping from which the element in question in isolated, if organized geometrically, will be perceived as warranting analysis; if organized organically, it may take on a more pictorial or spatial quality. SANG ZHANG/PARSONS SCHOOL OF DESIGN [LEFT], JESSIE GANG/SCHOOL OF VISUAL ARTS [RIGHT] UNITED STATES

While this issue is somewhat wrapped up in the perceptual psychology of form and meaning in images (or, "semiotics," discussed in-depth in chapter 4), it can not be ignored with regard to the basics of form language and its interaction in compositional space. In first confronting a visual communication, an audience will parse its totality and begin down a particular conceptual and emotional path. Every kind of decision the designer makes at this level has implications: the structure is organic or geometric, classical or evolutionary; edge proximities will induce comfort or anxiety; intervals may repeat with certainty or change discordantly; the space will be perceived either as ethereally deep or analytically flat and focused. Any of these qualities, or others—and combinations of them—may be useful at any given time; the designer must carefully consider the more practical, mechanical, purely visual aspects of working with form and space side by side with the goal of using them to evoke the right feeling or association and so appropriately underscore and enhance whatever complex, higher-level messages are to be found within the content.

The two posters above and the magazine cover at left all present compositions that are primarily grid based, but order material on their grids in very different ways—resulting in very different interpretations of the content. In the poster at top left, the grid units (and the images they contain) are very different in size and fit together in a kind of puzzle pattern, creating a sense of connected relationship but emphasizing differences in content meanings. In the poster at top right, the ordering is repetitive and even, creating a more analytical interpretation. In the magazine cover, the grid is regular, but its components are rotated, suggesting overall similarity but suggesting difference or variation
BARNBROOK UNITED KINGDOM [TOP LEFT]
L2M3 GERMANY [TOP RIGHT]
STUDIO DIEGO FEIJOO SPAIN [BOTTOM LEFT]

Perceptually flat space, as well as the presence of pronounced alignments, suggests the mechanical, intellectual, artificial, or factual. Deep illusory space and a lack of alignment among elements suggests the organic and experiential.
HAEHUN HAN/SCHOOL OF VISUAL ARTS UNITED STATES [TOP]
LABORATORIO SECRETO SPAIN [BOTTOM]

The Achievement of Totality The breadth and depth of everything to be considered in developing visual form language, especially with composition, can be overwhelming… and, admittedly, difficult to grasp piece by piece. Shown here is a dissection of all the formal and spatial decisions a designer could (and must) make in a single project. In summing up the concepts presented in this chapter, the poster, opposite, demonstrates the orchestration involved in creating a cohesive visual experience.

The design of this concert poster embodies the complexity of form language and composition that is typical of most design projects. While it includes such elements as typography and pictorial images that haven't been addressed yet, readers will see how these components similarly relate to the fundamentals of form language and composition that are the focus of our discussion here.
PAONE DESIGN ASSOCIATES
UNITED STATES

Dots

Lines

Planes

Geometric forms

Organic forms

Pattern

Texture

Figure/ground reversal

Positive/negative interplay

Movement

Rhythm

Illusory depth

Foreground elements

Middle ground elements

Background elements

Compositional structure

Symmetry or assymetry

Scale contrast

Contrast of angle to curve

Contrast in intervals

Proportional spatial breaks

Macro level elements

Micro level elements

Part-to-whole unity

Major hierarchy

Subhierarchies

Compositional flow

Identify each of the fundamentals of form and space in the poster and describe how they interact with each other to create a unified visual language. You may find that, as with many complex visual experiences, there can be more than one answer to the same question. In the next chapters, you'll see how these basic formal qualities relate to typography and images, as well as explore how color works.

PHILADELPHIA
YOUTH
ORCHESTRA
ANNUAL
FESTIVAL
CONCERT

Mahler
Resurrection
Symphony No.

2

Louis Scaglione
Music Director & Conductor

Michelle Johnson
Soprano

Chrystal E. Williams
Mezzo Soprano

**Mendelssohn Club
of Philadelphia**

Alan Harler
Artistic Director

**Sunday
2 June 2013
7:30 PM**

Verizon Hall
The Kimmel Center
for the Performing Arts

Tickets
$10 – $20
Ticket Philadelphia
215 893 1999

design: paone design associates

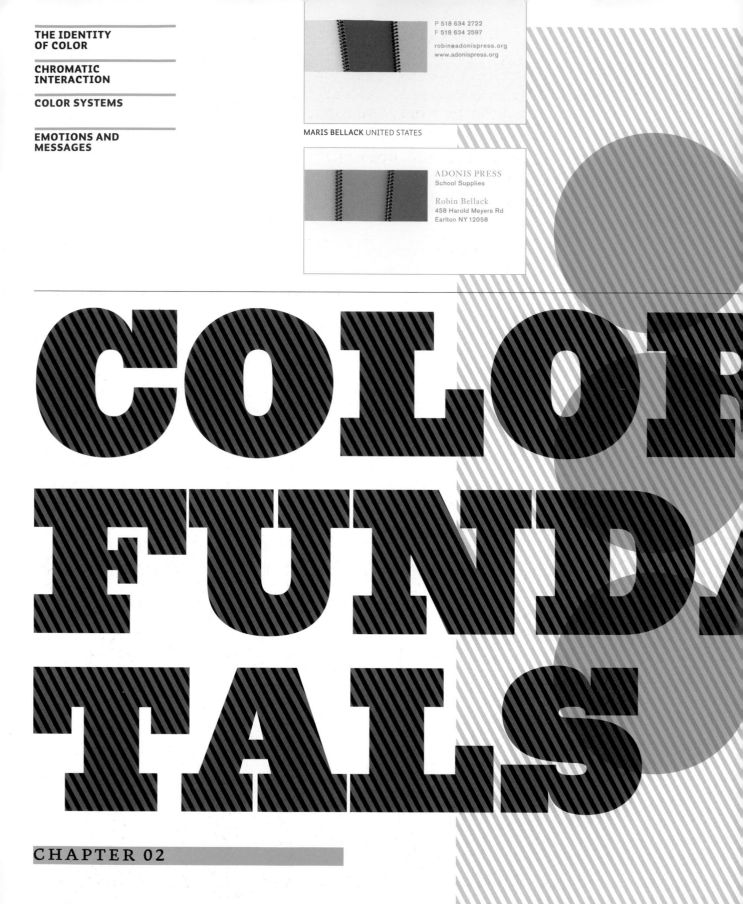

P 518 634 2722
F 518 634 2597

robin@adonispress.org
www.adonispress.org

MARIS BELLACK UNITED STATES

ADONIS PRESS
School Supplies

Robin Bellack
458 Harold Meyers Rd
Earlton NY 12058

COLOR FUNDAMENTALS

CHAPTER 02

> If one says "red" and there are fifty people listening, it can be expected that there will be fifty reds in their minds. And… all these reds will be very different. Colors present themselves in continuous flux, constantly related to changing neighbors and changing conditions.

JOSEF ALBERS / *Artist, visual theorist, and educator; from* Interaction of Color, *Yale University Press*

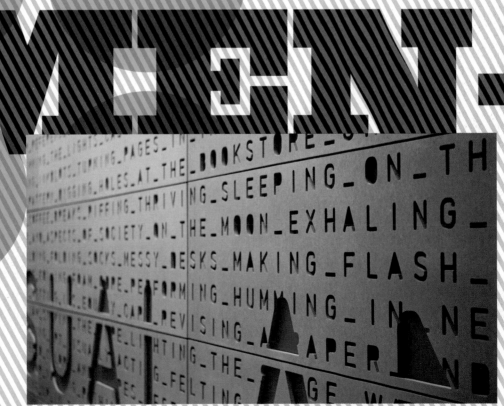

STUDIO BLUE UNITED STATES

There are few visual stimuli as powerful as color; it is a profoundly useful communication tool. But the meaning transmitted by color, because it results from reflected light waves transmitted through an imperfect organ—the eyes—to an imperfect interpreter—the brain—is also profoundly subjective. The mechanism of color perception is universal among humans.

What we do with it once we see it is another thing altogether, and controlling it for the sake of communication depends on understanding how its optical qualities behave.

A single color is defined by four essential qualities related to our perception of its essential nature as waves of light.

Hue A distinction between color identities as defined by their wavelengths

Saturation The relative dullness or brightness of a color

Temperature A color's perceived warmth or coolness

Value Whether a color appears light or dark

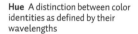

Color plays important, yet very different, communicative roles in these two logotypes. In the GEF logo, the dark blue of the color field feels stable and personable; the more vivid, lighter blue field in the Utopia logo is energetic and cool. The color break in the GEF logo creates a recognizable flag; in the Utopia logo, the color break enhances the lunar quality of the O form.
MADE IN SPACE, INC.
UNITED STATES [TOP]
RAIDY PRINTING GROUP LEBANON
[BOTTOM]

These two posters exemplify the different characteristics that define a color's identity and quality. The red poster is warm in temperature, darker in value, and more intense or saturated than the violet poster—which is cool in temperature and lighter in value.
PAONE DESIGN ASSOCIATES UNITED STATES

Color in typography is highly effective in enhancing spatial relationships, as well as creating relationships between text and image. In this brochure spread, the warm golden type helps push the type closer to the spatial position of the mantis but contrasts with the cool violet tones of the beetle, helping it to optically advance in space. CAROLYN CALLES/THE ART INSTITUTE, ORANGE COUNTY UNITED STATES

Hue This term refers to the identity of a color—red, violet, orange, and so on. This identity is the result of how we perceive light being reflected from objects at particular frequencies. When we see a green car, what we're seeing isn't a car that is actually green; we're seeing light waves reflected off the car at a very specific frequency while all other frequencies are absorbed. Of color's four intrinsic attributes, the perception of hue is the most absolute: we see a color as red or blue, for example. But all color perception is relative, meaning that a color's identity is really knowable only when there's another color adjacent with which it can be compared. Some hues we are able to perceive are absolutes of a sort, what we call the primary colors. These colors—red, blue, and yellow—are as different from each other in terms of their frequency as can be perceived by the human eye. Even a slight change in frequency in any one of the primary colors will cause the eye to perceive that it has shifted slightly toward one of the other primary colors.

When light is split by a prism, the separate wavelengths are perceived as individual colors. The same is true of light that is reflected by an object: the material of the object absorbs some wavelengths and reflects others; the reflected wavelengths are what cause us to understand an object to have a particular hue.

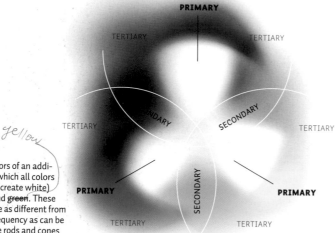

The primary colors of an additive system (in which all colors mix together to create white) are red, blue, and green. These wavelengths are as different from each other in frequency as can be discerned by the rods and cones in the human optical system. The secondary colors in an additive system—orange, green, and violet—represent shifts in frequency toward one primary color or another. The tertiary colors are still smaller shifts perceptible between the secondary colors and their parent primaries.

Although this brochure cover's colorful forms exhibit changes in their relative lightness and darkness, their color logic is mostly about hue: differences between elements that appear very clearly as blue, green, red, orange, and yellow. STAYNICE NETHERLANDS

When we are presented with a light frequency between those of two primary colors, we perceive a hue that evenly mixes them. These hues are the secondary colors: between red and yellow is the frequency perceived as orange; between yellow and blue, green; and between blue and red, violet. Further intermixing produces the tertiary hues: red orange, orange-yellow, yellow-green, blue-green, blue-violet, and violet-red.

Hue defines the essential identity of a color, based on its wavelength: yellow versus violet, for example.

Basic hue Identity is relative: both of the swatches above are red, but once adjacent, distinctions in temperature and value may be made.

Even when altered in value (top) and saturation (bottom), a hue still retains its essential identity (in this case, blue).

The primary text in this ad changes in hue but generally maintains similar value and intensity. Since hue is tied intrinsically to the perception of temperature, that variable also changes. PEOPLE DESIGN UNITED STATES

Red-orange and red-violet are loosely analogous, appearing on either side of red on the color wheel. The red component makes both colors feel a little passionate; the orange component adds adventure or risk; the violet component adds mystery and a touch of sensuality. AMES BROS. UNITED STATES

Saturation The color's saturation describes its intensity or brilliance. A saturated color is very intense or vibrant. Colors that are dull are said to be desaturated; colors in which almost no hue is visible—such as a warm gray or a very dull brown—are said to be neutral. As with hue, the apparent saturation of a color will change if it can be compared to an adjacent color.

The same hue seen in its pure, or saturated state (top) and desaturated or neutralized (bottom).

In their purest, or most saturated, states, some hues are yet intrinsically more or less saturated than others. Yellow is intrinsically more saturated than other hues.

Changing a hue's value typically diminishes its saturation.

Intensely saturated versions of the primary colors—magenta, cyan, and yellow—provide a bold experience in this film poster.
GERILYN HISIGER/PARSONS SCHOOL OF DESIGN UNITED STATES

Photographs of elegantly styled dishes define layout colors in this cookbook. Here, the dish's primary color is yellow—as are the background colors of the pages and text elements, simply desaturated to different degrees. SANG ZHANG/ PARSONS SCHOOL OF DESIGN UNITED STATES

Bringing together hues that are as different from each other in frequency as possible, meaning closer to either of the opposing primaries, will cause the intensity of both colors to increase dramatically. This effect is even more pronounced if the amount of the two colors is very different; the color present in a smaller amount will become much more intense against a large field of the second color. Interestingly, a small amount of a desaturated—even neutral—color, presented against a large field of another color, will appear to gain in intensity and shift hue toward the opposite end of the spectrum. Of equal interest is the effect of value on saturation. As a pure, saturated hue is lightened or darkened, its apparent saturation will diminish.

The value of the field on which a color sits also will affect its apparent intensity. For example, on a white background, primary yellow will appear somewhat less intense—white is the ultimate in saturation—but on a black background, the same yellow will become extremely intense. Against a middle value of gray, the yellow decreases in saturation unless the surrounding value is similar.

The background of this book cover is darker but less saturated than the type, which is lighter and more saturated (intense or vibrant). LSD SPAIN

The apparent saturation of a given hue also is affected by the relative intensities, values, and temperatures of hues that surround it. Here, the same violet is presented against fields of varied intensity and value. In general, as the saturation of the surrounding field increases or decreases, the violet's intensity will appear to do the opposite. This inverse relation is also true with regard to value (similar to what occurs with the yellow examples above). The more pronounced the temperature difference of the surrounding field, relative to the violet, the greater the violet's intensity.

Desaturated colors, all of a similar temperature, create a feeling of sophistication and repose in the splash page of this website. PEOPLE DESIGN UNITED STATES

Value A color's value is its intrinsic darkness or lightness. Yellow is perceived as being light; violet is perceived as being dark. Again, it's all relative. One color can be considered darker or lighter only compared to another. Yellow, even, appears darker than white, which has the lightest possible value of any color. An extremely deep blue or violet appears quite luminous against a maximal black, which has the darkest value of any color (black being technically the absence of any reflected light). Lightening the value of an intensely saturated hue tends to desaturate it. Darkening the value of a moderately to intensely saturated hue will initially intensify its saturation, but if the value is darkened too much, the hue will become less vibrant. Placing any color on a darker color will make it seem lighter, as will increasing the amount of a color. If you've ever had the unfortunate experience of picking out a paint swatch for your living room only to find that it's three or four values too light once you paint an entire wall, you already know this to be true. Bringing two hues of the same value together, regardless of their relative intensities, creates an odd "bleeding" effect that messes with our ability to see a sharp, distinct boundary between the two. The more different the two hues, or the more similar they are in intensity, the more pronounced this effect becomes;

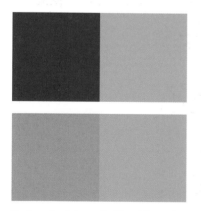

The effect of value relationships is shown here in a close-in comparison of two colors of relatively similar hue and intensity; the greater the difference in the value of either color—or of the color field on which it sits—the greater the effect on relative intensity. In the lower example, the deeper ochre becomes more intense as the yellow orange lightens.

The boundary between the blue-violet on the left and the blue-green on the right is easy to see in the top pair. Replace the darker color with a violet of similar value to the blue-green, however, and their boundary is more difficult to see and seems to vibrate.

Although the largest elements in a composition typically appear to advance, the enormous titling element in this page spread appears to recede, relative to smaller elements, because its value is the same as that of the background. RESEARCH STUDIOS UNITED KINGDOM

A simple, stark division in value between the upper and lower areas of this book cover layout is immediately apparent; the upper area, while overall light, is fluidly divided by very subtle changes in value. Similar subtlety of value shift also occurs in the text elements, helping to distinguish them as set in German or English. ANDREAS ORTAG AUSTRIA

at some magical intersection of hue and saturation, the boundary between two colors of the same value will be nearly impossible to see. Designers may exploit this optical vibration to great effect, but must be very careful when applying it to text—most often, it will cause small text to become completely illegible.

Absolute value identity is considered in terms of hues' similarity to a tone of black, which achieves the darkest value possible.

Every hue has an inherently lighter or darker value, relative to the others in the visible spectrum. The pure hue at top is deeper in value than the one below.

Saturation has an effect on the perception of value. Even though both of these colors are the same value relative to the gray strip, the more saturated one (top) appears lighter.

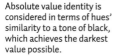

Like a photograph that is considered "good," this drawing exhibits a great deal of value change—a full range from deep shadows, through a generous number of middle tones, up through a bright highlight or white. However, the values are not distributed evenly across the format; they progress from one side to another, and they are concentrated in specific places to create contrast.
RAIDY PRINTING GROUP LEBANON

Temperature The temperature of a color is a subjective quality that is related to experiences. Colors considered "warm," such as red or orange, remind us of heat; cool colors, such as green or blue, remind us of cold objects or environments, such as ice. Colors of a particular temperature remind us of these specific kinds of objects or substances because those substances reflect similar wavelengths of light. The temperature of any color will be thrown

Every hue is intrinsically warm (such as the orange at top) or cool (such as the violet below), based on associations with real-world experience.

Any hue may be presented as cool or warm; the further the temperature shift from its pure form, the more likely the hue will be perceived as a different one; this is especially true of yellow, which shifts rapidly to orange or green, as seen above.

Extremely desaturated neutrals, even those devoid of any chromatic activity, may be distinguished by temperature. The top, absolute gray (a tonality of black) appears to take on warmth when adjacent to a subtly cool gray, a desaturated blue.

Warmer colors seem more aggressive and alive, while cooler colors seem more passive. In the right context, this contrast can convey a message that negates energy and, therefore, a sense of life. In this poster, the SOS in yellow-orange seems to call out urgently; the cooler blue overlapping the yellow-orange type quiets it down. This simple change alludes to flooding and, possibly, death.
STEREOTYPE DESIGN UNITED STATES

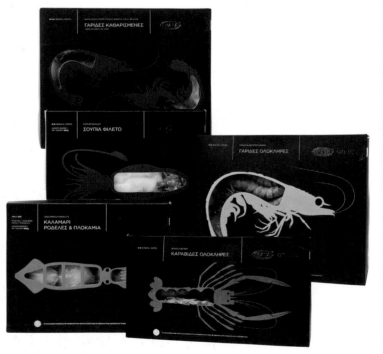

All of the illustrations on these packages are, technically speaking, in the red family—some are cooler, skewed toward the violet range, and others are warmer, skewed toward the orange range of the spectrum. **BEETROOT DESIGN GROUP** GREECE

in one direction or another if compared to any other color. Placing a hot red near an even hotter orange will make that red seem cool; conversely, placing a slightly cooler magenta next to the same hot red will simply enhance the perception of its intrinsic temperature. Temperature relationships need not be especially dramatic to be effective. Subtle shifts in warmth or coolness within a group of hues that are primarily blue, for example, or between a set of neutrals, are easily seen once the colors are in direct juxtaposition; exercising this kind of control in temperature offers rich possibilities for complexity, as well as subtlety, within a palette while maintaining overall unity among its components.

A color's perceived temperature is, of course, relative; even colors that are commonly experienced as cool or warm will demonstrate a shift in temperature when juxtaposed with another hue. In this example, a very cool green—cool, that is, when next to a warm orange—becomes unusually hot when next to an icy cool blue.

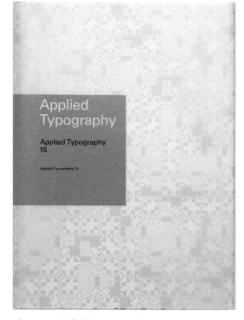

The warm, slightly desaturated orange square appears to advance, while the cool blue-green pattern appears to recede, enhancing the separation created by the translucent jacket. SHINNOSKE, INC. JAPAN

A cooler image on the left-hand page of this brochure spread—with blue-green and pale violet tones—contrasts with the warmth of the wood in the image on the right-hand page. The contrast is important to help add interest, as both images share a repeating pattern of linear, curving, and angular elements. NOT FROM HERE UNITED STATES

Color Relationships Since the fifteenth century, artists and scientists have been creating methods for organizing color perception in visual models. A color model helps a designer see these relationships for planning color ideas. Of these, the most common is the color wheel, developed by Albert Munsell, a British painter and scientist. Munsell's color wheel is a circular representation of hue—the differences in wavelength that distinguish blue from yellow from red—modified along two axes that describe the color's darkness or lightness (its value) and its relative brilliance (its saturation). Johannes Itten, a Bauhaus master at Weimar, Germany, in the 1920s, posited a color sphere—a three-dimensional model that integrates the value scale of Munsell's color wheel into a globe—in his landmark book *The Art of Color,* published in 1961. Both models focus on hue as color's defining aspect, radiating at full intensity around the outside of a circular form and decreasing in intensity toward the center. In Itten's sphere, the decrease in intensity toward the center of the solid globe is the result of mixing hues that are situated opposite each other (as they are on Munsell's color wheel) and results in a cancelling out toward a neutral. These color models were developed to describe how color works with refracted light, but, for the most part, graphic designers work with color derived

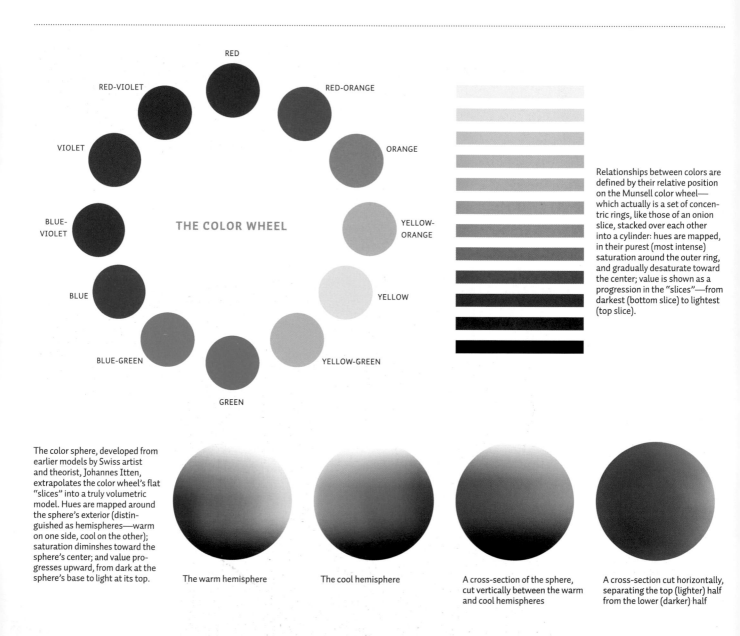

THE COLOR WHEEL

RED · RED-ORANGE · ORANGE · YELLOW-ORANGE · YELLOW · YELLOW-GREEN · GREEN · BLUE-GREEN · BLUE · BLUE-VIOLET · VIOLET · RED-VIOLET

Relationships between colors are defined by their relative position on the Munsell color wheel—which actually is a set of concentric rings, like those of an onion slice, stacked over each other into a cylinder: hues are mapped, in their purest (most intense) saturation around the outer ring, and gradually desaturate toward the center; value is shown as a progression in the "slices"—from darkest (bottom slice) to lightest (top slice).

The color sphere, developed from earlier models by Swiss artist and theorist, Johannes Itten, extrapolates the color wheel's flat "slices" into a truly volumetric model. Hues are mapped around the sphere's exterior (distinguished as hemispheres—warm on one side, cool on the other); saturation diminshes toward the sphere's center; and value progresses upward, from dark at the sphere's base to light at its top.

The warm hemisphere

The cool hemisphere

A cross-section of the sphere, cut vertically between the warm and cool hemispheres

A cross-section cut horizontally, separating the top (lighter) half from the lower (darker) half

from mixing chemical pigments—paint or inks. The relative color relationships described by these models, however, work in much the same way with mixed pigments; the difference is simply how these relationships are achieved in a physical sense. When working with inks (see page 116), the type of ink being used contributes to the designer's consideration of color relationships. If the inks being combined are solids, the beginning color relationships are much more direct and have a more aggressive effect on each other when added together; they will define the secondary and tertiary colors by virtue of their printing on top of each other. If color is being produced by a buildup of primary colors—as in process, or CMYK, printing—a wider range of colors is possible.

It should be noted that in order for color to affect the perception of space—or, for that matter, for there to be a color relationship within a composition at all—there must be interaction between at least two hues. A black-and-white composition that has been colorized, meaning that instead of tonalities of black, all the elements are presented in tonalities of blue, for example, is still a black-and-white composition and is not about color.

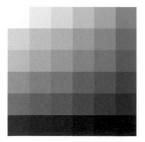

An abstracted model for additive, or light-based, color, forms the symbol for this media company's brand signature.
PAONE DESIGN ASSOCIATES UNITED STATES

This color study is interesting for its examination of relationships between warmer and cooler colors as well as between analogous and complementary colors.
DIANA HURD/CARNEGIE MELLON UNIVERSITY UNITED STATES

In a subtractive color model, such as that which defines ink mixtures for printing, successive layers of ink result in darker, more saturated colors, to a point. Once the ink layers no longer permit a substantial amount of light to reflect from the printed surface, the combined colors become less saturated and eventually neutral and black. Subtractive color is also altered by the chemical makeup of the pigments used to color the inks: rather than desaturating to a truly neutral gray (as with light), for example, a mixture of complements will typically desaturate to a muddy brown.

Two fundamental color relationships are at work to distinguish different areas and levels of content in this website: a hue/temperature relationship (yellow/warm against blue/cool); and a saturation relationship (saturated = more important, neutral = less important).
CONOR & DAVID IRELAND

Hue Relationships Designers can create interaction between different hues, independent of their saturation or value, according to where they lie on the color wheel. The closer together the colors appear on the wheel, the more similar their optical qualities and, hence, the more harmonious or related. The further apart colors are on the wheel, the more their optical qualities contrast.

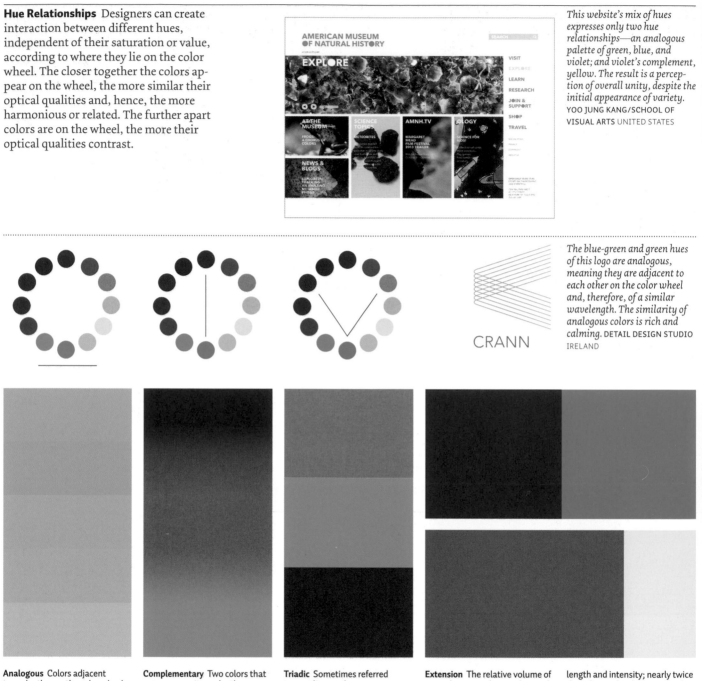

This website's mix of hues expresses only two hue relationships—an analogous palette of green, blue, and violet; and violet's complement, yellow. The result is a perception of overall unity, despite the initial appearance of variety. YOO JUNG KANG/SCHOOL OF VISUAL ARTS UNITED STATES

The blue-green and green hues of this logo are analogous, meaning they are adjacent to each other on the color wheel and, therefore, of a similar wavelength. The similarity of analogous colors is rich and calming. DETAIL DESIGN STUDIO IRELAND

Analogous Colors adjacent to each other on the color wheel are said to be analogous. Although noticeably different from one another, the relationship becomes more about temperature difference. Above, for example, a viewer will note a collection of green hues of varying warmth.

Complementary Two colors that appear opposite each other on the color wheel are complements of each other. Their mixture results in a neutral tone. With light, the neutral is a medium gray; with ink, it's a dull brown.

Triadic Sometimes referred to as split complements, a color triad involves three colors at 120-degree intervals from each other on the color wheel. One color is complementing the two colors equidistant from its true complement.

Extension The relative volume of one color to another, so that each seems to have the same presence, is a relationship of extension. The volume of a given color needed to support another color as equal in presence depends on its wavelength and intensity; nearly twice the volume of violet is required to optically satisfy the presence of a given amount of yellow.

The yellow-orange background of this webpage is complementary to the blue-violet inset images, and is analogous to the two colors wrapped around the central figure. SUBCOMMUNICATION CANADA

Blue-green and violet are loosely analogous, being separated by pure blue and blue-violet on the color wheel. TEMPLIN BRINK DESIGN UNITED STATES

Complementary colors buzz when they get close to each other and neutralize each other when mixed. If you cover up the heart and blur your vision, you'll perceive a less intense olive color where the pure red and green mix more evenly. The increase in red numbers in the heart area appropriately changes its relative intensity. GUNTER RAMBOW GERMANY

Simultaneous Contrast This optical illusion results in a perceived change of one color's identity when it comes into contact with other colors. In this example, the same blue appears surrounded by fields of different colors, but its apparent hue is different in each case.

Value Relationships Regardless of their specific hues, the colors selected for a palette will have relationships of darkness or lightness. By varying the number of jumps from value to value, or by how dramatically the values among the colors change, a designer can create contrast and rhythm among darker and lighter areas—even if the number of hues used, or how different they are, is limited.

The use of color in this poster is only about value—shades and tints of a single hue. In one way of thinking, this poster is essentially still black and white, as there is no true color relationship to be found—for there to be a color relationship, more than one hue must be present. Still, the dramatically luminous and dimensional qualities of the typographic forms, heightened through the use of light and dark, is optically compelling.
ARIANE SPANIER DESIGN GERMANY

Progressive A sequence of values among colors—in either optically even steps or optically geometric steps—is considered progressive if the overall effect is perceived as one of continual lightening or darkening within a given palette.

Analogous In a scale from lightest to darkest, two colors are considered to have analogus value if they exhibit the same (or very similar) darkness or lightness, relative to each other—regardless of saturation or hue. As colors approach each other in value, the ability to distinguish their boundary is diminished.

Rhythmic Extension A series of values, lighter and darker, is considered rhythmic if there are recognizable jumps between shades, relative to the extension or volume of each shade. The result is an optical proportioning of value similar to a spatial proportion system, but dependent on dark-to-light difference.

The boundary between adjacent colors, as we have seen, becomes difficult to distinguish when they are the same value. The effect is magnified when the colors are complements, as well as when two versions of the same hue—one intense, the other desaturated—are juxtaposed.

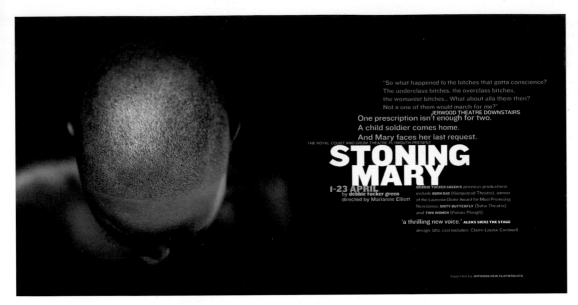

"So what happened to the bitches that gotta conscience?
The underclass bitches, the overclass bitches,
the womanist bitches... What about alla them then?
Not a one of them would march for me?"

JERWOOD THEATRE DOWNSTAIRS

One prescription isn't enough for two.
A child soldier comes home.
And Mary faces her last request.

THE ROYAL COURT AND DRUM THEATRE PLYMOUTH PRESENT

STONING MARY

1-23 APRIL
by debbie tucker green
directed by Marianne Elliott

DEBBIE TUCKER GREEN'S previous productions
include BORN BAD (Hampstead Theatre), winner
of the Laurence Olivier Award for Most Promising
Newcomer, DIRTY BUTTERFLY (Soho Theatre),
and TWO WOMEN (Paines Plough).

'a thrilling new voice.' ALEKS SIERZ THE STAGE

design: Ultz. cast includes: Claire-Louise Cordwell

Supported by JERWOOD NEW PLAYWRIGHTS

A change in value from dark to light among the type elements, culminating in the reversed white title, correspond to the value changes in the woman's head in the photograph.
RESEARCH STUDIOS UNITED KINGDOM

Using a lighter value for the word "taxi" in this logo makes it feel lighter, reinforcing the concept "eco," which appears in a deeper value.
KROPP ASSOCIATES
UNITED STATES

EARTH CONSCIOUS ORGANIC TAXI

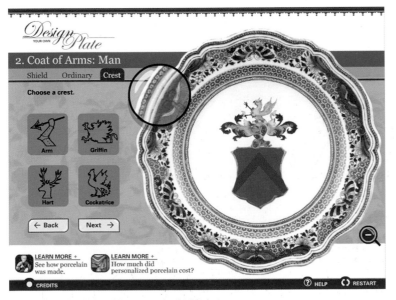

Value changes in the base blue are used to highlight important content and clarify navigation in this website.
SWIM DESIGN UNITED STATES

Simultaneous Contrast
This optical illusion results in a perceived change of one color's value when it comes into contact with colors of differing value. The effect in this case is that one color appears to be lighter or darker, depending on the values of colors surrounding it. In this example, a blue of the same value appears surrounded by fields of different value, causing it to appear lighter or darker in turn.

Saturation Relationships Saturation relationships may occur independently of hue relationships but will usually have an effect on value or temperature. As a hue is desaturated, it may appear to become darker adjacent to a different hue of greater saturation, but it may also appear to become cooler if the adjacent hue is a warm color. Grouping analogous hues of similar intensity, but changing the intensity of one, will create a rich, intimately harmonious palette. Grouping complementary hues, or split complements, all with similar values but different saturations, will create a rich experience.

Both of the featured photographs in these book spreads emphasize saturation as a primary chromatic element. The image at top shows a single hue (yellow) in varying degrees of saturation. The lower image shows a desaturated cool red contrasting a saturated warm red. JELENA DROBAC SERBIA

Analogous Any colors, regardless of hue, temperature, or value, that exhibit the same intensity or brilliance, are said to exhibit analogous saturation.

Diametric Opposition Similar to hue complements, but expressed in terms of saturation, this relationship concerns the juxtaposition of the most intense and almost completely desaturated versions of the same hue. The result of this kind of pairing is that while the desaturated component retains its base hue, its complement appears to be present because of what is called the "after-image" effect—an optical illusion in which the eye is stimulated by the saturated color so much that it triggers the perception of a "phantom" of its complement.

Extension Juxtapositions of two or more colors of similar intensity, but in different volumes, create effects of simultaneous contrast and after-image. Juxtaposing a small volume of a desaturated color with a large volume of an intensely saturated color creates hue-shifting; the intense volume acts on the desaturated color to skew it toward the intense color's complement.

Split Opposition The most intense version of a given color in relation to the nearly desaturated versions of its split complements creates a relationship of split opposition. The split relationship can also occur between the desaturated hue and the most intense versions of its split complements.

CREATIVE
T I L E
COMPANY INC.

The effect of diametric opposition occurs here; the more intense squares in this logo (T, E) cause the viewer to see the complement in the desaturated squares. Looking at the T and E tiles will cause the others to appear greenish. **DROTZ DESIGN** UNITED STATES

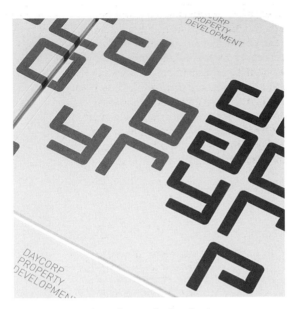

The pink of the letterform, whose value is also lighter, is less saturated than the red droplet, enhancing its vitality and symbolic quality. **LSD** SPAIN

A progression in value and saturation from less intense to more intense imparts rhythm and movement to the rigidly grid-shaped typography. **VOICE** AUSTRALIA

The idea of extension is manipulated for this book cover. The background yellow is relatively intense, more so than the medium gray of the title type; the effect of extension renders the type slightly bluish or violet, the complement of yellow. At the same time, the red elements are intensified through their analogous relationship—in hue and saturation—with the background. **RED CANOE** UNITED STATES

Simultaneous Contrast With regard to saturation, this optical illusion results in the perceived change of a color's intensity when it appears adjacent to colors whose intensity changes. In this example, the same blue-green appears surrounded by fields of different saturation, appearing more saturated in some contexts and less saturated in others.

Temperature Relationships Designers can establish relationships within a color palette based on relative temperature. Grouping colors with similar temperature, together with one or two variations on the same hues that are warmer or cooler—for example, a cool green, blue, and violet with a warmer green—can generate enormous possibilities for combining the colors while maintaining a tightly-controlled color environment.

Temperature relationships tie together each page of this magazine spread (note the locations of the warmer green elements) and separate elements in the hierarchy.
ADAMSMORIOKA UNITED STATES

Closed Extremely subtle, yet still perceptible, analogous shifts in temperature among a set of colors that, nonetheless, retain the same hue identity. Value and saturation changes of the same pure hue may accomplish this relationship.

Analogous Any sequence of colors that is adjacent on the color wheel so long as they are similarly warm or cool: red/orange/yellow, for example, or yellow/yellow-green/green, but not orange/yellow/green.

Progressive An analogous grouping in which temperature makes a markedly stepped transition, color by color, from cooler to warmer or vice versa.

Extension Between two colors sharing intensity and value, differences in volume will have the effect of changing the perception of their relative temperature. If two colors are both relatively close to each other in temperature, the one given in smaller volume will appear to shift temperature away from that given in greater volume.

LOOK UP

STUDY IN
NORWAY.

The analogous shift in temperature—added warmth that transforms a blue-green into green—not only adds visual interest, but evokes a sense of sky and landscape.
COBRA NORWAY

multipano

Each stroke of the M symbol becomes progressively cooler; the full logotype is the coolest. As green becomes cooler and deeper, it communicates less about refreshment and more about economic growth and stability. JELENA DROBAC SERBIA

An analogous hue change—here, for example, orange and red—is, for all intents and purposes, really a change in temperature. The orange is warmer than the red.
UMBRELLA DESIGN INDIA

Saraswat
Bank

So Ready
to Pop

A relatively subtle temperature difference between two red hues of analogous value provides enough visual separation between background field, foreground image, and type in this LP sleeve for a local Indie band—whose music draws upon psychedelic and 1960s underground music genres. TIMOTHY SAMARA UNITED STATES

This poster is printed in three ink colors, all of which could be characterized as cool if seen independently: a green-blue, a muted red violet, and a muted violet. In the context of the green-blue, however, the red violet (partly because it is desaturated) is perceived as a warm color. HELENA WANG / PARSONS SCHOOL OF DESIGN UNITED STATES

Simultaneous Contrast This optical illusion affects the apparent temperature of a color in much the same way it affects its hue, value, or saturation. A given color will appear warmer when situated against cooler colors but cooler when against warmer colors. In this example, the same green appears surrounded by fields of different warmth and coolness; the result is a corresponding change in the green's perceived warmth or coolness, in turn.

Color: Form and Space Colors exhibit a number of spatial properties: their relative temperatures, values, and saturations, in combination, will cause the forms to which they are applied to occupy an apparent foreground, middle-ground, or back-ground position in illusory space. Of the primary colors (in their pure states), blue appears to recede and yellow to advance, but red appears to sit statically at a middle depth within space. In general, against a white field, warm colors appear to advance into the foreground, and cool colors appear to recede; colors of darker value—or of greater intensity—appear to advance, while colors of lighter value—and those of lesser intensity—appear to recede.

These basic relationships will change, however, once the field, or negative space, also takes on a color. In such a case, the relative value, temperature, and saturation of the field will appear to draw those form elements whose values or temperatures are analogous to it—whether light in value or dark, warm or cool, saturated or desaturated—closer to a background position; those form elements whose values, temperatures, or saturations contrast those of the field

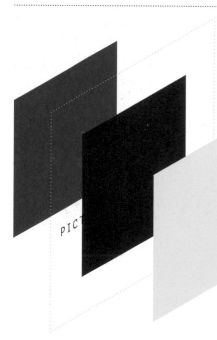

Our optical system (eyes and brain) perceive the three primary colors as existing at different depths in space, a function of how our brains interpret the wavelengths of these colors. Red appears stationary at a middle distance and seems to sit on the surface of the picture plane, neither in front of nor behind it. Blue appears to recede behind the picture plane, while yellow appears to advance.

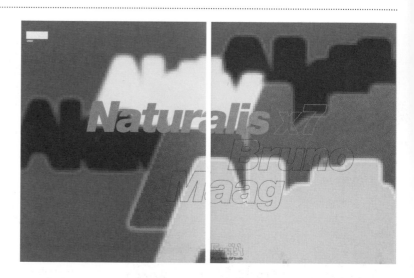

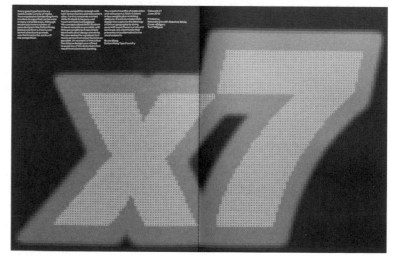

The designers of these page spreads play with the spatial properties of color in dramatic ways. In the top spread, colors that are cooler or more neutral act as expected—receding against warmer hues that advance. In the bottom spread, however, the cooler magenta hue appears to advance over the warmer yellow type due to its greater saturation. **SEA** UNITED KINGDOM

will appear to advance into the foreground. Given this possibility, therefore, it's entirely possible to cause warmly colored forms to fall into deep space and cool-colored forms to move into the foreground—if, for example, the field is itself a warm color. The volume of a given color present in a particular element, relative to its surrounding environment, will also have an effect on its apparent spatial position, as well as its overall value and intensity.

Consider, again, that colorizing a black-and-white composition will introduce no difference in the spatial relationships among the elements as they already exist, as defined by their absolute values. It is only through the interaction of two hues or more that applying color will add new kinds of perceived spatial interaction.

The amount of color that can be perceived—and its intensity and value—are all affected by volume. The orange of the narrow line appears darker and less intense against the white field of the page than either the thicker line or the larger square. The opposite is true when the same elements cross over a dark field.

Each color—blue, red, and yellow—assumes a place in space: blue recedes, red stays in the middle, and yellow advances. In this case, the application of color enhances the desired spatial location of each element.
THOMAS CSANO CANADA

Colors of similar value will appear to cluster together into one form, as do the grayish and olive green areas at the upper left of this study. Because their values are similar, the boundary between them appears less pronounced than those between other areas whose values are much different, even if their intensities are also very different. Note the relative lack of separation between the desaturated orange and light gray at the lower right.
JROSS DESIGN UNITED STATES

Color and Space Re: Visual Hierarchy

Applying color to a composition will have an immediate effect on hierarchy, the relative order of importance of the forms in space. The intrinsic relationships in a black-and-white composition might be exaggerated through the application of chromatic color or made purposely ambiguous. Color distinctions can greatly enhance the perception of spatial depth and force greater separation between the hierarchic levels. For example, if an element at the top of a hierarchy is set in a deep, vibrant orange-red, while secondary forms are colored a cool gray, these two levels of the hierarchy will be separated visually to a much greater degree. Although the values of the colors are similar, the saturated orange form will advance in space, and the cool gray one will recede. The application of color to the ground within a composition can further enhance the hierarchy.

A form in one color, set on a field of another color, will join closely with it or separate aggressively, depending on their color relationship. If the colors of foreground and background elements are related, the elements will occupy a similar spatial depth. If they are complementary in nature, the two will occupy very different spatial depths.

The result of color's appearance at different planar locations can have a tremendous impact on the perceived depth of forms in space and, consequently, on the order in which each form presents itself: the visual hierarchy. In this study, each form element—regardless of size or arrangement—is made to register in the foreground, then the middle ground, and then the background of the composition, merely by alternating the element to which each color is applied. The effect becomes even more dramatic when the background participates in the color swap.

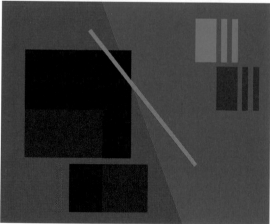

A black-and-white composition showing a major, two level hierarchy—as well as subhierarchies within—acts as a guidepost for a designer's application of color. A strong complementary relationship in the palette acts first to emphasize the top level of the hierarchy. This fundamental color contrast exaggerates the already dramatic distinction accomplished by size change and, being so strong, supersedes the contrasts that occur within the secondary level—all constrained within analogous relationships of hue and saturation.

A designer, therefore, must approach the application of color to elements within a visual hierarchy with the same sensitivity to overall difference (contrast) between hierarchic levels as he or she would the basic aspects of compositional contrast. The greatest degree of color contrast must be given to the elements at the top of the hierarchy, relative to the kinds and degrees of color contrast applied to the elements at the secondary and tertiary levels. The most effective way of successfully ensuring that this occurs is to first establish the composition's hierarchy in black and white. This allows the designer to understand the complexities of the hierarchic levels and the degrees of contrast needed to separate them (as well as those contrasts that are present within each level) without having to consider the wild variables that color will inevitably introduce. With the hierarchic distinctions clear in black and white, the designer creates a kind of reference map for assigning color relationships: What kind of hue/temperature/value/saturation qualities, together, will add to these distinctions, already in place?

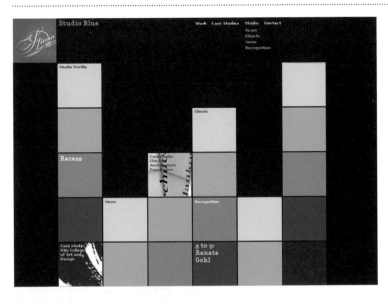

The spatial difference between the squares in this website creates hierarchy: The lighter squares advance and so become the more important, or sequentially primary, elements in the navigation.
STUDIO BLUE UNITED STATES

Differences in temperature between the primary hues of major elements in this ad—the cool violet and the warm red—enhance the hierarchy already established by value.
TIMOTHY SAMARA UNITED STATES

It's interesting to compare the effect of different color combinations on the same hierarchy in different instances. Note how the rectangular label element, in particular, appears to change in both apparent spatial position and emphasis relative to other elements in this system of packages. LOUISE FILI LTD. UNITED STATES

Color Logic: Defining a Palette Just as it's important for a designer to define a clear, unified form language and compositional idea—and one that includes contrast among these variables—so too must a designer establish an overall logic that governs the color within a project. This idea of color logic is more commonly referred to as a "palette," or a specific combination of hues that interact in specific relationships of value, temperature, and saturation.

The first direction a designer may pursue in developing a color palette for a project is that of optical interaction. Creating a rich palette depends on combining colors that can be clearly distinguished from each other but that also share some unifying optical relationships. Because of the strong opposition of complements, palettes based on this relationship tend to be the most optically dynamic—that is, cells in the eye are stimulated more aggressively, and the brain is provoked into greater activity as a result. Analogous colors, by their very similarity, create more complex, but less varied, palettes. Using such a basic relationship as a starting point guarantees a viewer's clear perception of a color idea; the designer may opt to maintain its simplicity, or introduce complexity—adjusting the value or intensity differences between the base colors, or adding colors that support and expand their relationship.

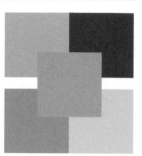

The process of defining a palette can begin very simply: choosing colors for their optical relationship—in this case, a pair of complements—because their interaction is so strong (top). Adjusting the relative values of the complements creates greater contrast without disturbing the clarity of the relationship (bottom).

Seeking a richer experience, the designer may shift the temperature of one or both complements, maintaining the essential relationship but skewing it slightly.

Altering the intensities of one or both introduces yet greater richness without sacrificing the fundamental logic of the palette.

The addition of a neutral version of one of the complements expands the palette; a second version of the neutral, lighter in value, introduces greater variation.

To this already complex mix, the designer lastly adds the analog of one of the base complements, adjusting its value and intensity to correspond more closely to one of the neutrals.

Each of these two ads, part of a campaign promoting a newspaper, presents a specific, focused palette of hues—and a specific set of hue, temperature, and saturation relationships. The ad at far left shows an analogous palette of reds and yellows, with greater contrast in saturation and value. The ad at near left shows a primary palette—a triadic relationship—of blue, red, and yellow, with overall diminished saturation and less contrast in value.
UMBRELLA DESIGN INDIA

Color, of course, can also mean something. Very often, that meaning is tied to associations we make between colors and objects or environments—but colors also evoke intangible feelings, whether by association or by the biological effects resulting from their perception. Further, colors carry cultural or social meanings, related to their use in religious ceremonies or iconography, or in heraldry, in flags, or historically in clothing or art.

Color is very effective for coding—that is, for identifying conceptual relationships in a hierarchy, sections in publications, or counterparts in a line of products. When using color this way, the designer's first concern must be the needs of the audience in terms of understanding how the coding relates the parts to each other. If the project is a packaging system, for instance, are all the products being packaged remarkably different or does each represent a grade or level? Is there one family of products, or are there several related lines, each with its own subproducts? The answers to questions such as these will help determine the complexity that the color coding must address and, therefore, how it will be useful to the audience.

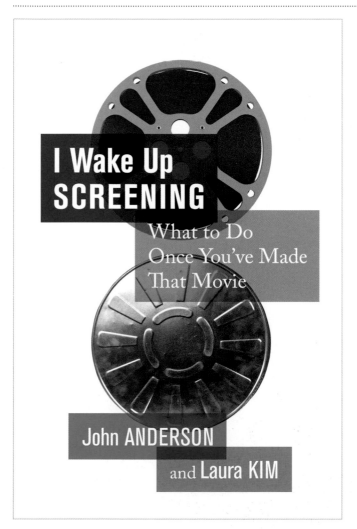

The designers of this book cover use a palette of disparate hues—red, green, blue, and orange—organized as pairs of complements. **THINK STUDIO** UNITED STATES

Working with richly colored photography can be inspirational for designers looking to establish a palette for a project. In this book about Scandinavian textiles, the designer has isolated a blue-violet hue that isn't literally to be found in the image, but is clearly related to the image's analogous colors. The designer followed this strategy for each section opening spread. YOO JUNG KANG/SCHOOL OF VISUAL ARTS UNITED STATES

Basic Optical Choices Establishing richness and flexibility in a palette is always important. Still, the palette must exhibit a clearly recognizable logic. This very often depends on limiting the number of hues and their interactions; as with form logic, composition, and hierachy, simpler is usually better. Grounding the palette in a fundamental hue relationship—analogous, complementary, or triadic—is a great place to start. If a two- or three-hue palette seems too limiting, an effective strategy is to develop a family of a few hues, whose interactions are constrained within a limited set of variables—only varying intensity, for example, while saturation among the hues remains constant—and swap the colors among the various parts of the project. Varying only one aspect of the palette creates the most clearly recognizable logic or system; altering two variables within the system adds complexity (and, of course, the possibility that the logic will become diluted or unrecognizable). Varying the extension, or the volume of each component in different combinations, can clarify the system while providing the flexibility to vary color impression on alternating pages within a website, to distinguish elements in a line of products, or to create a family of publications, all unique in tone yet clearly interrelated.

Color studies improve understanding of color in a deeper way than simply selecting colors strictly for a project. Each study pits relationships of value and intensity against the extension of colors of varying temperatures.
JROSS DESIGN UNITED STATES

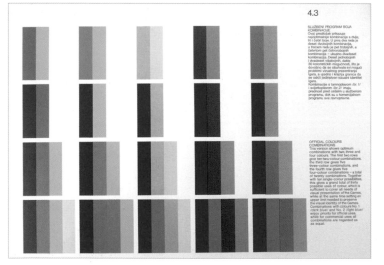

This page from an identity manual shows how colors from the supporting color palette can be combined with the primary corporate color in the system, the medium-value blue. The supporting colors are strictly controlled so that the corporate blue is always the deepest and most intense.
STUDIO INTERNATIONAL CROATIA

The color contrasts in this advertising photograph are limited primarily to two variables—temperature and value—while overall the hues and relative saturation of its elements are very similar. NAM JAPAN

SINGLE-VARIABLE SYSTEMS

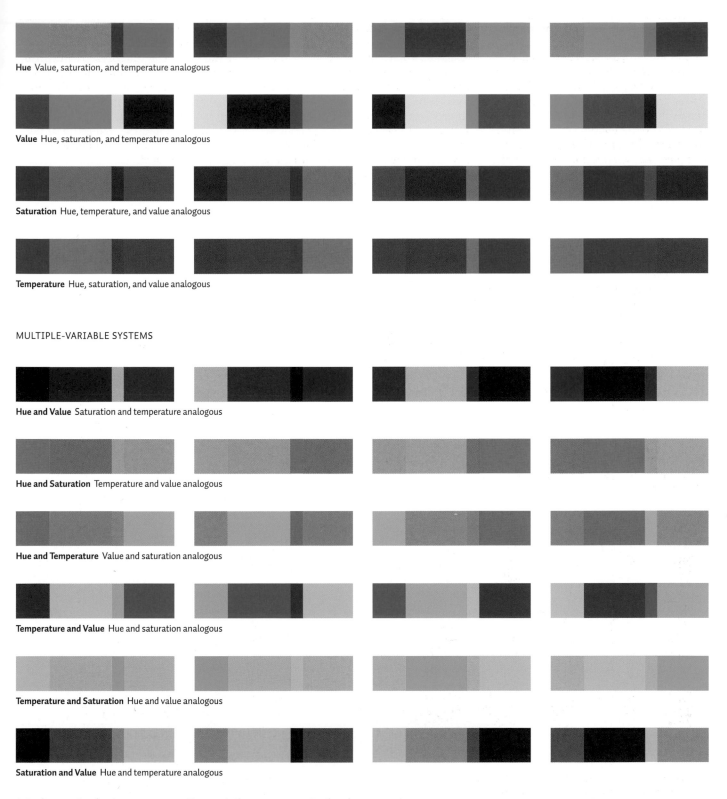

Hue Value, saturation, and temperature analogous

Value Hue, saturation, and temperature analogous

Saturation Hue, temperature, and value analogous

Temperature Hue, saturation, and value analogous

MULTIPLE-VARIABLE SYSTEMS

Hue and Value Saturation and temperature analogous

Hue and Saturation Temperature and value analogous

Hue and Temperature Value and saturation analogous

Temperature and Value Hue and saturation analogous

Temperature and Saturation Hue and value analogous

Saturation and Value Hue and temperature analogous

A simple proportional system is shown here as the basis for different color-coding relationships. The intervals within the composition remain the same throughout; the criteria for the coding system changes from series to series while, within a single series, the color components alternate position among the proportional intervals.

Limited Color Systems Using only three, or even two, colors can be the foundation of a surprisingly rich color language, whether used literally by printing in only two ink colors or limiting oneself in process-color (CMYK) print projects and digital (screen- or light-based) projects—where all colors, theoretically, are available. While a great number of projects call for full-color imagery, limiting the palette always creates a more recognizable and, therefore, more

memorable, experience. In printed matter, using only two "spot" color inks need not be limited to small-run or low-budget projects; a palette of even two thoughtfully-selected colors may communicate just as powerfully and further unify materials. This approach is particularly useful for branding, where the interrelation of inks can be used to clarify different publications in a literature system while reinforcing the identity of the brand.

When working with such a limited palette, choosing colors with dynamic chromatic interaction is of greatest concern: Without as many options, the designer must get as much flexibility as possible from the palette's two or three components. Choosing two complements as counterparts, for example, is an intuitive first possibility. Their complementary nature need not be exact; skewing this relationship can create equally dynamic combinations. Even an

Pure Complement

Complement
Same value, saturation shift

Near Complement
Cool

Near Complement
Warm

Near Complement
Saturation and value shifts

Split Complement

Analogous
Same saturation

Analogous
Different saturation

Analogous
Same value

Analogous
Different value

Analogous
Temperature shift: cool

Analogous
Temperature shift: warm

With a particular green as a starting point, different combinations with a succession of alternate counterparts create a variety of interesting possibilities. Each combination's specificity results in a clearly recognizable visual logic, especially useful for branding projects where color impression plays a dramatic role in brand memorability.

By limiting the value, hue, and intensity contrasts among warm-toned backgrounds and supporting details, the designer gives emphasis to full-color images and navigation while retaining a rich, textural experience in this website. TIMOTHY SAMARA [FOR LEXICON GRAPHICS] UNITED STATES

Simply replacing black ink with ink of another color—even in a one-color job—can give an extra punch to an otherwise mundane project.

analogous combination—a hot green and a cooler, bluer-green, for instance—can provide tremendous opportunities, especially if their values and/or intensities are radically different. Substantially limiting the color palette has some practical, as well as visual, benefits. In a digital environment, limiting the palette can help ease the effect of light on tiring the eyes; it also allows the designer to more clearly designate elements as interactive or noninteractive within a hierarchy. In printing, fewer inks means fewer printing plates and less time making technical adjustments, resulting in cost savings for the client.

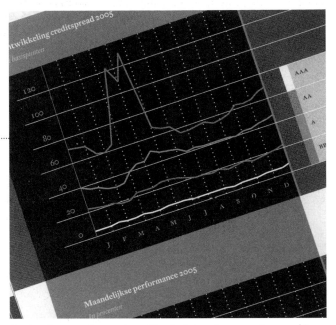

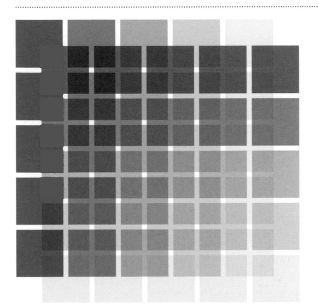

Overlapping spot colors creates a rich color interaction among typographic and graphic elements in this detail of a financial report. UNA [AMSTERDAM] **DESIGNERS** NETHERLANDS

Most printing inks are translucent, so a designer has the option not only to print each ink at full strength—or tinting them to lighten their values—but also to print the inks on top of each other, either at full strength or in combinations of tints. Printing one ink on top of another is called "surprinting," and creates new colors because of their overlap. Such new colors will vary in hue, saturation, and value, depending on the base ink colors selected; usually the resulting third color (and tinted variations) will be darker and less saturated.

If the base inks are very intense or pure, however, the surprint color will also be relatively intense. Choose two (or three) colors with value and saturation as considerations. The deeper, overall, and the closer the inks are in value and, the more saturated they are to begin with, the wider the range of possible combinations, and the greater their potential contrast.

Surprinting a field of red ink on top of found, make-ready sheets means budget-conscious production with interesting visual effects in this poster. The ink's transparency allows a haze of the surprinted image to show through. The result is that positive and negative space become more ambiguous. The red bar becomes flat against the photographs, but the reversed-out type seems to come forward, as does its positive repetition, below. Although the photographs seem flat toward the top, they seem to drop into a deeper space down below, as they contrast the flat, linear quality of the script type. BRETT YASKO UNITED STATES

Limited Palettes in Photographic Images

Photographic images or illustrations with varied tonality are excellent material with which to explore ink coloration: An image might be printed in one, two, three, or more spot colors, with different portions of the image's tonal range acted upon by the inks at different levels. Such options give the designer an opportunity to customize images for a client, enrich the dialogue of color among images, type, and other graphic elements, and to bring images into closer visual alignment with brand-related color messages. Even when full-color photography is not only available as an option, but desirable, limiting the palette within the imagery will help it integrate with the palette applied to nonphotographic forms and typography— such limitation can help focus attention on the most important components of the image's subject or emphasize important details. If the designer is lucky enough to have a budget that allows for commissioning original photography, he or she may art direct the photographer's use of lighting, props, backgrounds, and isolation of content in the frame to control the image's palette. A second option is to manipulate a photograph's native color using software to accomplish the same goal—for example, saturating the yellow components of an important subject in the foreground

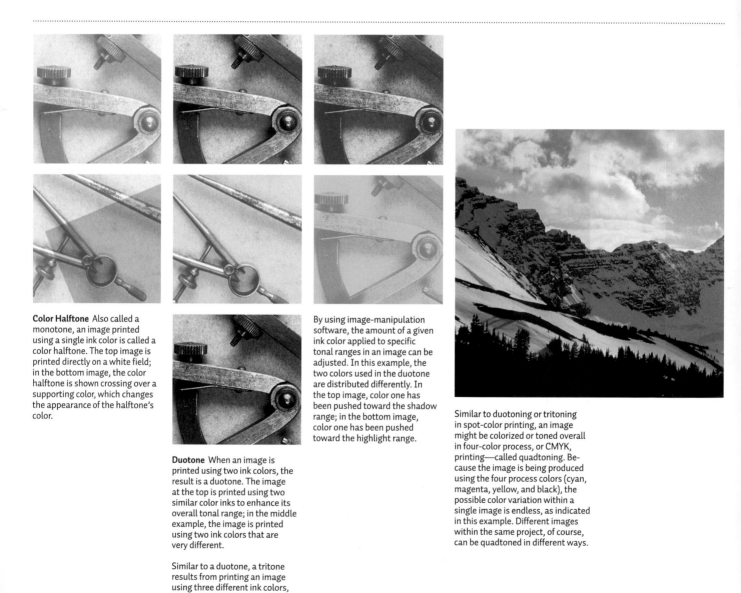

Color Halftone Also called a monotone, an image printed using a single ink color is called a color halftone. The top image is printed directly on a white field; in the bottom image, the color halftone is shown crossing over a supporting color, which changes the appearance of the halftone's color.

Duotone When an image is printed using two ink colors, the result is a duotone. The image at the top is printed using two similar color inks to enhance its overall tonal range; in the middle example, the image is printed using two ink colors that are very different.

Similar to a duotone, a tritone results from printing an image using three different ink colors, shown in the bottom-most image, above.

By using image-manipulation software, the amount of a given ink color applied to specific tonal ranges in an image can be adjusted. In this example, the two colors used in the duotone are distributed differently. In the top image, color one has been pushed toward the shadow range; in the bottom image, color one has been pushed toward the highlight range.

Similar to duotoning or tritoning in spot-color printing, an image might be colorized or toned overall in four-color process, or CMYK, printing—called quadtoning. Because the image is being produced using the four process colors (cyan, magenta, yellow, and black), the possible color variation within a single image is endless, as indicated in this example. Different images within the same project, of course, can be quadtoned in different ways.

and, subsequently, adjusting the color balance in surrounding areas to become cooler, even more violet, overall (skewing the tonality toward the yellow subject's complement, perhaps); the designer might further desaturate some features, or diminish their value contrast, to further emphasize the subject focus. That said, a designer may opt to completely change the color balance within a photograph for conceptual or formal effect: Who is to say that a photographic image must present the empirical (naturalistic) color as it appeared in nature? If the information the viewer needs from the subject doesn't depend on naturalistic color, radically altering the color of photographic images can accomplish a great deal.

FRENCH COUNTRY

Custom home designs inspired by the estates of rural France

DE MOLIERE
MARMONT
CHAUMURE
VOLNAY
BEAUX JARDIN

MEDITERRANEAN

Custom home designs inspired by the villas of Sienna and Tuscany

AMALFI
BELLA VISTA
AL HAMBRA
LA VENEZIA
PALLADIO

ENGLISH MANOR

Custom home designs inspired by the gracious estates of rural Engand

CODDINGTON
WELSH COTTAGE
GRAND TUDOR
IPSWICH
EDINBOROUGH

BRENTWOOD
CUSTOM HOMES

A three-color palette not only unifies the components in this literature system, it allows the designer to diferentiate different product offerings and still reinforce the core identity of the brand. The signature (logo) retains its color identity, and the components all seem intrinsically related to it, as well as to each other.
TIMOTHY SAMARA UNITED STATES

When styling a photograph, designers may make purposeful decisions about the coloration of propping, details, and lighting, in response to the subject's empirical color. The sandwiches in this photograph have been embellished with violet flowers and green leaves and shot against a cool, yet neutral, background. This affects the image's mood and establishes more specific chromatic interaction with the typography's color. MICHELLE LIV/ PARSONS SCHOOL OF DESIGN UNITED STATES

Tea Sandwiches

Tea
Sandwiches

Afternoon Tea

Color Stories: Coding with Color Within a complex visual environment, color can help distinguish different kinds of information, as well as create relationships among components or editions of a publication. A designer might develop, for example, a palette for graphic and typographic elements that helps readers distinguish between specific text components (headlines, subheads, and body) or between sections of information.

Or, a designer might use a general palette for all elements that is based on the color or thematic content of photographs. Perhaps, this palette has a consistent base, like a selection of warm neutrals that remains constant, while accent colors change.

To be effective, color coding must be easily identifiable and, therefore, relatively simple. Using more colors for coding creates confusion, as the viewer is forced to try to remember which color relates to which information. Color coding within a related set of hues—a deep blue, an aqua blue, and a green, for example—can help distinguish subcategories of information within an overall grouping but also ensure that the viewer is able to perceive the differences

Colors used to code a family of items need to be easily distinguished from each other. Triads, as well as large jumps in value or saturation within an analogous set, achieve this goal.

Within a relatively close-in analogous coding palette, an accent enriches the color language. For families of more than three items or levels, consider joining related palettes, especially if they will help identify subgroupings.

Changing the relative extension of a coding palette's component hues can add needed complexity if the number of items or levels is great. Reverse the proportional relationship between bases and accents to double the number of items that can be coded within the family while maintaining a close-in family.

Joshua Braun
EDITORIAL ASSISTANT

Christopher Mims
ONLINE PROJECTS MANAGER

In addition to the optical game created by the super-coarse dot screen, color relationships are used as part of the identity system in these business cards. SAGMEISTER+WALSH UNITED STATES

Groupings of analogous colors provide a flexible, yet very consistent, system for color coding in this packaging system. Each wrapper uses two analogous colors to identify its specific product in the system—blue-violet and aqua, red and yellow-orange, violet-red and orange—and each item's base color is also analogous in relation to each other. A10 DESIGN BRAZIL

between the colors. Pushing the colors farther apart in relation to each other might help—for example, the deep blue might be skewed toward the violet while yellow is added to the green. If the number of items to be coded is great—within an extensive line of products, or complex levels of information within a typographic hierarchy—creating analogous subsets within a still-limited palette of hues can be effective: for example, three analogous greens for one group, three analogous violets for another, and so on. Wide-ranging sets of hues can be unified using an accent color that appears throughout the coded material.

Each series of booklets is grouped in terms of a color relationship. At top, the grouping is by intensity and temperature; the bottom grouping is based on intensity and hue. LEONARDO SONNOLI ITALY

A rich set of analogous colors is used to code three different beverage products while maintaining a clear unity between the products in the family. There are three hues, and each is a specific value. In each bottle's wrapper, the three hues are swapped between the background and the different text elements; as a result, each bottle is first differentiated by the color of the wrapper's background color. NINE DESIGN SWEDEN

The Psychology of Color With color comes a variety of psychological messages that can be used to influence content—both imagery and the verbal meaning of typography. This emotional component of color is deeply connected to human experience at an instinctual and biological level. Colors of varying wavelengths have different effects on the autonomic nervous system—warmer colors, such as red and yellows, have long wavelengths, and so more energy is needed to process them as they enter the eye and brain. The accompanying rise in energy level and metabolic rate translates as arousal. Conversely, the shorter wavelengths of cooler colors—such as blue, green, and violet—require far less energy to process, resulting in the slowing of our metabolic rate and a soothing, calming effect. The psychological properties of color, however, also depend highly on a viewer's culture and personal experience.

Many cultures equate red with feelings of hunger, anger, or energy because red is closely associated with meat, blood, and violence. By contrast, vegetarians might associate the color green with hunger. In Western cultures, which are predominantly Christian, black is associated with death and mourning, but Hindus associate the color white with death. Christians associate white with purity or cleanliness. Because of the history of Western civilization, violet

This vibrant color is among the most noticeable. Red stimulates the autonomic nervous system to the highest degree, invoking the "fight or flight" adrenaline response, causing us to salivate with hunger, or causing us to feel impulsive. Red evokes feelings of passion and arousal.

The power of blue to calm and create a sense of protection or safety results from its short wavelength; its association with the ocean and sky account for its perception as solid and dependable. Statistically, blue is the best liked of all the colors.

Associated with the Sun and warmth, yellow stimulates a sense of happiness. It appears to advance spatially in relation to other colors and also helps to enliven surrounding colors. Yellow encourages clear thinking and memory retention. A brighter, greener yellow can cause anxiety; deeper yellows evoke wealth.

The association of brown with earth and wood creates a sense of comfort and safety. The solidity of the color, because of its organic connotation, evokes feelings of timelessness and lasting value. Brown's natural qualities are perceived as rugged, ecological, and hard working; its earthy connection connotes trustworthiness and durability.

Unknowable and extreme, black is the strongest color in the visible spectrum. Its density and contrast are dominant, but it seems neither to recede nor to advance in space. Its indeterminate quality reminds viewers of nothingness, outer space, and, in Western culture, death. Its mystery is perceived as formal and exclusive, suggesting authority, superiority, and dignity.

Violet is sometimes perceived as compromising—but also as mysterious and elusive. The value and hue of violet greatly affect its communication: deep violets, approaching black, connote death; pale, cooler violets, such as lavender, are dreamy and nostalgic; red-hued violets, such as fuchsia, are dramatic and energetic; plumlike hues are magical.

With the shortest wavelength, green is the most relaxing color of the spectrum. Its association with nature and vegetation makes it feel safe. The brighter the green, the more youthful and energetic. Deeper greens suggest reliable economic growth. More neutral greens, such as olive, evoke earthiness. However, green, in the right context, can connote illness or decay.

A mixture of red and yellow, orange engenders feelings similar to that of its parent colors—vitality and arousal (red) and warmth and friendliness (yellow). Orange appears outgoing and adventurous but may be perceived as slightly irresponsible. Deeper orange induces salivation and a feeling of luxury. Brighter orange connotes health, freshness, quality, and strength. As orange becomes more neutral, its activity decreases, but it retains a certain sophistication, becoming exotic.

The ultimate neutral, gray may be perceived as noncommittal, but can be formal, dignified, and authoritative. Lacking the emotion that chroma carries, it may seem aloof or suggest untouchable wealth. Gray may be associated with technology, especially when presented as silver. It suggests precision, control, competence, sophistication, and industry.

In a subtractive color model, white represents the presence of all color wavelengths; in an additive model, it is the absence of color. Both of these models help form the basis for white's authoritative, pure, and all-encompassing power. As the mixture of all colors of light, it connotes spiritual wholeness and power. Around areas of color activity in a composition—especially around black, its ultimate contrast—white appears restful, stately, and pure.

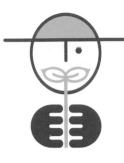

The reliability and strength of brown protect the growing green plant. SOHYUN KIM/IOWA STATE UNIVERSITY UNITED STATES

conveys authority, status, and luxury to members of that culture. Most cultures respond to blue with an association of water and, therefore, of life. Blue is also often perceived as deeply spiritual or contemplative, perhaps because of this particular association. Clearly, selecting a color for specific words in a composition can add meaning by linking its associations to the verbal message. A headline or title set in one color might take on additional, or completely different, meaning when set in another color. Comparing color options for type simultaneously helps determine which color may be the most appropriate for a given communication.

The rooster appears in a field of friendly, dynamic orange. APELOIG DESIGN FRANCE

The elegance of black and the passion of red unite in a rhythmic branding language used on shopping bags. JEONG WOO KIM/SCHOOL OF VISUAL ARTS UNITED STATES

Blue and blue-violet are cool and waterlike. In this poster, their calming quality represents the ocean as a contrast to the hectic movement of the red title. GUNTER RAMBOW GERMANY

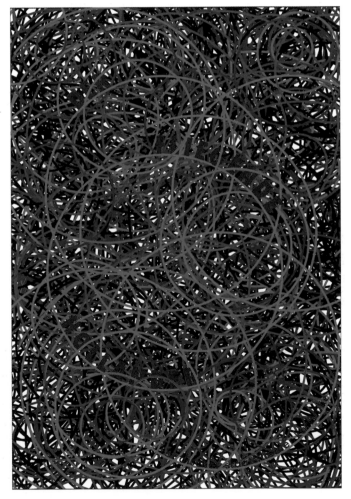

Changing Color, Changing Meaning

Because color so strongly evokes emotional response, its effect on imagery—both abstract and representational—is of great concern to the designer. First, the issue of "local color" in subject matter—the empirical color of objects—comes into play, influencing emotional responses in the viewer. For example, a corporate executive in a blue suit is approachable, but in a dark gray suit, possibly arrogant or shady; wearing a striped green tie, inexperienced, but wearing a solid red one, commanding and assured. Second, manipulation of the overall tonal balance of an image—warm or cool, intense or dull, greenish or blueish—will usually skew an image's feeling in one direction or another. Last, in considering color application to typography or abstract form elements, the designer must anticipate the powerful directness of any associations created for their relevance.

In attempting to identify a form and thereby assign it some meaning, viewers will focus on color after they appreciate the form's shape—but the two messages are nearly simultaneous. As a result, the color message will exert tremendous force on perception. Comparing the dots above, guess which is being presented as a Sun, and which the Earth.

QUIET

QUIET

QUIET

Color forcefully changes the feeling of words, sometimes enhancing their meaning and sometimes opposing the meaning or altering it. Subdued colors, especially those that are cool or desaturated, enhance the meaning of the word "quiet;" interestingly, the word's meaning is intensely appreciated when set in a vibrant color.

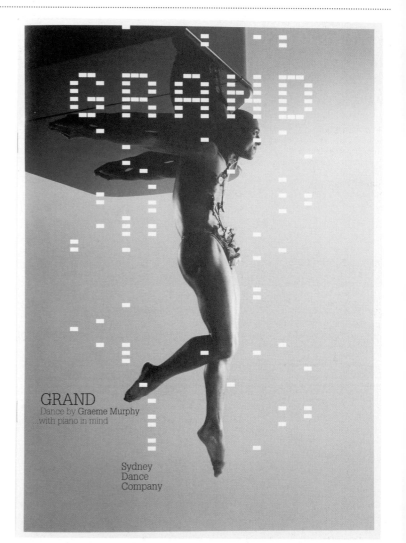

GRAND
Dance by Graeme Murphy
with piano in mind

Sydney
Dance
Company

A greenish-blue haze transforms the upside-down figure into one that appears to be floating in water.
FROST DESIGN AUSTRALIA

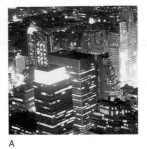    

A   B   C   D   E

Manipulating the overall color or color balance of an image will change a viewer's feeling about the image's content. When the original image (A) is presented in black and white (B), it becomes more documentary; printed in a duotone of intense colors (C), the image takes on a surreal and illustrative quality; skewing the image's color balance makes it refreshing (D) or somber (E). These dramatic changes show the potential of color alteration on a more metaphorical or conceptual level, as opposed to those shown in the sequence below.

A   B   C   D

This image has been manipulated on press by raising and lowering the density of the four process inks to correct and enhance the color balance and saturation: (A) original image; (B) cyan decreased and yellow increased; (C) cyan increased again, yellow decreased, and magenta increased; (D) yellow increased slightly, black increased. The results, subtle enough to be appreciated intellectually when compared side by side, nontheless improve the perception of the fruit's freshness, a desirable manipulation of feeling and message in this context.

Rich sepia coloration augments the fragmented, historical quality of this treated photograph; the deeper values add a somber, reflective note. THOMAS CSANO
CANADA

When altering the color in images that include people, considering the effect on skin tones becomes extremely important. While some color alterations will add energy or seem fun, others may unintentionally add negative connotations; in this example, the greenish toning produces a sickly feeling, while the blueish toning makes the people seem cold and dead.

Color Experience and Conventions While every client and project is different, the color language of many business sectors often respects convention that is usually tied to a given color's common psychological effects: Many financial institutions, for instance, use blue in their communications because of its perceived reliability and calming quality. Consumer expectations are a driving force behind color decisions in design related to products or lifestyle and subculture. Although differentiation through color in a crowded market is paramount, designers must still respect some conventions when it comes to communicating associations such as cleanliness, strength, masculinity or femininity, youth or maturity, heritage, comfort, and luxury. Earth tones are traditional, black and gray are chic, blues and grays mean business, and violets and pinks are feminine. Again, these color concepts, although rooted in convention, provide a grounding for overall communication, to be combined or altered appropriately for more specific messages.

The selection of red-oranges, pinks, and yellow-greens for this logo evokes the farmer client's farmland in Autumn. MINAH KIM / SCHOOL OF VISUAL ARTS UNITED STATES

Deep olives and browns evoke a sense of history, especially in the context of photographs, which were tinted brownish and sometimes olive in the early stages of photography. STUDIO BLUE UNITED STATES

Pink was once associated strictly with femininity. This book uses that color to evoke the time period in which that idea was prevalent. RED CANOE UNITED STATES

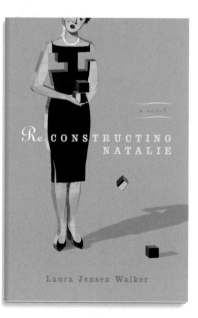

Cooler hues—specifically green and blue—are most often associated with the financial and scientific industries. DETAIL DESIGN STUDIO IRELAND

People generally associate a combination of red, white, and green with Italian culture, because of the foods in its cuisine, as well as the colors of the country's flag. BRUKETA+ZINIC CROATIA

Progressive

East Indian

Medieval

Babies [for adults]

Gardening

Sinister

European

Renaissance

Toddlers/Kids

Contemporary
Home Furnishings

Refreshing

African

Art Nouveau

Teens

Bath [traditional]

Artificial

South American

Art Déco/Streamline

Young Adults

Electronics/Gaming

Organic

Middle Eastern

Post-War/Baby-Boomer

Mature Adults

Eco-Friendly Laundry Products

Elegant

Japanese

Swinging 1960s Mod

Mass-Market Cosmetics

Automotive [sporting]

Romantic

Spring

1960s Folk/1970s Earthy

Men's Grooming

Consumer Health Care

Comical

Summer

New Wave Pop

Women's Luxury Apparel

Pharmaceuticals

Friendly

Autumn

New Age Millenial

Men's Business Apparel

Financial Services

Urban

Winter

Internet Futurism

Women's Fragrance

Telecommunications

Complex moods and emotions
are easily captured in palettes
that combine the psychological
aspects of individual hues, as well
as manipulations of their relative
values and intensities.

Along with emotional ideas,
palettes may suggest place—
distilled from various cultures' art
and textiles—as well as the time
of day or year.

Various periods in Western
history can be quickly identified
by colors that are related to
materials that were prevalent or
color schemes that were in vogue,
during that era.

Particular color palettes are often
associated with, and sometimes
identified as desirable by, specific
age groups and subcultures, especially those related to fashion
and gender conventions.

Very specific color palettes are
identified by consumers as
related to particular industries,
product types, and services.

CHOOSING AND USING TYPE

LEONARDO SONNOLI ITALY [ABOVE]

CHAPTER 03

> The typographer's one essential task is to interpret and communicate the text. Its tone, its tempo, its logical structure, its physical size, all determine the possibilities of typographic form. The typographer is to the text as the theatrical director to the script, or the musician to the score.

ROBERT BRINGHURST/*Typographer and poet; from his book,*
The Elements of Typographic Style, *Hartley & Marks Publishers*

L2M3 GERMANY

Sie können zupacken, jeder Handgriff sitzt, und ganz bestimmt fassen sie die Autos nicht mit spitzen Fingern an. Doch bei der Sternmontage gehören weiße Handschuhe zur Arbeitskleidung. Es gibt natürlich auch Frauen, die sie tragen.

Zu Land, zu Wasser und über den Werkszaun?

Visionen haben Gottlieb Daimler beflügelt, neue Ufer zu erreichen. So stehen die drei Zacken des Sterns für die Elemente Erde, Wasser und Luft. Nun ermöglicht diese Ausstellung den Blick über den Werkszaun und eröffnet ungewöhnliche Perspektiven.

Magnetische Farbe?

Vor dem Lackieren wird der Lack elektrostatisch aufgeladen. Dadurch »schlüpft« die Karosserie regelrecht in ihr farbiges Gewand. Die Farbe wird magnetisch von ihr angezogen. Das sieht faszinierend aus, und außerdem ist diese Technik höchst effizient: Bis zum letzten Tropfen landet die Farbe dort, wo sie hingehört.

Die Mitarbeit Endkontrolle Qualitätsans werden – zum lose Oberflä sie Augenma gefühl. Das

The Nuts and Bolts The letters of the Western alphabet are built from a system of lines with intricate visual relationships that are nearly invisible. With letters at a standard reading size, the eye perceives letters to be all the same weight, height, and width. This is the most critical aspect of type: stylistic uniformity discourages distraction during the reading process. When the same type is enlarged, minute changes in character height, stroke width, and

shape become apparent. Becoming sensitive to these optical issues and understanding their effect on spacing, organization, stylistic communication, legibility, and composition is crucial.

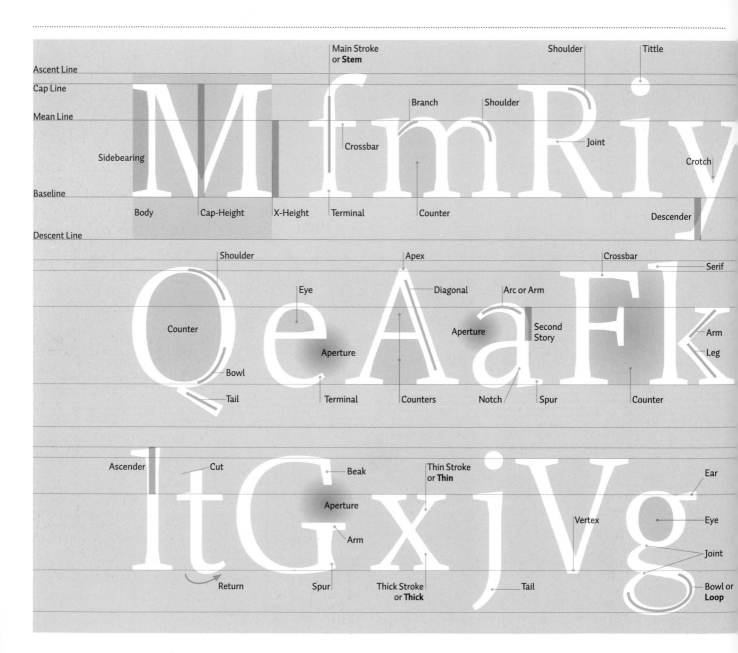

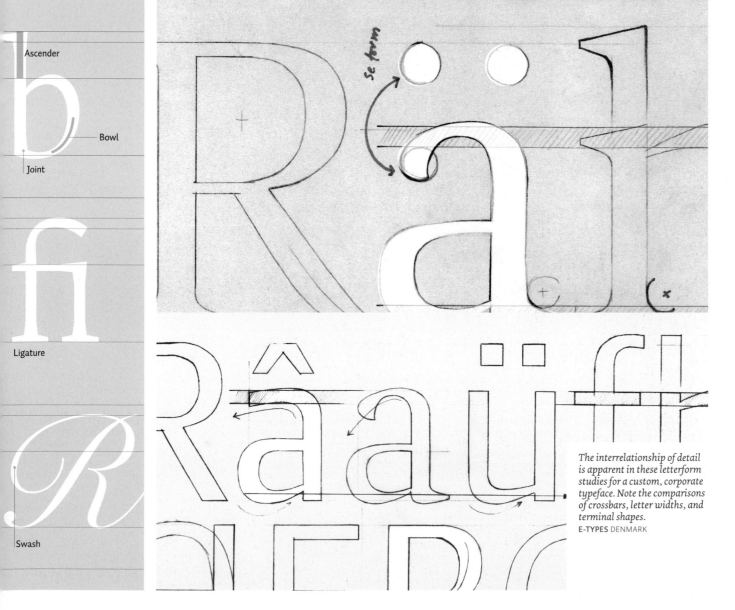

Enlarging letters reveals the tiny adjustments made by their designer to overcome optical characteristics and unify them. Differing angles, stroke shapes, and overall size changes, evident in a large setting, disappear in a text-sized setting. The same is true of corrections for weight and width in a family of typefaces.

Ascender

Bowl

Joint

Ligature

Swash

The interrelationship of detail is apparent in these letterform studies for a custom, corporate typeface. Note the comparisons of crossbars, letter widths, and terminal shapes.
E-TYPES DENMARK

Form and Counterform: The Optics of Structure The spacing of letters in words, sentences, and paragraphs is vital to create a uniform gray value for minimal reader distraction. Every typeface has a distinct rhythm of strokes and spaces. This relationship between form and counterform defines the optimal spacing of that particular typeface and therefore of the overall spacing between words, between lines of type, and among paragraphs.

Looking at letters set together as a word offers a clue as to how they should be spaced in that particular typeface and size. Creating a consistent gray value in text depends on setting the letters so that there is even alternation of solid and void—within and between the letters. A series of letters that are set too tightly, so that the counterforms within the letters are optically bigger than those between letters, creates noticeable dark spots in the line: the exterior strokes of the letters bond to each other visually where they come together. At the other extreme, letters that are set too loosely become singular elements, divorced from the line and recognizable as individual forms, making the appraisal of words difficult. Evenly set sequences of letters show a consistent, rhythmic alternation of black and white—form and counterform repeating at the same rate from left to right.

words

words
Mathematical spacing

words

words
Optically normal spacing

words
Overly tight spacing

words
Overly loose spacing

words
A

words
B

words
C

TYPOGRAPHY
The art of designing letters and text
Default spacing

TYPOGRAPHY
The art of designing letters and text
Corrected spacing

To   To
Ty   Ty
Tr   Tr
We   We
Wo   Wo
Ae   Ae
Pe   Pe

Optical spacing for the Univers regular weight is shown, compared to mathematically spaced or overly tight or loose spacing. The optimally spaced lines (second line) show a consistent rhythmic alternation between dark (the strokes) and light (the counterforms), both within characters and between them. Dark spots are evident in the examples spaced too

tightly, where the strokes are closer together between letters than within them. Compare the normal spacing of these faces to those of the bold condensed style of Univers (A), the italic serif (B), and the high-contrast modern serif (C); note how the internal logic of the stroke-to-counter relationship in each provides the clues to their optimal spacing.

Uppercase letters are more uniform in width and shape than lowercase letters, as well as optically more dense; to enhance their look and legibility, all-uppercase setting must always be spaced a little more loosely than normal.

Tightening or loosening the spacing between these pairs of letters corrects for the awkward counterspaces inherent in their forms. Shifting the lowercase y to the right, under the right crossbar of the T, for example, allows the spacing between them to become optically similar to that of subsequent letters.

The primary difficulty in achieving evenly spaced type is that the letters are of different densities. Some letters are lighter or darker than others. Added to this phenomenon are the directional thrusts of different strokes and the varied sizes and shapes of the counterforms. Some are very open, some are closed, and some are decidedly uneven in relation to the distribution of strokes in a given letter. To correct for these disparities, digital typefaces are programmed to add and subtract space from between different pairs of letters, depending on what the combinations are. These sets of letters, called "kerning pairs," provide for most circumstances of letterform combination, but not all. Invariably, a designer will need to correct unusual spacing that the computer's software is unable to address.

In this logotype, loose letterspacing makes a more distinct rhythm, improves the legibility of the all-uppercase setting, and obviates spacing problems that might have occurred among certain letter combinations (for example, X and P) if they had been spaced normally. **PAONE DESIGN ASSOCIATES** UNITED STATES

LIQUID

Default spacing

LIQUID

Corrected spacing

Always evaluate the spacing needs of a type component on a case-by-case basis. Some letters in a particular word are going to cause unresolvable problems, either because of their dramatic asymmetry, deep counters, or overall density. When presented with a word (or phrase of reasonable length), take time to correct the spacing throughout based on this worst-case scenario. In this word, nothing really can be done about the enormous counter following the L. To make sure it doesn't make more of itself than it needs to, the remainder of the line was spaced more loosely (still in the "normal" range) to minimize the effect of the L counter.

The rhythmic relationship between strokes and counters in letters are consciously overlooked in text, they are called out in bold relief when type becomes very large, as seen in this dynamic poster. **2X GOLDSTEIN** GERMANY

Type Sizes and Spacing The drawing of a typeface has an impact on the perception of its size. A sentence set in an oldstyle serif and a similar-weight sans serif at the same point size will appear to be two different sizes. The discrepancy results from the sans serif's larger x-height: its lowercase letters are larger in relation to the cap height than those of the serif. The difference in set size and apparent size can vary as much as two or three points, depending on the face. A sans-serif face such as Univers might be perfectly comfortable to read at a size of 9 points, but an oldstyle such as Garamond Three at that size will appear tiny and difficult to read. Setting the Garamond at 11 or 12 points will make it more legible as well as make it appear the same size as the Univers.

Historically standard type-size measurements use the point measuring system, based roughly on the height of the capital M. Sizes above 14 points are considered display sizes, to be used for such items as headlines or call-outs; sizes between 14 points and 9 points are considered text sizes; and sizes smaller than 9 points are considered caption sizes.

Note the disparity in size between sans-serif examples (left column) and serif examples (right column) of the same point size. Always evaluate the appearance of type, set in a particular typeface, to determine whether it's set at an appropriate size, rather than assuming that a 9-point "text size" will be legible. The oldstyle face Garamond, for example, will be difficult to read when set at 9 points, while the sans serif Helvetica will seem gigantic.

M M	72
M M	60
M M	48
M M	36
M M	30
M M	24
M M	18
M M	14
M M	12
M M	10
M M	9
M M	7
M M	6

Trip Trip Trip

The same word is set here in three faces at 36 points. The oldstyle serif appears smallest; its lowercase letters have a proportionally small x-height. Because the sans-serif lowercase letters are larger in proportion to the cap height, they appear larger; the same is true of the modern serif to the right.

Spacing must change at different sizes.

Spacing must change at different sizes.

Spacing must change at different sizes.

The same words, set first at 14 points in size and again at 6 points. Uncorrected, the spacing in the smaller type is inadequate for good character recognition. Adding space between letters in the bottom line greatly improves their legibility and their look.

Printing exacerbates the issue of space between letters, especially at smaller sizes. Ink bleeds when it hits paper; as a result, the space between and within letters is made smaller. Trying to judge proper spacing on a monitor, with its coarse resolution, is nearly impossible; a laser printer or an inkjet printer creates some bloating in the type but not nearly as much as will happen on press. A designer's prior printing experience will help him or her judge these spacing issues.

Setting type smaller or larger than the optimal reading size for text also has an impact on spacing. Comfortable and efficient reading of long texts, such as books, newspapers, or journals, takes place when the type size ranges between 9 points and 14 points—the texture of the type is a uniform gray and the letterforms are small enough that their details are not perceived as distinct visual elements. Optimal spacing at reading size means that the strokes and counterforms are evenly alternating. As type is decreased in size, the letterspace must be increased to allow the eye to separate the letters for clarity. At the other extreme, the space between letters must be decreased as the type size increases beyond reading size.

"Be open to change — it's another word for innovation."

MACKEY J. MCDONALD *Chairman, President and Chief Executive Officer*

Last year at this time, we talked about our expectations for another record year in 2004, and projected a 5% increase in both sales and earnings. I'm pleased to report that we had a banner year, substantially exceeding those projections. In 2004 sales jumped 16%, topping the $6 billion mark for the first time in VF's history. Earnings increased 17% to a record $4.21 per share. Sales benefited from growth across most of our core businesses, plus the addition of three terrific new brands: *Vans*, *Napapijri* and *Kipling*.

The larger type on this brochure spread needs to be set a little tighter than normal to account for the apparent size of the counters as it increases in point size; the tighter spacing compensates for the spread of ink that will very slightly decrease the thickness of the reversed white strokes. The smaller caption type, however, has been set more loosely. **AND PARTNERS** UNITED STATES

The strength of a typeface's stroke weights, at any size, will present optical size disparities between type printed positive, on a light background, and in reverse, on a dark background. Generally, a typeface will appear smaller and denser if reversed from a solid field. Typefaces with small x-heights, extreme contrast, or extremely thin strokes overall usually need to be enlarged slightly to ensure their strokes are robust enough to hold up against ink gain that might affect their legibility.

Type changes when printed positive or reversed from color.

Use a face with uniform stroke weights for knock-outs when possible.

Especially if it's small! You might also want to **beef up the weights of small, kmockout elements.**

Type changes when printed positive or reversed from color.

Use a face with uniform stroke weights for knock-outs when possible.

Especially if it's small! You might also want to **beef up the weights of small, kmockout elements.**

kmockout

Visual Variations The letterforms in all typefaces vary from their archetypes in only six aspects: case, weight, contrast, width, posture, and style. Type designers, referring to historical models, subtly alter and combine the variables in these six aspects to create individual type styles that, although appearing remarkably different, all convey the same information about the letterforms in the alphabet. Different approaches to the drawing of typefaces have evolved, become popular, or been discarded over time; as a result, the formal aspects of particular typefaces often carry associations with specific periods in history, cultural movements, and geographic location—some typefaces feel "modern" or "classical," while others feel "French" or "English." More important, the drawing of a typeface will often exhibit a particular kind of rhythm, or cadence, as well as provide a distinct physical presence in a design that may connote feelings—fast or slow, aggressive or elegant, cheap or reliable. Consider that not all viewers will perceive the same associations in a given typeface; the designer must carefully evaluate his or her typeface selection in the context of the audience for a particular piece. Additionally, mixing typefaces that are incongruous with the subject matter—for example, using an archaic Roman capital in a flyer promoting a concert of Electronica—will

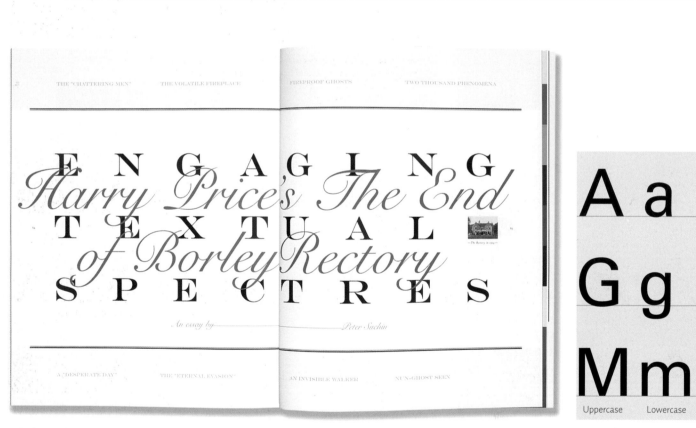

The degree of stylization or neutrality in any typeface is relative, much like the relativity of color: any typeface becomes more neutral when something more stylized appears next to it. These two faces share contrast in stroke thickness but are completely opposed in terminal shape, ductus, width, and posture. Both faces are generally considered somewhat stylized, but the script is more stylized than the all-uppercase serif.
CHK DESIGN UNITED KINGDOM

Uppercase   Lowercase

Case Every letter in the Western alphabet occurs in a large form—the capital or uppercase—and a small, more casual form—lowercase. The uppercase requires added space between letters to permit easier reading. The lowercase is more varied and more quickly recognized in text.

often add surprising layers of communication. Further, the drawing characteristics of typefaces affect their functional qualities, making some more legible at certain sizes or affected by color in particular ways. Recognizing and understanding the six fundamental aspects of alphabet variation is an important first step in being able to select and combine appropriate typefaces for a project.

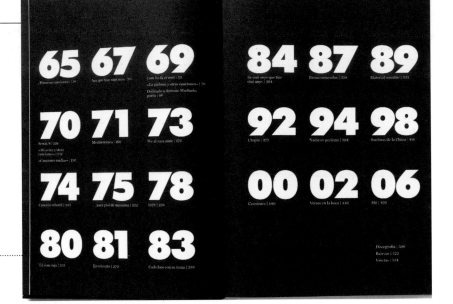

The designer of this book uses letterform variation to achieve extraordinary contrast—a difference in weight (light and extra bold) and a difference in style (serif and sans serif).
STUDIO ASTRID STAVRO SPAIN

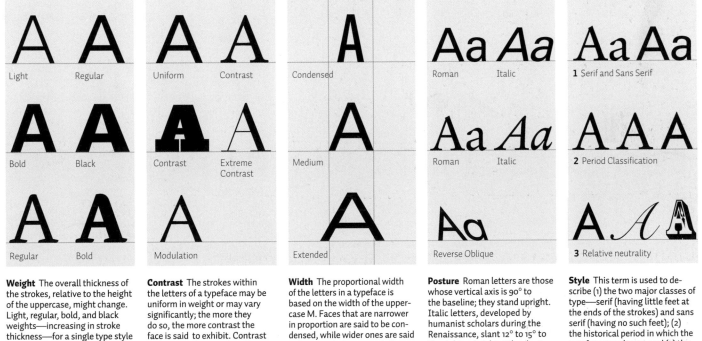

Weight The overall thickness of the strokes, relative to the height of the uppercase, might change. Light, regular, bold, and black weights—increasing in stroke thickness—for a single type style define a type family. Variation in weight helps to add visual contrast as well as to distinguish between informational components within a hierarchy.

Contrast The strokes within the letters of a typeface may be uniform in weight or may vary significantly; the more they do so, the more contrast the face is said to exhibit. Contrast within a stroke—such as flaring from thin to thick—is called "modulation"; the rate at which this occurs is referred to as the typeface's "ductus."

Width The proportional width of the letters in a typeface is based on the width of the uppercase M. Faces that are narrower in proportion are said to be condensed, while wider ones are said to be extended or expanded.

Posture Roman letters are those whose vertical axis is 90° to the baseline; they stand upright. Italic letters, developed by humanist scholars during the Renaissance, slant 12° to 15° to the right, mimicking the slant of handwriting.

Style This term is used to describe (1) the two major classes of type—serif (having little feet at the ends of the strokes) and sans serif (having no such feet); (2) the historical period in which the typeface was drawn; and (3) the relative neutrality or decorative quality of a typeface. Typefaces that are neutral are closest to the basic structure, while those with exaggerated characteristics are said to be stylized, idiosyncratic, or decorative.

Style Classifications Classifying type helps a designer grasp the subtle differences among styles, organizing them in a general way and further helping to select an appropriate typeface for a particular project; sometimes, the historical or cultural context of a particular style will add relevant communication to a typographic design. Classification is by no means easy, however, especially as our typographic tradition becomes increasingly self-referential and incorporates historical formal ideas into modern ones. The typeface Meta, for example, drawn in 1994 by the German designer Erik Spiekermann, is a modern sans-serif face sharing characteristics associated with oldstyle serif types: contrast in the stroke weights, modulation of weight within major strokes, an oblique axis, and a bowl-formed lowercase g. A number of systems for classifying type have been developed during the past several decades. Today, as then, these classifications often change—but a few basic categories remain constant.

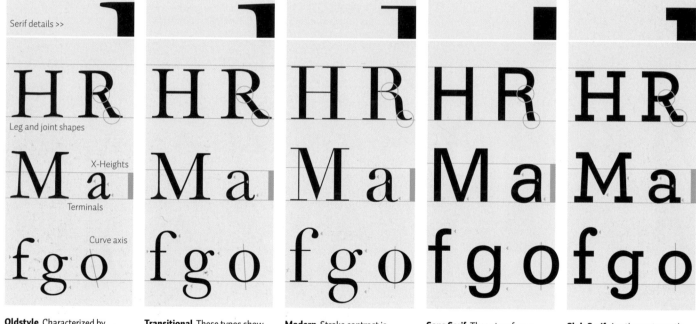

Serif details >>

Leg and joint shapes

X-Heights

Terminals

Curve axis

Oldstyle Characterized by organic contrast of weight in the strokes—from brush or pen drawing; an angled, or oblique, axis in the curved forms; and a notably small x-height defining the lowercase letters. The terminals are pear-shaped and the apertures in the lowercase letters are small.

Transitional These types show an evolution in structure. Stroke contrast is greatly increased and more rationally applied—its rhythm is greatly pronounced. The x-height of the lowercase is larger; the axis is more upright; and the serifs are sharper and more defined, their brackets curving quickly into the stems.

Modern Stroke contrast is extreme—the thin strokes are reduced to hairlines, and the thick strokes made bolder. The axis of the curved forms is completely upright, and the brackets connecting the serifs to the stems have been removed, creating a stark and elegant juncture. The serifs in a number of the lowercase characters have become completely rounded, reflecting the logic of contrast and circularity.

Sans Serif These typefaces are an outgrowth of "display types" of the nineteenth century, designed to be bold and stripped of nonessential details. They are defined by a lack of serifs; the terminals end sharply without adornment. Their stroke weight is uniform, and their axis is completely upright. Sans-serif types set tighter in text and are legible at small sizes; during the past fifty years, they have become acceptable for extended reading.

Slab Serif Another outgrowth of display types, slab serif faces hybridize the bold presentation of a sans serif and the horizontal stress of a serif face, characterized by an overall consistency in stroke weight. The serifs are the same weight as the stems, hence, "slabs;" the body of the slab serif is often wider than what is considered normal.

One of the most damaging scourges in a vineyard is small birds which peck at the fruit, leaving them to rot. We control these birds by deterring, rather than destroying them. Scraps of offal littered around the vineyard during the ripening season attract a family of hawks, whose menacing presence deters the smaller birds. ☙ The shadowy spectre of these hawks, eerily floating over the vines, lends its name to this fine range of varietal wines – Sparkling Chardonnay Pinot Noir, Chardonnay, Shiraz and Merlot.

BLACKWING

These are wines where oak and extreme winemaking influences are kept to a minimum, to ensure all you see is the epitome of varietal character. ☙ The wines are deliberately selected to be rich, full flavoured, and yet round and soft, leaving a most memorable lingering impression on the back palate. ☙ They are classy, rich and sophisticated but always approachable and arguably represent the best value for money.

The iconic bird drawing, which refers to a specific time and place, has its very own language of line and mass. The inline capitals used for the page title echo these linear qualities, but they also are classical capitals with their own history. The supporting text is a sans serif with similar width proportions as the capitals, but it contrasts their thins and thicks with a uniform weight that is clearly modern. VOICE AUSTRALIA

Graphic These typefaces are the experimental, decorative children of the display types. Their visual qualities are expressive but not conducive to reading in a long text. This category includes specimens such as script faces, fancy and complex faces inspired by handwriting, and idiosyncratic faces that are illustrative or conceptual.

Stylistic differences in a selection of typefaces give voice to the varied writing styles of Irish authors in this festival program. STUDIO AAD IRELAND

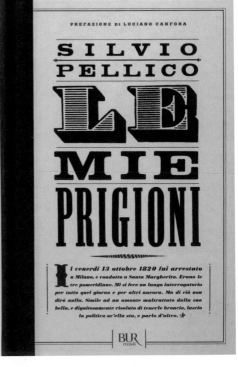

A combination of Victorian wood types emphasizes the visual contrasts of weight, width, mass, and line. LOUISE FILI LTD. UNITED STATES

Choosing the Right Face Whatever other goals a designer may have when deciding on the typeface(s) to use for text elements, his or her first consideration must be its legibility. Of the 150,000 fonts available, a relative few are considered useful for continuous text—500, perhaps. Of those, even fewer are considered to be well constructed and aesthetically pleasing. The subjective nature of "pleasing" means there can be some allowance for individual taste, but, typically, one must repress stylistic biases in favor of functionality. There are a small number of faces, often referred to as "workhorses" for their reliably utilitarian, time-tested quality of construction, that designers often choose for the kinds of details that ensure legibility: a large x-height in the lowercase, open counters, relatively little stroke contrast, even optical widths among characters, and evenly balanced upper and lower propor- tions. These faces eschew idiosyncratic details, such as exaggerated serif shapes, unusual joint formations, and unexpected changes in width—leaning toward the neutral, archetypal forms. Knowing what to look for among these details is impor- tant; designers must be intimately familiar with the drawn characteristics of many faces to compare their varied effects on legibility, as well as overall feeling.

Structural Proportions
The body widths of alphabetic characters—how tall they are compared to their height—vary from typeface to typeface, creat- ing a specific rhythm between strokes and counters. The coun- ters in condensed typefaces be- come similar to the weight of the strokes as the overall letter width decreases, creating a rapid alter- nation of positive and negative that may seem to speed up the reading rhythm, adding increased energy or tension. Conversely, the counters in extended faces tend to slow the reading rhythm. The ratio of the lowercase letters to the uppercase letters, or their x-height, is extremely important to consider. The larger the x-height is in relation to the cap height, the more open and inviting the counters of the low- ercase letters will be, increasing their legibility. At the same time, a larger x-height means the low- ercase is expanding to decrease the amount of space between lines, resulting in an appearance of greater density and a larger point size.

Bowls, Shoulders, and Axes
The lower part of such large circular forms as O, D, and G (the bowls), and the upper part of such curves, as well as the upper curves on the uppercase R, or the lowercase P and F (shoulders)— might be rounder or elliptical or squared off. Comparing these forms within the same face will reveal subtle variations, but these curves will share a logic that will be very different compared to another typeface, even within the same class. The axis of the curved forms changes also, being slanted in older styles and completely upright in more modern ones.

Apertures and Eyes The entry into the counters of letters such as the lowercase E and A, what is called the "aperture," may be tight or more open. Small, closed-off counters, or "eyes," appearing in letters such as the lowercase E and G, also vary considerably in shape and proportion.

Ascenders and Descenders
The movement and extension of these strokes above and below the body of the lowercase are important details. Some as- cenders strike the capline, while others rise above it; descenders, too, may be deep or shallow compared to the body of the text. The larger the x-height, the more shallow the ascenders and descenders tend to be, creating greater density. The height and depth of these strokes influence how tightly lines of a given type- face must be leaded, as well as on feeling or character.

Selecting a typeface for its feeling or mood is a tricky endeavor based on a designer's gut reaction to the rhythm or shapes inherent in a particular style. Every typeface, whether neutral or stylized, will feel either fast or slow, heavy or light, sharp or soft; these qualities, too, are attributed to the interplay of counterspaces, stroke weights and contrasts, joints, and so on. The drawn details of a typeface may further involve shapes that evoke associations or physical experience: sinewy, curved shoulders that seem to sprout from the vertical stems of letters, or organically shaped terminals, for example, may allude to natural forms such as plants or animals. When thinking about choosing an appropriate typeface, look at the images that accompany the text or think about objects or places related to the text's subject matter as inspiration. Many typefaces also conjure associations with cultural motifs because of their common use in advertising or other pop-culture venues for specific kinds of subject matter: gothic blackletters or textura faces, for example, commonly evoke horror or fantasy because they are tied to certain historical time periods and because they have been used widely in posters and advertising for movies and books in this genre. Being conscious of all these aspects of typeface design will help narrow the choices and result in the most appropriate decision.

Terminals, Serifs, and Spurs
The shapes of a typeface's terminals affect its apparent sharpness and rigidity, causing it to seem casual or elegant, older or newer, or comforting or more austere. Terminals might end perpendicular to the angle of a stroke or might be angled against it. Serifs vary in shape as well; they might be angled or perpendicular, softer or more sharply cut, and even round. Spurs (terminals that extend away from a stroke's expected cutoff) are vestiges of older, brush-drawn styles—but also are found in sans serif faces. The lowercase A is often the site of a spur, as is the lowercase G and B.

Joints and Branches
A great deal of a typeface's character is found where the strokes of letters meet: when these joints are smooth and fluid, the typeface may feel organic, relaxed, or casual; faces with abrupt joints may seem geometric or formal.

Stroke Formation
Letters of uniform stroke weight produce a consistent, less energetic, rhythm across a line; letters with contrasting stroke weights will seem to pulse or move across the line with greater energy. Some faces show contrast within a single stroke—usually a flaring in thickness from the midpoint of the stem outward to the terminals. This feature, called "modulation," is typical of older styles. The "speed" of the transitions between thicks and thins is called the face's "ductus." Pronounced modulation, and quicker ductus, also impart a more vigorous feeling; less modulation, and more passive ductus, result in the opposite.

Graphic Details
Many faces are distinguished by decorative details whose qualities often carry specific associations. There's no way to compare these typefaces since they vary so much, other than to appraise the effect of the graphic details on legibility (stylized face are likely useful only for larger-sized display applications); on their ability to visually relate to other kinds of elements in a layout; and to evoke visceral emotional and conceptual responses that are relative to the content.

Lorem ipsum dolor sit amet, consectetur adipiscing elit. Vivamus iaculis tincidunt nisi ut facilisis. Fusce accumsan blandit.

LOREM IPSUM DOLOR SIT AMET, CONSECTETUR ADIPISCING ELIT. VIVAMUS IACULIS TINCIDUNT NISI UT FACILISIS. FUSCE ACCUMSAN BLANDIT ODIO.

Lorem ipsum dolor sit amet, consectetur adipiscing elit. Vivamus iaculis tincidunt nix.

LOREM IPSUM DOLOR SIT AMET, CONSECTETUR ADIPISCING ELIT. VIVAMUS IACULIS TINCIDUNT NIX.

Lorem ipsum dolor sit amet, consec tetur adipiscing elit. Vivamus iaculis tincidunt odio ut facilisis accum san.

Lorem ipsum dolor sit amet, consec tetur adipiscing elit. Vivamus iaculis tincidunt odio ut facilisis accum san.

Lorem ipsum dolor sit amet, consec tetur adipiscing elit. Vivamus iaculis tincidunt odio ut facilisis accum san.

Lorem ipsum dolor sit amet, consec tetur adipiscing elit. Vivamus iaculis tincidunt odio ut facilisis accum san.

All of the details within a typeface, working together, render it as useful (or not) for extended reading. The overly stylized nature of the typefaces applied to the text specimens at top prevent serious consideration of them for anything but headlines or, perhaps, short callouts. Still, startling distinctions in tone and energy accompany typefaces that initially appear far more neutral and are, therefore, functional for extended reading: compare the dramatic differences each time in the feeling of the same text, set in comparatively neutral, "workhorse" faces.

MAGNIFICENT

MAGNIFICENT

MAGNIFICENT

Magnificent

Magnificent

DASTARDLY

DASTARDLY

DASTARDLY

dastardly

Dastardly

ALONE

ALONE

ALONE

ALONE

Alone

Three different words, each loaded with different potential meanings, are set in a selection of typefaces—the same faces every time. It's interesting to note how each typeface affects the perception of a given word, calling attention to a particular meaning or sense … and how the same typeface affects each of the other words, as well.

MAQUILLAGE

gorenje

INTEGRINE

pearlsoft

ergon

CAMINOS MADRID

Take a look, too, at the logos above to see how decisions in typeface selection—based on such details—affect their meanings or emotional qualities. Even more so than in the setting of extended texts, the different graphic qualities of typefaces have a profound impact on communciation when they appear in brand identity marks—either as individual symbol elements, acronyms or monograms, or wordmarks.

Logos, top to bottom:
HELMUT SCHMID DESIGN JAPAN
JELENA DROBAC SERBIA
APELOIG DESIGN FRANCE
GRAPEFRUIT ROMANIA
MADE IN SPACE UNITED STATES
IGAWA DESIGN UNITED STATES
MANUEL ESTRADA SPAIN

Combining Type Styles The conventional wisdom for mixing typefaces is to select two type families for a given job. In one sense, this rule is predicated on the notion of establishing clear hierarchy; the greater the variety of typefaces, it is reasoned, the more difficult it will be for a reader to categorize and remember the meanings of different treatments among informational components. In another sense, this rule is about aesthetic unity in the visual language (no less relevant in the context of type). Context, of course, plays an important role in deciding whether or not to adhere to such a limitation. If the complexity or expressiveness of a job requires seven or eight typefaces to communicate appropriately, so be it—but choose wisely. The only reason to change a typeface is to gain an effect of contrast, and so the contrast achieved by the combination should be relevant and clearly recognizable.

Opposing the extremes of weight, width, or style is a natural starting point. But somewhere in the mix, among extremes, a formal relationship must exist between the selected fonts to enrich their visual dialogue. Choosing a sans serif and a serif that are similar in weight or width, for example, creates a tension of similarity and difference that is quite sophisticated, as is selecting two serif faces that are similar in weight, but very different in contrast.

dynamic **dynamic**
dynamic dynamic
dynamic dynamic
dynamic dynamic
dynamic dynamic
dynamic *dynamic*
dynamic ***dynamic***

Within a single family, variations on weight, width, and posture lend an extraordinary range of textural and rhythmic changes that might have an effect on communication. Note how the word "dynamic"—set in members of the Univers family—changes in presence, cadence, and spatial location (foreground or background) as width, weight, and posture are changed in each.

each **incidence**

each **incidence**

Sometimes, the reason for mixing faces is functional: The bold weight of this text face isn't much different from the regular weight; a bold face from an alternate, yet similar, family can be substituted. Note the similarity of the spurs, terminals, and other details between the two faces.

BbAa
BbAa
OoSs
OoSs

In choosing to mix typefaces, select counterparts with enough contrast, but be aware of their similarities as well. In this example, the serif and the sans serif are radically different in stroke contrast and detail, but their construction is similar—take note of the slight angularity of the curves; the oblique emphasis in the O's; the joint angle in the lowercase a; the abrupt joint in the lowercase b.

Lorem ipsum dolor consectituer
RUNNING TEXT

Lorem ipsum dolor consectituer
PULL-QUOTE

Lorem ipsum dolor consectituer
CALLOUT

Lorem ipsum dolor consectituer
Duis autem velure nunc et semper
CAPTION [TITLE AND TEXT]

LOREM IPSUM DOLOR
TITLING

The designer of this book selected one typeface style (whether a singular font or a family) for each kind of information—running text, image captions, callouts, and titling. Each face shares some attribute of proportion or detail while contrasting others.
VERA GORBUNOVA/SCHOOL OF VISUAL ARTS UNITED STATES

Recognizing the differences in the details among a selection of faces from which to choose is an important step in making a choice for a clear combination. Generally, avoid combing two faces of a similar style unless the difference is pronounced enough for the average reader to notice. Combining Caslon and Baskerville, for example—two transitional serifs with similar axis, weight, width, and terminal shapes—isn't such a great idea. But combining Bodoni—a modern serif of extreme contrast—with Glypha—a slab serif of uniform stroke weight but similar width and axis—might be effective. As another possibility, similar faces set at dramatically different scales might be unified by the weight of their strokes at these different sizes. For example, 7-point Futura Heavy capitals, which are very dotlike, might correspond in overall weight to the strokes of Univers 45 set at 13 points in size on the same page. Both are sans serif; their different sizes create contrast in their counters and linearity even as the overall weight of the smaller Futura begins to approach the stroke weight of the larger Univers 45.

AaBbRrMmGg
AaBbRrMmGg

Combining two typefaces of the same style classification typically results in stylistic confusion. The two transitional serifs seen here, for example, aren't different enough to be appreciated as different.

AaBbRrMmGg
AaBbRrMmGg
AaBbRrMmGg

Replacing one of the transitional serifs above with a slab serif delivers recognizable contrast; another slab serif with more uniform stroke weight, but dot-like serifs, creates a different, more subtle contrast.

AaBbRrMmGg
AaBbRrMmGg

The geometric slab serif above is paired, this time, with a modern or Neoclassical serif for an extreme contrast.

AaBbRrMmGg
AaBbRrMmGg

This combination of two sans serifs—the stylistic differences of which are even more subtle than those of serifs—is almost pointless: it seems as though the designer couldn't decide on one, or couldn't tell the difference between them.

AaBbRrMmGg
AaBbRrMmGgKkQqTtXxSs

AaBbRrMmGgKkQqTtXxSs
AaBbRrMmGgKkQq

The roundness and heaviness of the geometric sans serif, paired here with a more graceful, condensed sans serif, establishes a stark dot-to-line contrast as well as one of weight. Adjusting the sizes of each face to more closely match each other's weights maintains this formal relationship (and its contrast) while creating a more quiet impression.

A popular—and decisive—approach to combining type styles is to choose a sans serif and a serif. In the book design above, a bold sans serif for headings is supported by a ligther weight of the same sans, and text is set in a serif with which it shares some structural qualities. STUDIO ASTRID STAVRO SPAIN

*Mixing together many typefaces in one logo, headline,
or other composition is perfectly fine as long as the
typefaces chosen have a relationship in weight, width,
texture, or contrast, as is the case in this logotype.*
RAIDY PRINTING GROUP LEBANON

*All of the typefaces combined in this logo share pro-
nounced contrast in stroke weight, which helps unify
them given their radically different stylistic traits and
proportions. Each element has been scaled, relative to
the others, to standardize the weights of the thin and
thick strokes among the varied forms.*
C. HARVEY GRAPHIC DESIGN UNITED STATES

The historical quality of typefaces may
also play a role in how they are combined.
Since the average reader usually associates certain qualities with a given typeface
because of its classical or modern drawing
qualities, mixing typefaces from related—
or dramatically different—periods might
help generate additional messages. A
Roman capital, such as Trajan, in combination with a geometric sans serif, such
as Futura, not only presents a great deal
of contrasting typographic color but also
alludes to a historical association: old and
new, continuum, evolution, innovation,
and so on. In this particular case, both
Trajan and Futura are based on Roman
geometric proportion, despite being separated by 2,000 years of history.

Assessing Character Count, Leading, and Paragraph Width The width of a paragraph depends heavily on the size of type being used and, therefore, how many characters can be fit onto a single line. Regardless of the type size or the reader's maturity, between fifty and eighty characters (including spaces) can be processed before a line return. With words averaging between five and ten letters, that means approximately eight to twelve words per line. Achieving this character count determines the width of a paragraph. The proportions of the page format—and how much text must be made to fit overall—might affect paragraph width, but character count is the best starting point for defining an optimal width.

Lorem ipsum dolor sit amet consectitur adipscing elit in nonum erat summa es |50

Lorem ipsum dolor sit amet consectitur adipscing elit in nonum erat summ |50

Lorem ipsum dolor sit amet consectitur adipscing elit in nonum est |50

Lorem ipsum dolor sit amet consectitur adipscing elit in nonum erat summa est nunc |50

Lorem ipsum dolor sit amet consectitur adipscing elit in nonum |50

Lorem ipsum dolor sit amet consectitur adipscing elit in nonu |50

Lorem ipsum dolor sit amet consectitur adipscing elit i |50

Lorem ipsum dolor sit amet consectitur adipscing elit in nonum erat s |50

Lorem ipsum dolor sit amet consectitur adipscing elit i |50

Lorem ipsum dolor sit amet consectitur adipscing el |50

Lorem ipsum dolor sit amet consectitur adipsc |50

Lorem ipsum dolor sit amet consectitur adipscing elit in no |50

Lorem ipsum dolor sit amet consectitur adipscing elit in nonum erat summa es nunc et semper quam gloriosa de duis autem velure quod vam uns erat lorem ipsum dolore sit amet consectitur adipscit

Lorem ipsum dolor sit amet consectitur adipscing elit in nonum erat summa es nunc et semper quam gloriosa de duis autem velure quod vam uns erat lorem ipsum dolore sit amet consectitur adipscit

Lorem ipsum dolor sit ame consectitur adipscing elitin nonum erat summa es nun cet semper quam gloriosa e deduis autem velure quod vamuns erat lorem ipsum doloresit amet consectitura

Lorem ip consecti nonum e et sempe

Lorem i consecti nonum e et sempe

Lorem i consecti nonum e cet semp

A comparison of character count for a selection of typefaces, at varying sizes, is shown set on the same paragraph width. As with all typographic rules, there is a range to what is comfortable for the average reader. Given a fifty- to eighty-character comfort range, it is easy to see that a paragraph must widen as the type size increases and narrow as it decreases, to maintain the optimal number of characters on a line.

Comfortable interline space, or leading, varies according to several characteristics in typeface style and size; but generally, the interline space should seem a point or two larger than the height of the lowercase running as text. Because the x-height varies so much among faces, a designer will need to judge the leading appropriate to the appearance of the lowercase, rather than try to assign a leading to a point size by way of a specific formula.

The leading of the lines, as noted, depends somewhat on the width of the paragraph, the type size, and its spacing. The space between lines should be noticeably larger than the optical height of the lines, but not so much that it becomes pronounced. Similarly, the leading must not be so tight that the reader locates the beginning of the same line after the return and begins reading it again. As paragraph width increases, so must the leading, so that the beginnings of the lines are more easily distinguished. Oddly, as the width of a paragraph narrows, the leading must also be increased: otherwise, the reader might grab several lines together because the snapshots he or she takes while scanning encompass the full paragraph width.

Une pièce gentille sur des gens sympathiques

(Een vriendelijk stuk over aardige mensen)

Personnages
SOFIA
MICHAEL
GABRIËL

Résumé
Les noms des personnages de cette pièce d'Esther Gerritsen, écrite pour la troupe Keesen & Co, sont significatifs. Michael, Gabriël et Sofia sont des amis de jeunesse «qui essaient de passer un bon moment ensemble les uns chez les autres». La connotation religieuse et philosophique n'est pas gratuite. Tout dans les pièces de Gerritsen est motivé et renvoie au thème central : le manque de sens entrave l'homme moderne et empêche ou interdit le contact avec son prochain.

La manière sèche, observatrice et pragmatique avec laquelle les personnages analysent les choses les plus variées et les nomment très précisément, est à la fois comique et grinçante. Elle enlève toute évidence aux choses les plus banales. Chaque scène constitue une variation sur le même thème : nous voulons nous connaître les uns les autres, mais ne savons parler que de nous et des autres, au lieu de nous parler les uns les autres, malgré tous nos talents et en dépit de nos défauts, dont nous connaissons la liste de fond en comble. La présence inattendue, dans la cuisine, d'un évêque s'amusant avec de la crème chantilly, ne fait que semer la panique – et suscite le rire chez le spectateur.

Une pièce gentille sur des gens sympathiques a été représentée pour la première fois le 27 mars 2002, dans une mise en scène de Willibrord Keesen et produite par Keesen & Co.

Commentaires de la presse ·
«Les acteurs sont parfaits dans cette étonnante pièce de Gerritsen, à la fois absurde et aliénante, parfois comique, souvent laborieuse. L'aspect dramatique se développe tout d'un coup pour ensuite s'arrêter. Ici, elle tente d'élucider tous les mystères du monde en bloc et nous entraîne vers des sphères nébuleuses, ailleurs les trois acteurs se penchent sur des banalités comme le fromage fondu pour petits-fours. La pièce a une dimension profonde car Gerritsen aspire, plus que dans ses œuvres précédentes, à une dimension métaphysique. L'apparition trompeuse de l'évêque dans la cuisine se situe exactement sur ce niveau. Ce personnage par excellence de l'intrus de Pinter qui fait tout disjoncter.» *NRC*, Kester Freriks, 4/4/2002.

«Cette nouvelle pièce d'Esther Gerritsen (l'un des meilleurs jeunes dramaturges du moment) est un exercice de réflexion poussé jusqu'au bout. Elle l'a écrite à la demande de la compagnie «Keesen & Co» d'Arnhem. (…) Pour lancer la soirée, [les personnages] nomment tout ce qui transforme un rendez-vous en une agréable soirée, ce qui a pour résultat des scènes très pince-sans-rires. Gerritsen y analyse avec précision le comportement imposé par les conventions de politesse qui vont de soi dans les tentatives de socialisation. La force dramatique des œuvres de Gerritsen repose sur une vision absurde du quotidien, doublée dans *Une pièce gentille* d'une portée philosophique. Vers la moitié de la pièce, les trois acteurs sont fascinés par «l'évêque dans la cuisine». Cette formule devient non seulement la blague récurrente mais aussi le symbole du hasard auquel nous sommes tous soumis. (Gabriël : «Franchement, combien de fois tu trouves chez tes amis un évêque dans la cuisine ?» Michael : «Exactement. Cela sert à ça, le hasard.»). Puis ces personnages montrent qu'ils veulent devenir des hommes en acceptant dans leur vie soit le hasard soit la malchance.» *De Volkskrant*, Annette Embrechts, 2/4/2002.

Extrait de Une pièce gentille sur des gens sympathiques / 1

Sofia et Gabriël viennent chez Michael. Ils viennent d'entrer. Ils ont encore leurs manteaux sur eux et ne s'apprêtent pas à les enlever.

SOFIA Je suis une autorité. Dans le domaine de l'océanographie. Je suis l'auteur de nombreux ouvrages de référence que tout étudiant en océanographie trouvera dans sa bibliographie. Je suis également professeur de génétique moléculaire. Je découvre les secrets moléculaires de la vie à l'aide du vers *elegans*, une petite bête bien ordonnée de seulement 302 neurones. Je suis une femme intéressante et une oratrice charmante. Je suis une amatrice de l'œuvre de Proust. Disons : une spécialiste de Proust par excellence. On dit parfois que j'ai une personnalité charismatique. J'ai la réputation d'être une mordue de water-polo et d'avoir un niveau plutôt honorable. Le record mondial de saut de haies est à mon nom. Ce record tient depuis des années et l'on ne prévoit pas qu'il soit prochainement battu. Je suis ce que l'on appelle un être exceptionnel doué de dons extraordinaires. Donc si tu me dis : «Sympa que tu sois là », bien sûr, cela ne m'étonne pas. Il est évident que tu es content que je sois là. On aime me voir tout simplement. J'ai une allure plaisante et une voix agréable. J'ai un caractère foncièrement bon et des centres d'intérêts très variés. Le violoncelle par exemple est l'une de mes grandes passions. Non seulement le violoncelle, mais j'aime aussi jouer du piano. Tout comme la guitare, le violon, la cithare, l'orgue, la flûte traversière, la clarinette. Je n'ai pas de préférences. Je joue de tous les instruments, je parle toutes les langues, je pratique tous les sports. Je sais tout faire.
Mais ce n'est pas important. Ce n'est pas non plus un mérite. Je ne l'ai jamais «voulu». C'est indépendant de ma volonté que je sache tout faire. Que je parle toutes les langues, pratique tous les sports et tombe tous les hommes, cela est pour moi aussi évident que l'est pour d'autres le fait de respirer. Oui, en effet, je ne compte pas les handicapés ni ceux qui sont gravement malades et qui racontent dans les spots de publicité informative que respirer n'est pas pour tous une évidence. Je parle ici d'adultes normaux en bonne santé. Non pas d'handicapés, de malades, de vieux séniles, d'enfants,

38

39

The optimal quality of the column widths for the running text in this page spread is evident in lines of relatively consistent length, a comfortable rag, and notably few occurrences of hyphenated line breaks. This column width also appears to accommodate heads and subheads of different sizes.
MARTIN OOSTRA NETHERLANDS

Alignment Logic Text type can be set in several different configurations called "alignments." It can be set so that every line begins at the same left-hand starting point (flush left) or right-hand starting point (flush right), or with an axis centered on the paragraph width (centered). In this case, there are two options: In centered type, the lines are different lengths and are centered over each other on the width's vertical axis; in justified type, the lines are the same length, aligning on both the left and the right sides. Justified text is the only setting in which the lines are the same length. In text set to align left, right, or centered, the uneven lengths of the lines create a soft shape on the nonaligned side that is called a *rag* (in the UK and Europe, the rag is referred to as the *range*). The alignment of text has an effect on the spacing within it and, therefore, on the search for a desirable text setting.

Only two kinds of alignment are considered permissable for setting estensive volumes of text—more than thirty to fifty words: Flush left, ragged right (FLRR) and justified. The other two kinds of alignment, flush right, ragged left (FRRL) and centered axis, are considered inappropriate for extensive texts because their optical qualities dramatically impair comfortable reading. In text set FRRL, the reversal of the aligned edge to the right of the paragraph—

Think of the blank page
as alpine meadow, or as the
purity of undifferentiated
being. The typographer enters
this space and must change
it. The reader will enter it later,
to see what the typographer
has done there. The underlying
truth of the blank page must
be infringed, but it must
never altogether disappear.

Flush left, ragged right

Think of the blank page
as alpine meadow, or as the
purity of undifferentiated
being. The typographer enters
this space and must change
it. The reader will enter it later,
to see what the typographer
has done there. The underlying
truth of the blank page must
be infringed, but it must
never altogether disappear.

Flush right, ragged left

Think of the blank page
as alpine meadow, or as the
purity of undifferentiated
being. The typographer enters
this space and must change
it. The reader will enter it later,
to see what the typographer
has done there. The underlying
truth of the blank page must
be infringed, but it must
never altogether disappear.

Center axis, or Centered

Think of the blank page as
alpine meadow, or as the
purity of undifferentiated
being. The typographer
enters this space and must
change it. The reader will
enter it later, to see what
the typographer has done
there. The underlying truth
of the blank page must be
infringed, but it must never
altogether disappear.

Justified

Text excerpted from *The Elements of Typographic Style* by Robert Bringhurst

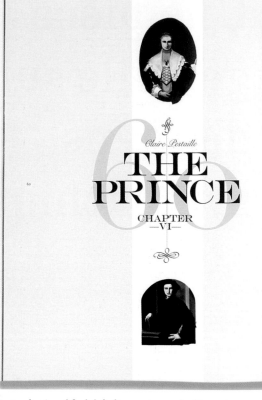

Centered-axis and flush-left alignments are mixed to great effect in this classically influenced page spread design. The margins of the flush-left, asymmetrical text set on the right-hand page are symmetrical and optically balanced with the material on the left. CHK DESIGN UNITED KINGDOM

opposite that which is considered the starting point of reading sequence in Western languages—creates a disturbing verbal disconnect for readers. The problem with text set centered is that its outer contour's shape visually overpowers the perception of the internal lines' linearity; the eye, constantly drawn to appreciate the cluster form, is continually distracted from following the sequence of text line by line—which can be annoying after a while.

In a paragraph set flush left, ragged right, the word spaces are uniform. The word spaces in a justified paragraph, however, vary because the width of the paragraph is mathematically fixed, and the words on any given line must align on both sides—no matter how many words or how long they are. In justified text, word spacing variation is the single most difficult issue to overcome. The result of poorly justified text in which the word space constantly

changes is a preponderance of rivers—chains of word spaces that visually connect from line to line. Text set ragged avoids the spacing issues inherent in justified text; it also introduces the pronounced textural effect of an organic edge whose opposition to the hard edge of the alignment imparts an immediate visual contrast to the page, as well as provides optical separation between horizontally arranged paragraphs.

This justified setting uses wide margins to create focus on the text block. The internal spacing of the text is relatively consistent.
ADAMSMORIOKA UNITED STATES

Text in this brochure spread is primarily set flush left, ragged right, with a callout on the left-hand page set in lines that stagger left to right, without a specific alignment structure.
C+G PARTNERS *United States*

Exploring the Ragged Edge The rag of a paragraph might be deep or shallow, active or subtle, but its uniformity and consistency from the top of a paragraph down to the bottom are what make it desirable. The ragged line endings are considered optimal if they create an organic, unforced "ripple" down the edge of the paragraph, without pronounced indents or bulges. In an optimally ragged paragraph, the rag becomes invisible: The reader is never aware that the lines are ending at their natural conclusion. If the alternating lines end short and very long, the rag becomes active and calls attention to itself, distracting the reader from following the content of the text. That said, a deep rag is acceptable if it remains consistent throughout the text.

A designer might opt to mitigate a deep rag by introducing more interline space. What is never desirable, however, is a rag that begins at the outset of a paragraph guided by one kind of logic but transforms into another kind of logic as the paragraph progresses in depth; a rag that shows excessive indenting from the right; or sharp, angular inclusions of space created by lines that become sequentially shorter. The overall unity of a rag can be easily compro-

Think of the blank page as alpine meadow, or as the purity of undifferentiated being. The typographer enters this space and must change it. The reader will enter it later, to see what the typographer has done. The underlying truth of the blank page must be infringed, but it must never altogether disappear—and whatever displaces it might well aim to be as lively and peaceful as it is. It is not enough, when building a title page, merely to unload some big, prefabricated letters into the center of the space, nor to dig a few holes in the silence with typographic heavy machinery and move on. Big type, even huge type, can be beautiful and useful.

Think of the blank page as alpine meadow, or as the purity of undifferentiated being. The typographer enters this space and must change it. The reader will enter it later, to see what the typographer has done. The underlying truth of the blank page must be infringed, but it must never altogether disappear—and whatever displaces it might well aim to be as lively and peaceful as it is. It is not enough, when building a title page, merely to unload some big, prefabricated letters into the center of the space, nor to dig a few holes in the silence with typographic heavy machinery and move on. Big type, even huge type, can be beautiful and useful.

Think of the blank page as alpine meadow, or as the purity of undifferentiated being. The typographer enters this space and must change it. The reader will enter it later, to see what the typographer has done. The underlying truth of the blank page must be infringed, but it must never altogether disappear—and whatever displaces it might well aim to be as lively and peaceful as it is. It is not enough, when building a title page, merely to unload some big, prefabricated letters into the center of the space, nor to dig a few holes in the silence with typographic heavy machinery and move on. Big type, even huge type, can be beautiful and useful.

Example of a paragraph showing a desirable rag (left), and two paragraphs whose rags are fraught with problems: The rag is either too deep or active; shows sharp inclusions of negative space

and protrusions of long lines; a contour with a noticeable shape; or irregular width overall from top to bottom.

Think of the blank page as alpine meadow, or as the purity of undifferentiated being. The typographer enters this space and must change it. The reader will enter it later, to see what the typographer has done. The underlying truth of the blank page must be infringed, but it must never altogether disappear—and whatever displaces it might well aim to be as lively and peaceful as it is. It is not enough, when building a title page, merely to unload some big, prefabricated letters into the center of the space, nor to dig a few holes in the silence with typographic heavy machinery and move on. Big type, even huge type, can be beautiful and useful.

Think of the blank page as alpine meadow, or as the purity of undifferentiated being. The typographer enters this space and must change it. The reader will enter it later, to see what the typographer has done. The underlying truth of the blank page must be infringed, but it must never altogether disappear—and whatever displaces it might well aim to be as lively and peaceful as it is. It is not enough, when building a title page, merely to unload some big, prefabricated letters into the center of the space, nor to dig a few holes in the silence with typographic heavy machinery and move on. Big type, even huge type, can be beautiful and useful.

Think of the blank page as alpine meadow, or as the purity of undifferentiated being. The typographer enters this space and must change it. The reader will enter it later, to see what the typographer has done. The underlying truth of the blank page must be infringed, but it must never altogether disappear—and whatever displaces it might well aim to be as lively and peaceful as it is. It is not enough, when building a title page, merely to unload some big, prefabricated letters into the center of the space, nor to dig a few holes in the silence with typographic heavy machinery and move on. Big type, even huge type, can be beautiful and useful.

A ragged edge is considered appropriate for a given paragraph setting if it varies within a fifth to a seventh of the paragraph's width. A much more active rag, however, also is visually interesting; the designer must, however,

ensure that the rag throughout the project remains consistent in its activity, rather than changing from page to page or even from column to column. The more active the rag—meaning, the greater the difference between

short and long lines—the more attention is due the rag of both the exterior edge formed by the long lines and the interior edge formed by the short lines.

The even, unforced ripple in the rags of these text columns (seen in the enlarged detail of the page spread, above) is considered desirable in text that is lengthy and intended to be read continuously. The designer has achieved this evenness in the rag's rhythm by balancing the variables of point size and column width, along with manually breaking lines.
ANDREAS ORTAG AUSTRIA

mised by the single occurrence of two short lines that create a boxy hole. In an optimal rag, the depth hovers between one-fifth and one-seventh of the paragraph's width. Word order and word breaks across lines also affect the rag. Problems in ragged-right setting commonly arise when a series of short words—of, at, it, to, we, us—are broken to align at the left edge, creating a vertical river running parallel to the aligned edge; and when short words appear at the end of a long line between two shorter lines, appearing to break off and float. In such cases, the designer must weigh the consequences of rebreaking the lines to prevent these problems against their effect on the rag as a whole. Similarly, the breaking of words across lines by using a hyphen can also be problematic if left untreated. From an editorial perspective, two successive lines ending with hyphens is undesirable. If a text is hyphenating excessively—more than once every ten lines or so—the problem lies in the relationship between the text's point size and the width of the paragraph; one or the other must be adjusted to correct the problem. Although a text free of hyphens would be best, this state of perfection is rarely possible; indeed, some designers argue that hyphenating words here and there helps contribute to the uniformity of the rag by allowing lines to remain similar in length.

Think of the blank page as alpine meadow, or as the purity of undifferentiated being. The typographer enters this space and must change it. The reader will enter it later, to see what the typographer has done. The underlying truth of the blank page must be infringed, but it must never altogether disappear–and whatever displaces it might well aim to be as lively and peaceful as it is. It is not enough, when building a title page, merely to unload some big, prefabricated letters into the center of the space, nor to dig a few holes in the silence with typographic heavy machinery and move on. Big type, even huge type, can be beautiful and useful.

Think of the blank page as alpine meadow, or as the purity of undifferentiated being. The typographer enters this space and must change it. The reader will enter it later, to see what the typographer has done. The underlying truth of the blank page must be infringed, but it must never altogether disappear–and whatever displaces it might well aim to be as lively and peaceful as it is. It is not enough, when building a title page, merely to unload some big, prefabricated letters into the center of the space, nor to dig a few holes in the silence with typographic heavy machinery and move on. Big type, even huge type, can be beautiful and useful.

Think of the blank page as alpine meadow, or as the purity of undifferentiated being. The typographer enters this space and must change it. The reader will enter it later, to see what the typographer has done. The underlying truth of the blank page must be infringed, but it must never altogether disappear–and whatever displaces it might well aim to be as lively and peaceful as it is. It is not enough, when building a title page, merely to unload some big, prefabricated letters into the center of the space, nor to dig a few holes in the silence with typographic heavy machinery and move on. Big type, even huge type, can be beautiful

Text excerpted from *The Elements of Typographic Style* by Robert Bringhurst.

Hyphenated word breaks are a constant source of frustration for a designer. Too many hyphens in a row are considered undesirable, and a slight adjustment in text size or paragraph width might correct the problem. The three paragraphs shown here are set in the same size text, with subtle differences. The first paragraph shows uncorrected hyphenation and rag. The second shows a more active rag but no hyphens—a toss-up between desired goals. The third shows a slightly wider paragraph and a more even rag; the only hyphen appears in the second line. One hyphen every ten lines or so is optimal.

Although the designer has set this book text on a wide paragraph, she has decided to limit the rag activity. The soft rag keeps the page quiet in general and it strives not to detract from the indents that define the beginnings of paragraphs. CHENG DESIGN UNITED STATES

HASHIDATE-YU Seattle / Washington (WA)

The Hashidate-Yu operated out of the basement of the Panama Hotel, a single room occupancy (SRO) hotel in what is now known as Seattle's International District, for more than 50 years — from 1910 until the mid-1960s — closing only during the evacuation and relocation period associated with Japanese internment during the Second World War. All indications are that the bathhouse was built at the time of the hotel's construction in 1910 by the first Japanese architect to practice in the city, Saburo Ozasa. The location of the Hashidate-Yu bathhouse at Sixth and South Main put it at the heart of Seattle's Nihonmachi, which served as a regional draw for Japanese immigrants who had settled on the urban periphery, as well as a residential center in its own right.

Immigrants came to soak at the sentos because life was hard, the hot water was relaxing, bathing facilities were scarce in prewar housing, and it was a traditional cultural activity. Japanese bathing traditions are at least twelve centuries old and have taken many forms. Bathhouses have existed in Japan since the eighth century, when they were a central feature of Buddhist temples. The earliest public bathhouses were connected with temples and monasteries, such as the one in the Second Month Hall of the Todai-Ji Temple in Nara. Built on a natural spring, the temple served as a bathhouse for the monks as well as a site of Buddhist purification rites.

Buddhist temples provided baths as resources for the general public, who lacked private facilities.¹ Although its religious connotations eventually faded, the act of bathing persisted in Japan. Bathhouses became social gathering places for urban dwellers. The first sento was established in Osaka in 1590; and by the mid 1800s there were 550 bathhouses in Tokyo alone. Neighborhood bathhouses in the eighteenth century were often two-story structures, with a room (or rooms) on the second level for relaxing, chatting, eating, drinking, and playing games.

Natural bathing facilities such as hot springs or onsen have been highly valued by Japanese for their healing capabilities. Bathing is still a valued tradition in Japan and was among the most significant traditional cultural practices to be brought over to the United States by the first Japanese immigrants. The furos, or soaking tubs, that Japanese immigrants constructed in American Nihonmachis are among the few surviving elements of the built environment that reflect a distinctively Japanese American heritage.

Several Japanese bathhouses were located within Seattle's Nihonmachi. Those who lived outside of the city frequently would visit Japantown on the weekend to do shopping and attend events at

Natural bathing facilities are highly valued by the Japanese for their healing capabilities. At right, the women's bath at Makiba-no-ie Ryokan in Yufuin, Japan, 2000.

HASHIDATE-YU Seattle / Washington (WA)

The Intricacies of Justification Setting text justified creates an exceptionally clean, geometric presentation within a layout. The problems this alignment structure creates, however, are formidable, both from the standpoint of comfortable reading and aesthetics. Well-justified text can be sublimely beautiful in a stark, austere way; achieving the sublime requires that all the internal word- and letterspacing is absolutely consistent, producing the appearance of a continuous, uninterrupted gray value. The first challenge to overcome, as noted previously, is that of the inconsistency of spacing that naturally attends justification: different numbers of words, of different lengths, forced to fit within a fixed width. And there are actually three problems this state of affairs creates: the first is rivers—chains of word spaces that join from line to line—and the others are: distracting changes in the visual density of the lines (some appearing open and light, others appearing compressed and dark); and excessive hyphenation, even more than is typically present in ragged text. To minimize these problems, the designer must first find the optimal number of characters and words (see page 155) that comfortably fit upon the justified width and so mitigate the potential for undesirable spacing. A slightly wider paragraph than that which would be truly optimal

An ancient metaphor: thought is a thread, and the raconteur is a spinner of yarns—but the true storyteller, the poet, is a weaver. The scribes made this old and audible abstraction into a new and visible fact. After long practice, their work took on such an even flexible texture that they called the written page a textus, which means cloth. The typesetting device, whether it happens to be a computer or a composing stick, functions like a loom. And the typographer, like the scribe, normally aims to weave the text as evenly as possible. Good letterforms are designed to give a lively, even texture, but careless spacing of letters, lines, and words can tear this fabric apart.

Another ancient metaphor: the density of texture in a written or typeset page is called its color. This has nothing to do with red or green ink; it refers only to the darkness or blackness of the letterforms in mass. Once the demands of legibility and logical order are satisfied, evenness of color is the typographer's normal aim.

An ancient metaphor: thought is a thread, and the raconteur is a spinner of yarns—but the true storyteller, the poet, is a weaver. The scribes made this old and audible abstraction into a new and visible fact. After long practice, their work took on such an even flexible texture that they called the written page a textus, which means cloth. The typesetting device, whether it happens to be a computer or a composing stick, functions like a loom. And the typographer, like the scribe, normally aims to weave the text as evenly as possible. Good letterforms are designed to give a lively, even texture, but careless spacing of letters, lines, and words can tear this fabric apart.

Another ancient metaphor: the density of texture in a written or typeset page is called its color. This has nothing to do with red or green ink; it refers only to the darkness or blackness of the letterforms in mass. Once the demands of legibility and logical order are satisfied, evenness of color is the typographer's normal aim.

Text excerpted from *The Elements of Typographic Style* by Robert Bringhurst

This specimen exhibits all the hallmarks of exquisitely well-justified text: lines that are consistently spaced and that appear the same in overall density (none tighter and darker, nor looser and lighter); the word spaces are normal (not relatively tight or loose compared to the letterspacing for this type style); there are no rivers; and the presence of hyphens is minimal.

Poorly justified text displays wildly varied word spaces and rivers, lines whose density alternates between very dark and very light, and excessive hyphenation. To correct these problems, a designer must continually adjust text size and paragraph width, move text from line to line, and selectively tighten and loosen spacing.

(in general) allows greater flexibility in how words may be moved or broken from line to line. No matter how consistent the spacing this strategy initially achieves, inevitably the designer must shift words—or parts of words—from line to line for finetuning. He or she must then select individual words, groups of words, single spaces, or entire lines and manually tighten and loosen their spacing. Correcting excess hyphenation also comes about this way.

And, then, there are the aesthetic issues. From a classical standpoint, justified setting is considered only truly beautiful when all of its components align: both horizontally (the baselines of text in adjacent columns) and vertically (the tops and bottoms of paragraphs or columns. Achieving this goal is challenging due to the unpredictable length of text at any given time. Further, it tends to limit the designer's options for separating para-

graphs (see page 157); only those that maintain the alignment among baselines between adjacent paragraphs will seem appropriate. Special attention must also be given to punctuation that occurs at the beginnings and ends of lines because of the way quotation marks, periods, and so on appear to "bite into" the clean edges of the justified text block. The reward for all this hard work, of course, is beauty: elegant, crisp, and controlled.

The tightly justified columns of text in this asymmetrical layout reinforce the geometry of the page. Weight changes within the text add contrast, and the spacing is consistent.
BRETT YASKO UNITED STATES

hought is a thread, and
er of yarns—but the true
weaver. The scribes made
straction into a new and
ractice, their work took
texture that they called
tus, which means cloth.
whether it happens to be
sing stick, functions like
grapher, like the scribe,
e the text as evenly as
ns are designed to give a
areless spacing of letters,
r this fabric apart.
etaphor: the density of

PROPOR
WITHIN TH

HORIZONS BEY

"To say the least, the a
from within," recount
describing the scenar
hardened through ye
It was the result of a l
exasperated, looking
kinetic rhythm toward
(approximately 50 tim
per the data) in which
grossly underestimat

contemporary visual and entertainment media, including film, fashion and design. Since the 1986 debut of Peter Gabriel's *Sledgehammer* video, artists working in new media, especially animation, have taken many cues from MTV. Despite music video's evolution outside of art traditions and venues, it is now thoroughly integrated in the contemporary art world with many artists straddling the high/low culture realms. For example, one of the successful directors in this exhibit, Chris Cunningham (director of Björk's *All is Full of Love*), is represented by a New York gallery and exhibited in the 2001 Venice Biennale.

The guest curator of this exhibit, Ed Steinberg, has chosen music videos produced since 1982, the year following an explosion in budget and distribution with the growth of cable television and MTV. The typical budget grew exponentially, from the low tens of thousands to nearly half a million dollars with Michael Jackson's *Beat It*. Despite their economic ramifications and impact, Steinberg based his selection of music videos on their creative qualities and innovation. To provide the fullest exposure, the 14 DVDs in this exhibit are projected continuously on large screens on a rotating basis.

Steinberg gravitates toward works that do not conform to the formulaic. They span a variety of productions by both industry directors and artist directors. The former include F. Gary Gray, Michel Gondry, Hype Williams, Mark Romanek, Anton Corbijn, Chris Cunningham, Jim Yukich and Spike Jonze, while the latter include Damien Hirst, Andy Warhol and Doug Aiken. Remixed dance videos, spotlights on particular recording artists (such as compilations of Madonna and Björk) and "random cool" videos also add to the mix. Steinberg is open about trusting the opinions of practitioners in the field—the artists, themselves.

rapid editing are often employed, borrowed from the advertising industry. Like ads, music videos must forge an instant connection with audiences, but also withstand the repetitive play endemic to the entertainment industry and essential to its success. Numbing is inherent to any repetition, so the challenge is to sustain those instant connections through content and quality.

important sources of reference. For this catalogue's design, we thank Brett Yasko; for its editing, we thank Kristen Fair and Sharmila Venkatasubban.

The installation staff of Wood Street Galleries (George Dun, Tom Hall, Thaddeus Kellstadt, Chris Korch, George Magalios, Erin O'Neill, Drew Pavelchak and Shaun Slifer) has been outstanding, rising once again to the occasion by meeting the challenge of media-based work. Finally, we wish to thank Ed Steinberg; his enthusiasm for the project made our involvement an honor and pleasure.

Murray Horne
Curator
Wood Street Galleries
The Pittsburgh Cultural Trust

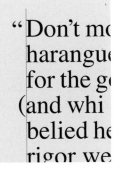

"Don't m
harangu
for the g
(and whi
belied he
rigor we

"Don't m
harangu
for the g
(and whi
belied he
rigor we

The goal of justified setting is absolute, geometric cleanliness—and so rigorous control of its external shape has historically been considered important. The baselines of lines of text in one paragraph, or column, are typically made to align with others in paragraphs or columns to the left and right—across a page or spread; the upper and lower edges of paragraphs and columns are made to align with each other: everything justifies with everything else.

Further, such annoying details as quotation marks, commas, periods, and other punctuation that disturb the perfection of the aligned edges must be spaced—and sometimes hanged outside the aligned edges—to prevent them from creating holes that appear to "bite" into the text block.

The Optimal Paragraph A desirable paragraph setting is one in which a constellation of variables achieves a harmonic balance. Since extended running text is such an important consideration for a publication, finding the optimal paragraph is one way to begin developing overall typographic structure. A designer might first make some assumptions about the text typeface, based on his or her sense of its appropriateness from a conceptual standpoint and in consideration of its visual attributes—the relative height of the lowercase letters, the general weight of the strokes and any contrast within them, the height of the ascenders and descenders—and set a text paragraph at an arbitrary width and arbitrary text size. Judging from this first attempt, a designer might opt to adjust the size of the text, loosen or tighten its overall spacing, open and close up the leading, and change the width in successive studies. By comparing the results of these variations, a designer will be able to determine the most comfortable text setting for extended reading. At what point is the type size too small—or uncomfortably large? Are the lines relatively even in length or varying a lot? Is excessive hyphenation occurring, meaning that the paragraph is too narrow to allow a useful character count? Is the leading creating too dense a field of text to feel comfortable?

A "what if" book, *The Switch* is inspired by the blood-boiling enmity of polar opposites found in all spheres of life: families, shared living spaces, war-zones, ideological divides, and places of work. *What if* there was a compulsory shoe-swapping day? *What if* flashes of light lit up dark pockets of hate and misunderstanding all over the world, even for only a moment? Can empathy be cajoled or would it make no difference at all?

The Switch was published by Jewel Weed Press, Middletown NY, a garage-based small press owned by a former High School of Printing classmate, Ronald Hodamarsky. Although Jewel Weed's list focused mainly on books written by Ronald's wife Pat Hodamarsky, Ronald really dug the premise of *The Switch* when I pitched it to him over the phone. He agreed to publish the book if I would pay for all the printing and binding expenses including the costs of having their small second-hand offset press fixed. Published in an edition of 400 copies, my first novel was reviewed in two obscure literary journals—favorably in one and very unfavorably in the other. The reviewer of the pan was particularly irritated by the book's structure: "It is dizzying enough slogging through

The Switch *a novel*

One morning, a woman wakes to find she's living the life of her number one nemesis. Her nemesis has become her as well, at least for the day. They witness themselves in each other. It seems, on this one day at least, these switches have occurred all over the world. *The Switch* chronicles the day in the lives of six sets of switched enemies: three pairs who are face to face enemies, and three pairs who never even met but despise the very thought of the other.

1978, Jewel Weed Press, Middletown, NY

THE SWITCH

excerpt

Joanne, in the person of Carlotta, feeling the weight of a body sixteen pounds heavier than her own, sees herself coming down the hallway and wants to duck into the bathroom or turn around and head the other way. Carlotta feels so much revulsion associated with this person walking towards her, the feeling is physical. Her neurons hurl frantically over synapses in search of a means of escape, her stomach knots, her fingers and toes tremor. She recalls a dream where Joanne is nice to her, confides in her. In the dream, the two of them were singing a song together and embraced each other in the way old friends do. Whose dream was that? Joanne's? Carlotta's? Both? Neither? Carlotta decides to keep walking, say good morning, maybe ask Joanne how her dad is doing or something about the Anderson case.

Carlotta, in the person of Joanne, decides not to go into the mailroom after all. Instead she ducks into a stairwell. Joanne despises the way Carlotta tries to engage her in small talk. *It's so dishonest. We both detest each other, why bother acting like it's any different.* Joanne will take truth over niceness any day of the week.

Two people disliking each other, even with great intensity, is not a serious problem in and of itself. It is a serious problem for Joanne and Carlotta because they are both intellectual property lawyers at Bennett and Bennett and have no choice but to work together on at least one third of their cases. Truth is, Joanne doesn't care for 90% of her colleagues at Bennett and Bennett. She considers most of them immoral, shiftless hypocrites. She hates working there but would never leave the firm because it's pretty much her whole life. Carlotta dreamed of working at Bennett and Bennett ever since she was a pre-law student reading about the firm's landmark class-action suits against big pharmaceutical companies. It's not a huge firm but it has an excellent reputation and they let her take on a lot of pro bono cases. Still, she often considers leaving, primarily because of Joanne. As a lawyer, Carlotta prides herself in finding solutions that avoid having to go to court. She's a mediator by nature and considers it a personal failure that she's never been able to reach some kind of common ground with Joanne. She loses sleep over the conflict and has named a deepening worry line in her forehead after her nemesis.

Carlotta believes that Joanne is not, deep down, a bad person. She is just severely fucked up, clinically depressed, and probably had a very difficult

a book where every character is simultaneously someone else, but then halfway through *The Switch*, the reading orientation flips 180 degrees forcing the reader to physically turn the book upside down. Once vertigo sets in you realize this device is nothing but a trick to get you to notice the book's palindromic cover design which forms a face from both orientations. Cute, but it doesn't make up for the preposterous premise and the altogether convoluted read. Switch it off!"

46   47

Three styles of text set on different widths are also set in three different sizes to achieve as near-to-optimal relationships between type size and column width as possible—approximately thirty characters per line for short bursts of reading, fifty to seventy characters for extended reading. The wide, primary text column is likely too wide to be optimal, but the designer has increased the leading, relative to the point size, to make it more comfortable. EARSAY UNITED STATES

During this study, it might become clear that several options for width and leading are optimal, but a designer will need to choose one as a standard for the publication. The choice that the designer makes has implications for the page size, the number of columns of text that might fit on it, and optimal sizes for other text groupings, such as captions, callouts, introductory paragraphs, and so on.

In this study of a paragraph, the variables of type size, spacing, leading, and paragraph width are tested to arrive at a text setting that results in the most comfortable spacing, the least hyphenation, and a decisive rag.

Text excerpted from *The Elements of Typographic Style* by Robert Bringhurst

Think of the blank page as alpine meadow, or as the purity of undifferentiated being. The typographer enters this space and must change it. The reader will enter it later, to see what the typographer has done. The underlying truth of the blank page must be infringed, but it must never altogether disappear— and whatever displaces it might well aim to be as lively and peaceful as it is. It is not enough, when building a title page, merely to unload some big, prefabricated letters into the center of the space, nor to dig a few holes in the silence with typographic heavy machinery and move on. Big type, even huge type, can be beautiful and useful.

Initial Setting Set solid; the activity of the ascenders and descenders, and a relatively large x-height, create an uncomfortably dense setting. Furthermore, the rag shows indecisive lengths, as well as inclusions, and there are two hyphenated breaks in sequence.

Think of the blank page as alpine meadow, or as the purity of undifferentiated being. The typographer enters this space and must change it. The reader will enter it later, to see what the typographer has done. The underlying truth of the blank page must be infringed, but it must never altogether disappear—and whatever displaces it might well aim to be as lively and peaceful as it is. It is not enough, when building a title page, merely to unload some big, prefabricated letters into the center of the space, nor to dig a few holes in the silence with typographic heavy machinery and move on. Big type, even huge type, can be beautiful and useful.

Second Setting Same leading; adjusting the size to 8 points alleviates the density and somewhat improves the rag shape; however, the size is too small for the width of the paragraph to be optimal (fifty to seventy characters on each line).

Think of the blank page as alpine meadow, or as the purity of undifferentiated being. The typographer enters this space and must change it. The reader will enter it later, to see what the typographer has done. The underlying truth of the blank page must be infringed, but it must never altogether disappear—and whatever displaces it might well aim to be as lively and peaceful as it is. It is not enough, when building a title page, merely to unload some big, prefabricated letters into the center of the space, nor to dig a few holes in the silence with typographic heavy machinery and move on. Big type, even huge type, can be beautiful and useful.

Third Setting Same size and leading, but substitution of a face with a smaller x-height. This face appears too small to be comfortable, however, and the width is still too wide for an optimal character count.

Think of the blank page as alpine meadow, or as the purity of undifferentiated being. The typographer enters this space and must change it. The reader will enter it later, to see what the typographer has done. The underlying truth of the blank page must be infringed, but it must never altogether disappear—and whatever displaces it might well aim to be as lively and peaceful as it is. It is not enough, when building a title page, merely to unload some big, prefabricated letters into the center of the space, nor to dig a few holes in the silence with typographic heavy machinery and move on. Big type, even huge type, can be beautiful and useful.

Fourth Setting A return to the typeface of the initial settings, but narrowing the paragraph, retains legibility, optimizes the character count (to sixty-five per line) and creates a more active rag. The leading still seems a bit dense, and there are problems with the rag and excessive hyphenation.

Think of the blank page as alpine meadow, or as the purity of undifferentiated being. The typographer enters this space and must change it. The reader will enter it later, to see what the typographer has done. The underlying truth of the blank page must be infringed, but it must never altogether disappear— and whatever displaces it might well aim to be as lively and peaceful as it is. It is not enough, when building a title page, merely to unload some big, prefabricated letters into the center of the space, nor to dig a few holes in the silence with typographic heavy machinery and move on. Big type, even huge type, can be beautiful and useful.

Final Setting Another slight decrease in the paragraph width, an added point of leading, and decisive rebreaking of the lines yields a paragraph with a comfortable texture, an optimal line count, minimal hyphenation, and a beautiful rag. From this ultimate paragraph, the typographer is ready to consider how to structure columns and supporting treatments for elements such as callouts and captions.

Separating Paragraphs As recently as the fifteenth century, text was set continuously without breaks; the definition of the paragraph as an informational nugget emerged in the 1500s as a way of helping readers navigate text. Initially, a paragraph change was indicated by a larger space after the period following the last sentence of one paragraph; a later evolution introduced graphic elements, such as squares or bullets, as paragraph separators—but still

Bold subheads with a slight indent, along with a full return, distinguish the paragraphs within the columns of this layout.
CLEMENS THÉOBERT SCHEDLER AUSTRIA

The beginning of each paragraph, along with an interval of space, is indicated by a bold lead line. C+G PARTNERS UNITED STATES

A simple proportional return separates the paragraphs within the text column of this brochure spread. Sometimes, a full return of the same leading—leaving a full line open between paragraphs or double the leading—will be too much, appearing to disconnect the paragraphs from each other and disturb the continuity of the text in the column. In such cases, setting a leading measure between paragraphs that is less than twice the text's leading will create enough distinction without also creating a distracting gap. VOICE AUSTRALIA

there was no break in the text, such as a line return. Eventually, columns were set with a line return, but without space between paragraphs; instead, the beginning of a new paragraph was indicated by an indent—where the first line of a new paragraph starts a few character-widths in from the left alignment. This treatment works particularly well in justified setting. The depth of the indent is subjective but must be noticeable. The indent must be deeper if the leading is loose; more interline space normalizes the perception of the column's width and a bigger "hole" must be cut into the paragraph. Sometimes, a designer will exaggerate the indent for visual effect. If the paragraphs are long and set in relatively wide columns, this treatment often will help to break up the wall of text by introducing a rhythm of cuts into the columns. Indents are usually not a great idea if the text is set ragged right. Since the rag is already changing the line lengths on the right edge of the column, the indent on the left side loses some of its visual power, and may appear sloppy. Beyond indents, spaces of differing intervals may be introduced between paragraphs, of course, as well as supporting graphic elements, unusual treatments to the first lines of paragraphs—a designer's options for accomplishing the goal of separation are nearly endless.

abitur nec nisi maecrena hicula odio sed urna. Nas enim, fringilla vita, temp mollis eturna. Phaselus a
   Vestibulum blandit ne amet furpis. Suspendisse Aliquam posuere aliquet Phaselus aliquet nisl vita coelis in semper qua dolc

One-Em Indent

abitur nec nisi maecrena hicula odio sed urna. Nas enim, fringilla vita, temp mollis eturna. Phaselus a

Vestibulum blandit nequ amet furpis. Suspendisse Aliquam posuere aliquet Phaselus aliquet nisl vita

Full Leaded Return

consectur adipiscing eli ur suspendiso semassa, c
   Abitur n
   maecren
   hicula oc
urna. Nasunio enim, frir vita, tempean mollis etu Phaselus adipe poiup we Vestibulum dof blandit r

No Return: Multiple-Line Deep Indent

abitur nec nisi maecrena hicula odio sed urna. Na enim, fringilla vita, temp mollis eturna. Phaselus a
   ﷽
Vestibulum blandit nequ amet furpis. Suspendisse Aliquam posuere aliquet Phaselus aliquet nisl vita

Full Return: Dingbat Divider

abitur nec nisi maecrena hicula odio sed urna. Nas enim, fringilla vita, temp mollis eturna. Phaselus a
   Vestibulu blandit neque sit amet fu pis. Suspendisse lect Alic posuere aliquet nurp Pha aliquet nisl vitae ni coeli:

Deep Indent

abitur nec nisi maecrena hicula odio sed urna. Nas enim, fringilla vita, temp mollis eturna. Phaselus a

Vestibulum blandit nequ amet furpis. Suspendisse Aliquam posuere aliquet Phaselus aliquet nisl vita

Proportional Leaded Return

abitur nec nisi maecrena hicula odio sed urna. Nas enim, fringilla vita, temp mollis eturna. Phaselus a

Vestibulum bland amet furpis. Sus isse lect. Aliquam posue aliquet nurp Phaselus al

Ascending Cap: Full Return

abitur nec nisi maecrena hicula odio sed urna. Nas enim, fringilla vita, temp mollis eturna. Phaselus a
_____
Vestibulum blandit nequ amet furpis. Suspendisse Aliquam posuere aliquet Phaselus aliquet nisl vita

Full Return: Rule Divider

abitur nec nisi maecrena hicula odio sed urna. Nas enim, fringilla vita, temp mollis eturna. Phaselus a
■ Vestibulum blandit ne amet furpis. Suspendisse Aliquam posuere aliquet Phaselus aliquet nisl vita coelis in semper qua dolc

Indent with Graphical Embellishment

abitur nec nisi maecrena hicula odio sed urna. Nas enim, fringilla vita, temp mollis eturna. Phaselus a

Quae Coelis Sum
Vestibulum blandit nequ amet furpis. Suspendisse Aliquam posuere aliquet Phaselus aliquet nisl vita coelis in semper qua dolc

Bold Subhead: Full Return

ur suspendiso semassa, c abitur nec nisi maecrena

Vestibulum blandi sit amet furpis. S pendisse lect. Ali posuere aliquet nurp Pha aliquet nisl vitae nicoelis semper qua dologi uiou

Drop Cap: Full Return

abitur nec nisi maecrena hicula odio sed urna. Nas enim, fringilla vita, temp mollis eturna. Phaselus a

Vestibulum blandit neque sit furpis. Suspendisse lecfk Aliquam posuere aliquet Phaselus aliquet nisl vita

Hanging Indent

abitur nec nisi maecrena hicula odio sed urna. Nas enim, fringilla vita, temp mollis eturna. Phaselus a

Vestibulum blandit nec amet furpis. Suspendisse Aliquam posuere aliquet Phaselus aliquet nisl vita

Lead Line: Style Change

abitur nec nisi maecrena hicula odio sed urna. Nas enim, fringilla vita, temp mollis eturna. Phaselus a

Vestibulum blandit nequ amet furpis. Suspendisse Aliquam posuere aliquet Phaselus aliquet nisl vita

Proportional Return: Reversed Lead Line

There are as many ways to separate paragraphs as there are to decorate a cake. Indeed, this often-overlooked detail of typesetting can offer a beautiful opportunity and add contrast and texture as a way to relieve text's relentless monotony on the page. Shown here are a few of the most common approaches. Variations on a particular method—or combinations of related methods—can create a deeper expression of a project's typographic language or help distinguish between different kinds of breaks in the sequence of content.

OK, Now Deal with It: The Finer Points of Text Typography Very little attention is paid to the crafting of type beyond composition and style. The tiny details of text setting are equally, if not more, important to ensure smooth reading and grammatical correctness, and are often overlooked. Knowing these fundamental rules for clean text setting keeps the designer alert to potential spacing problems and helps improve the look and readability of running text.

The designer of this page has carefully considered the editorial and visual qualities of the text components. List numbers hang outside the columns to maintain the clarity of alignment; the title is distinguished by its italic setting; callouts are pronounced in a bolder weight; and each different kind of text content is given a distinct stylistic treatment.

FINEST MAGMA GERMANY

The Page Begins Here

Lorem ipsum dolor sit amet, consetetur sadipscing elitr, sed diam nonumy eirmod tempor invidunt ut labore et dolore magna aliquyam erat, sed diam voluptua. At vero eos et accusam et justo duo dolores et ea rebum. Stet clita kasd gubergren, no sea takimata sanctus est Lorem ipsum dolor sit amet. Lorem ipsum dolor sit amet, consetetur sadipscing elitr, sed diam nonumy eirmod tempor invidunt ut labore et dolore magna aliquyam erat.

A New Sequence Begins

At vero eos et accusam et justo duo dolores et ea rebum. Stet clita kasd gubergren, no sea takimata sanctus est Lorem ipsum dolor sit amet. Lorem ipsum dolor sit amet, consetetur sadipscing elitr, sed diam nonumy eirmod tempor invidunt ut labore et dolore magna aliquyam erat. At vero eos et accusam et justo duo dolores et ea rebum. Stet clita kasd gubergren, no sea takimata sanctus est Lorem ipsum dolor sit amet.

Duis autem vel eum iriure dolor in hendrerit in vulputate velit esse molestie consequat, vel illum dolore eu feugiat nulla facilisis at vero eros et accusan et iusto odio dignissim qui blandit praesent luptatum zzril delenit augue duis dolore te feugait nulla facilisi.

Ut wisi enim ad minim veniam, quis nostrud exerci tation ullamcorper suscipit lobortis nisl uta aliquip ex ea commodo consequat. Duis autem vel eum iriure dolor in hendrerit in vulputate velit esse molestie consequat, vel illum dolore eu feugiat de nulla facilisis at vero eros et accusan et iusto odio dignissim qui blandit praesent luptatum zzril delenit augue duis dolore te feugait nulla facilisi.

Ut wisi enim ad minim veniam, quis nostrud exerci tation ullamcorper suscipit lobortis nisl uta aliquip ex ea commodo consequat. Duis autem vel eum iriure dolor in hendrerit in vulputate velit esse molestie consequat, vel illum dolore eu feugiat de nulla facilisis at vero eros et accusan et iusto odio dignissim qui blandit praesent

To indent or not to indent? In setting text in which paragraphs run together, separated by indenting the first line, the first paragraph on the page should have no indent. Every paragraph thereafter is then indented—until the next major sequential break or subheaded paragraph, which should not be indented.

and whatever displaces it might well aim to be as lively and peaceful as it is. It is not enough, when building a title page, merely to unload some big, prefabricated letters into the center of the space, nor to dig a few holes in the silence with typographic heavy machinery and move on. Big type, even huge type, can be beautiful and useful.

Care for the widows. Never allow a single word (a widow) to end a paragraph. If widows constantly appear in the rough setting of a body of text, the column width should be adjusted. Ideally, the last line of a paragraph should be more than half the paragraph's width, but three words (no matter their length) are acceptable.

whenever she seems ti
period (let's face it) org

whenever she seems ti
period (let's face it) org

Keep 'em upright. Use upright parentheses and brackets, even if the text in which they appear is italic. These marks, in their sloped versions, appear weak and usually exacerbate the spacing problems associated with them.

---

122   Interview

www.borsellino.net

Piero Borsellino wird 1975 als Sohn sizilianischer Eltern in Frankfurt geboren. Mit 14 beginnt er sich sein Taschengeld mit dem Organisieren von Parties, dem Schreiben von Sponsoring Konzepten für Markenartikler sowie dem Entwerfen von Logos zu verdienen. Mit 16 macht er sich selbständig, wechselt jedoch mit 17 zur PR Agentur Leipziger & Partner und wird mit 18 Art Director der Plattenfirma des damaligen Nena und Bodosatz Managers. Mit 21 gründet er sein eigenes Designbüro und arbeitet fortan für Kunden aus Musik, Mode und Kultur. 1999 gründet er sein erstes Modemagazin, 2001 folgt sein zweites Magazin namens 14XI, welches 2002 in M.Publication umbenannt wird. Für sein Design - zuvor für Kunden als auch aktuell für M - erhielt er mehrfach Auszeichnungen.

10.2/Piero Borsellino

Sex, Drugs and Rock'n'Roll.

01 \5 **Was gefällt dir an deinem Beruf?**
Sex, Drugs and Rock'n'Roll: Seine eigenen Ideen zu entwickeln und umzusetzen ist wie ein Orgasmus, ein süchtigmachender Rausch und ein gutes Konzert zugleich. Wer das nicht verspürt, sollte den Beruf wechseln.

02 \5 **Wer waren bzw. sind deine Vorbilder?**
Früher: Adriano Celentano, heute: Renzo Rosso (Diesel Chef).

03 \5 **Machst du freie Projekte?**
Freie Projekte? Hört sich absurd an. Auch wenn ich weiss was mit der Frage beabsichtigt ist, wundere ich mich über diese Bezeichnung. Kreative schaffen sich sogenannte "freelance projects", damit sie ganz ohne Vorgaben und Kundenwünsche Schalten und Walten können - sich "selbst-verwirklichen" können. Hört sich sehr arty an. Und vor allem so, als würden sie in der anderen Zeit nur "unfreie" Projekte verwirklichen. Was bin ich Dienstleister oder Künstler? Das zeigt, dass die kreativen Berufe, sei es Designer, Photograph, Illustrator, Texter oder Regisseur, immer nach größtmöglicher Freiheit (ja einem "Director's Cut") heischen. Der Idealfall: Versuchen Kunden zu finden, die von einem den Director's Cut und nicht das Gegenteil verlangen. Wie war noch mal die Frage? Aaah, ja ich mache freie Projekte!

04 \5 **Was sind Computer für dich?**
Moderne Mittel zum Zweck.

05 \5 **Mit was spielst du?**
Mit dem Feuer.

06 \5 **Wie bringst du Familie, Freizeit und Beruf unter einen Hut?**
Momentan in der genau umgekehrten Reihenfolge: Erst der Beruf, dann die Freizeit und dann die Familie. Kann sein, dass sich die Reihenfolge in einigen Jahren ändert. Und zwar wenn ich Papa werde.

07 \5 **Was magst du an deinen Arbeiten, was nicht?**
Die Freude ist meistens nur von kurzer Dauer, weil ich mit

getaner Arbeit das Kapitel beendet habe. Umso mehr freue ich mich über Arbeiten, die noch nach Jahren wirken.

08 \5 **Dein Lieblingsfluch?**
Minghia! (Sizilianisch für "Schwanz", wie Fuck!).

09 \5 **Was machst du nachdem du aufgestanden bist?**
Meistens urinieren.

10 \5 **Empfehle drei Feinde:**
Die Ablenkung, den Perfektionismus und die Müdigkeit. Alle drei Kosten Zeit. Dies fordert wiederum die Disziplin.

11 \5 **Wo würdest du gerne leben, wo arbeiten?**
Beides in New York, Sizilien oder in der Renaissance.

12 \5 **Design und Politik - ist das ein Thema für dich?**
Nicht direkt. Beides ist abstrahiert gesehen ein Gestaltungsprozess. Gute Gestaltung gibt eine Richtung vor. Leitet die Massen. Dies wiederum verleiht Macht. Manifestiert eine Aussage. Kommt nur, wie immer, darauf an, welche Interessen(gemeinschaften) sich dahinter verbergen.

13 \5 **Wiedergeboren werden als?**
Wind. Mal ist man da, mal nicht. Mal stärker, mal schwächer.

14 \5 **Was sammelst du?**
Erfahrungen aller Art.

15 \5 **Wie findest du Prince, Prince Charles, Charles Bronson?**
Überragender Geist, geisttötend, tötender Mundharmonikaspieler.

16 \5 **Was würdest du gerne erfinden?**
Das Glücksrezept.

17 \5 **Wobei kannst du am besten entspannen?**
In der Sauna und beim Sex.

18 \5 **Die größte Revolution war/ist:**
Der Mikrochip.

19 \5 **Wen würdest du gerne einmal treffen?**
Denjenigen, dessen Idee "Adam & Eva" war.

20 \5 **Dein Lieblings-Buchstabe in deiner Lieblings-Schrift?** *Mir gefällt das grosse "S" in der Akzidenz Grotesk Black ganz gut.*

\5.02.06.THEMEN .... Schriften\\Digi8a Text\Monopoint\Gringo Tuscan\Copy ....

When the editor and designer pay careful attention, bad line-breaking will be radically reduced. It's always best to break a word to leave a desirable syllable of four letters.

will be presided over by Ellen Mac-Murray and her partner, Roberto M. Castiglioni, along with Joy Adams.

(f) [f] {f}   *(f) [f] {f}*

(f) [f] {f}   *(f) [f] {f}*

erview Terrace •Luna Park, New Jerse
erview Terrace •Luna Park, New Jerse

erview Terrace •Luna Park, New Jers

erview Terrace · Luna Park, New Jers

erview Terrace ·Luna Park, New Jers

Watch the breaks! Avoid breaking words across lines (hyphenating) so that short or incomplete stubs begin the line following: -ed, -er, -ing, -tion, -al, -ly. Make sure there are at least four letters in the word ending the line before athe break. Try to avoid breaking names from one line to another. If absolutely necessary, however, break right before the last name—never in the middle of a name and never before an initial.

Avoid a serious crash. The content within parentheses and brackets usually will benefit from additional space to separate it from these marks, especially italic forms with ascenders that are likely to crash into the marks if left at the default spacing. In particular, lowercase italic f, l, k, h, and many of the uppercase letters will need this adjustment.

Style your bullets. The default bullet is usually enormous and distracting compared to the typeface in which it appears. The bullet needs to be noticeable but not stick out; slightly heavier than the text's vertical stroke weight is enough. Feel free to change the bullet's typeface—or use a dingbat or even a period, shifted off the baseline—to bring it stylistically closer to the surrounding text.

host *delicious* cakes fo

host *delicious* cakes fo

Don't cross the channels. When possible, avoid hard returns between paragraphs aligning (or nearly aligning) between adjacent columns. As the horizontal negative channels created by the returns approach each other, not only do they become distracting, but they also tend to redirect the eye across the columns and break reading sequence.

Italic type needs spacing, too. Italic used for emphasis within text sometimes appears smaller and tighter than its roman counterpart. Always evaluate the italic and adjust its size or spacing to fit most seamlessly with its surrounding text.

(by listening to the sea) will c
determined, and thought it
"Think carefully," he said, ag
foremost a kind of singular

• Optional leather seats and dash board
• Five-speed transmission
• ABS breaking system with titatnium discs
• Power steering and automatic mirrors

Hang your punctuation. Most punctuation marks—especially quotations—should hang outside the aligned text if they occur at the beginning of a line. This rule sometimes applies to bullets as well; a designer might opt to maintain the alignment of the bulleted text and hang the bullets in the margin or gutter.

whenever possible. A special

whenever possible. A special

not always, however, because

not always, however, because

Think of the blank page as alpine meadow, or as the purity of undifferentiated being. The typographer enters this space and must change it. The reader will enter it later, to see what the typographer has done. The underlying truth of the blank page must be infringed, but it must never altogether disappear—and whatever displaces it might well aim to be as lively and peaceful as it is. It is not enough, when building

ize; however these

ize; however these

you say? That's pr

you say ? That's pr

Mind the gaps. A single word space, never two, follows a period before the initial cap of the next sentence. Furthermore, the space before a comma or a quotation mark should be reduced; these marks "carry" additional space above or below them. Similarly, the word space following a comma, apostrophe, or quotation mark should also be slightly reduced.

Too much is just too much. In justified setting, adjusting the letterspacing to avoid rivers is inevitable, but don't adjust too much. Like rivers, overly tight—and therefore very dark—lines of text are distracting.

Push and pull. Colons and semicolons need additional space preceding them and less space following them. Exclamation points and question marks often benefit from being separated from their sentences by an extra bit of space. A full word space is too much, as is half a word space; but +20 tracking, is usually sufficient.

n the year 1254 before moving on to
n the year 1254 before moving on to

n the year 1254 before moving on t
n the year 1254 before moving on t

10,336.00   10,336.00
135.36   135.36

Look at the figures. Numerals always need spacing adjustments, especially in sequences. Lining numerals, which extend from baseline to cap height, usually require extra letterspacing, even though they're more varied in form than uppercase letters. Numerals in complex arrange-ments, such as tables, are generally tabulated—arranged flush right or around a decimal point in vertical arrangements of figures. In such situa-tions, the lining figures are preferred to ensure vertical alignment for making calculations.

dolor sit amet, consetetur sadipscing.

Elitr, sed diam nonumy eirmod tempor invidunt ut labore et dolore magna aliquyam erat, sediam volu ptua. At vero eos et accusam et justo duo dolores et ea rebum. Stet clita kasd gubergren, no sea takim ata sanctus est Lorem ipsum dolor sit amet. Lorem ipsum dolor sit amet, consetetur sadipscing elitr, sed diam nonumy eirmod tempor invidunt ut labo re et dolore magna aliquyam erat.

At vero eos et accusam et justo duo dolores et ea rebum. Stet clita kasd gubergren, no sea takim ata sanctus est Lorem ipsum dolor sit amet. Lorem ipsum dolor sit amet, consetetur sadipscing elitr,

Lorem i
elitr, sed
labore e
ptua. At
ea rebu
ata sanc
ipsum d
sed dian
re et dol
duo dole
no sea ta
amet. Lo
sadipsci
invidun

Save the orphans. Don't allow the last line of a paragraph to begin the top of a column. This "orphan" is especially distracting if there is a space separating the paragraph that follows and really irritating if it occurs at the very beginning of the left-hand page. Run the text back so that the new page starts a paragraph, or space out the preceding text so that the paragraph continues with at least three lines after the page break.

ıe new AIGA building

ıe new AIGA building

ıe new AIGA building

Uh-oh . . . Small caps! Small caps used for acronyms, although smaller than uppercase letters, still need additional space around them to improve their recognition. The small caps of many fonts are too small and appear lighter in weight than surrounding text. Adjust their point size up by as much as two points to achieve uniform weight and spacing, but not so much as to confuse them with the uppercase.

the final chap
the final cha
the final ch

A clue to optimal: the ligatures. Ligatures—specially drawn characters that optically correct for spacing difficulties in particular combinations of letters— provide a clue to the optimal spacing of a given font. Since ligatures are drawn with a fixed space between the characters (for example, an "fi"), a designer can assume that the font's creator determined this fixed space as optimal for the ligated pair based on his or her appraisal of what optimal spacing for the entire font should be. If the ligatures within running text appear more tightly—or more loosely—spaced than the nonfixed characters around them, it means either the font either needs to be respaced accordingly or the designer needs to replace the ligature with the two independent characters instead.

as Thoreau[2] said, the

arently CH_2O_3 will ca

Find a formula for supers and subs. The size and spacing of subscript and superscript characters, which are used to indicate footnotes or in chemical formulas, must be determined in relation to a given font size and the leading within paragraphs. Typically, the subscript or superscript character is just shy of the x-height in size, although, in an oldstyle face with a small x-height, this measure might prove too small. The subscript character should be set shifted below the baseline so that it rests on the descent line but does not extend upward to the mean line; a superscript character should hang from the capline and rest marginally below the mean line. In terms of letterspacing, the subscript or superscript character should be set to follow the same optical rhythm of the surrounding charac-ters. With an uppercase A, a following superscript character might benefit from being tucked a little closer to compensate for the A's inward diagonal thrust and, therefore, intrusive counterspace.

"Hey!"   Dad's

"Hey!"   Dad's

Hey! Yeah, you! Use the right marks! There is no quicker giveaway that the designer of a text is a total amateur than the use of prime marks (or "hatch marks" as they're sometimes called) in place of the punctuation that's supposed to be there. Prime marks are used to indicate foot and inch measures. The most egregious error—and, oddly, the most ubiquitous—is the substitution of a prime mark for an apostrophe. Just don't do it. Second in line: substituting prime marks for quotation marks. There are two versions of quotation marks: an open quote and a closed quote. One is used to indicate the beginning of a quotation (the ones called "66" because of their shape), and the other is used to end a quotation (the ones called "99"). Please use accordingly.

in-depth look

Hyphen Combines words or breaks them between lines

100–200 pages
6:00–9:00pm

En-Dash Separates ranges of figures or durations in time

beware—it is the

Em-Dash Separates evolutionary phrases within text

DUIS AUTEM VEL eumriure doloreme in henderit in vulputate velit esserati molestie consequat, vel illum dolore eu feugiat nulla facilisis at vero eros et accu sant et iusto odio dignissiquit blandit praesenta luptatum zzril delenit augue duis do.

Nalora ipsum dolor sitamet, consetetur sadipscing elitr, sed diam nonumy eirmo tempor invidunt ut labore et doloret magna aliquyam eratsediam wohp tua. At vero eos et accusam et justivi duo dolores et ea rebum. Stet clita kasd gubergren, no sea takimata san ctus est Lorem ipsum dolor sit ame. Lorem ipsum dolor sitamet, consec tetur sadipscing elitr diam nonumy

LOREM IPSUM DOLOR sit amet, consec tetur sadipscing elitr, sed diam non my eirmod tempor invidunt ut labore et dolore magna aliquyam eratse dia wolu ptua. At vero eos et accusam et justo duo dolores et ea rebum. Stelita kasd gubergren, no sea takimata san ctus est Lorem ipsum dolora sit amet. Lorem ipsum dolor sit amet, consec etur sadipscing elitr diam nonum sui eirmod tempor invidunt ea reabum

Subheading
Lorem ipsum dolor etur sadipscing elit my eirmod tempor et dolore magna iam wolu ptua. At v am et justo duo dol Stet clita kasd gube kim at sa sanctus est sit sit amet. Lorem amet, consetetur sa

---

ina@rockpub.com
ina@rockpub.com
earing and/or verti
earing and/or verti

Know your dashes. There are three horizontal punctuation lines—the hyphen, the en dash, and the em dash. Use the correct one for its intended function, and adjust the spaces around them so that they flow optically within text. A full word space on either side is too much, although there are times when this might be appropriate. The default lengths and baseline orientation of each mark might need to be altered to improve their relationship to surrounding text; the hyphen often sits low, and the em dash is sometimes too long.

Include with clarity. Text inclusions, such as drop caps, lead lines, and subheads, should exhibit some clear logic in their appearance. Drop caps should sit on a baseline three, four, five, or more lines from the top of the column. A lead line should be a consistent number of words in the first line or, alternatively, used to treat complete introductory phrases in a consistent way. A sub-head, when appearing at the top of one column, should be consistently aligned with the text in columns preceding or following—optically.

So it's not a letter. The appearance of analphabetic symbols, such as the @, #, $, and %, and some linear punctuation marks, such as the forward slash "/," are improved by slight spatial adjustments. The @ usually appears too high on the line; a slight shift below the baseline causes the character to center optically on the line of text. The # and % display a diagonal thrust akin to italic forms, and decreasing the space preceding them—but increasing the space following them—helps them participate in the overall rhythm of the letterspaces and word spaces. The "/" tends to benefit from additional space on either side, although a full word space is far too much; +20 to +30 tracking is comfortable.

---

6 VAN LANSCHOT INVESTMENT FUNDS NV

Bedragen in duizenden euro's

Van Lanschot Investment Funds nv (Totaal)	2005	2004	2003	2002	2001
Resultaten					
Som der bedrijfsopbrengsten	29.290	21.773	13.968	− 59.267	− 83.661
Som der bedrijfslasten	3.271	3.236	2.410	1.678	3.620
Resultaat	26.019	18.537	11.558	− 60.945	− 87.281
Balansgegevens, ultimo boekjaar					
Financiële beleggingen	286.874	304.760	305.238	85.483	16.525
Vorderingen en overige activa	6.150	9.279	6.575	2.879	11.670
Eigen vermogen	292.846	313.878	311.655	88.235	179.075
Kortlopende schulden	178	161	158	127	120
Per aandeel van € 1,– nominaal, ultimo boekjaar					
Beurskoers (x € 1)	n.v.t.	n.v.t.	n.v.t.	n.v.t.	n.v.t.
Intrinsieke waarde (inclusief dividend) (x € 1)	n.v.t.	n.v.t.	n.v.t.	n.v.t.	n.v.t.
Dividend over boekjaar (x € 1)	n.v.t.	n.v.t.	n.v.t.	n.v.t.	n.v.t.
Aantal uitstaande gewone aandelen	7.878.446	9.421.697	10.274.914	6.642.644	7.924.894

De in de jaargegevens opgenomen resultaten zijn inclusief waardeveranderingen van beleggingen en exclusief de (variabele) kosten van aan/afgifte van aandelen conform de in het boekjaar zorg gewijzigde grondslagen voor resultaatbepaling. Voor wat betreft de (variabele) kosten van aan/afgifte van aandelen zijn de kerncijfers voor 2001 niet herrekend.

Structuur

Algemene informatie

Van Lanschot Investment Funds nv is een beleggings-maatschappij met veranderlijk kapitaal. De vennootschap is opgezet volgens een zogenaamde paraplu-structuur. Dit betekent dat het gewone aandelenkapitaal is verdeeld in verschillende series van gewone aandelen, Fondsen genaamd, waarin het vermogen van de beleggings-maatschappij is belichaamd. De Fondsen als zodanig hebben geen rechtskarakter; zij vallen onder één en dezelfde rechtspersoon: Van Lanschot Investment Funds nv. Het geplaatste kapitaal van iedere serie vormt een Fonds, met een eigen beleggingsbeleid, risicoprofiel en koersvorming. Ook de administratie van elk Fonds is geschieden door het gebruik van separate rekeningen. Het op een afzonderlijke serie (Fonds) gestort kapitaal wordt afzonderlijk belegd. Zowel de kosten als de opbrengsten worden per Fonds afzonderlijk verantwoord. Waardestijgingen en waardedalingen in de portefeuille van een Fonds komen uitsluitend ten goede aan of ten laste van de houders van de desbetreffende serie. Hoewel sprake is van (administratief) afgescheiden vermogens blijven de Fondsen in juridische zin deel uitmaken van Van Lanschot Investment Funds nv.

Binnen Van Lanschot Investment Funds nv bestaan per 31 december 2005 vier van dergelijke Fondsen, te weten:

Fonds A	Van Lanschot Dutch Equity Fund;
Fonds C	Van Lanschot Far East Equity Fund;
Fonds D	Van Lanschot ICT Fund;
Fonds E	Van Lanschot Euro Credit Fund.

De verschillende Fondsen hebben, zoals gezegd, alle ook hun eigen aspecten van het beleggingsbeleid, welke onder 'Kenschetsen afzonderlijke Fondsen' nader worden toegelicht.

Verhandelbaarheid

De afzonderlijke Fondsen zijn aan de effectenbeurs van Euronext Amsterdam nv genoteerde beleggings-instellingen met een (semi) open-end structuur. De beurs-koers volgt de intrinsieke waarde van de aandelen binnen nauwe grenzen. Behoudens wettelijke bepalingen en uitzonderlijke situaties is de directie met inachtneming van het navolgende verplicht aandelen af te geven en in te kopen. Deze afgifte en inkoop geschieden uitsluitend via

E. van Lanschot Bankiers nv, waarmee een contractuele verbintenis is aangegaan als liquiditeitsverschaffer in de aandelen van de afzonderlijke Fondsen. Met deze verbintenis wordt, voor zover mogelijk binnen het handelssysteem van Euronext Amsterdam, bewerkstelligd dat intervenie in de markt door inkoop of uitgifte zodanig plaatsvindt dat de prijs inclusief kosten van de aandelen op de effectenbeurs van Euronext Amsterdam zich in principe steeds beweegt tussen intrinsieke waarde plus of min een maximaal bepaalde bandbreedte. Onderstaand wordt een actueel overzicht van de gehanteerde spreads ten opzichte van de intrinsieke waarde bij aan- en verkoop van aandelen voor de diverse Fondsen weergegeven.

	Aankoop	Verkoop	Maximale spread
Fonds A	+0,50%	−0,50%	0,70%
Fonds C	+0,75%	−0,50%	1,25%
Fonds D	+0,50%	−0,50%	1,00%
Fonds E	+0,50%	−0,50%	0,90%

In het algemeen zal een deel van de gehanteerde op- en afslagen ten goede komen aan de liquiditeitsverschaffer en een deel aan het Fonds (met uitzondering van Fonds E, Van Lanschot Euro Credit Fund, 0,1%) ter dekking van transactiekosten bij de belegging van verkregen middelen dan wel bij de verkoop van bestaande beleggingen. Onder omstandigheden kan besloten worden de inkoop van aandelen op te schorten.

Risicoprofiel

Aan een belegging in een van de Fondsen zijn risico's verbonden, welke in het algemeen gepaard gaan met het beleggen in aandelen en/of obligaties. De koersvorming van aandelen wordt beïnvloed door de resultaten van de individuele ondernemingen waarin belegd wordt, de verwachtingen hieromtrent en het beursklimaat in het algemeen. Het beleggen op basis van een thema brengt specifieke risico's met zich mee. Voor obligaties is de waarde-ontwikkeling in de eerste plaats afhankelijk van de ontwikkeling van de kapitaalmarktrente. In de tweede plaats is aan een belegging in obligaties debiteurenrisico verbonden. Verder bestaat er, indien van toepassing, het risico van valutaschommelingen. Voor een uitgebreide risicoparagraaf en het door de directie van de vennoot-

---

The text and tabular data in this spread from a financial report have been carefully and clearly styled to impart a sense of credibility and attention to detail, appropriate to the sober, accurate nature of the material. Clear hanging indents, comfortable spacing for figures, and easily distinguished alignments all contribute to the report's exquisite craftsmanship.
UNA [AMSTERDAM] DESIGNERS
NETHERLANDS

Type Is Visual, Too Design students and novices often make the mistake of ignoring the abstract visual nature of type and, as a result, use type in a heavy-handed way that doesn't correspond with image material—in effect, separating the two things completely. Type is visual; in space, it acts the same way that dots, lines, planes, and fields of texture do in any composition… Because it is, in its essence, dots, lines, planes, and fields of texture. Type doesn't stop being abstract form material simply because it says something. Recognizing this truth about type, understanding it and feeling it intuitively, is challenging. It's very difficult to divorce one's appreciation of its formal aspect from its verbal aspect: One is constantly struggling to stop reading a text to focus on what it looks like. But that is exactly what a designer must do to move beyond the merely mechanical concern of creating a functional reading

> The new time sense of typographic man is cinematic, sequential, pictorial.
>
> **Marshal McLuhan**
> *The Medium is the Massage*
> Penguin Books, 1967

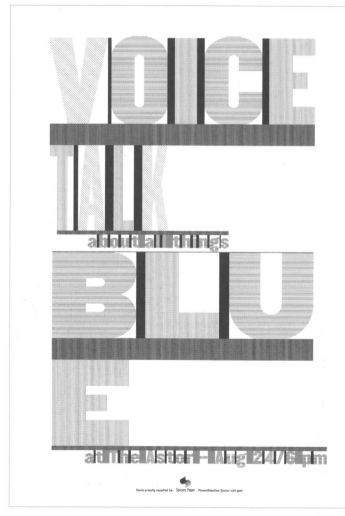

Although all of the typographic elements on this poster are printed in the same ink color, changes in size, weight, density, and spacing create what is considered a very "colorful" example of typographic composition.
VOICE AUSTRALIA

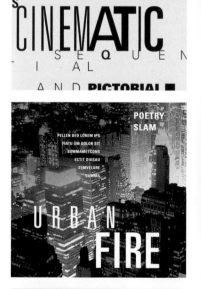

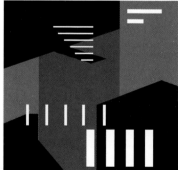

experience toward an optical experience of the text that gives it added meaning. Typography isn't simply the fact of the text; if it were, typographic design would be as simple as printing out a word-processed document in Times Roman, with the text all at one size, spread from margin to margin. This is what is called "writing." To become typography, the neutral fact of the text must be transformed into an expression of what it means, as well as crafted into a beautiful form. There's a saying among architects (the analogy of typography to architecture is telling) that designers would do well to reflect upon: "All architecture is building; but not all building is architecture." Legibility and functional reading are givens in typography, as doors, windows, adequate spaces, and a structure that won't fall down are in architecture. Approaching the text components of a project as images, in consideration of their shapes, proportions, values, contrasts, and movement—just as one would with pictorial image material—ensures that the type becomes not only yet another vehicle for conceptual narrative, but also that it integrates with, and fully unifies with, such other material: type and image become equal players.

At left, the same text information is treated differently in each composition—first, in a static and relatively neutral way, without much color; and second, with great variation in letterspacing, line spacing, width, size, and weight. Note how the negative spaces created by the type participate in the composition—some engaged as active players in the type treatments themselves, and others creating a proportional counterpoint to the type's rhythm and texture.

The visual quality of type is recognizable when it's further abstracted into its base components: dots, lines, planes, and masses. The freedom that simplicity implies—the liberty to move type around as freely as one might move the lines of a drawing around—becomes even more dramatic in the examples in which type is related to image: see how each pictorial element and each type element plays off the other, responding to their individual compositional qualities. The type isn't on top of the layout or next to the picture. The picture and the type take on the same value.

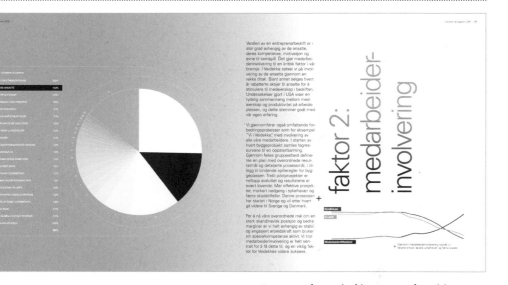

Every type element in this page spread participates in visually resolving the composition and activating space. The size of the dotlike chart weights it in relation to the texture of the column and the vertical motion of the large, rotated headline; the rhythm of positive and negative from left to right uses repetitions of specific intervals; and the type elements have a decisive up-and-down motion relative to each other.
COBRA NORWAY

The abstract formal nature of letterforms is easier to appreciate when they are integrated with pictorial matter as individual characters, rather than grouped together as words. In this poster (in which, surprisingly, actual words are spelled out), each character's particular shaping, stroke weights, proportions, and details respond to these aspects in other forms around it, as well as to those of other characters.
BARNBROOK UNITED KINGDOM

Typographic Color In addition to how type is placed within a format, its rhythmic, spatial, and textural qualities are important considerations. The term for these qualities is "typographic color." Typographic color is similar to chromatic color—like red, blue, or orange—but deals only with changes in lightness and darkness or value. Moreover, it is different from the qualities of chromatic color in that it describes changes in rhythm and texture. Changing the typographic color of typographic components separates them from the surface and introduces the illusion of spatial depth and a sense of changing rhythm. A larger chunk of type, for example, appears closer than a smaller one, while a lighter element appears to recede into the distance. A texture appears to flatten out because perception of its shape and uniform value determine its spatial depth more so than its components.

A line appears to come forward regardless of its weight, although a heavier line comes farther forward than a narrow line. Because the continuous value of text has the potential to be overwhelming—creating a kind of gray wall that can be daunting to look at (never mind dull and lifeless)—and because each specific thought, or informational component, within a text will benefit from a visual change, typographic color, composition, and verbal clarity are inseparable.

This web page is typographically very colorful, even though it uses only black and tints of gray. The callout of the word "One," by setting it in solid black, reinforces the brand image and idea of singularity. The deeper density of the second paragraph makes the call to action more pronounced; secondary information is set smaller and in lighter tints of gray to help clarify the hierarchy.
RESEARCH STUDIOS UNITED KINGDOM

The designers of this foldout brochure have focused on textural density, the proportions of columns and negative spaces, and contrasts between dot-like and linear formations (achieved through spacing changes). The linearity and textural qualities of the text are a stark contrast to the giant image dots. LSD SPAIN

Jakarta
2 0 0 7
Indonesia
POST **75**

Jakarta
2 0 0 7
Indonesia
POST **75**

Jakarta
2 0 0 7
Indonesia
POST **75**

Nam liber tempor cum soluta no
bisar eleifend option congue nih
m perdieti domine id quod maz
merti placerat facer possimsum
Loremipsum dolorsit amet con
ectetuer adipiscing elit sed dian
nonum nibu reuismodi tincidun
summa nunci et sem per dierae
bisar eleifend option congue nih
m perdieti domine id quod maz
merti placerat facer possimsum
Loremipsum dolorsit amet cons
ectetuer adipiscing elit sed dian

Nam liber tempor cum soluta no
bisar eleifend option congue nih
m perdieti domine id quod maz
merti placerat facer possimsum
Loremipsum dolorsit amet cons
ectetuer adipiscing elit sed dian
bisar eleifend option congue nih
m perdieti domine id quod maz
merti placerat facer possimsum
Loremipsum dolorsit amet cons

Nam liber tempor cum soluta no
bisar eleifend option congue nih
m perdieti domine id quod maz
bisar eleifend option congue nih
m perdieti domine id quod maz
merti placerat facer possimsum
Loremipsum dolorsit amet cons

COMPRESSION

COMPRESSION

C O M
PRES S
I O N

Lorem ipsum dolor sit amet, conetetur adipscing elit sed diam nonumy eirmod tempor invidunt ut labore et dolore magna aliquyam erat, sediam volup tua. At vero eos et accusam et justo duo dolores et. Stet clita kasd gubergren, no sea takimata sanctus est Lorem ipsum dolor sit amet.

Lorem ipsum dolor sit amet, consetetur sadipscing elitr, sed diam nonum eirmod tempor invidunt ut labore et dolore mag na aliquyam erat, sediam volup tua. At vero eos et accusam et justo duo dolores et ea rebum. Stet clita kasd gubergren, no sea takim ata sanctus est Lorem ipsum dolor sit amet. Diam nonum eirmod tem por invidunt ut labore et dolore magna aliquyam erat, sediam volup.

Lorem ipusum dolor
sit amet, consetetur
sadipscing elitar, sed
diam nonum eirmo
d tempor invidunt ut
labore et dolore mag
na aliquyam erat, se
diam volup tua. Vero
eos et accusam et jus
to duo dolores et ea
rebum. Stet clita kasd
gubergren, no sea ta
im ata sanctus. Lorem
ipsum dolor sit amet.

COMPRESSION

COMPRESSION
COMPRESSION

He ran **quickly,**
fast as he could —
but the distance
seemed to
stretch out
and he **could** not escape!

[TOP] Changes in size create differences in perceived density and weight change, despite all the elements being regular weight.

[MIDDLE] This strategy is enhanced by changing the weights of selected type elements as well.

[BOTTOM] The application of bold weight has been swapped among the various components for a different spatial effect.

[TOP] This example shows tight leading; the interline spaces appear the same as word spaces. The type is more texture than line; it is optically the darkest of the examples.

[MIDDLE] The texture and linearity of normal leading are evenly balanced, appearing lighter than the previous example.

[BOTTOM] When leading is loose, linearity dominates; the text has the lightest value.

[TOP] Extremely tight spacing, and the resulting overlap of strokes, creates pronounced dark spots; the individuality of the letters is compromised in favor of overall linearity and mass.

[MIDDLE] In normal spacing, the linearity of the word dominates the individuality of the letters, but the alternation of stroke and counter is more regular.

[BOTTOM] Loose letterspacing causes the dotlike individuality of the letters to dominate.

[TOP] Horizontal emphasis, or movement, dominates the vertical in a wide paragraph.

[MIDDLE] Although physically wider than deep, the optimal paragraph's width-to-depth ratio results in a comfortable stasis.

[BOTTOM] In a deep, extremely narrow paragraph, the vertical emphasis dominates the horizontal; the paragraph takes on an especially linear quality.

[TOP] The word, set in a condensed face, contracts inward.

[MIDDLE] The same word, set in an extended face of the same weight, expands outward—and more so when set in a bold extended face.

[BOTTOM] Dramatic compression and expansion in visual density (and enhanced communication) are achieved by combining varying widths and weights of text within the same line.

THE PAPER OF RECORD   MONDAY

6 | 20

NOW

that the Democrats have given up on this absolutely vital part of American life, where can we turn to stop this selfish and evil descent back to the dark ages of the twenties and thirties? – Bill Messina, NY

I FEEL THAT I AM LIVING IN AN EVER-DARKENING NIGHTMARE.

WE ARE NOT LIVING IN NORTH KOREA OR CHINA.

I HAVE GROWN FROM A GAY TEENAGER INTO A GAY MAN

CLARENCE WAS SPRINGSTEEN, AND SPRINGSTEEN WAS CLARENCE.

IT IS ALSO WORTH NOTING THAT RATIONAL CHOICE IS A MYTH

ALL THE LITTLE PRETTIES RAISE THEIR HANDS

A change of color automatically alters not only the spatial and textural quality of the type, but its meaning. As much as one must, at times, disconnect from the verbal content of text to concentrate on its visual qualities, one must always keep this fundamental inseparability of form and meaning top of mind—it has profound implications on establishing informational hierarchy (see page 170 in *Type as Information*).

In the design of this newspaper masthead, exceptionally stark—even jarring—contrasts of weight among the text elements carves the format space into areas of tremendous mass and acutely sharp, delicate detail.
TRIBORO DESIGN UNITED STATES

The Texture of Language More than simply a tool for clarifying hierarchy, the variation of typographic texture—changes in boldness, size, linearity, texture, and rhythm—is an outgrowth of the way we speak or write . . . and the way we speak or write is a source for typographic color. Slowly spoken phrases contrast with sharp, abrupt outbursts. Long, contemplative soliloquies provide rest against erratic, fractured thoughts. These qualities of spoken and

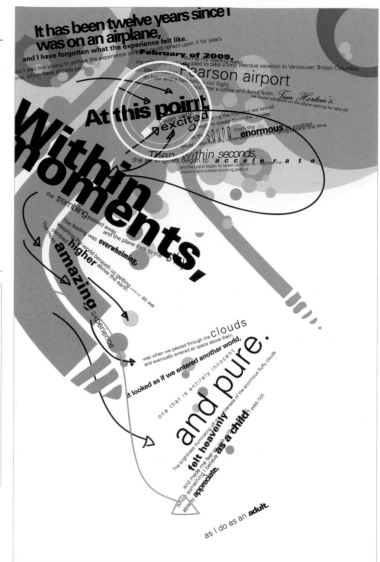

Sound and rhythm influence the designer's choice of each text element's size, weight, style, spacing, and positive or negative presentation in a still from a motion sequence that educates viewers about the musical genre "dubstep." SEOUNGJUN LEE/SCHOOL **OF VISUAL ARTS** UNITED STATES

The performative quality of a text—its assumed volume and cadence changes—is a great source for typographic style. In this example, weight and size change reflect changes in volume and emphasis in the text.
MAREK OKON CANADA

The sound and the meaning of words are often connected; in these examples, sound and meaning are linked through visual expression.
CHRISTINE CHUO [FAR LEFT]
MICHAEL SUI [MIDDLE]
TAMMY CHANG [NEAR LEFT]
CARNEGIE MELLON UNIVERSITY,
UNITED STATES

written language can be made visual, not just to provide intriguing eye candy, but to help an audience feel the author and the emotional import of his or her words. Changing sizes, weight, or posture within lines of running text, even within individual words, can make a dramatic, evocative statement without sacrificing clarity. It might even improve readability—the quality of and the degree to which the type engages its readers and leads them

through the experience of the content. Bolding a subhead that begins a paragraph accomplishes this—making it seem louder and, therefore, a point of focus—but in an almost totally neutral, objective way. It's about giving the reader the chance to find something of interest or heightened importance.

But strategically approaching typographic material in a sensory way, giving it the visual quality of its sounds and cadence, is a powerful method designers can employ in creating a more vivid verbal experience.

Our time is a time for crossing barriers, for erasing old categories— for probing around.

When two seemingly disparate elements are imaginatively poised, put in apposition in new and unique ways...

... startling discoveries often result.

Our time is a time for *crossing* **barriers...** for e r a s i n g old categories— **for probing around.**

When two seemingly disparate elements are imaginatively poised, **put in apposition** in new and unique ways... *startling discoveries* often result.

Our time is **a time** for **crossing** barriers, for *erasing* old categories— for **probing** around.

When two seemingly **disparate** elements are imaginatively poised, put in **apposition** in new and unique ways, startling **discoveries** often result.

The text in these examples is powerfully altered by changing the typographic color of its internal parts. In the first version, a strategy of overall size change affects the sense of the text's loudness, creating a crescendo.

In the second version, calling out specific parts through changes in weight, posture, width, and spacing produces a rhythmic journey—slowing down, speeding up—for the reader. In the third version, color changes are

applied to distinguish linguistic and conceptual relationships among different parts of the text; the result is rhythmically dynamic and supports the interrelationships of the author's ideas. This approach provides the added

bonus of giving the reader a snapshot of the content before fully engaging the text.

The changing alignment of the paragraphs, along with small text details and complex negative spaces, creates a geometric and rhythmic color in this page from a book spread. EARSAY UNITED STATES

Alignments, Masses, and Voids Dividing space creates structure, which unifies disparate elements in a composition. Several lines of type together create a different kind of structural relationship to the format than a single line of type; the grouping relates to the single line but visually contrasts with it. This mass of texture further defines the space around it into channels that correspond to its height and depth and between itself and the format in all directions. Separating elements within a group maintains a sense of the mass; it also introduces a greater complexity of structure by further subdividing the space. Visual structure must evolve out of the verbal structure of language. The verbal sense helps define what material within it might be mass or line. A continuous sequence of thoughts likely will be clarified if they cluster together; a distinct thought might benefit from being separated from

The tension between positive and negative space—and the invisible linear connections between elements—is what drives typography. Here, the proportions of the negative spaces are created by the positive type elements, alternately contrasting and restating them. Alignments between the edges of positive forms establish potentially meaningful relationships and help activate spaces across the composition.

This poster demonstrates the visual power a designer commands with regard to creating rigorous compositional structure and activating space—using only four small elements. While the three heavy elements optically splice the format into an upper and lower area and create a triangular axis, it is the very light column of text that most emphatically establishes a set of proportionally related rectangles of negative space.
STUDIO ASTRID STAVRO SPAIN

Visual structure, relative to the format, is created when the elements are positioned decisively to subdivide it and, thereby, create differentiated shapes of negative space. Still, the type elements exhibit no structural difference to help distinguish them. Massing some elements and separating others creates focus and movement. The alignment of particular elements establishes a similarity of meaning among them; separating an element from the primary alignment creates distinction or emphasis.

Design Elements
Understanding the rules and knowing when to break them
Timothy Samara
Form; Color ; Type
Image; Layout
Rockport Publishers
Gloucester, MA

Design Elements

Understanding the rules and knowing when to break them

Form
Color
Type
Image
Layout

Timothy Samara

Rockport Publishers
Gloucester, MA

the others. Both kinds of type elements are positive forms: the figures within the composition. They are in contrast with each other, as well as to the spaces, or voids, around them. The relationship of the typographic mass to the voids within the format is essential to defining typographic space in composition, just as it is in defining the rhythm of letter spacing and the space within a paragraph. Regular intervals between masses and voids—unlike in letter spacing, word spacing, and leading—are undesirable because regularity implies sameness, and not all the type elements are the same: they mean different things. Smaller spaces between masses of text help improve the understanding that they are related, while greater spaces between or within typographic masses indicate that the masses are different in meaning. On a visual level, the designer creates contrast and rhythm within the composition by changing the proportional relationships between solids and voids. As type elements divide space in proximity, their points of alignment become important. Aligning elements augments the sense of a relationship between them. Further, alignments between elements help create directional movement through the elements in the format.

The edges of letter strokes in the gigantic title are used as alignment points for text and for intrusions of geometric negative space into the column; this spatial area is activated by the large red callout. **FROST DESIGN** AUSTRALIA

The interaction of positive and negative drives the dynamic composition of type and image in this brochure spread. The type breaks the space into decisively different intervals; in addition, the shifting negative spaces and the rotation of some type elements restate the structural qualities of the photograph. **RESEARCH STUDIOS** UNITED KINGDOM

Establishing Hierarchy Information is systematic. Most often, it appears as a collection of parts, each having a different function: for example, callouts, captions, and sidebars in magazine articles; or the primary content, supporting content, and menus on a webpage. These various parts often repeat, appear within the same space, and support each other. One of the designer's most important tasks is to give information an order that allows the viewer to navigate it. This order, called the "informational hierarchy," is based on the level of importance the designer assigns to each part of the text. "Importance" means "the part that should be read first, second, third . . ." and so on; it also refers to the "distinction of function" among the parts: running text (the body of a writing), as measured against other elements such as page folios, titles and subheads, captions, and similar items.

Creating informational hierarchy applies the formal aspects of purely visual hierarchy to the parts of language present in the format or field at hand and results from reading the text and asking some simple questions: What are the distinguishable parts of the information to be designed? Which part (or parts) should be the main focus of the reader's attention? How do the parts that are not the main focus relate to each other? How do these relate to images

A quick illustration of the simultaneity of visual hierarchy and verbal hierarchy: how the compositional strategies discussed in the first chapter (page 80) are directly relevant to typographic and pictorial elements. As is most often the case, dark value elements appear to advance and rise to the top of the hierarchy, while elements of lighter value recede. In the actual newspaper cover, however, note that the hierarchic position of some elements is indeterminate—the large red elements, especially the numeral 50, occupy different levels of visual importance relative to other elements in different locations. BACHGARDE DESIGN SWEDEN

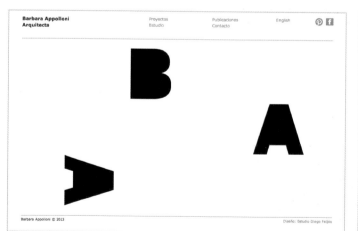

On the landing page of this website, large, bold letters visually assume a dominant position, but allow much smaller navigational text to become more relevant. On the subpage, however, the text content is given hierarchic dominance by assigning it the greatest width (and, so, increasing its mass). Organizing the text content below a set of thin lines further separates it from the navigation above, which—together with the large graphic initials—have diminsihed in relative importance. STUDIO DIEGO FEIJOO SPAIN

Table variant 1

isang yun (1917–1995)

	41' 58"	naui dang, naui minjokiyo! my land, my people! for soloists, chorus and orchestra (1987)	chorus and state symphony orchestra of the democratic peoples republic of korea conducted by byung-hwa kim
1	07' 42"	rjoksa (history)	cpo 999 047-2
2	14' 26"	hyon-shil I (presence I)	
3	06' 17"	hyon-shil II (presence II)	
4	13' 26"	mi-rae (future)	

myung-sil kim soprano	young-ok kim alto	sun-chai pak tenor	yong-yin han bass

Table variant 2

isang yun (1917–1995)

41' 58"	naui dang, naui minjokiyo! my land, my people! for soloists, chorus and orchestra (1987)

1	07' 42"	rjoksa (history)	myung-sil kim soprano
2	14' 26"	hyon-shil I (presence I)	young-ok kim alto
3	06' 17"	hyon-shil II (presence II)	sun-chai pak tenor
4	13' 26"	mi-rae (future)	yong-yin han bass

chorus and state symphony orchestra of the democratic peoples republic of korea conducted by byung-hwa kim

cpo 999 047-2

Table variant 3

isang yun (1917–1995)

naui dang, naui minjokiyo! my land, my people! for soloists, chorus and orchestra (1987)	41' 58"
1 rjoksa (history)	07' 42"
2 hyon-shil I (presence I)	14' 26"
3 hyon-shil II (presence II)	06' 17"
4 mi-rae (future)	13' 26"

chorus and state symphony orchestra of the democratic peoples republic of korea conducted by byung-hwa kim

myung-sil kim, soprano
young-ok kim, alto
sun-chai pak, tenor
yong-yin han, bass

cpo 999 047-2

Differentiating spaces between columns with similar proportions and between informational components within columns—as well as changing vertical positioning—keeps positive and negative areas proportionally unified but easily distinguishable from each other.
HELMUT SCHMID JAPAN

Purple

'He wrapped himself in quotations – as a beggar would enfold himself in the purple of Emperors.'
Rudyard Kipling

Did you know that

... purple is the bee's favourite colour? More specifically, the European buff-tailed bumblebee (*Bombus terrestris*) prefers violet flowers to blue ones. A study has shown that violet flowers in the vicinity of beehives were far more popular than the insect's second choice: blue blossoms. Bee colonies with access to purple flowers harvested more nectar. Past research has shown that animals often have favourite colours, smells and signals when it comes to choosing a mate, but little research has been done on how such sensory preferences affect searches for food.

... the popularity of purple in Roman times led to the near extinction of the murex family of shellfish? The natural dye of the murex was extracted to produce purple. The dye was very expensive, because it took over 8000 shellfish and a great deal of intensive labour to make a single gram of purple dye.

... the first mass-produced synthetic dye was mauve, a rather pale shade of purple? The dye was discovered, more or less by accident, in 1856 by William Henry Perkin, who called it 'mauveine'. His invention marked the beginning of the chemical and pharmaceutical industry.

... the official name of Beijing's famous 'Forbidden City' is 'The Purple Forbidden City', a reference to a secret purple area of heaven thought to be near the North Star?

... in Thailand purple is worn by a widow mourning her husband's death?

... Leonardo da Vinci believed the power of meditation increases ten times when you're bathed by purple light, such as daylight streaming through purple stained glass?

... if you're born 'in the purple' you are a member of a royal or other high-ranking family?

... early life on earth might have been purple? In 2007 a team of geneticists at the University of Maryland suggested that whereas plants now use chlorophyll to harness the sun's rays, primeval microbes may have used retinal (a form of vitamin A) to photosynthesize. Retinal is a simpler molecule and easier to produce in a low-oxygen environment, such as that which characterized early life on earth. Because retinal absorbs green light and reflects red and violet light, the microbes would have appeared to be purple.

... in 2003 a very odd species of purple frog was found in the Ghat hills of India? *Nasikabatrachus sahyadrensis* ('nose frog from Sahyadra') is a 7-cm-long, dark-purple blob with a pointy snout. It spends its time buried underground feasting on termites, surfacing for only two weeks a year to mate. The males make a loud chicken-like sound. The purple frog is unique: its closest relatives live in the Seychelles, but it split from them more than 130 million years ago.

... purple fruits and vegetables are rich in flavonoids, which are the most abundant and powerful of all the phytochemicals contained in the foods we eat? One of the many categories of flavonoids helps make blood vessels healthier. Purple foods include plums and aubergines, as well as certain types of cabbages and potatoes. Purple food has even rocketed into space. The 'Purple Orchid Three' is a sweet potato now being cultivated in Hainan Province, China, from seeds that were on the nation's Shenzhou VI rocket in 2005.

... February is associated with the colour purple? The birthstone for those born in February is amethyst, which is also a sacred stone for Tibetan Buddhists, who use it to make prayer beads.

... in the United States, the poker chip worth the most ($5000) is purple?

178

Stay cool
Blue has long possessed a calming effect on the mind. Light, medium and deep blues convey a sense of quietness, clarity and serenity. The soothing quality of blue makes it ideal for pyjamas — an aid to a good night's sleep.

Trust in me
Loyalty and trust are inseparable. Blue is the number-one choice for use in corporate branding. Research has shown that blue is the most popular colour in the world.

Spiritual calling
Blue expresses an air of introspection that is associated with spirituality. The ancient Egyptians chose lapis lazuli to represent the afterlife. Painters have often used blue to represent heaven, and in Christian works of art the Virgin Mary is frequently depicted wearing blue garments.

Stand by me
The tranquility and permanence of blue is translated into loyalty and faithfulness: a 'true blue' friend remains steadfast, evoking an image of dependability that may also imply conservativeness.

Serve and protect
Navy blue is often associated with authority, law and order: the uniforms of police and military forces worldwide are a good example, as are the many national flags that feature dark blue. Blue has been used as protection against witches, and Egyptian pharaohs wore blue to ward off evil.

Power hungry
In the Christian West, blue emerged in the 12th century. Initially, blue pigments were rare and affordable only to the wealthy, hence the association with aristocracy, royalty and the term 'blue blood'. Prestige ultimately gives rise to power and praise: the award for first prize is a 'blue ribbon'.

Away and beyond
Blue suggests a feeling of distance and is used to show perspective. Symbolically, it communicates a broad vista of the universe beyond these earthly bonds. Adventuring into the unknown is to go 'into the wild blue yonder'.

Speak easy
All shades of blue encourage easy communication, invite contact and promote interaction. Notes written on blue paper are recommended for remembering important information. In certain Eastern religions, blue represents the throat chakra, which enables the expression of thoughts and feelings.

Spick-and-span
The obvious relationship between blue and water also explains the connection between blue and cleanliness. Delving even deeper into this alliance with water, we find a reference to Earth – covered largely by oceans – as the 'Blue Planet'.

Feeling blue
To 'feel blue' is to feel sad. Blue – and especially the darker shades, which may be perceived as cold and melancholy – can convey gloom. In India and Iran, for example, blue is associated with mourning.

179

b l u e

Blue

'Blue colour is everlastingly appointed by the Deity to be a source of delight.'
John Ruskin

In this page spread, two items immediately demand attention because of their size and weight: the letters that spell "blue," and the horizontal callout at the top of the left-hand page. Notice that the callout at the bottom of the right-hand page isn't as dominant—this is because it is visually overpowered by "blue," and because it is also near the bottom of the format. The callout at upper left is located in the area where readers expect to begin reading, so once the viewer has focused on "blue," the next search is for that text which will lead the reader into the article.
MARIELLE VAN GENDEREN + ADRIAAN MELLEGERS NETHERLANDS

---

that accompany the text elements in the layout? Does the viewer need to see (and understand) a particular grouping of words before they begin to focus on the main part? The answers to these questions are often common sense. On a publication's cover, for example, the masthead or title is most important, so it makes sense that it should be the first type the viewer sees. In a table of financial information, the viewer needs to understand the context of figures being presented, so the headers, which describe the meaning of the figures, need to be located easily. Within a publication's pages, where running text may interact with captions, callouts, and other details, the running text needs to occupy a consistent area and be visually noted as different from these other elements. The effect of these decisions, as noted previously, becomes simultaneously verbal and visual.

All text looks equally important in raw form. If placed within a format as is, the words form a uniform field of texture. By manipulating the spaces around and between text, the designer's first option is to create levels of importance through spatial distinction. The designer might group the majority of elements together, for example, but separate a specific element—maybe a title—and give it more space. The uniformity that is usually desirable to keep the reader moving is thereby purposely broken, creating a fixation point that will be interpreted as deserving attention and, therefore, more important than the other elements. Enhancing such spatial separations by changing the typographic color of separated elements will further distinguish each from the other.

The masthead occupies the top of the hierarchy because of its size but, more importantly, its color. The large content listing below the photograph reads second in sequence, and weight change distinguishes page number from story listing within this group. COBRA NORWAY

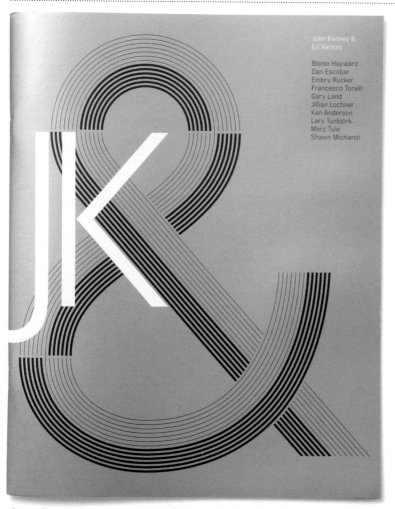

The eye distinguishes groups, and elements within groups, based on differences among them. In this brochure cover, the first distinction is the JK& combination, based on relative size; the second, in which the JK combination is differentiated from the ampersand, derives from value relationships; the JK is also flat and simple, compared to the texturally complex ampersand. TRIBORO DESIGN UNITED STATES

Despite the density of the darker blue text in this layout, the lighter green paragraph wins out in the hierarchy because of its positioning at the natural, upper-left entry point for reading.
CLEMENS THÉOBERT SCHEDLER AUSTRIA

Similar to the way that viewers rely on visual comparisons of form to help identify their meaning, so too do they make assumptions about the roles of informational components because of their appearance. More than simply establishing a level of importance, creating hierarchy also means clarifying the function of informational components through their formal relationships: whether they are grouped together or separated; whether they appear in a consistent location; and how they are treated with regard to typeface, size, spacing, and so on. Blocks of information that are treated similarly will be assumed to mean similar things or be closely related in function—captions in this book, for instance, are assumed to function differently (or carry a different kind of content) than the running text because of a difference in treatment. The captions are no less important than the running text, but both play important roles, which the viewer learns by seeing how they behave in the page layouts and associating this behavior with each of their roles. The designer, in effect, must visually categorize each kind of information for the viewer to identify and, most importantly, learn how to associate each identified kind of information with every other.

this text is less important
most important
this is not important
other text is more important
some text is important

Change in Size

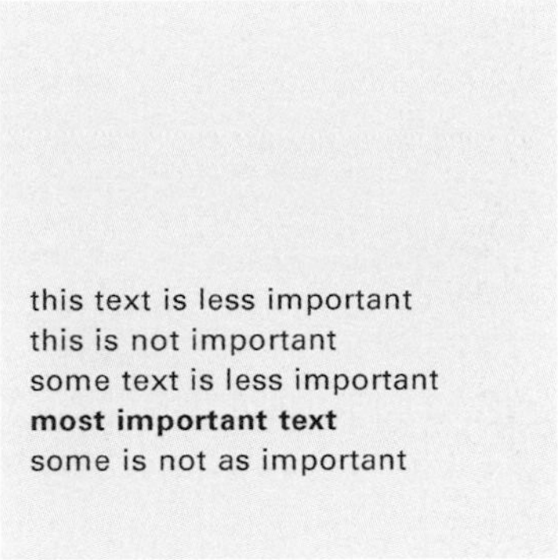

this text is less important
this is not important
some text is less important
most important text
some is not as important

Change in Weight

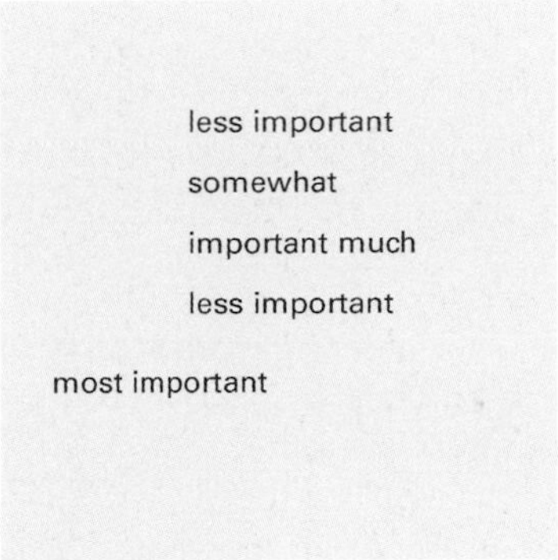

less important

somewhat

important much

less important

most important

Change in Alignment

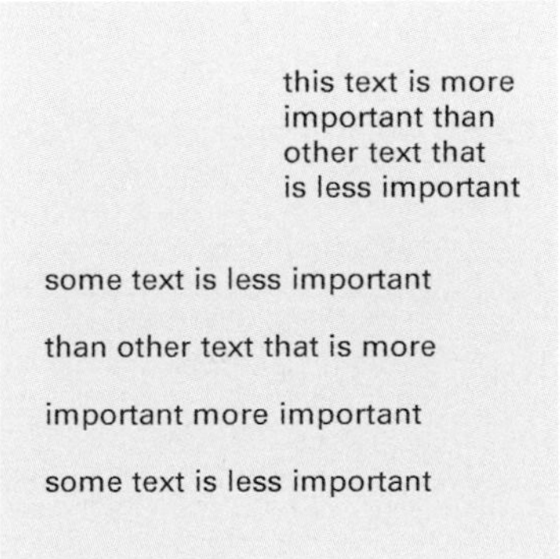

The designer has, at his or her disposal, a great variety of approaches for establishing the relative importance of typographic elements to each other. As can be seen here, even type that is all one color—and even the same weight or size—can be effectively differentiated using extremely simple means.

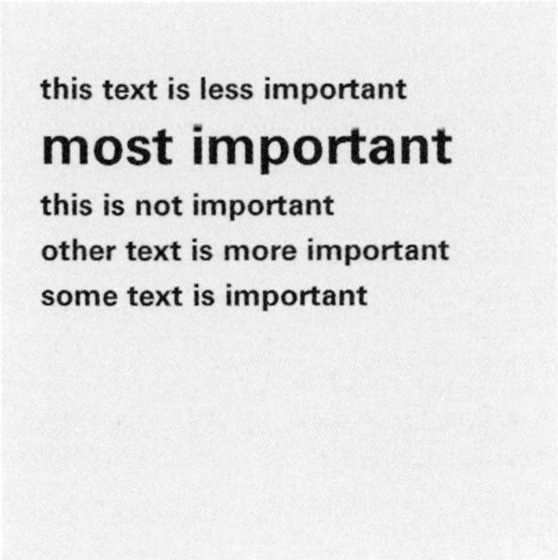

this text is more
important than
other text that
is less important

some text is less important

than other text that is more

important more important

some text is less important

Change in Rhythm

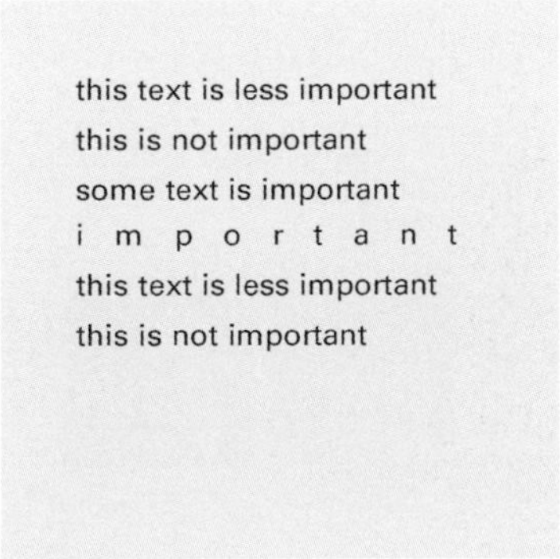

this text is less important

this is not important

some text is important

i m p o r t a n t

this text is less important

this is not important

Change in Spacing

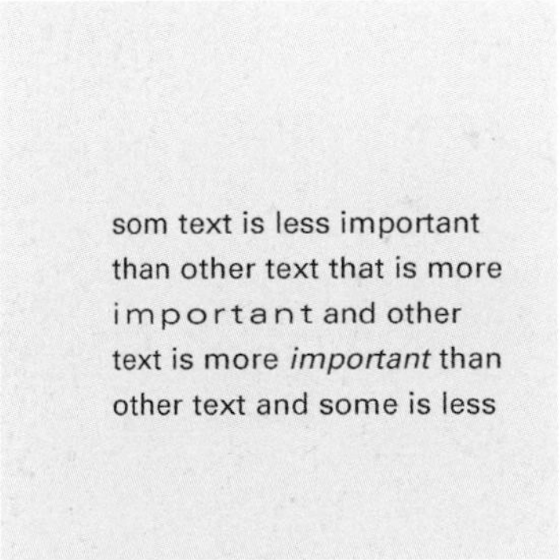

som text is less important
than other text that is more
i m p o r t a n t and other
text is more *important* than
other text and some is less

Change in Width or Posture

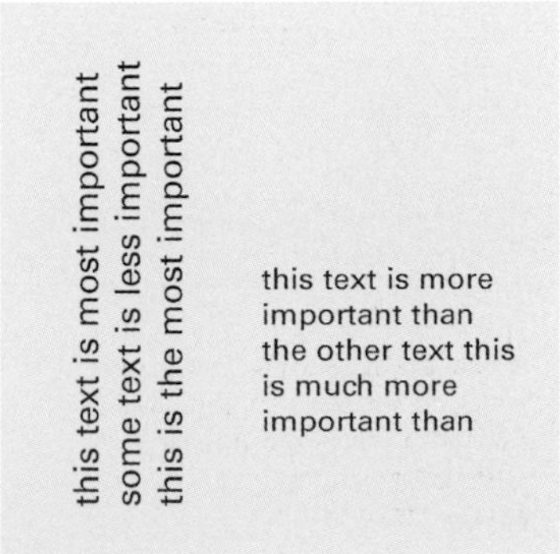

this text is most important
some text is less important
this is the most important

this text is more
important than
the other text this
is much more
important than

Change in Orientation

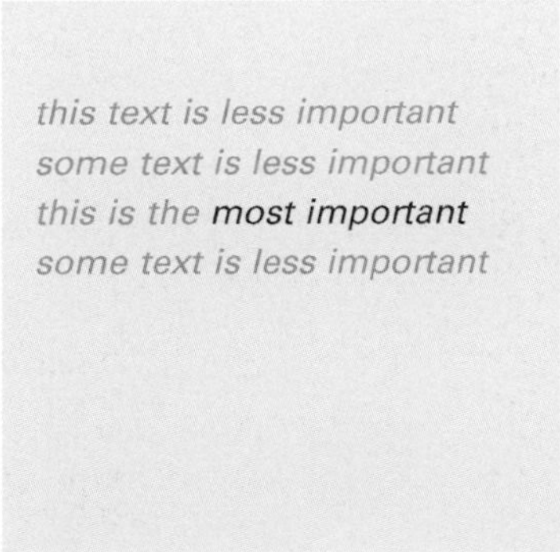

this text is less important
some text is less important
this is the **most important**
some text is less important

Change in Gray Value

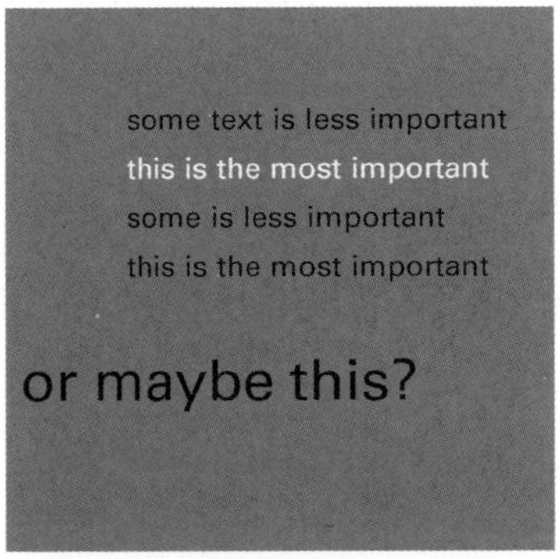

some text is less important
this is the most important
some is less important
this is the most important

or maybe this?

Change in Background Contrast

Distinction and Unity Just as viewers will assume that abstract shapes that share similar attributes are related to each other (and those that are formally different are unrelated), viewers will also make the same assumption with regard to text elements. Interrelationship among a hierarchy's visual qualities is important, but so too are clear contrasts important for hierarchic clarity. Too much difference among the hierarchic components, however, will create a visual disconnect: The danger of pushing stylistic differences between informational components is that, as a totality, the project will appear busy and lack a fundamental cohesion or "visual voice." This is one reason why designers are admonished to employ only two or three type styles in a project and, as often as possible, to combine styles that share substantially similar qualities. The reader need not be hit over the head with an optical baseball bat every time the content requires differentiation. Minute changes are easily recognized; the reader need only be shown an appreciable, yet decisive, difference among hierarchic components to clue them in. Limiting the varieties of stylistic difference to just what is needed to signal a change in information allows the reader to understand such changes while maintaining visual unity and more clearly creating interrelationships within the content.

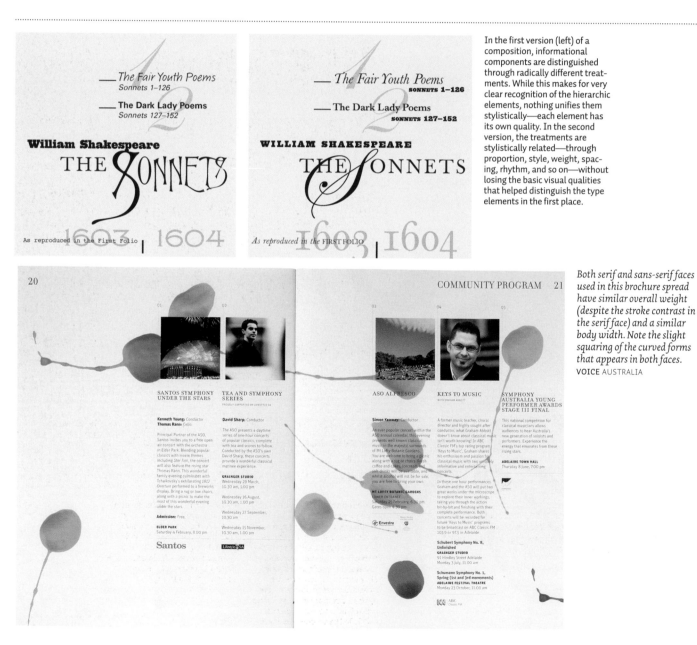

In the first version (left) of a composition, informational components are distinguished through radically different treatments. While this makes for very clear recognition of the hierarchic elements, nothing unifies them stylistically—each element has its own quality. In the second version, the treatments are stylistically related—through proportion, style, weight, spacing, rhythm, and so on—without losing the basic visual qualities that helped distinguish the type elements in the first place.

Both serif and sans-serif faces used in this brochure spread have similar overall weight (despite the stroke contrast in the serif face) and a similar body width. Note the slight squaring of the curved forms that appears in both faces. VOICE AUSTRALIA

Typographic Color: Scales of Contrast

To meet these dual goals (distinguishing and unifying), consider hierarchic levels in terms of how separate in emphasis they need be, along with what they share in informational structure—and apply typographic color to each to correspond with the degree of difference or similarity. It's sort of like a song: The melody, harmonies, supporting instrumentation, and percussion are each a level in a hierarchy. Each level can be separated because of some degree of sonic difference; the separation between melody and harmony is relatively little, while the separation between those and the instruments is pretty big. Even so, the instrumentation restates components of the melody; and, one could say that the "proportion" of difference between melody and harmony (in pitch and volume) is echoed by a similar kind, but much greater, pitch and volume difference that separates the instruments. Typographic experience can be made to operate this same way by establishing a "scale" of difference in color between hierarchic levels—in which the degree of difference between each level's color is "proportionally" related to the others; and in which sublevel treatments work to distinguish material within them, while echoing or varying treatments that appear in different levels. How much difference in presence between levels may be required—

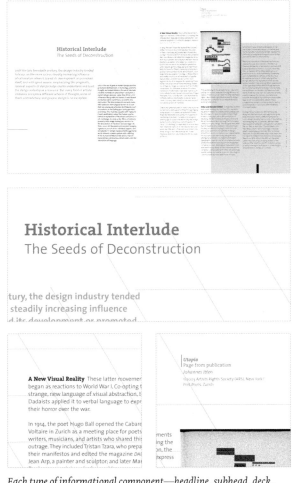

Each type of informational component—headline, subhead, deck, text, caption, and subcaption—is given its own unique style, but all the styles are selected from related families: a sans serif and a serif that have been designed to work with each other.

TIMOTHY SAMARA UNITED STATES

Ipsume
Headline
46 points

Duis autem velu nunc et semper
Deck or callout
23 points

Proin condimentum sit amet metus in dimenti donec erat lectus, suscip arcun ec, fermentum lobortis. Pellentesque habitant morbi tristi senectus et netus.
Running text
11.5 points

Ipsum dui
Headline
35.25 points

Duis autem velure nunc et semper ix
Deck or callout
20 points

Proin condimentum sit amet metus in dimenti donec erat lectus, suscip arcun ec, fermentum lobortis. Pellentesque habitant morbi tristi senectus et netus.
Running text
11.5 points

The notion of scaling the use of typographic color is illustrated here by two sets of text specimens, each representing three levels in a hypothetical hierarchy. In the first specimen, top, size and weight relationships among elements in the top level are halved at a secondary level, and again at a tertiary level; the scale ratio of difference in presence is 2:1. In the second specimen (bottom), the ratios of difference between levels is 3:2, offering less of a distinction but greater continuity. Scales of differentiation in typographic color may be defined mathematically but, more often than not, they are established intuitively.

and, how extreme the difference in presence between top-most and bottom-most levels must be—derives from the nature of the project. A poster, for example, is a format that requires three scales of information: It must deliver a substantial amount of information from a distance, at a quick glance, but it then invites the viewer to come closer, to glean information at an intermediate level; once there, the viewer may also be presented with further

material at an intimate scale. The jumps in presence between each scale may be extreme, supported by the physical size of the poster format: one scale may be very large and another extremely small. A book or web page, on the other hand, requires many more scales, and these scales may be separated in their presence by only smaller degrees. In each case, the designer must determine what kinds of typographic color and stylistic changes apply to each

scale level, as well as which scales are closer to each other in relative presence. With regard to the poster, for instance, the designer may establish that the top- and intermediate-level scales must be less different as compared to the intimate-level scale. "By how much?" is the next question: "Proportionally, are they twice as different (together) in presence as compared to the intimate scale?" Quantifying this difference may suddenly take on a mathematical

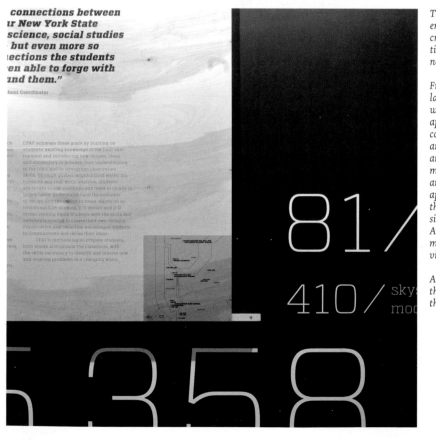

The design of this exhibition employs typographic color to create varied scales of interaction and color contrast that are nonetheless unified.

From a distance, looking at large-scale information on a wall display, viewers first appreciate its specific scale of color contrasts in size, weight, and spacing between primary and secondary levels of information; the larger type sizes and the bolder weights used appear so much larger or bolder than accompanying medium sizes and lighter weights. At this distance, sublevels of more detailed information are virtually invisible.

As viewers approach the wall, the upper-level elements and their color so extreme that

they advance past the viewer's frame of reference, seeming to disappear as a sublevel of information presented on wood plaques comes into focus. At this point, the viewer comes to appreciate the same, or similar, degrees of typographic color contrast among informational levels that they have encountered in the large, upper level. This transition creates both a stylistic and intellectual cohesion between the levels so that they flow into each other.
POULIN+MORRIS UNITED STATES

aspect in an attempt at clarification: Maybe the two larger scales, in totality, are presented in type that is twice the point size, or twice the boldness, of that used for presenting the material at the intimate level. Within the intimate level, then, perhaps there is a similar 2:1 ratio scale that governs the size and weight distinctions used to organize its internal components.

The discussion here has focused on size, primarily, but this thinking can apply to stylistic variation, as well. Along with size difference, for example, perhaps the most emphatic level makes use of four typefaces, the intermediate level uses two of the four, and the intimate level, only one. Or, conversely, one face is used for the top level (being the simplest information), two for the intermediate level, and four (incorporating those already used) at the intimate level, where the information's greater complexity requires greater differentiation. By extension, this scale logic implicates visual aggressiveness or passivity as aspects of scale, as well as the repetition, or restating, or sharing of formal or stylistic aspects among the scales so that, although clearly separated, they yet show relationships that help harmonize typographic color and style throughout all the project's parts.

The number, and proportional ratios of presence among, scales of typographic color are somewhat tied to the nature of a given project. A poster embodies three scales of hierarchic interaction—one scale seen from a distance, a second negotiated at a middle range, and an intimate scale. The difference from one scale level to the next is typically extreme, as shown in the schematic at left.

Lorem
DOLOR SIT AMETSIS

Consectituer
Adipscing elit

Duis Autem
Nonum eratues fiat ad nunc et semper coelis *in glorios* ex eternam

MAGNIFICATOR
Nonum eratues fiat adi nunc et semper coelis **duis autem** velure sunt, ex odio pelleteat

A book, on the other hand, presents multiple scales whose ratios of difference tend to be more varied but also more closely constrained: In a poster, size and weight contrast are the governing aspects of typographic color that define the scale levels and the degree of difference among them. In a book spread, where such extreme variation in size is impossible, contrasts in weight, spacing, value, and style do the work of identifying each scale level.

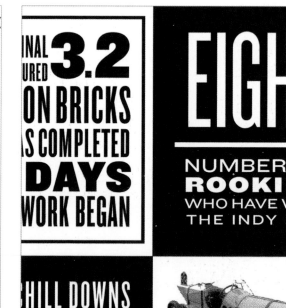

This informational poster about the Indianapolis 500 motor race presents a wealth of statistics and historical facts about the event. Because the information is so dense, the designer decided to break it into discrete units. This strategy initially resulted in a busy appearance that was generally lacking in contrast; the designer solved this problem by alternating between positive and negative blocks. The complete poster appears at far left.

At the macro level of distance viewing, the typographic color was so extreme that information within each unit also needed to be treated with extreme contrast; otherwise, the information would have

been overly textural and, therefore, would have disintegrated against the boldness of the black-and-white upper level. At near right is a detail of the poster at actual size, showing the dramatic degree of size, weight, and width contrasts within the units.
KIM FOSTER/SCHOOL OF VISUAL ARTS UNITED STATES

Structure, Detail, and Navigation

Structure itself—axis relationships created by alignments and groupings, along with the interplay of masses and voids—helps readers locate, separate, or connect pieces of information … or, more simply, to "navigate" them. Aligning shallow columns of text horizontally across a format, for example, will indicate that they share some verbal relationship and may indicate a temporal sequence—a series of steps that builds in meaning. Creating a band of space between one horizontal text alignment and another will keep the two sequences clearly defined, but the fact of their similar horizontal structure may indicate that they are interrelated—or perhaps they communicate two sequential processes for launching a software program. Running text vertically in columns enhances the sense of continuity between paragraphs. Grouping several vertical columns together, while introducing a space to separate this grouping from another, may imply that the two groups are unrelated, or it may signal a pause for the reader to assimilate the content of one grouping before proceeding to the next. Keeping consistent spaces between groups that are related in meaning, and increasing the space between groups that are unrelated in meaning, is an easy way of helping readers navigate among more general

Four studies for a book cover (left) demonstrate how dramatic changes in spacing can completely alter the reading order—and meaningful interrelationships—of informational components. In the second study, for example, the reader will move from the title down to the three last names of the artists, directly linking their last names with the subject matter. In the last study, the title (and, therefore, subject matter) of the book becomes secondary as a result of its position, emphasizing the identities of the artists.

JROSS DESIGN UNITED STATES

sections of information and among sub-groups of information within those sections. Alignments between the edges of individual lines, clusters, columns, or groupings thereof create optical paths along which the eye will flow from one part or section to another. A designer cannot only help readers organize informational groupings, but also guide them through their intended sequence.

In this website for an architecture firm, succeeding levels of navigation expand from left to right, aligned horizontally at the top. The axes of their flush edges create similar divisions between levels of content above and unify the two informational spaces. PISCATELLO **DESIGN CENTRE** UNITED STATES

Thin vertical lines establish intervals of time in this infographic and help the reader assess the relative number of years between events within a given interval. STRUKTUR DESIGN UNITED KINGDOM

Sometimes, it is difficult to remember that type is just a collection of lines, dots, and shapes, and that they behave in the same way their simplified components do. Integrating such visual forms can also enhance hierarchy and clarify navigation through text. The focal power of a dot, which defines a location in space, can indicate the beginning or ending point of a text element (for example, using bullets to call out items in a list), correspond to alignments, activate

Although color and value changes clarify the hierarchy of information vertically, thin horizontal lines create connections between informational components from left to right.
RESEARCH STUDIOS
UNITED KINGDOM

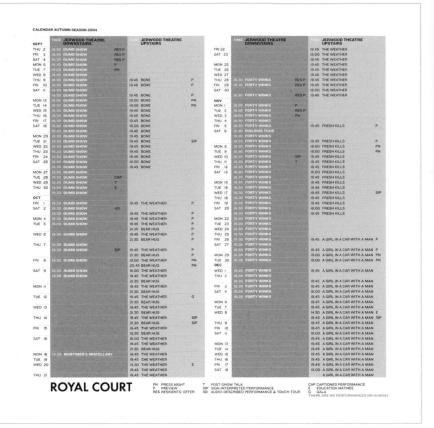

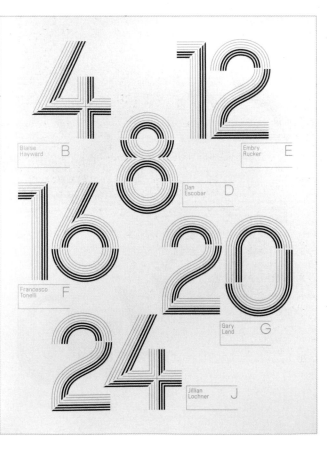

Sharp architectural line configurations enclose and embellish editorial elements such as section headings, list items, and captions in this brochure for a photographers' representative, taking their cue from the linear, patterned numerals that relate to the company's branding.
TRIBORO DESIGN UNITED STATES

spaces within a composition, and separate informational material linguistically, like an exaggerated form of punctuation. Lines, too, can perform a variety of useful functions to enhance hierarchy and navigation: separating, enclosing, emphasizing, or augmenting structural relationships, and activating space. Graphical lines, after all, are visually similar to lines of type, and relationships of contrast—in weight, solidity, directionality, and so on—operate the same way between them as they do among lines of type. Horizontal and vertical line configurations visually correspond to this intrinsic quality of text. Lines that are angled, curved, or wavy starkly contrast this "orthogonal" logic. Geometric shapes, whose hard-edged quality can be visually similar to that of letters, can act as inclusions or details among letters or words—as well as supports for clusters of text, operating as fields upon which the type lies or passes between. Because geometric forms integrate so well with type forms, but retain their identity as images, they can also be used to create visual links between type and other pictorial elements.

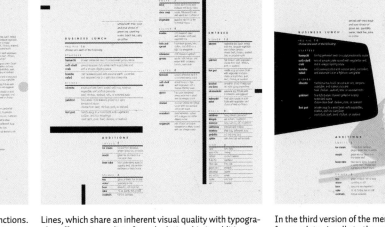

In the first version, left, dots perform a variety of functions. The large dot acts as a focal point, bringing its associated type element to the top of the hierarchy. A system of smaller dots is used to highlight structural alignments and to denote a specific sublevel in the hierarchy. Still other dots activate negative spaces in the format.

Lines, which share an inherent visual quality with typography, offer an immediate formal relationship in addition to whatever functions they serve. In the second version of the menu, heavy lines separate clusters of information that are unrelated, while lighter lines help distinguish clusters that share a relationship. In addition, the lines also activate space and help add movement to the composition.

In the third version of the menu, right, planar geometric forms relate visually to the geometry of letterforms, but contrast with the texture and linearity of type. As fields or containers for informational elements, they can help reinforce hierarchic distinctions among groupings of content; in this particular case, they also create a visual link between the type and the imagery while honoring the layout structure.

In all versions of a menu shown above, the same simple structure of varied column widths separates different kinds of information; columns of similar width, spaced more tightly together, establish the similarity of information they contain. Alignments between columns act in different ways: those between the major groups create compositional interaction, while those within groups serve either to distinguish subgroups (among categories of food) or to create directional flow between steps in a process (how to eat the food). In each of the three versions, dots, lines, and planar elements, respectively, add compositional vitality and informational support for the basic structure that helps readers navigate.

What Happens Now? Type in Color

Chromatic color can greatly enhance the textural qualities of type—its boldness, lightness, openness, density, and apparent location in three-dimensional space (called "typographic color")—reinforcing these qualities as they already exist in black and white by adding the optical effect of a true color. As we have seen, different hues appear at different locations in space; cool colors appear to recede, while warmer colors appear to advance. Applying a warm color to a type element that is large and important will enhance its contrast against other type elements. The relative value of colors is the most critical aspect of color in regard to how it affects type—especially its legibility—for example, when colored type sits on a colored background. As their values approach each other, the contrast between type and background diminishes, and the type becomes less legible.

Two versions of a composition of numbers demonstrate the effect of chromatic color on hierarchy, showing the layout in the same set of colors, but with the colors distributed differently among the numbers in each version. In one version, the numbers read in the correct sequence; in the other, they do not.

Changes in value and saturation add to the rhythmic typographic color of this page spread.
LSD SPAIN

A palette of analogous hues differentiates major sections in this website; a kind of animation results as the site rapidly auto-scrolls between sections when the user navigates. Each section exploits variations in the value, saturation, and temperature of its base hue to unify content in that section, while differentiating between hierarchic levels. The potential effect of color contrasts on legibility is readily apparent, underscoring the need to consider them carefully.
TIMOTHY SAMARA UNITED STATES

Color and Hierarchy All the qualities of chromatic color have a pronounced effect on hierarchy because of the way they change the apparent spatial depth and prominence of the typographic elements to which colors are applied. Color presents the possibility of altering the meaning or psychological effect of words by introducing a layer of meaning that is independent of—yet becomes integral to—the words themselves. Applying color to a black-and-white typographic composition will have an immediate effect on hierarchy. For this reason, it's a good idea to understand how the hierarchy works in black and white first, separating the typographic components through their typographic color—their density and rhythm, linearity and mass. Consider chromatic color as an added bonus, but make sure the hierarchy is clear by virtue of size changes, changes in weight, spacing, and so on. If the different levels of importance in the hierarchy are clearly established, further distinguishing each level with a difference in color can force greater separation between them. For example, if the information at the top of a hierarchy is set in a vibrant orange-red, while the secondary information is set in a cool gray, the two levels of the hierarchy will be separated visually to a much greater degree. Although the values of the colors are similar, the saturated

leonardo sonnoli
tassinari/vetta

The complex spatial changes created by the colored type forms—blues and violets receding, reds and yellows advancing—is further complicated and enriched by the use of transparency. **LEONARDO SONNOLI** ITALY

Value and temperature differences between text and background create a simple hierarchy without sacrificing legibility. **LOEWY** UNITED KINGDOM

Note the cool gray numerals set against the supersaturated yellow field, and compare their apparent spatial position with the reversed white numeral and the diagonal orange text. Because the gray and yellow hues are the same value, their physical boundaries become less distinct; but their temperature and saturation differences are adequate for legibility.
Also consider how the yellow appears to change identity, from that of a positive element on the white surface (the vertically rotated yellow type) to that of a deep spatial field. **PAONE DESIGN ASSOCIATES** UNITED STATES

orange type will advance in space, and the cool gray type will recede. The application of color to the ground within a composition can further enhance the hierarchy. Type of one color, set on a field of another color, will join closely with it or separate aggressively, depending on their color relationship. If the colors of type and background are related, the two elements will occupy a similar spatial depth. If they are complementary in nature, the two will occupy very different spatial depths. It is important to maintain considerable contrast between the type color and the background color so that the type remains not merely visible, but readable.

Color can also be used for coding, much as it may be applied in pictorial or abstract forms or textures. Color may link related informational components within a single composition, like a poster, or between multipart, serial, or sequential fomats—throughout pages in a website; between entry signage and directional signs in an environmental wayfinding program; across otherwise color-coded packages within a line of packaging, and so on.

In these ads, from a series, the value and intensity of the three primary hues changes, relative to the background, causing each to appear in a different spatial position in different instances.
ROBERT MCCONNELL/PARSONS SCHOOL OF DESIGN UNITED STATES

The Arabic text in this brochure, produced in the Middle East, is made dominant by applying the same hue to headings and text, while the English translation is downplayed in a lighter-value, neutral hue. Only the English heading—to be picked out rapidly by English readers scanning for material they can read—is set in a darker value. VCU QATAR QATAR

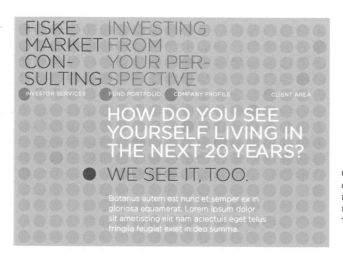

Compared to text and graphical elements whose analogous cool hues, limited value range, and lack of intensity group them together as a background, the vivid, warm orange text is the most emphatic.
TIMOTHY SAMARA UNITED STATES

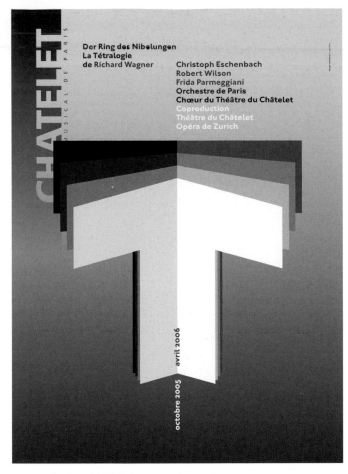

Intense red callouts highlight important elements in this poster's hierarchy, contrasting with the analogous blue and gray tones that recede in space.

DESIGN RUDI MEYER FRANCE

Color acts as information in these book spreads about New York City neighborhoods. In the overview map, each location's color is made different enough to clearly separate them; in subsequent detail maps, the specific coloration of a location indicates that this is the subject currently in focus. Color connects map locations with associated text, as well as the time of a visit to that location displayed in the chronological list at the right.

MYUNG HA CHANG SCHOOL OF VISUAL ARTS, UNITED STATES

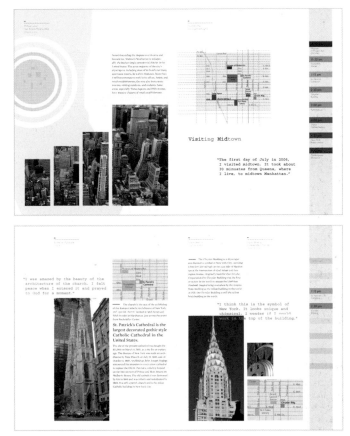

In a poster for an event, for example, all the information related to the time and place of the event might be assigned a particular color, which may relate to the color assigned to the title of the event. The color relationship of the two components creates a meaningful link for the viewer and serves to clarify the information. In a far more complex example—that of wayfinding, for instance—the headings of various departments on entry signage at reception may be color coded typographically; as a visitor travels through the department area itself, the color may then be applied to sign mounts or furnishings, while a different set of colors is then assigned to the typography that delineates administrative offices, research areas, and functional services such as restrooms. These colors may be consistent in all the departments, in contrast to each one's base color. Further, an accent color may highlight the office of the department's director, again used consistently for all directors' offices, regardless of department. Such color coding is exceptionally useful for labels in charts and graphs, to create links with supporting text, and for those in complex infographics or diagrams. And last, but not least, it bears repeating that color can radically alter the feeling or connotation of text— this too, is a kind of coding or hierarchic relationship that may be defined.

THE NATURE OF IMAGES

MEDIA AND METHODS

PRESENTATION OPTIONS

CONTENT AND CONCEPT

THE WORLD IMAGE

CHAPTER 04

Images are no longer just representations or interpreters of human actions. They have become central to every action that connects humans to each other…as much reference points for information and knowledge as visualizations of human creativity.

RON BURNETT/*Design educator and author; from* How Images Think, *The MIT Press: Cambridge, MA, 1993*

BIG ACTIVE UNITED KINGDOM

FLORENCE TÉTIER FRANCE

What Images Are Image making is perhaps one of the most complex and ecstatically human activities. An image is a powerful experience that is far from being inert—a simple depictor of objects or places or people. It is a symbolic, emotional space that replaces physical experience (or the memory of it) in the viewer's mind during the time it's being seen. This is true of images that are strictly representative of a real place, people, or objects, as well as of images that are artificial—either contrived representations or abstract configurations of shapes. In the hands of a designer who knows how to command composition on a purely visual level, and who can conceptually select and manipulate content, an image is by far the most profound communication tool available. In graphic design, there are myriad image possibilities—symbols and photomontage, drawing and painting, and even type—that perform different functions. Images provide a visual counterpoint to text, helping to engage the audience. Images also offer a visceral connection to experiences described by written language. They can help clarify very complex information—especially conceptual, abstract, or process-oriented information—by displaying it concisely: "at-a-glance." They can add interpretive overlay in juxtaposition with literal text or images. It's foolish to think that simply picking

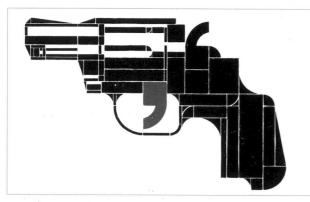

Poster image SAGMEISTER + WALSH UNITED STATES

Book cover THIBAUD TISSOT
GERMANY

Poster MUNDA GRAPHICS AUSTRALIA

Poster DOCH DESIGN GERMANY

Pasta packaging
ANDREW GORKOVENKO RUSSIA

Painting for illustration series SEAN RYAN UNITED STATES

a photograph of a particular object will alone solve a communication problem in its entirety. The relevance of an image to a design solution isn't simply wrapped up in its subject matter. An image becomes relevant when its composition and production technique, as well as its subject matter, are working in concert with other material to create an integrated message.

Newsletter masthead PAONE DESIGN ASSOCIATES
UNITED STATES

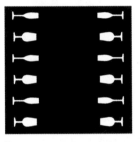

Logo MANUEL ESTRADA SPAIN

Icon TEN-DO-TEN JAPAN

Website home page ISHAN KHOSLA DESIGN INDIA

Book cover system CARDON WEBB UNITED STATES

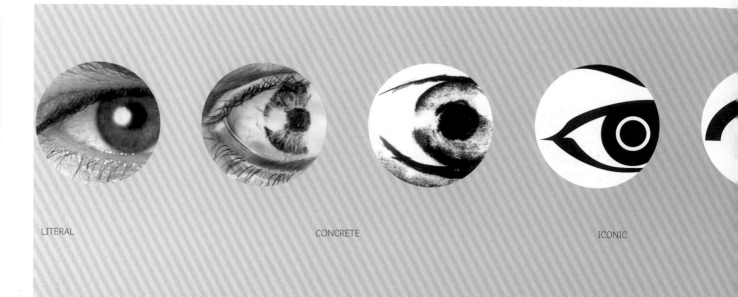

LITERAL CONCRETE ICONIC

PICTORIAL

Pictorial images show such recognizable subjects as objects, figures, and spaces.

Empirical pictorial images depict the characteristics of objects and scenes as they are observed in space. Their primary purpose is description, explanation, or the suggestion that their message is grounded in real life, concrete and accessible: The content demands a clear, journalistic delivery. Photographic images, one could argue, are the most empirical of all pictorial images.

Pictorial images of subjects in which a designer noticeably exaggerates elements, edits out information, or imposes a formal conceit (while retaining a generally naturalistic quality), inhabit a subterritory called **stylization:** The image exploits the recognizability of the concrete but adds conceptual or metaphorical overlay. As a bonus, the stylistic qualities that are exaggerated or imposed will likely integrate more fluidly on a visual or formal level with other material, such as typography. A pictorial image in which the form language is dramatically simplified—as in a graphic translation or icon—is said to be **reductive.** The even more stylized quality of such images radically augments both specificity of message and metaphorical power; it creates a bold optical presence that facilitates perceptual immediacy and deep imprinting, making them especially useful for logos and critical informational messages. In such images, empirical form and purely abstract visual qualities assume a simultaneous, even equivalent, presence, delivering a visceral and vital tension between the concrete and the conceptual.

The Spectrum of Representation The presentation of images falls on a spectrum defined at one end by the pictorial and at the other by abstraction—nonpictorial form. Images that lie closer to the pictorial end of the continuum are more literal; images that approach abstraction are more interpretive. An image might be mostly pictorial or abstract (nonpictorial), but it always will be a mixture of the two—and it will always communicate or represent something. At the macro level, images range between these two major territories: they either depict some subject or content that corresponds to observable experience (pictorial); or they are made up of graphic forms that don't appear to have a source in physical reality (nonpictorial); or they may lie somewhere in between.

Both major territories contain subterritories, and their boundaries are fluid and mutable: The aspects of any image are likely to cross from one territory to another or exhibit characteristics from several, depending on the designer's goal. In the right context, a simple yellow circle becomes the Sun. A composition of lines in dynamic rhythms might communicate a subtler message about movement or energy, not necessarily referring to some

DIAGRAMMATIC

CONNOTATIVE

SYMBOLIC

NONPICTORIAL

Nonpictorial images consist of abstract graphic forms—dots, lines, planes, and patterns.

Many nonpictorial images also inhabit a reductive geography. These include bold, minimal shape configurations, for example, or textures and patterns, and abstract symbols. Symbols are used to convey extraordinarily complex ideas and narratives; consider any religious symbol, the recycling symbol, or the biohazard symbol—as a surgically concise, immediate form.

Environmental or expansive fields of marks and shapes, similar to empirical, pictorial images, also establish a sense of complex, articulated space governing objects or figures. Such images are often used as an alternative to pictorial depiction where

high-level conceptual messages are concerned (intangibles such as music, poetry, and emotions). They are also useful in creating metaphorical and visual bridges between other compositional elements—for instance, in a branding system where a relevantly meaningful pattern is used to support type and photographic imagery, as well as the system's various applications (ads, website, etc.).

Typography, being a system of lines, planes, and pattern that denies reference to the physical world, is the ultimate reductive nonpictorial form—even more so, one could argue, than the elemental dot, which itself may easily be interpreted as a reference to some natural form (cell, planet, molecule, eye, etc.). Further, typographic forms are symbols of sounds and, therefore, verbal or conceptual content, positioning them in a starkly abstract visual territory.

literal object or experience. Even a photograph that presumably shows something real is an abstraction on some level—it depicts a state of activity that is no longer happening and flattens it into a two-dimensional form. Portions of it might not even be real, but instead, contrivances set up by the photographer or by the designer directing the creation of the photograph. Using the intrinsic messaging of abstract form described in chapter 1 to influence a

photograph's composition will enhance its messaging potential. Similarly, suggesting concrete literal experience within an abstract composition will help ground the message in reality for a viewer, making it more accessible without sacrificing the abstraction's simplicity and visceral evocative power. Creating or selecting appropriate imagery for an intended communicative purpose necessitates understanding how images work: what their parts are, how we

identify those parts and assign meaning to them and, further, how those parts can be manipulated to assure a reliable interpretation and a compelling experience.

Semiotics: How Images Communicate

The processes of perception and cognition, or what the brain does with visual form to arrive at understanding, are the focus of a branch of visual anthropology called "semiology," developed in the 1800s. Visual stimuli, or "signs," consist of two parts: the signifier (the visual form itself), and its signified (the concept it calls up). In working with an image, or sign, a designer must always be conscious of two aspects—its syntax, or purely formal qualities (what it looks like) and its semantics (what it means) ... and of their mutual interplay, as these aspects of a sign may be adjusted independently. Many kinds of syntax may point to the same signified, or semantic meaning; and many kinds of meaning may be embodied in a single kind of syntax. In the simplest terms, a viewer first assimilates, or perceives, the syntax of a sign and then compares it to prior knowledge to identify it—which may involve "template matching," against copies (templates) stored in memory from past experiences, or "protoype matching," an averaging of features to arrive at a generalization, rather than a perfect match. These are examples of "top-down" processing, meaning that the viewer has some basis for comparison; but a viewer may have no such basis, relying instead on "bottom-up" processing— parsing individual features in relation to

The simple, clear visual form of the type's arrangement creates an easy template match for the viewer, that of a flag.
MANUEL ESTRADA SPAIN

All of these signs, of varied syntax, can signify the same idea: New York City.

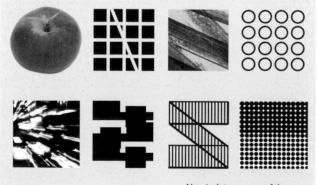

Now isolate any one of them and list for yourself all of its other possible meanings.

Viewers will quickly template-match the subjects "human figure," and "praying gesture," but the replacement of the head with that of an animal, and juxtapositions of incongruous elements, will require the viewer to process from the bottom up to gain deeper understanding. ZOVECK ESTUDIO MEXICO

different experiences to find commonality and, thereby, inferring a possible identity. Template matches are essentially literal images—useful as basic information, but not especially interesting in their immediate and summary recognizability. With prototype matches and, more so, images requiring bottom-up processing, designers more effectively engage viewers: the added effort to decode such images generates interest and forces a viewer to draw upon

varied associations and experiences—and this is where emotion, association, reinvention, and metaphor come into play. A designer may easily alter a template match, or literal, image with unexpected syntax, forcing bottom-up processing as a viewer resolves the incongruity (e.g., replacing a figure's head with a graphical form). And literal images become suddenly interesting in juxtaposition: upon identifying each individually, a viewer seeks a relationship.

Therefore, it's the relationships between syntactic, or form, elements that tell the story. As discussed in the first chapter (page 26), form language and composition establish the first understanding to which a viewer will come. Identifying the nature of a form, noting how it behaves in space, and comparing the behaviors of individual forms to others, is the foundation of communicating at even the most basic, abstract or nonpictorial level.

Unexpected discrepancies in signifieds are opportunities rich with metaphor, relying on the viewer to make connections. This illsutration accompanied an article on charity and wealth disparity. CATHERINE CASALINO UNITED STATES.

A hybrid of two iconic, easily recognized subjects establishes causality and/or equivalence, or parity, between their identities—and all the meanings inherent in them. OLIVER MUNDAY GROUP UNITED STATES

The specific syntax of each pattern skews its signification—one is recognized as Art Déco ornament, the other is interpreted as a psychedeleic experience.

CORALIE BICKFORD-SMITH [LEFT]
UNITED KINGDOM
ZHU ZIPENG/SCHOOL OF VISUAL ARTS
[RIGHT] UNITED STATES

Appreciating Form Syntax All forms carry meaning, no matter how apparently simple or elemental they may be. As noted, this is because the brain relies on the analysis of visual stimuli, relative to prior experience, to ultimately make decisions based on the result of that comparison. The shape, size, linearity or mass of a perceived form tells us what it is; and, conversely, knowledge of forms that look a certain way cause us to project that understanding onto a form in a new context. For example, we know from experience that the Sun, Moon, cells, water droplets, and other such things are round: Therefore, when confronted with a circular plane, we identify it correspondingly—a circular form means "natural." Conversely, a square means the opposite—artificial, intellectual, architectural—its equivalent angles and parallel sides occur only in the works of humanity. Further, forms become significantly more meaningful when they can be compared. If they exhibit parity (are similar), they must be equivalent in meaning; if not, they must be different, and the quality of this difference will contribute additional meaning. All of this information is acquired just from a form itself, never mind what it is appears to be doing.

Identifying a pictorial form includes assessing its abstract syntax, which underscores the more complex, specific understanding acquired via further template matching: The circularity of the flower supports, the understanding of its organic nature. Greater complexity confronts a viewer when two recognizably different signifieds, or concepts, share a form identity: Both the flower and the car wheel are circular ... so now, what interrelationship exists in their presumedly different meanings?

Asked to project meaning onto a circle, all viewers will offer the same responses: the Earth, Sun, or Moon; unity, continuity, the cycles of nature—all that which is organic. In contrast, the universal responses to a square will be associations with the intellectual or man-made: shelter, order, mathematics, and so on.

Combining lines with dots offers a powerful visual contrast and, in this logo, creates meaning.
LSD SPAIN

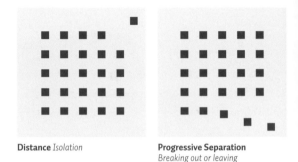

Distance *Isolation*

Progressive Separation
Breaking out or leaving

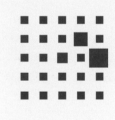

Progressive size change
Increased importance; growth

Direction *Movement or energy*

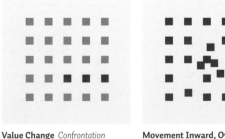

Value Change *Confrontation*

Movement Inward, Overlap
Interference; assembly

By differentiating elements (or groups thereof) from others within an overall grouping, a designer instigates comparisons that elicit several questions: "What is the nature of each grouping? How are they different? What does this difference signify?" Shown here are a number of examples that illustrate simple comparative formal interactions.

Interplay Makes a Message Forms acquire new meanings when they participate in spatial relationships; when they share or oppose each other's mass or textural characteristics; and when they have relationships because of their rotation, singularity or repetition, alignment, clustering, or separation from each other. Each state tells the viewer something new about the forms, adding to the meaning that they already might have established. Forms that appear to be moving, or energetic, because of their spatial arrangement, mean something very different from those arranged statically. The degree of difference between elements can be subtle or dramatic, and the designer can imply different degrees of meaning by isolating one group or part more subtly, while exaggerating the difference between others. Because tiny adjustments in form are easily perceived, the difference between each group can be precisely controlled.

There are numerous strategies for creating such interplay. Of course, which strategy to employ will depend on the message the designer must convey; he or she will trigger very different perceptions of meaning by alternating smaller and larger sizes, as opposed to increasing them in a progression. In the first instance, the difference may be perceived as a change in energy; in the second, the difference may be perceived as growth or a focusing in energy.

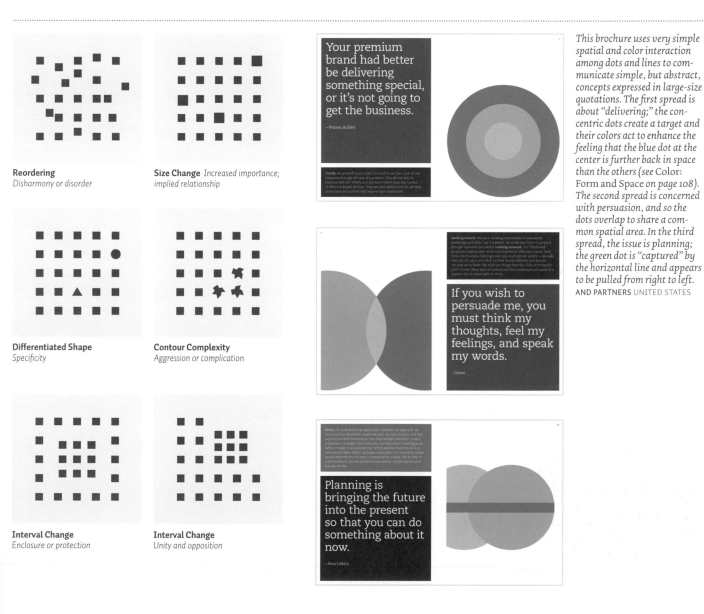

Reordering
Disharmony or disorder

Size Change *Increased importance; implied relationship*

Differentiated Shape
Specificity

Contour Complexity
Aggression or complication

Interval Change
Enclosure or protection

Interval Change
Unity and opposition

Your premium brand had better be delivering something special, or it's not going to get the business.
– Warren Buffett

If you wish to persuade me, you must think my thoughts, feel my feelings, and speak my words.
– Cicero

Planning is bringing the future into the present so that you can do something about it now.
– Alan Lakein

This brochure uses very simple spatial and color interaction among dots and lines to communicate simple, but abstract, concepts expressed in large-size quotations. The first spread is about "delivering;" the concentric dots create a target and their colors act to enhance the feeling that the blue dot at the center is further back in space than the others (see Color: Form and Space on page 108). The second spread is concerned with persuasion, and so the dots overlap to share a common spatial area. In the third spread, the issue is planning; the green dot is "captured" by the horizontal line and appears to be pulled from right to left.
AND PARTNERS UNITED STATES

Complex Abstract Messages The seemingly generic and intangible qualities of abstraction belie its profound capacity to convey messages on a universal perceptual level that viewers very rarely are able to acknowledge. Ever more specific interpretations deriving from cultural context, individual experience, and emotional life compound the common and universal, and every level of interpretive response mutually colors the others. The more primal an intended message, the more common its form language and its reliability in communicating to a diverse audience. Conversely, the more intangible or culturally specific a communication, the more variable will be its form language, and the fewer reliably similar interpretations.

While interpretations of abstract imagery are often emotional, a quality designers may use to subliminally manipulate more concrete imagery, abstract form languages may be used independently to communicate any number of concrete subjects, not only intangible ones. Through the combination of form language, structure, and positive/negative interaction, abstract imagery may capture a feeling or represent a physical activity; it may connote a time

Architecture

Evolution

Intimidation

Dissolution

Traffic

Unity

Ephemeral

Sensuous

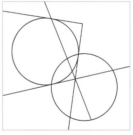

Precision

Conflict

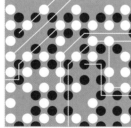

Technology

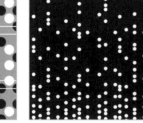

Effervescence

Monumental

Mapping

Winter

or place. In place of recognizable pictorial subjects, such narratives may be suggested by simplified allusions to physical experience, in effect, translating shapes and actions through implication and inference, in a diagrammatic way. Formations of arcing lines may capture the influence of wind on branches; masses compressing against each other and expanding may tell a story about conflict and intimidation, or bodies undulating in the throes of passion.

Introducing abstract imagery into compositions that also include pictorial subjects invites speculation about the juxtaposition. Used as fields or backgrounds, such imagery creates a new context in which to frame understanding of a naturalistic subject; used within, or on top of, pictorial images—even photographic ones, whose typically evidentiary literalness is difficult to dismiss outright—can have dramatic consequences on that image's presumed

meaning. And given that one important task for a designer often is to clearly, and memorably, differentiate a visual experience from other, competing ones—super critical in branding—abstraction, being profoundly unique, offers a completely custom experience for a client's audience.

Elegantly swirling curves—whose fluid movement, precision weight contrasts, and surface sheen all communicate notions of luxury—are applied to the walls of a home furnishings shop to enhance the appeal of the products on display. **A10 DESIGN** BRAZIL

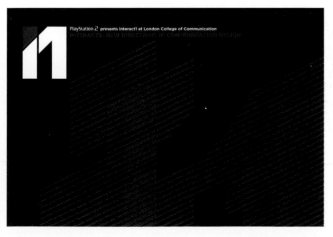

Repeated patterns of lines create vibration and the illusion of three-dimensional planes that may be interpreted as printed surfaces, video texture, and ideas related to transmission associated with communication design. **RESEARCH STUDIOS** UNITED KINGDOM

Modes of Pictorial Signification A designer might choose to represent an idea pictorially by using photographs, illustrations (drawings or paintings), or a hybrid: manipulated photographs or drawn images in combination. Decisions such as these result from evaluating the content and its conceptual functions. The images must provide informational clarity, but they must do so in a way that resonates and delivers secondary and tertiary messages—associational or branded messages—as well. The form of an image's representation is called its "mode," and this includes its fundamental syntax (and its resulting degree of naturalism), as well as the way that it points to, or signifies, its intended meaning. A designer must consider a number of things in choosing the right image mode, or modalities, to use. Among these are the evocative, emotional qualities of the project's content; the number of different modes needed to differentiate specific kinds of messages; and the expectations of the viewing audience for certain image experiences over others, because of their demographic makeup or the social and historical context of the project's content.

An icon is a visual sign that shares a structural similarity with the object it signifies. Usually, icons are devoid of detail and are literal representations of their signified object.

An indexical sign, or index, is a visual sign that points to its signified object indirectly, or "indexes" it—for example, a nest indexes a bird.

A symbol is a pictorial or abstract image whose form is unrelated to its signified object or idea; it derives its power from the arbitrary agreement of the culture that uses the symbol. The context in which a symbol appears—cultur-

ally or subculturally—will alter its symbolic meaning: consider the difference in meaning between the same symbol element in these various environments.

A photograph may be considered an icon if it depicts its subject neutrally and acts as pure description. As with graphical icons, such an image will signify only its subject unless it is somehow given a new context or altered. In this study, the neutral icon "book" is manipulated to create specific meanings. In the example at top, the image has been burned, suggesting intellectual repression (or a famous work of science fiction, Farenheit 451, by Ray Bradbury). In the example at bottom, the application of a digital filter to pixellate the book's pages signifies electronic media. KELLY CHEW/ PARSONS SCHOOL OF DESIGN UNITED STATES

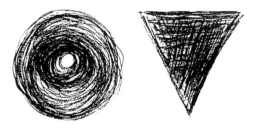

Symbols are highly mediated forms of image, drawing on common understanding that elevates them beyond mere representation. Consider the depth of meaning in these two images that symbolize which public restroom to use. ART: TECAJI SLOVENIA

A supersign integrates more than one sign (and often more than one type of sign) in a single, gestalt combination in which all the signs included are visible and accessible immediately; a logo is a good example. On this page are examples of supersigns that combine: icons with icons; icons with indexes; icons with letters; letters with indexes; and icons with letters and symbols.

This supersign uses a letterform as a base, altered only by the addition of two small dots to create added meaning. LSD SPAIN

Highly resolved integration of car and bicycle icons begins to suggest some relationship between them; the addition of the cautionary yellow striping evolves the message further. THOMAS CSANO CANADA

Wasseem Mohanna
IT Consultant

The elegant W and M lockup, while still clearly letters, has also formed an iconic representation of wires. Further, as a logo it acts as a symbol. RAIDY PRINTING GROUP LEBANON

This poster creates a political statement by verbally qualifying a powerful combination of two icons into a supersign. LESLEY MOORE NETHERLANDS

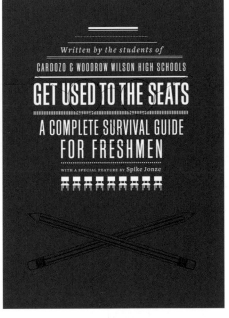

The supersign in this book cover pokes fun at the tribulations of student life, using type and supporting icons to create a gestalt image. OLIVER MUNDAY GROUP UNITED STATES

This illustration for a newspaper article about global economics in the digital age forms an icon of a brain from numbers and symbols. TIMOTHY SAMARA UNITED STATES

In semiotic terms, an image may be presented in one of three modes—that of icon, index, or symbol. The first mode, "icon," has a variety of meanings that can cause some confusion. Technically, an icon is a drawing whose syntax shares a structural similarity with the object it signifies. Usually, icons are literal, graphic representations of their signified object, edited to essentials, utterly neutral, identifying. An image of iconic modality, however—which could be a photograph, as opposed to a drawing—follows this basic precept: the image looks like what it represents. But it is also possible to use pictorial images that are representational but that are not pictures of the signified itself. This kind of image is called an "indexical sign" and refers to its subject indirectly: An image of an egg or nest may "index" a bird. A pictorial image whose form is physically unrelated to its signified object or idea is a "symbol"; it derives its power from the arbitrary agreement of the culture who uses the symbol. A dove, for example, is a symbol of peace in Western culture. Context may have a dramatic impact on how the audience perceives the symbolic signified: consider the image of an apple in various contexts. A symbol may be either pictorial or abstract.

The Medium Is a Message A line is a line is a line … or not. Every mechanical method of creating an image has specific properties, or makes characteristic marks, that contributes a specific kind of visual language to the image. These languages have a powerful effect on an image's communicative value, not just on its visual qualities relative to other elements in a design solution. Above and beyond the overall territory (pictorial or abstract)

and the the semiotic mode (of a pictorial image)—the medium a designer chooses with which to create the illustration carries meaning. This meaning may be imparted through the perceived feel of the medium (softness, hardness, fluidity, or stiffness) and, sometimes, through its conceptual or allusory aspects (for example, using a drawing tool native to a certain region or historical period for a project related to that region or period).

How far from its "natural" reference an image becomes through the designer's intervention with medium (or stylization, discussed in the next section) is described as how "mediated" it is. The level of an image's mediation can be evaluated in a couple of ways. First, it can be considered in terms of its physical expression and its mode; for example, a realistic drawing shows a greater level of mediation than a photograph of the same subject; a reduc-

Photograph

Toned Photograph

Filtered Photograph

Stipple Drawing

Vector Drawing

Graphite

Charcoal

Ink

Paint

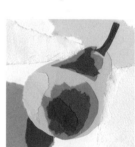

Cut Paper/Collage

Engraving

Linocut or Wooodcut

Experimenting with the mark-making possibilities intrinsic to different tools shows the endless potential for expression in an illustrated image. Here, the same subject is illustrated using different tools to show how powerful the effect of the medium could be on communication in different contexts.

The choice of image used for one of several wall panels in a French cultural center—Guignol, a puppet character from a child's story—is symbolic of French culture. Its historical stature is altered through mediation: representing the image in a digital pixel pattern that makes it contemporary.
APELOIG DESIGN FRANCE

tive icon is more mediated, still). Second, an image's level of mediation can be considered in terms of how direct, or indirect, the messaging in the image is—a somewhat literal drawing of a subject is less mediated than is a caricature (mediated by humor) or a cubist drawing (mediated by time deconstruction).

The question of mediation and credibility comes to the fore in comparing these two illustrations. Both are fabrications—but which one seems more real? If you decided that the corncob person does, you're probably *not alone: its empirical, photographic qualities make it more believable as "real" than the invented space and painterly texture of the drawn image on the right.*
CHRISTOPHER SHORT [LEFT] / CYR STUDIO [RIGHT]
UNITED STATES

All these images depict the same subject—a figure—but their differing syntax intrinsically mediates the subject to varying degrees. The "pure" photograph is the least mediated of the three. The two drawn images are inherently more mediated than the photographic image but, between the two, the naturalistic drawing is less mediated than the other.

Viewers will suspend their disbelief when confronting a highly mediated image of empirical experience.
TIEN-MIN LIAO UNITED STATES

Stylization To stylize an image means to purposely alter or edit the visual language used to represent its subject—to mediate it—away from a naturalistic presentation toward one that is, in essence, more of an abstraction. Stylization emphasizes awareness of the image as a contrivance, or an intellectually calculated, sign. In selecting the details of the idea or subject to be represented, the designer looks for elements that are the most universally recognizable—for example, the fundamental shapes and qualities of a cat (ears, tail, a common posture, whiskers, paws, and so on)—rather than those that are specific—particular ear shapes, markings, or short or long hair. In arranging the elements, the designer invents a particular graphic language—an internal logic of positive and negative relationships, an emphasis on curved or angular forms, and an integration of line and mass—that will make the image live as its own unified idea rather than simply reproducing the likeness of the object. A stylized image may intend to communicate on an objective, universal, and neutral level by distilling its subject's features to those that represent its fundamental "truth"; at the other extreme, the designer's use of form language and medium may interfere with this semiotic purity. In giving the form its own identity, the designer selectively interprets aspects

One of the decisions a designer must make is the degree to which evidence of the means of the image's creation will be explicit or downplayed. A designer may decide in favor of a "clean" presentation: An imposed imperceptibility of the image's creation that suggests "realism" or objectivity.

Works in which the image-making process is visible start down the road of stylization. This may be purposely exaggerated, and the designer may further impose a contrived form language; both carry subjective or emotive qualities. When form language itself becomes a purposeful component of an image, it takes on a dual role—acting as a vehicle for viewers to recognize the subject it represents, and as an independent experience that adds some other knowledge about the subject. The form language used to stylize may directly refer to observed elements in the subject: short, tufted marks, for example, may texturally represent leaves or trees themselves, rather than be used as secondary components to construct a naturalistic illusion of leaves or trees—effectively referring to them in shorthand. The degree of stylization within an image alters a viewer's intellectual focus. Toward the realistic end of the spectrum, the subject's literal meaning takes on more importance; as it becomes more stylized, the gesture, the quality of the marks, and associations or symbolic messaging that these impart become more important.

It's easy to identify stylization in a drawn or painted image; to a certain degree, the fact of the medium, if visible in the image's execution, already alerts a viewer to its stylized nature. Stylization in photographic images is more subtle, usually embodied in consciously unnatural lighting or coloration, more extreme viewing angle or cropping, and clearly artificial propping or presence of materials that are out of context.
ANDREW GORKOVENKO [LEFT] RUSSIA
LA BOCA [RIGHT] UNITED KINGDOM

of the form, skewing the communication in one direction or another. Following the cat example further, the designer might emphasize a crouching position, possibly communicating readiness for action, or might emphasize the cat's claws, a message that might mean power or aggression. The angularity of the drawing, or how weight is distributed, might add interpretation, such as restful and contemplative, or quick and agile, qualities; further rendering the overall form as a pattern of differently weighted lines might exaggerate the interpretation of kinetic potential, as well as introduce some conceptual association with technology—relevant, perhaps, in a communication for an energy utility or manufacturing company.

Pictorial images that engage the form language on a dual level as an aspect of the stylization merge pictorial and nonpictorial—their syntactic components have a life of their own while still serving a depictive function. In these drawings, the marks of the tool and the gesture of their form represent treebranches in wind and rain without literally describing them.
EVA SURANY/UNIVERSITY OF THE ARTS UNITED STATES

The stylized, linear, and planar form language in these two posters distracts the viewer from the literal identities of their subjects to focus on their metaphorical messages.

[TOP] The iconic outer form of the lightbulb is elevated to translation status by virtue of its indistinct, sparkling inner contour—a formal adjustment that suggests the bulb's function. The filament is made symbolic through translation into circuits that also appear to represent leafy branches.

[BOTTOM] An icon of a hand becomes doubly symbolic as the string around the finger— a symbol for remembering something—is transformed into a power cord. TEMPLIN BRINK DESIGN UNITED STATES

Photography The "pure" photographic image has become the preeminent form of imagery used in visual communciations in recent years. One reason for this might be the speed at which photographs transmit information—their realism and directness allow a viewer to enter the image and process it very quickly, rather than get distracted by abstract pictorial issues such as texture, medium, and composition. Access speed in imagery has become important because the flood of visual messages encountered by the average viewer requires images to compete robustly for attention; the faster a viewer is able to recognize an image's subject and understand its significance, it may be reasoned, the more likely they are to invest continued attention—or, at the very least, retain some information if they decide to move on.

While composition plays an important role in the quality of the photographic image and its messaging potential, its presence as a mediating phenomenon is much harder to recognize and, therefore, is often overlooked on a conscious level by the viewer. This suggests another reason for the primacy of photographs as communicators: the fact of the image's mediation (or manipulation)—through composition, selective focus, lighting, cropping, and

A

B

C

As with any other imagery, photographic content must be decisively composed. The photographer has two opportunities to control the image's composition, however: first, within the frame of the camera's viewfinder; and second, during the printing process in the darkroom (or in cropping a digital photograph using software). In this study, a minor shift in camera angle produces a variation on an already decisive composition of elements (A, B). Radically changing the viewpoint (C) creates a very different composition while retaining the identity of the content.

Clean, neutral daylight and meticulous styling capture the the product's wholesome and sensuous qualities; the intimate cropping exudes warmth and honesty. WALLACE CHURCH
UNITED STATES

Along with their common full-frame use, photographic images also may be used as independent elements within collages or in concert with typography.
MANUEL ESTRADA SPAIN

other techniques—is secondary to the acceptance of photographic images as "real." This provides the designer with an upper hand in persuasion, on behalf of a client, because the work of convincing a viewer that he or she can believe or trust the image is already well on its way to being achieved: "I saw it with my own eyes." Today's average viewer, although much more sophisticated and attuned to the deceptive potential of photography than viewers in previous generations, is still much more likely to accept the content of a photograph as truth than that of an illustration, simply because the illustration is obviously contrived; the contrivance possible in a photograph is not so readily appreciated. On a purely practical level, photographs—in the form of stock, or ready-made images—are abundantly available, and often far less expensive and time consuming to acquire than either commissioning a photographer for original work or, for that matter, inventing imagery oneself in some other way. Although useful in a pinch, such images create a few potential pitfalls: they very often are generic or cliché, and the designer runs the risk of an image he or she has used in a particular context appearing in another one entirely, diluting the specificity of its impact and possibly confusing viewers who see it in more than one place.

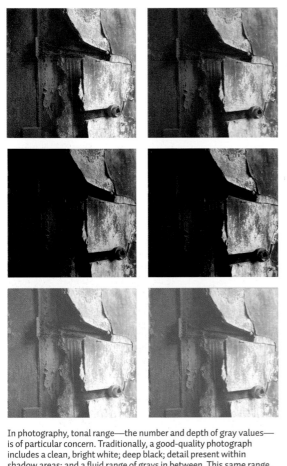

In photography, tonal range—the number and depth of gray values—is of particular concern. Traditionally, a good-quality photograph includes a clean, bright white; deep black; detail present within shadow areas; and a fluid range of grays in between. This same range, from darkest shadow to brightest highlight, also is desirable in color photographs. Pushing the tonal range toward generally brighter values decreases the contrast in the image and, to some degree, flattens it out; pushing the tonal range toward the shadow end also tends to flatten the image but increases contrast and causes highlight areas to become brighter and more pronounced. These effects of tonality shift are shown in the accompanying images, in both black and white and color. Note the contrast differences between corresponding images.

A clever viewpoint and stark, high-contrast lighting render a typically complex subject as a cluster of revealing dots and lines. KING 20G [FELIX HEYES/JOSH KING/ PAUL NELSON/BEN WEST] UNITED KINGDOM

Illustration One is not limited, of course, to photography alone as a means of introducing imagery to a project. The choice of illustration over photography opens up tremendous possibilities for transmitting information. The designer is not only unencumbered by the limitations of real-world objects and environment but also given the potential to introduce conceptual overlay, increased selectivity of detail, and the personal, interpretive aspect of the designer's visualization—through choice of medium, composition, and gestural qualities. The term "illustration" is used here in the broadest sense: it technically refers to drawings or paintings that show, very literally, what a text describes (most commonly, in a literary context, to create a visualization of a setting or action)—but it can can refer to any nonphotographic, designed image that supports text. It's advisable to avoid a literal use of illustration, as well as redundancy—visually repeating information that a text has already provided. An illustration should always add to, or evolve, a viewer's understanding of what a text presents verbally; the designer must orchestrate a relationship between text and illustration so that each contributes information that, together, is more complete and meaningful than what either presents individually.

The rich, almost collagelike mixture of tools used to create this image— airbrush, pen, digital images, flat ink—contributes textural contrast and multiple layers of meaning to consider. MACIEJ HAJNRICH POLAND

The drawing of the house using simple lines becomes symbolic by transforming the lines into circuits. DROTZ DESIGN UNITED STATES

A texture of illustrated insects reveals a numeral 5 in this panel from a parking garage signage system. Illustrating the insects gives the designer control over their visual presentation rather than relying on finding or photographing images of real insects. STUDIO WORKS UNITED STATES

As with all types of images, an illustration can be concrete, objective, or realistic in how it presents its subject, or it can become abstracted and symbolic; the designer can add details that normally would not exist in a real scene or can exaggerate movement, texture, arrangement, space, and lighting. Choosing illustration for image presentation, however, means potentially sacrificing a kind of credibility or real-world connection for the viewer.

Despite the fact that most audiences realize that a photograph might just as easily be manipulated and, therefore, made misleading, the audiences will still instinctively respond to a photograph as though it were reality. The power of illustration over photography, however, is to communicate with a visual sensitivity that is emotional, poetic, organic, and innately human. An illustration can also integrate with other visual material, such as type, abstract

graphic elements, and even the paper stock or other finishing techniques, on a textural level that is impossible with a conventional photograph. The designer must weigh these aspects carefully and select which mode of representation will best suit the communication.

The decision to illustrate the vegetables on this label, rather than to photograph them, ensures their absolute perfection and freshness. WALLACE CHURCH UNITED STATES

....

Photography becomes especially intriguing when used in a nonrealistic way, as seen here in an editorial illustration for a lifestyle magazine. As surreal and contrived as this collection of objects is, somehow it will be perceived as grounded in the real world. SUPERBÜRO SWITZERLAND

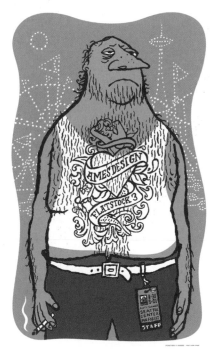

The scraggly outline and cartoonish forms of this illustration mix humor and pathos. AMES BROS. UNITED STATES

Drawing and Painting The directness of hand-generated images is universally appealing. Through drawing and painting, the designer taps into a viewer's own sense of creativity and connects on an extremely personal level—there is a genuine, honest, and warm quality to an illustration that might be lacking in the slick and seamless realism of a photograph. An illustration's success lies in the appropriateness of its style to the subject matter at hand.

The majority of illustration is contracted from specialists, who cultivate a particular style to find a niche in the market, but this doesn't preclude designers themselves from taking on the role of illustrator. A designer wanting to illustrate will be intimate with the subject matter of the project and other relevant graphic elements—including type and finishing techniques. As a result, he or she might be able to build images that are even more appropriate and integrated with other elements than would be likely if working through an outside source. Many designers, however, neglect the possibility of drawing and painting due, perhaps, to a sense of intimidation—"I can't even draw a stick figure." Drawing is a skill that, like any other, can be learned. Some people demonstrate a superlative native talent for it, just as they might for working with typography or taking photographs; others must work on honing it

Scratchy, almost distraught cross-hatching, produced with pen and ink, enhances the mysterious and slightly sinister quality of the image. **AMES BROS.** UNITED STATES

Illustration, even if naturalistic, still liberates the designer to reinvent space and abstractly combine disparate elements that would otherwise be empirically impossible. **CYR STUDIO** UNITED STATES

as they would for any other skill. It's very interesting to consider that children draw intuitively as part of their early development, consistently showing a remarkable level of visual sophistication in their work. At issue here is confidence; young children fearlessly accept their skill and the expression that results without the judgment that adults impose on themselves. Somewhere along the way, though, many of us lose that fearlessness; our intellectual development cuts us off from one of the most provocative, human modes of storytelling and narrative. Illustration can be many things; regardless of native talent or the academic naiveté with which it is created, it can exhibit a compelling, forceful presence in designed communication. What is really most important is authenticity of feeling and the relevance of that feeling, in its form, to the intended message. Bluntly and roughly tracing photographic reference and freeing oneself from the need to create a realistic depiction—or, more radically, interpreting ideas in a nonpictorial way—are valid possibilities that cannot only help designers become confident in their own image-making abilities but also yield unique, powerfully memorable experiences.

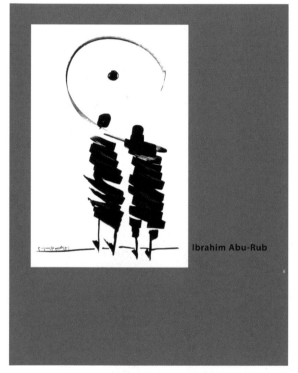

A lively dialogue between abstract gestural mark and figural representation lends humanity and depth to the illustration. VCU QATAR QATAR

Hand drawing and vector drawing are combined with xerographic effects to produce a high-tech image for this CD cover, nonetheless retaining a human touch. GLASHAUS DESIGN GERMANY

The doodle-like quality of the line work in these juice package illustrations extends into the drawing of all the text, delivering a spontaneous, refreshing, and direct quality while clearly describing the contents. BILLIE JEAN UNITED KINGDOM

Graphic Translation One particular kind of stylized illustration—known as "graphic translation"—evolved from the poster traditions of Switzerland and Germany in the early part of the twentieth century. Graphic translation combines some attributes of both icon and symbol. It depicts subjects in a literal way, like an icon, but also in a self-consciously abstract way that takes on symbolic qualities. A translation attempts to convey the concrete, fundamental truth of a subject, without details that are specific to that one particular instance of it; for example, a translation of a cat strives to be about the idea "cat," but not about a specific cat; that is, how long its hair is or the markings of its particular breed. Unlike an icon, however, which is strictly about shape, the textural and volumetric qualities of the subject are important considerations in finding an appropriate language with which to translate it: the cat translation must indicate that cats, in general, are soft or furred, that they are slinky and athletic, and so on. A translation might be simple and stylized, or it might be relatively naturalistic, taking on characteristics such as surface detail or effects of light. Graphic translation differs from conventional illustration in that its visual language, or "form language"— the marks used to make the drawing—is reduced to the point that there's nothing extra, only

These leaf translations all share the quality of recognition, but the language of each one is different, affording knowledge of specific aspects of the idea "leaf" from alternately physical and metaphorical viewpoints.

The translation language used to portray U.S. President Abraham Lincoln uses the interaction of light and shadow but renders these shapes with texture that suggests this image is a statue of Lincoln, further enhancing his status as a historical and cultural icon.
METROPOLITAN GROUP
UNITED STATES

Bold, naturalistic—yet simplified—translations of tools give an authentic brand voice to the website of a longtime, family-owned construction business.
TIMOTHY SAMARA
UNITED STATES

In a nod to illustration styles of the mid-twentieth century, this translation focuses on a simplified breakdown of light and shadow to clarify the form, while specific details—the bright buttons and the shine of the boot—add information. RESEARCH STUDIOS UNITED KINGDOM

the shapes and marks needed to describe the subject. The medium used for the drawing is important only if its characteristic marks help describe the subject's form or feeling. A scratchy texture made by charcoal, for example, might be appropriate in describing the fragility or dryness of an autumn leaf, but the texture does not exist for its own sake. Most often, a translation is developed simultaneously with other visual material in a layout—the designer chooses translation as the illustrative option in advance—so that its shape, details, and textural qualities are dynamically integrated with photographs, typeface selection, abstract elements, and their positioning, in combination with the qualities of the translation.

Clever reversals of positive and negative, together with the exaggerated undulation of the octopus's tentacles, imparts the sinuous action of the animal's movement. GREG FALCONI/UNIVERSITY OF THE ARTS UNITED STATES

The massive dark forms in this translation of a bear are supported by its expression and sharp, jagged contour lines that bring out its inner beast. SARAH BIRMINGHAM/ UNIVERSITY OF THE ARTS UNITED STATES

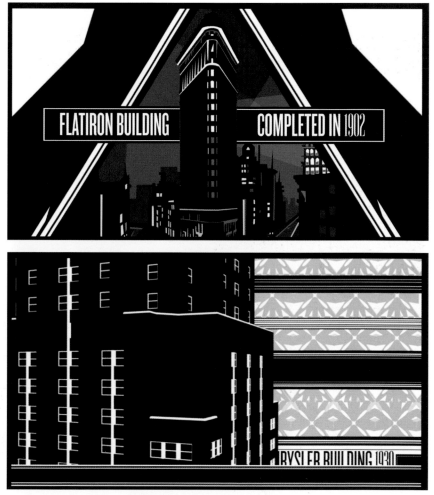

This motion sequence about the history of iconic, twentieth-century skyscrapers delivers its information with translations and graphic patterning that echoes the design aesthetics of the time period. LLOYD KIM/SCHOOL OF VISUAL ARTS UNITED STATES

Collage: Old and New Assembling graphic elements in a free pictorial composition, called "collage," is a relatively recent development in illustration. It derives from the evolution of representation in fine art from depicting a strictly singular viewpoint through the construction of multiple viewpoints, or cubism, into incorporating multiple viewpoints of several, possibly physically unrelated, scenes or references. Collage was initially used to add two-dimensional printed or found material—labels, fabric, bits of newspaper, flat pieces of wood, and so on—into paintings, but, with the rise of photography as a medium, it quickly incorporated photographic images. Collaging photographic images, rather than illustrative images, is usually called "photomontage" and has been a popular method of illustration since the 1920s. Collage is a highly intuitive illustrative approach that takes into account not only the possibility of disparate subjects appearing in one space but also the nature of the combined elements—meaning how exactly they were made. Drawn and painted components can coexist with cut or torn pieces of textured paper, cropped images, scraps of fabric, parts of actual objects, and other drawn, painted, or printed material. Given that the pictorial space in a collage is abstract because of its fragmented construction, the designer must resolve

Examples of collage show the varied possibilities in combining material: cut and torn paper; found text and images; three-dimensional material. Digital collage allows for photographic effects—transparency, blending, blurring, intricate silhouetting, and masking not possible with conventional, cut-and-paste techniques.

Collage offers the designer of this book tremendous variety in formal qualities that add contrast and vitality to simple shapes. Typography, found engraving, paint marks, transparent overlays, and crinkled texture all combine to resolve the movement and spatial interaction of the composition.
ANDREAS ORTAG AUSTRIA

compositional issues similar to those in any other image; but he or she must also address each item's internal visual qualities—overall visual activity, flatness of color relative to texture, and recognizability of the source material (such as printed words or croppings of image).

In particular, because the source components of a collage might be recognizable, the conceptual relationship between abstract and representational elements is extremely important. Integrating recognizable imagery, with its own subjects and messages, helps direct the message and adds degrees of meaning. Collage is still a common approach to illustration and page layout in the digital environment, where not only scanned images of found

or hand-generated material can be combined with photographic material, but also where photographic effects such as transparency, multiple exposure, blurring, and silhouetting—techniques made possible only by the computer—can be investigated.

The cutout letters of the word "democracy" hint at the political dialogue inherent in that social system. The scissors and the work gloves suggest democracy's constructive nature. STUDIO INTERNATIONAL CROATIA

Enormous digital collages of spliced photographs and rhythmic lines of type wrap the walls of the administrative offices of Madison Square Garden, an iconic venue in New York City. POULIN+MORRIS UNITED STATES

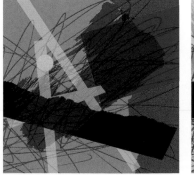

In this study, the message changes as the content of the collage's components is changed. As the content becomes more recognizable, the collage transmits a more literal and, therefore, more specific message.

Type as Image When a letter or word takes on pictorial qualities beyond those that define their form, they become images in their own right and their semantic potential is enormous. Words that are also pictures fuse several kinds of understanding together: they are supersigns. As their meaning is assimilated through each perceptual filter—visual, emotional, intellectual—they assume the evocative stature of a symbol. Understanding on each level is immediate, and a viewer's capacity to recall images makes such word pictures highly effective in recalling the verbal content associated with them. As is true with so many aspects of strong typographic design, making type into an image means defining a simple relationship between the intrinsic form of the letters and some other visual idea. It is easy to get lost in the endless possibilities of type manipulation and obscure the visual message or dilute it.

A viewer is likely to perceive and easily remember one strong message over five weaker ones—complexity is desirable, whereas complication is not. Type can be transformed into an image by using a variety of approaches. Each provides a different avenue of exploration, and several might be appropriate both to the desired communication and to the formal aspects of the type itself.

Logo TIEN-MIN LIAO UNITED STATES

Exhibition poster TIMOTHY SAMARA UNITED STATES

Logo TIMOTHY SAMARA UNITED STATES

Title treatment LEONARDO SONNOLI ITALY

Wordmark study YOOJUNG KANG UNITED STATES

Logo RAIDY PRINTING GROUP LEBANON

Logo DEBRA OHAYON UNITED STATES

Title treatment PAONE DESIGN ASSOC. UNITED STATES

Form alteration changes the structural characteristics of type elements, manipulating them to communicate nonliteral ideas.

Deconstruction changes the visual relationships between the parts of text, calling out the relation of its structure to its meaning or spoken rhythm.

Form substitution is a strategy in which a type form is replaced by an icon or symbol whose visual structure still reads as that of the type it has replaced.

Illustration CATHERINE CASALINO UNITED STATES

Winery logo JELENA DROBAC SERBIA [L]
BiblioMetro logo MANUEL ESTRADA SPAIN [R]

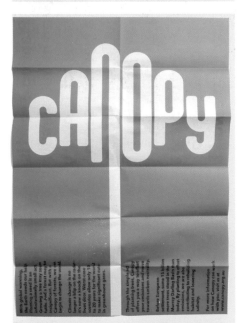
Eco-services poster PARALLAX AUSTRALIA

Logo SOOIM HEO/SVA UNITED STATES [L]
Logo EUIKYUNG LEE/SVA UNITED STATES [R]

Logo MV DESIGN UNITED STATES

Concert poster MIXER SWITZERLAND

Logo DEBORAH GRUBER UNITED STATES

Logo C+G PARTNERS UNITED STATES

Book cover LOUISE FILI LTD. UNITED STATES

Title treatment FINEST MAGMA GERMANY

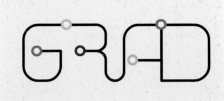
Transit logo BRUKETA+ZINIC CROATIA

Pictorialization occurs as the result of typography becoming a representation of a real-world object or taking on the qualities of something from actual experience.

Pictorial inclusion refers to bringing illustrative elements into the type forms so that they interact with its strokes or counterspaces.

Ornamentation Typography can be transformed with graphical details, such as borders, dots, lines, dingbats, and other embellishments.

Strategies for Composition Composition in an illustrated image is of great concern. In creating a drawn image—especially one that is naturalistic—designers sometimes forget that they are not bound by the realities of arrangement imposed by the scene they are rendering. Using the formal relationships of figure and ground (see chapter 1, page 32) on an abstract level—particularly within a realistic representation—contributes to the illustration's power to communicate beyond the literal as well as helps engage the viewer and direct the eye. To simply place the subject in the central area of the illustration, without regard to the subject's outer contour, tension, and contrast of negative space, and so on, prevents the illustration from being resolved and creates a static presentation. Just as cropping, position, relative sizes of elements, and contrast between linearity, mass, angles, and curves are intrinsic to the decisive layout of graphic elements and typography in a page environment, so too is their refinement within an illustrated image of utmost importance—and such considerations apply equally to photographed images.

Massing the collaged elements along a horizon lends concrete spatial realism to the scene, despite its textural and abstract surface qualities. The massing of dark areas also forces a sense of perspective that draws the viewer inward; this triangulated movement is counteracted by the circular title cluster at the top. 2FRESH TURKEY

Fragmented, overlapping photographs and text elements create a dimensional space that speaks of a Holocaust survivor's shattered childhood. LABORATÓRIO SECRETO BRAZIL

The positioning of the three highly reductive graphical figures of soldiers in the lower part of this LP sleeve's format causes them to appear to "slide" along the horizon; the evenness of their spacing and the cropping of the two outer figures—each to a different degree—enhances the sense of regular, marching movement. Breaking this regimented movement by turning the middle soldier's head downward draws attention to this figure, who now personifies the contemplative question of the LP's title.
BIG ACTIVE UNITED KINGDOM

A pictorial image is deconstructed here to show the various compositional strategies—beyond the selection of subject and medium—that the designer has considered in creating a well-resolved image. Each aspect of the composition reinforces the others.

Positive and negative shapes

Contrast between mass and line

Optical weight distribution

Value distribution

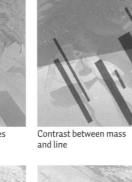

Perspective and spatial depth

Directional movement

Color relationships

Contrasts in surface activity

Mixing Image Styles As with all compositional strategies, creating contrast among visual elements is key to surprising, refreshing, and enlivening layouts—and this is no less true for imagery. Aside from the big-picture contrasts afforded by changing sizes, shapes, color, and spatial arrangement, combining different modes of image offers an important and highly effective method for introducing contrast. Very textural, linear illustration, for instance,

This concise (yet by no means comprehensive) table compares the same pair of subjects presented in various combinations of image mode. Evaluate each pairing for similarities, as well as disparities, in visual form; which combinations produce the most unified visual relationships, and which have the most contrast? Then consider which combinations might also be the most useful for comparing related concepts, and which offer the richest interplay of concept.

The decision to present the background image in illustrative form stems from the need to solve two problems. First, the designer wanted to avoid visual conflict between two photographs; the flatness of the illustration style visually separates it from the photograph and causes it to recede into the background. Second, the illustration enhances the temporal metaphor created by the two images—one showing a historical stage in cultural development, the other showing a developmental stage in education. TIMOTHY SAMARA
UNITED STATES

From the moment they enter the world, children are gathering information. At first, learning is random—sights, sounds, tastes, textures. But before long, their natural curiosity demands more.

At Manlius Pebble Hill, students from Pre-K to postgraduate study find a colorful world of creativity and discovery. Enthusiastic, innovative faculty keep learning activities exciting and interesting; in turn, students are enthusiastic and highly motivated.

They're comfortable too. Although we refer to Lower, Middle and Upper schools, MPH is really one integrated school. Upper grade students become friends and mentors by "adopting" lower grades and through our Peer Leadership program. And because our classes are small, students and teachers really get to know each other.

Children Become Students at Birth

The result is no surprise. Our students learn more and learn better in a caring, respectful setting.

More important, they want to learn—it's fun!

"We have homework this year. That's different from last year. We're doing a lot of cut out pages...and CSMP; that's the way we do math. I like that."

Kelsey Kelly Weiner
Class of '10

STONEHENGE

CA . 2500 BC

will contrast richly with photography—which tends to be continuous in tone—as well as with flat, solid graphic elements. It's important that, while the different styles being combined contrast with each other decisively, they also share some visual qualities. Similar to how these other decisions radically affect communication (as well as compositional quality), the decisions a designer makes regarding image types—icon, symbol, textural drawing, lush photograph—affect communication as well. Each kind of image brings certain associations with it. Photographs are associated with documentation or assumed to represent reality. They are concrete, pure, environmental, and reliable. Illustrations are perceived as "created" and personal, readily showing their method of creation; they evoke fantasy, display impossible or ideal situations, and portray their content in a subjective way—even if they are naturalistic. Icons, symbols, and translations distill and simplify complicated, abstract ideas; they are most often associated with diagrams, navigation, and identification. The designer must combine image styles selectively to support a given purpose, using the qualities of each to appropriately convey intended messages and interact with each other in a unified visual language that assimilates their differences as part of their logic.

A sparkling, pixellated texture, rendered in multiple colors, merges with the photographic environment to suggest the improvisational vitality of a musical genre. **HELMO** FRANCE

Imagery that lies between the abstract and the concrete offers the viewer multiple levels of intrigue. Which is the real image in this poster detail; which is the abstraction? One kind of image, an icon or abstraction of sound waves as seen digitally, is used to create the lights and darks of a larger image: a face. **MIXER** SWITZERLAND

Selecting and Manipulating Content

A picture, as the saying goes, is worth a thousand words. Which words those are, however, is up to the designer and—in the context of photographic images, especially—by the designer and/or a photographer. A designer inventing an illustrative image from scratch naturally must select all the components (figures, objects, or otherwise) to be included. While this is equally true when conceiving a photograph to be taken, many designers overlook a similar level of calculation that photographs require—themselves fooled by the idea that the photograph is an image of "reality," they make the assumption that it will simply capture what is needed from whatever happens to exist within the viewfinder … and that they need accept it as is. The choice of the pictorial elements contained or not within a photograph, regardless of subject matter, is entirely their own, and has tremendous implications for meaning. Given a similar assumption that viewers will make upon seeing a photographic image—that everything about it is real—every aspect of what it shows, and how, must be considered.

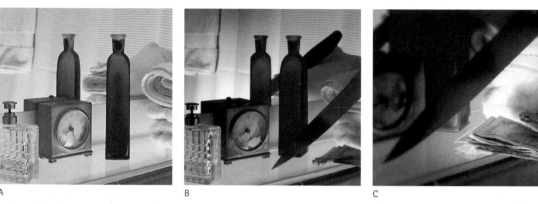

A   B   C

In this study of an image for a mystery novel's cover, the information conveyed by the image is altered—sometimes subtly, and sometimes dramatically—as a result of changes in content and composition. In the first version of the image (A), the content and lighting provide neutral facts: The viewer is in a bathroom, probably at a hotel. In version (B), this content is clarified by the addition of a hotel key—but altered through the addition of the knife and money, signifying foul play. The dramatic change in lighting, from even to more extreme, as well as the unusual direction of the light, enhances the sinister mood and further hints that something is wrong: Why is the light on the floor? In the final version (C), a closer viewpoint helps create a feeling of paranoia—what's happening beyond the frame is unknown—and focuses attention on specific details: the time on the clock, the point of the knife, the money, and the hotel key. The manipulation of the light, as well as selective focus, helps draw attention to elements that may be relevant to the story.

The same figure is shown here photographed from the same viewpoint in different environments. Although the figure is the focus of the message, the environment affects the tone of the message, adds secondary meaning, and positions the figure in different relationships to the viewer.

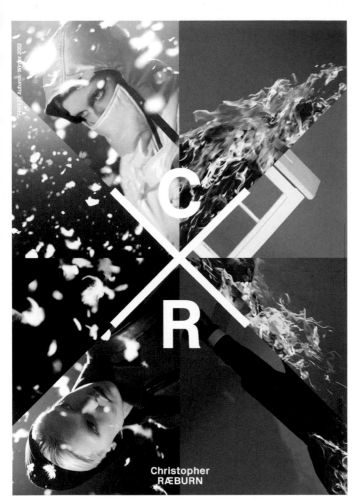

The photographs in this fashion ad are reasonably direct—using simple props to suggest seasons—but they take on a metaphorical quality when rotated in a quadrant formation, evoking the endless turning of the fashion industry's seasons.
RÉGIS TOSETTI UNITED KINGDOM

Conscious artifice informs these two photographs. The image at top crops the figure out of the frame in favor of her ephemeral reflection; the image at bottom uses a prop—an award medal—to dramatize quality and personify the product. RESEARCH STUDIOS UNITED KINGDOM [TOP] / VOICE AUSTRALIA [BOTTOM]

Subject and Context An image's primary subject is important, of course, but equally (and sometimes, more critically) important are the elements that surround it, and with which it interacts. That is, the fact of the primary subject is a given, and it's the story around them that really matters. Clothing catalogs, for example—often use setting and props to convey concepts about lifestyle by showing people wearing the clothes in particular locations or situations. While such images demonstrate the look of the clothes on real people, they position the clothes relative to a lifestyle: The scene or set, as well as objects included as props, are actually delivering the important information. Similarly, leaving certain facts out of a photograph might be just as influential as choosing what to include. Cropping an image, or adjusting the viewpoint, to edit unnecessary information, is important to keep viewers focused on a subject without distraction. More extreme cropping may further alter that focus or create mood: Cropping a portrait tightly to a subject's face may emphasize his or her emotional life. Finally, it almost goes without saying that software allows a designer to completely change the context in which a subject appears, thereby constructing its reality—and its narrative—in whatever way will be most relevant or beneficial for the intended communication.

Subject Alteration Even if a designer's sensibility—or the tone of a particular project—leans toward a photographic approach, there's no requirement that the photographic material be deployed in its unadulterated form. Tonal changes (discussed in the second chapter, page 86) whether through color enhancement or the use of ink separations (duotoning and tritoning) are, of course, useful options. In addition, montage and overlay of multiple images, and hybridizing elements from different photographic sources, present numerous interesting possibilities. Surprisingly, even the most surreal combinations of unexpected subject elements, when made from photographic ingredients, often will be perceived by viewers as convincing because of their expectation that the medium relies on capturing subjects that actually exist. Radical alteration of a photographic object may, in fact, not only be overlooked as physically impossible, but may sometimes add such a viscerally experiential quality that a viewer will perceive it as more "real" an experience than if they had been confronted by the subject in its natural state—transforming the neutral image of a clock into that of a reverberating alarm by intensifying its saturation and overlapping it in repetition, for example, or selectively blurring a sharply static image of a car in a way that

Because photographic images are so readily perceived as depictions of reality, designers have incredible leeway in manipulating them without sacrificing believability. Despite the surreal situation depicted in the top image, for example, viewers will find it easy to accept the scene as credible. Further, this automatic assumption about the veracity of a photograph permits designers to evoke sensory experiences through their manipulation. Presenting a graphically exaggerated photograph of an object, as seen in the lower example, trades on its believability and the corollary common understanding of its function to create an immediately recognizable aural experience.

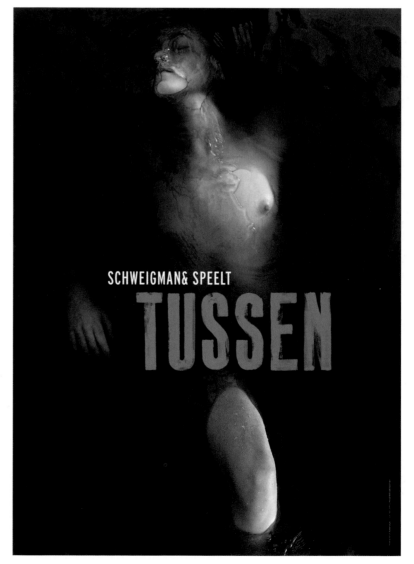

The lighting in this image is purposely cast from a low angle to illuminate only certain parts of the body.
STUDIO JONA NETHERLANDS

throws it into motion. From a purely practical standpoint, altering photographs in a dramatic way that appears purposeful can erase unwanted problems and mask the poor quality of images over which the designer has no control—for instance, those supplied by a client with no budget for commissioned, or even stock, photography. Blemishes from damaged prints, dust and spots from poor scans, uneven lighting, and pixellation created by enlarging small, low-resolution images—all these, and more, may be obviated by the clever use of textural filters and overlays of graphical patterns, as well as by selective changes in an image's tonal levels. In addition to overcoming a poor-quality image's challenges, a designer may find that he or she also has created something entirely new and far more interesting than even a high-quality image may have provided from the outset.

Altering a photograph is also a means of hiding the inferior quality images that are sometimes supplied by clients: poor lighting, surface problems from scratched prints or bad scans, and blurring or softness from low-resolution images. Selectively adjusting contrast levels in an image's tonal areas, or applying textural effects or filters available in software can dramatically improve an image by introducing new syntax, rather than through an attempt to fix the problems.

The photographic subjects in these annual report spreads are altered simply through mono-tone coloration—and more complexly, by splicing them to create hybrids as they cross the page gutter to transform into another subject.
BRUKETA+ZINIC CROATIA

Narrative Interplay A single photograph delivers a powerful punch of "semantic" content—conceptual, verbal, and emotional meaning that likely includes messages that are not literally represented in its subject. Putting photographs together increases their semantic power and creates narrative or storytelling; the instant two images can be compared, whether juxtaposed or arranged in sequence, a viewer will try to establish meaningful connec-

tions between them. Every photograph will influence any others around it, changing their individual meanings and contributing to a progression in narrative as a result. For example, a viewer might see an image of a biker and a second image of a man in a hospital bed and construct a story about a biking accident. Neither image represents this idea; the narrative occurs in the viewer's mind. Even concluding that the man in the hospital bed is the same biker is an

assumption the viewer creates. This distance between what is shown in two images and what the viewer makes happen internally is a kind of "semantic gap." Substituting the hospital image for one that shows a biker at the finish line of a race changes the narrative. The semantic gap is smaller and, therefore, a more literal progression, but the gap exists because the viewer still assumes the two bikers are the same person. As more images are juxtaposed or added in

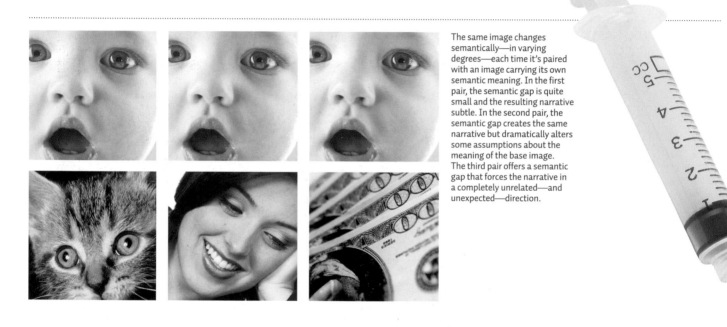

The same image changes semantically—in varying degrees—each time it's paired with an image carrying its own semantic meaning. In the first pair, the semantic gap is quite small and the resulting narrative subtle. In the second pair, the semantic gap creates the same narrative but dramatically alters some assumptions about the meaning of the base image. The third pair offers a semantic gap that forces the narrative in a completely unrelated—and unexpected—direction.

In this comparison of two sequences beginning with the same base image, the narratives are wildly different, but the narrative momentum of each concludes with assumptions that you, the viewer, has made that aren't necessarily true. The rubble in the last image of the lower sequence is not, empirically, that of the building shown earlier in the sequence. What assumptions have been made about the information in the other sequence that cannot be proven true?

sequence, their narrative reinforces itself based on the increasingly compounded assumptions initially made by viewers. By the time viewers have seen three or four images in a sequence, their capacity to avoid making assumptions decreases and they begin to look for meaning that completes the narrative they have constructed. This "narrative momentum" increases exponentially to the point that viewers will assume the semantic content of any image appearing later in the sequence must be related to that delivered earlier, even if details in the later image empirically contradict those of the first images.

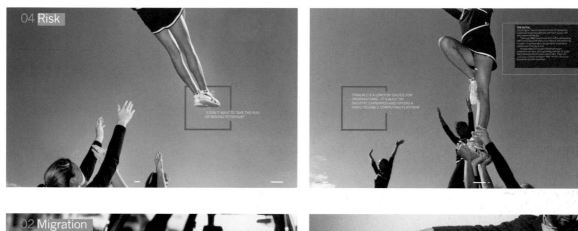

In addition to whatever semantic content an image offers, viewers will project meaning on the image themselves, based on personal, as well as cultural, experience. In the current American cultural context, viewers are likely to project meaning related to "illegal drug use," even though the image doesn't offer any explicit reason for doing so.

Sequencing related images from one spread to the next creates distinct narratives in each set of two page spreads shown at left. In both sequences, the repetition of recognizable, remembered subject components—the cheerleader, the couch—creates narrative momentum: The viewer recognizes a kind of cause and effect because the same object appears in each step of the narrative. In the cheerleader sequence, the semantic or narrative gap is relatively small: The cheerleader is in flight and then is caught and is assumed safe. The gap in the couch sequence is more extreme: We don't see the couch move from one location to the next, but it exists in a very different state in the second spread. We assume that it has been moved and now is being put to use.
LOEWY UNITED KINGDOM

Word and Image: Brainwashing the Narrative Pictures greatly influence each others' meaning … and words, even more so. As soon as words—concrete, accessible, seductive—appear next to an image, the image's meaning is altered forever. Just as there is a semantic gap between images that are juxtaposed, so too is there such a gap between words and pictures. The gap might be relatively small, created by a direct, literal relationship between the two players. Or, the gap may be enormous, allowing the viewer to construct a narrative that is not readily apparent in the image when it appears by itself. The word "death," placed next to an image of a skull, for example, produces a relatively small semantic gap—although not as small a gap as the word "skull" would produce. Consider, however, the same skull image adjacent to the word "love;" the tremendous distance between what is shown and what is told, in this case, presents a world of narrative possibility. Every image is susceptible to change when words appear next to it—so much so that a designer can easily alter the meaning of the same image over and over again by replacing the words that accompany it. In a sequential arrangement in which the same image is repeated in subsequent page spreads but is accompanied each time by a new word or phrase, new experience and knowledge about the image

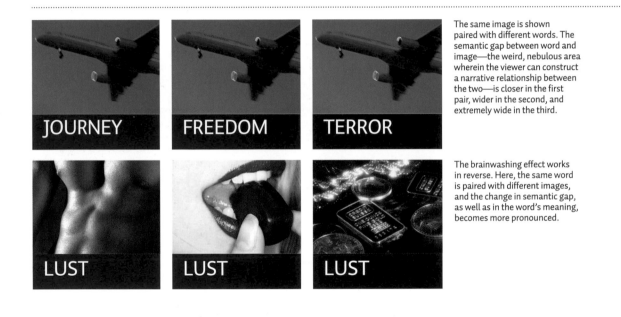

The same image is shown paired with different words. The semantic gap between word and image—the weird, nebulous area wherein the viewer can construct a narrative relationship between the two—is closer in the first pair, wider in the second, and extremely wide in the third.

The brainwashing effect works in reverse. Here, the same word is paired with different images, and the change in semantic gap, as well as in the word's meaning, becomes more pronounced.

Two images of the same person, juxtaposed with two different headlines, create a double identity for the man as teacher and companion. COBRA NORWAY

are introduced to the viewer. Once this knowledge is introduced, the viewer will no longer be able to consider the image in its original context. The meaning of the image, as far as the viewer is concerned, will be the composite meaning that includes all the information acquired through the sequence. Not surprisingly, the ability of images to change the meanings of words is equally profound. This mutual brainwashing effected by words and images depends a great deal on the simultaneity of their presentation—that is, whether the two are shown together, at once, or in succession. If seen simultaneously, word and image will create a single message in which each reciprocally advances the message and neither is truly changed in the viewer's mind—the message is a gestalt. However, if one is seen first and the other second, the viewer has a chance to construct meaning before being influenced. In such cases, the semantic gap is greatly widened and the impact of the change is more dramatic: The viewer, in the short time given to assimilate and become comfortable with the meaning of the first word or image he or she has seen, must give up his or her assumptions and alter his or her mindset.

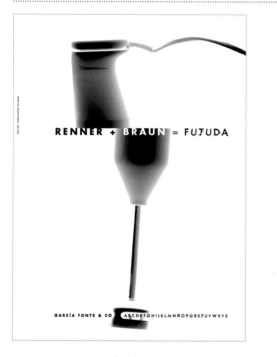

The poster at far left plays on the word Futura, *the name of a typeface, and the Spanish slang term* Futuda, *which means mixed up or messed up (although more vulgar than that). The play on words describes the mixer as a metaphor for remixing or deconstructing to promote a reworked version of the classic sans-serif face. The poster at left presents what seems like a simple tableau in a common room; the word* Jesus *transforms it into an altar of personal domesticity.*
LSD SPAIN [LEFT]
FINEST MAGMA GERMANY [RIGHT]

Although the difference between the sharp photograph in the television and the blurred image that follows it creates a sense that the blurred image is a televised image, the juxtaposition of the words creates a different—yet possibly related—meaning for the viewer: that real life is less tangible than that depicted on television. BRETT YASKO
UNITED STATES

Ever Metaphor? In writing and speech, a metaphor is an expression—a word or phrase—that refers to an intuitively unrelated idea, creating additional meaning. A sensitive young man's intense romantic yearning may be described in terms of a delicate, but clinging, vine; the exceptionally productive woman in one's office may be labeled a "machine." Images can be used in much the same way: A designer may present an image that means something else entirely, refers to a much broader concept, or combines concepts to evoke a third concept that is not explicit in either of the combinants. "Visual metaphors" are messages of parity; a literal subject is recast as equivalent to another subject. One option is to depict one thing behaving, pictorially, like another—presenting products in an urban cosmetics brochure, for instance, configured as a city skyline. Yet another possibility is to combine two or more seemingly unrelated images to suggest another form with its own meaning, implying some narrative connection between ideas—showing a corn cob with wheels to suggest the idea of plant-based auto fuel. A designer may also consider altering one image by having another act upon it—chopping the first image up, mixing it into a texture, pushing it out of the way, making it vibrate, and so on.

The graphic shape of the cigarette creates a focus of attention, letterboxing the action in this sequence of frames from a public service commercial. It also confines and traps the people and then metaphorically burns them to ash. 2FRESH TURKEY

By presenting the text in this poster as though it is actually on the reverse and then folded forward, the designer transforms the printed communication into a metaphor for the architectural and gestural qualities of the dance it promotes. SULKI+MIN SOUTH KOREA

The placement of the repeated, green logotype at floor level along the glass wall creates a grassy environment, bringing the outdoors inside and vice versa. PEOPLE DESIGN UNITED STATES

Trading on audiences' cultural, political, historical, and personal experiences by merging or altering commonly agreed-upon symbolic or allusive meanings is a strategy designers may utilize to deliver startling messages—startling and eminently powerful because they not only tend to necessitate unique inventions of form but, more importantly, because they draw upon deeply-ingrained understanding, memory, and social themes to provoke exaggerated responses that resonate deeply in a target audience. Symbols are signs that hold meaning that comes to be understood through socialization, an "agreed upon" signification in which the members of a social group participate. Symbols have ritual depth and significance; simply juxtaposing certain ones, or constructing one using another, equally symbolic image, is bound to elicit a dramatic (and potentially provocative) metaphor.

Transforming lipsticks into bullets creates a metaphorical dialogue about the nature of gender relations and aggression. **THOMAS CSANO** CANADA

The meaning of the elements brought together in a collage is important—and not just what the images portray but their medium of creation as well. In these two posters for a film festival, the film reel is iconic and modern and both times portrayed as an apple whose symbolic meaning is one of knowledge. The engraved images connote a connection to history, and the photographic transparencies and gradation changes suggest the element of light. **ADAMSMORIOKA** UNITED STATES

In this conceptual promotional piece, small cubes of sugar are wrapped in typography that expresses ideas about "sweetness" from a survey and packages them together. **COMA** NETHERLANDS

Visual forms or styles associated with particular events, cultural contexts, or day-to-day experience—what is referred to by the term "vernacular"—may be invoked to create a form language that makes this connection for the viewer. One might, for example, lay out an invitation to a travel-themed fund-raising event to look like an airline ticket, using the type styles, colors, and other visual details—even the format and production techniques—of such tickets as a source. Or, as another example, a blog devoted to exposing potentially sinister or laughably inept political conduct might be designed to mimic the cover designs of pulp fiction or horror novels, or comic books. Aesthetic styles from times past present a rich treasure trove of metaphorical possibilities—evoking the authoritative pomp of medieval heraldry for a manufacturer of luxury handbags, for instance, or aligning a contemporary furniture company with the experimental, aspirational energy of the early twentieth century's avant-garde movements.

The floral wallpaper used to cover this book evokes the tasteful parlors of higher class English culture. MICHELLE LIV/PARSONS SCHOOL OF DESIGN UNITED STATES

This CD cover appropriates the vernacular language of scribbled high school binders. STEREOTYPE DESIGN UNITED STATES

```
211
rfd


Dean, Rebecca F.
Library Science Consultant
beccadean@riseup.net
347 834-6740
```

The typography of this card is a metaphor for the client's area of practice. MARIS BELLACK UNITED STATES

Typographic form, of course, when used as image (see page 214 in this chapter), is rich with possibilities for creating metaphor; but even before explicitly creating an image through pictorialization or more radical form-alteration approaches, the selection of a particular typeface can easily call to mind a particular region, time period, or other metaphorical reference (also see chapter 3, page 138). There are as many ways to create metaphors as there are ideas and images—in short, an endless array limited only by imagination. While the literal content of images provides a baseline communication, a thoughtful designer can evoke higher-level concepts above and beyond what they merely show. The result is a richer, more inventive, and more memorable and meaningful experience for the audience.

The two digits in the infamous date fall into a cascade of dominoes, implying the resulting political and cultural ramifications of a terrorist attack.
LESLEY MOORE NETHERLANDS

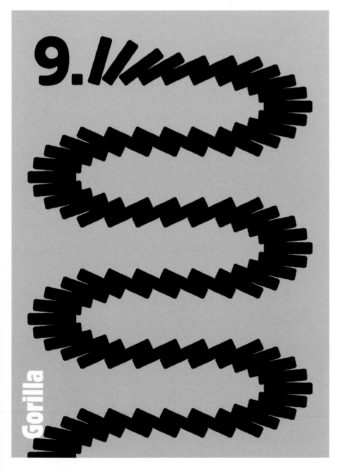

Presenting the numerals as large architectural elements is a kind of photographic pictorialization that metaphorically supports the subject matter of the poster but also transforms the text—verbal ideas—into concrete constructions. STUDIO INTERNATIONAL CROATIA

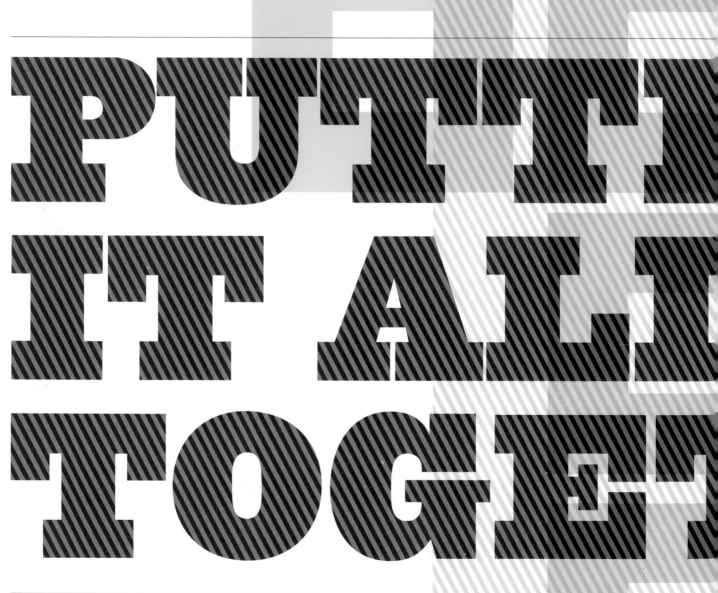

PUTTING IT ALL TOGETHER

CHAPTER 05

> There is no recipe for a good layout. What must be maintained is a feeling of change and contrast.

ALEXEY BRODOVITCH/*Pioneering graphic designer and art director*

Two Things Becoming One In the simplest terms, every design project incorporates just two different parts—type and image—and so the most important question to address, therefore, is: "How exactly do I put these two different things together?" Getting type to interact dynamically with imagery, in a unified way, poses a serious problem for many designers. The challenge stems from the fundamental differences between type and everything else.

Sure, type behaves in accordance with the same visual rules that apply to images (as we have seen), but while images exhibit formal qualities in staggering variety, type is always type: graphical lines, making patterns of other lines. And these lines are all words—they mean something, which inevitably creates a strange disconnect for designers when trying to analyze its very specific visual qualities relative to the more intuitively understandable visual

qualities of pictures and graphical shapes. The results of poorly integrated type and image fall into two categories: The first includes type that has nothing in common with the images around it; the second includes typography that has been so aggressively integrated with image that it becomes illegible or unnavigable. Overcoming type's stark, alien difference from other visual material and, in so doing, avoiding either of the aforementioned

Alternating dark and light typographic elements in the upper portion of this brochure cover repeat the dark and light value breaks in the landscape image.
ANDREAS ORTAG AUSTRIA

The text, inset images, and linear graphic forms are organized on a grid of vertical and horizontal axes to unify their proportions. LSD SPAIN

Both the type and the spliced image are composed on a symmetrical axis; the headline's staggered overlapping, as well as the informational text's deep rags, echo this irregular movement in the image.
JUNE KIM/PARSONS SCHOOL OF DESIGN UNITED STATES

scenarios depends on finding more particular areas of common ground between the limited formal qualities that type exhibits and the more varied kinds among images. Laying type into or across an image is a quick way of finding visual relationships. Their immediate juxtaposition will reveal similarities among elements in each, as well as opposition among others. The rag of a short paragraph might have a similar shape as a foreground element in a photo-

graph, for instance, even while the paragraph's optimal width, being horizontal in proportion, opposes the same foreground element's verticality. The fundamental difference between type's linear patterning and the photograph's continuous tonality is unavoidable; even so, commonality is present in at least one aspect between them—shape—in similar, as well as opposing, ways. And, there are likely other such relationships to be found as well.

So, to simplify matters for the sake of this discussion, it's easiest to break down these two states of possible type/image relationship—formal congruence, or similarity, and formal opposition, or contrast—into categories that concern only four different attributes: shape, texture, value, and rhythm. Initially concerning oneself only with these attributes makes it easier to integrate typography and image overall.

Both the wide callout on the left-hand page of this spread and the group of shallow columns on the right share proportions with elements in the image. The relative positions of the two groupings restate the image's major diagonal axis. LOEWY UNITED KINGDOM

Combining vertical and horizontal positioning of type elements helps integrate the linear movement of both type and image, as well as permits the currency's denomination to be read when the bill is held at either angle. MARCIA LISANTO/ LAGUNA COLLEGE OF ART AND DESIGN UNITED STATES

The staggered movement and size change of the type correspond to the vertical movement of the sewing machine needle—contrasting it with horizontal motion— and the flow of fabric through the sewing machine. VCU QATAR QATAR

Formal Congruence Similarities between type elements and pictorial elements make a strong connection between the two. When typographic configurations display similar attributes to an adjacent image, or expand on those attributes, the type and the image are said to be formally congruent. Such similarities are to be found in four basic attributes: those of shape, texture, value, and rhythm.

The attribute of shape includes the exterior planar contours of both text and image elements (rectilinear, curvilinear, and so on), as well as their proportions (tall versus wide); and on the internal shapes of a text element's line breaks or rag. Restating the shape of a building in the contour of a text block, for instance, or breaking lines of text to mimic the rhythm of inward and outward shaping of a city skyline are both examples of shape-based congruence.

The attribute of texture focuses on typeface: the apparent surface activity it imparts to a field of text; and the graphical qualities of its characters' details. In the first instance, the roughness of a stone wall in an image might correspond to an irregular, weight alternation in a paragraph of serif text; in the second instance, it may be that details in an image of a wrought iron fence are picked up by ball serifs and swashes in a chosen font.

Formal congruence between type and image in this magazine spread—separated from each other on facing pages—helps unify the distinct halves of the layout.
STUDIO VIE AUSTRIA

Shape Congruence
The title, deck, and horizontal set of columns echo the horizontal intervals in the image; the thin vertical line restates the vertical axis of the figure.

Texture Congruence
Through the choice of typeface, a serif with pronounced contrast, the blocks of text exhibit strong surface activity that relates to the surface textures in the image. The loose spacing of the headline in two weights reflects the pattern of light and dark linear elements on the wall behind the figure.

Value Congruence
The type is distributed spatially from top to bottom such that its dark form and the light negative spaces in between groupings relates to the alternating rhythm and proportions of light and dark in the image.

Rhythm Congruence
The strong optical pull of the image's central axis is restated by the thin vertical line but also through the contrast of the horizontally proportioned elements pulling inward and pushing outward from the center.

Value—just as it is with regard to color—is an attribute focused on relative lightness and darkness and, similar to the attribute of shape, immediately distinguishable. A type element may be similarly as dark as, or as light as, some component of an image. This relative darkness or lightness may be the result of scale change (in a big, bold, element), a spacing change (looser versus tighter), or a transparency change (solid color versus a tint of that color).

The attribute of rhythm is, perhaps, the most subtle relationship of congruence to define and exploit. It focuses primarily on interval (spacing) relationships: how close or far apart are elements within an image, as compared to how so among blocks or lines of text; but it may also, on a smaller scale, have to do with the internal stroke/counter rhythm within a body of text.

Formal congruence between type and image may be a direct, one-to-one relationship—the type element literally repeats the image attributes in every way—or indirect, extrapolating the attributes' logic. An image may be composed of curves and circles, for example; the type that accompanies it need not be shaped and positioned in direct repetition—simply curving the type in arcs or forming paragraphs into rounded clusters is enough.

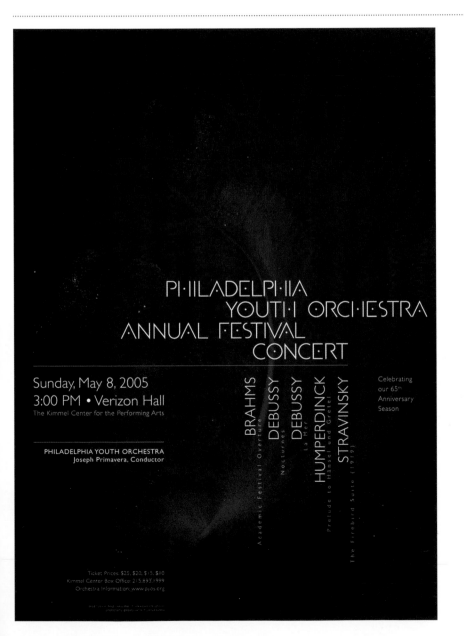

Shape Congruence
The curving form of the feather image is echoed by the optical curves implied by the type's masses and positions.

Texture Congruence
The feather's wispy, linar fronds are restated by the delicate, linear typeface and by the irregular rag shapes created by the type's varying line lengths.

Value Congruence
The bright value of the reversed type corresponds in its position to the brighter-value areas within the image.

Rhythm Congruence
The vertical and lateral push-and-pull of the feather's contours and areas of visual emphasis are restated by similar emphases in the type, established in the positions of wider and narrower, larger and smaller, clusters of text.

Careful attention to relationships in texture, movement, and visual stress and openness between type and image establish their formal congruence. PAONE DESIGN ASSOCIATES UNITED STATES

Formal Opposition Relating typographic elements to images by contrasting their visual characteristics is also a viable way of integrating them. Although seemingly counterintuitive, creating formal opposition between the two kinds of material actually can help clarify their individual characteristics. In doing so, the fundamental quality of the attribute being thus contrasted comes to light as a kind of "after-image": An image may be dramati-cally divided into horizontal bands by a boundary defined by value, for example, while the text juxtaposed with it is set in a vertically-proportioned block. The discrepancy between the image's horizontal logic and the type's vertical logic calls to mind a commonality: both relate to the attribute of shape. All four of the major attributes that serve as sources for congruence may act as sources for opposition. The greater the intermingling of congruence and opposition among these attributes, the richer the type-to-image relationships become. The caveat is that some congruence between the elements must also exist so that the opposing characteristics are brought clearly into focus. In the same way that a hierarchy is destroyed if all the elements are completely different, the strength of the contrast in opposing forms is weakened if all their characteristics are completely different.

In this page spread of a season program for a theater, the type and the image exhibit clear contrasts in their organization and textural qualities. The presence of each kind of contrast calls attention to its opposing quality in each component.
VOICE AUSTRALIA

Shape Opposition
The main image element is a vertical form of narrow proportion; the clustered typography creates a wide horizontal shape of deep proportion.

Texture Opposition
Most of the surfaces and contours visible in the image are smooth and lack texture. The typography, in contrast, is exceptionally textural—both in the brushy quality of its drawing and in the heavily irregular contours of its external and internal stroke edges.

Value Opposition
While the image is light in value, and shows little contrast in tonal range, the type is generally dark and exhibits a great degree of light and dark change within it.

Rhythm Opposition
The mannequin form is static and visually concise; the type opposes this quietness with a tremendous amount of inward and outward movement among strokes, shifting height positions for internal elements, and complex edge contours—as well as apparent shifts in relative foreground/background position of elements.

Accomplishing this state of tension is most easily achieved by using what could be called the "seesaw" method—establishing degrees of congruence and opposition that create a kind of equilibrium. Maybe all the type elements juxtaposed with an image share attributes of shape, texture, and rhythm, but two of the type elements severely oppose the image in terms of value. Or, perhaps each individual type element's attributes are congruent with just one of the attributes of each of the image's elements—but opposes each with regard to a different attribute. As one increases the kind (and degree) of opposition in one or more attributes, between more elements, it becomes important to establish simpler, more pronounced kinds of congruency between others to ensure that the oppositional qualities don't dominate and cause the unity between type and image to disintegrate.

Shape Opposition
The shapes within the image are very specific—a half-dot and a radial configuration of tringles—and their relative scales are very similar. The type elements are very different in size and show a variety of shapes.

Texture Opposition
The type is primarily pattern-like in the typeface chosen for the title and in the small-scale informational text; the image is made up primarily of flat color fields.

Value Opposition
Dark and light elements—of both the typography and the image—alternate with each other in position, rather than follow each other around the format.

Rhythm Opposition
The image's contour exhibits a radially organized, inward and outward movement; the type, on the other hand, is made up of many small clusters that appear scattered around the central area of the format, lurching to the left and right, up and down.

The scale differences and textural variation of this poster's typographic elements oppose the more regular structure, rhythm, and large-scale planar forms of the nonpictorial image forms.
STUDIO LESBEAUXJOURS FRANCE

Spatial Considerations Another aspect of integrating type and image is the consideration of relationships between the image's field and the type element relative to that of the negative space in a given format. Images may be presented in three ways: silhouetted (retaining their contours or being "cut out" so they "float" within the format); "full bleed" (filling the format from edge to edge in all directions); or inset (cropped into a shape, such as a rectangle,

that is appreciable as a compositional form even if it bleeds [touches] one or two edges). In whichever of these states an image appears, the positional relationship of any accompanying type engenders a new question: Is the type on top of the image, embedded within it, or simply next to it?

Type adjacent to an image remains a totally separate entity. Its relationship to the image depends on its positioning and any correspondence between its compositional elements and those in the image. This will be true whether the image itself is silhouetted or cropped into a shape and inset. The relative visual density, scale, or value of the two will cause one or the other to be perceived as occupying either a foreground or background position. Alternatively, the

When images are discrete compositional objects within a space, type elements may appear adjacent to them. In doing so, congruence and opposition in shape between type and image dominates; the attribute of value is of secondary concern; and the attributes of texture and rhythm are the least pronounced.

Type may easily overlap image elements, whether they are silhouetted or inset, creating the perception of a pronounced foreground/background relationship. Two different possibilities, both resulting in the same effect, are shown here: one in which the type originates within the image's boundaries and extends into the surrounding space; and another in which the type orginates and terminates in the space but traverses the image.

The vertical, overlapped title—as well as the geometric blocks of white and yellow—appears to float in front of and over the image on an invisible foreground plane, thanks to their enormous scale and tremendous value contrast with the image. Oddly, the subtitle occupies a space inside the white bar at the top.
THOMAS CSANO CANADA

type might cross the image and connect the space around it to its interior—beginning inside the image's boundaries and extending beyond them into the surrounding format space, or beginning and ending within the format space but overlapping a portion of the image. In such circumstances, the type will usually appear as a foreground element that is "sliding past" or "over" the image. Again, this will be true whether the image in question is silhouetted or inset within a shape. Type that is placed within the field of an image, on the other hand, becomes part of it. In a situation in which the image element creates an independent shape within a format, the type that is contained within it will be completely disconnected from the surrounding space and, so, from nearly all other compositional relationships that may exist outside the image. If the image is full bleed, the type takes on a more ambiguous quality. Being contained entirely within the image field, it becomes part of the image; but even so its elements establish independent compositional relationships of congruence and opposition with the image elements that exist around and under it.

Typographic material that exists solely within the confines of an image's boundaries becomes part of that image and disconnects in nearly every way from potential visual relationships that may exist in the surrounding space.

Within a full-bleed image—one that completely fills a format from edge to edge in all directions—typographic elements exhibit a strange duality. They become new compositional elements that are part of the image itself; but in so doing, they also retain their compositional independence to a certain degree.

For all appearances, the chapter title on this book spread is situated on the gallery wall at the back of the image. **FINEST MAGMA** GERMANY

All of the text is contained within the full-bleed image's field; but the text that appears at lower right is separated from the full bleed image as a foreground element. **KATE HOOVER** UNITED STATES

Interacting with Silhouettes Silhouetted images share a visual relationship with the rags of paragraphs or columns but also share an opposing relationship with their alignments. Type adjacent to a silhouetted image offers more or less contrast, depending on its location relative to the image. If the rag leads into the image contours, the two elements flow together, and the type might seem to share the spatial context of the image. Bringing the vertical alignment of a column into proximity with an image's irregular contour produces the opposite effect: the type advances in space and disconnects itself from the spatial context of the image. It's equally important to be conscious of formal elements contained within the silhouetted image—finding congruence between its internal material and the typographic language that exists outside of it—so as to ensure integration, despite the image's qualities of irregularity.

Despite silhouettes' irregular contours, geometry underpins their structures; internal axes may define options for positioning type elements for greater integration. Look to play type off other visual syntax as well: dark-value elements and boundaries between contrasting forms; tonal changes that may present possibilities for adjusting text values; and shapes or surface activity within the silhouette may relate to stroke and terminal details in a typeface.

Geometric silhouettes—the circular teacups and the triangular potting marker—are contrasted by the irregular silhouettes of the flowers and leaves. Both types of silhouettes contrast the angular and linear aspects of the type structure. RED CANOE UNITED STATES

Position silhouetted images to ensure they flow smoothly into the type's geometry without seeming awkwardly out of place. Note the alternation of hard edges and organic ones in multiple directions. The relationship between the image shape and the rag becomes dominant if the rag enters into the image's contour; the geometric alignment in the same block of text will naturally counter the irregular forms within the silhouetted image. Allowing text to overlap the silhouette helps further integrate the two.

Immediately recognizable is the type's repetition of the diagonal axis within the image. Also note the alignments between the upper and lower edges of columns with major focal points contained within the image—notably, the thumb. FROST DESIGN AUSTRALIA

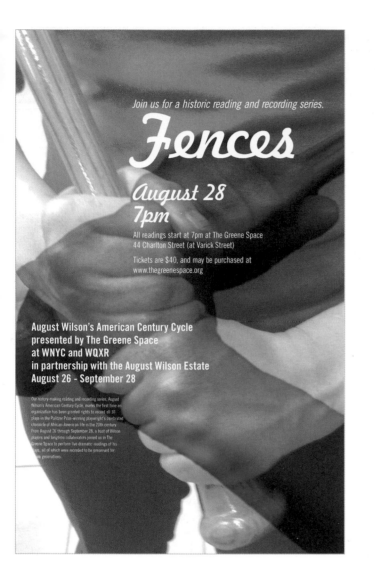

While the type in this poster takes advantage of large, tonally simple areas, the designer has left the majority of the interesting spaces untouched. HELENA WANG/PARSONS: THE NEW SCHOOL FOR DESIGN
UNITED STATES

The designer of this book cover uses diagonal rotation of the type to oppose the dotlike central form in the image, but staggers the lines of text to create inward and outward movement that echoes similar movement in the clouds and stars. Despite the volume and size of the text, valuable negative space is retained to prevent visual cluttering. DECLAN ZIMMERMAN UNITED STATES

Type and Full-Bleed Images Type that is placed within the field of an image must respond to the image's composition as though it is one made of independent compositional forms. Although the type has become part of the image, it must still engage in specific instances of congruence and opposition with the internal components of the image, just as it would in any other circumstance. The most challenging aspect of composing type within a full-bleed image is that of ensuring legibility through adequate contrast between the type's value and that of whatever is behind it. Finding a relatively open, simple area within the image—one that is overall dark or overall light, and devoid of changes in value or small, complicated detail—will generally allow the type to be set in a value that is the opposite. One danger here is the potential to fill up the negative spaces in the image that contribute to its own compositional dynamism. The joy of working with type in full-bleed scenarios is that the type becomes so dimensional and integrated; but this depends on the image retaining its own spatial characteristics.

Integrating Inset Images Inset images correspond most directly to the geometric characteristics of type. An image may be inset, or cropped into, any kind of planar shape: circles and ellipses, organic blobs, triangles, trapezoids—not only within rectangular boxes. For that matter, one may even crop an image into a line, if the line's proportions permit enough of it to show. Given this explicit geometric quality, creating congruence between text and inset images focuses primarily on shape and proportion, but also implicates alignment and interval logic within a format. Once an inset image enters the field, the presence of the axes created by its edges—top, bottom, left, and right in a rectangular form—cannot be ignored; the axes automatically create a compositional condition that must be addressed. Type may "hang" from an edge or "sit" upon it; the aligned edge of a text element may follow an axis or, in the case of nonorthogonal polygons, be anchored under or across from the point where two edges meet. It may be equally clear and dynamic, however, for text elements to not align with the edges or axes of an inset image; just make sure the misalignment is decisive.

The axes created by the edges of any angular, geometric form offer possibilities for positioning type elements to establish alignment relationships. The aligned edge of a text element may travel along an axis or anchor to it orthogonally.

Lorem ipsum dolor sit amet, consectetur adipiscing elit. Pell entesque est sed risus tincidunt, ut mollis.

Lorem ipsum dolor sit amet, consectetur adipiscing elit. Pell entesque est sed risus tincidunt, ut mollis.

Lorem ipsum dolor sit amet, consectetur adipiscing elit. Pell entesque est sed risus tincidunt, ut mollis.

Lorem ipsum dolor sit amet, consectetur adipiscing elit. Pell entesque est sed risus tincidunt, ut mollis.

Lorem ipsum dolor sit amet, consectetur adipiscing elit. Pell entesque est sed risus tincidunt, ut mollis.

The outer edges of circular forms, if large enough, also present axes, although these need not be considered solely orthogonal ones. The internal symmetrical axes (vertical and horizontal) of a circular form are also valid for establishing alignment relationships.

Lorem ipsum dolor sit amet, consectetur adipiscing elit. Pell entesque est sed risus tincidunt, ut mollis.

Lorem ipsum dolor sit amet, consectetur adipiscing elit. Pell entesque est sed risus tincidunt, ut mollis.

Lorem ipsum dolor sit amet, consectetur adipiscing elit. Pell entesque est sed risus tincidunt, ut mollis.

Lorem ipsum dolor sit amet, consectetur adipiscing elit. Pell entesque est sed risus tincidunt, ut mollis.

These two versions of a book's table of contents—by different designers—demonstrates different possibilities for relating text to inset images: reinterpreting shapes and axes from within the images themselves.
JIL GUYON [TOP], DECLAN ZIMMERMAN [BOTTOM]
UNITED STATES

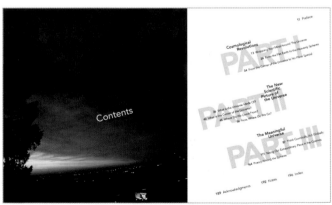

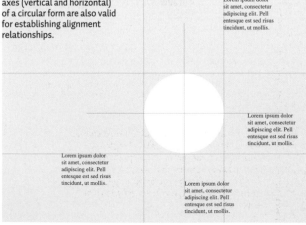

Working from the inset image's internal composition offers very rich, and sometimes far more interesting, opportunities. Look for strong vertical, horizontal, or diagonal breaks or movement within the image as potential sources for alignment; clearly defined shapes within the image—especially if different from the shape of the box into which it is cropped—may similarly provide inspiration for the shaping of text blocks.

Orthogonally shaped inset images—that is, rectangular ones—may arguably relate best to the vertical and horizontal axes that are intrinsic to typographic structure; the mutually enhancing geometry of these two becomes more significant, and rigorous, when there are multiple images (and multiple text blocks). Using a grid to organize such material is an intuitive next step a designer may consider, discussed in depth in the following section.

The positions of this poster's type elements refer to the circular inset image's outer contour, central axis, and to axes contained within it.
TIMOTHY SAMARA UNITED STATES

Inset images cropped into rectangles exhibit strong horizontal and vertical axes, as well as alignments and positive/negative alternation, to which the type responds in counterpoint.
ONLAB GERMANY

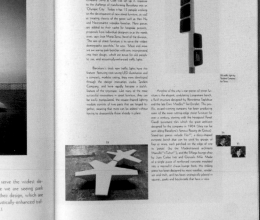

Another example of rectangular inset images, following similar alignment and rhythmic positioning strategies as in the spread above—here, however, the images and text appear to move more fluidly, rather than appear anchored to a strong architectural geometry.
FOLCH STUDIO SPAIN

The Grid System All design work involves problem solving on both visual and organizational levels. Pictures, fields of text, headlines, and tabular data: all these pieces must come together to communicate. A grid is an organizational framework of vertical and horizontal axes that may be used to govern alignment and proportional relationships among such elements—and it is simply one approach to achieving this goal. Grids can be loose and organic or they can be rigorous and mechanical. Among other things, a grid is suited to helping solve communication problems of great complexity. The benefits of working with a grid are simple: clarity, efficiency, economy, and continuity. Before anything else, a grid introduces systematic order to a layout, helps distinguish between various types of information, and eases a user's navigation through them. Using a grid permits a designer to lay out enormous amounts of information in substantially less time because many design considerations have been addressed in building the grid's structure. The grid also allows many individuals to collaborate on the same project or on a series of related projects over time, without compromising established visual qualities from one instance to the next.

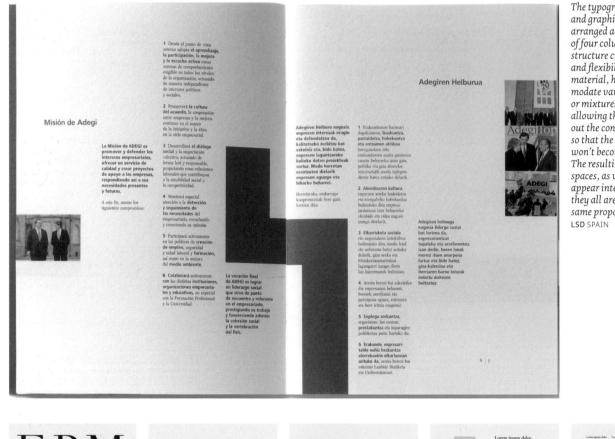

The typography, images, and graphic elements are arranged across a structure of four columns. The grid structure creates unity and flexibility among the material, helping to accommodate various amounts or mixtures of content and allowing the designer to lay out the content in variations so that the sequence of pages won't become monotonous. The resulting negative spaces, as well as the type, appear interrelated because they all are based on the same proportions.
LSD SPAIN

To some designers, the grid represents an inherent part of the craft of designing, the same way joinery in furniture making is a part of that particular craft. The history of the grid has been part of an evolution in how graphic designers think about designing, as well as a response to specific communication and production problems that needed to be solved. Although grids may seem overtly intellectual and mathematical, the notion of this structural approach grows quite organically from the nature of typographic form. At its most fundamental level, type is a system of vertical lines (these being the primary element of all the letters in the Western alphabet). Sequenced side by side to form words, and then sentences, the verticals form a horizontal line. Stacking horizontal sentences below each other creates a new vertical line—the column—and columns appearing side by side establish yet another horizontal structure.

Grid Anatomy A grid consists of a distinct set of alignment-based relationships that serves as a guide for distributing elements across a format. Every grid contains the same basic parts, no matter how complex the grid becomes. These parts can be combined as needed or omitted from the overall structure at the designer's discretion, and the proportions of the parts is similarly dependent on the designer's needs. This book, for example, is structured on a fifteen-column grid to address several issues: an optimal column width for running text and captions; a static navigation system at the far left; consistent proportions between diagrams and caption text-widths; and flexibility to size and arrange contributor design projects. While text and diagram widths necessitate a greater number of columns left to right, the need for flexibility in positioning dictates that no flowlines be established top to bottom.

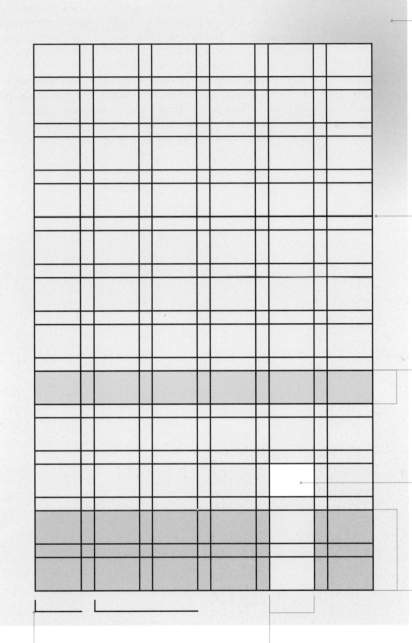

Margins are the negative spaces between the format edge and the content, that surround and define the live area where type and images will be arranged. The proportions of the margins bear a great deal of consideration, as they help establish the overall tension within the composition. Margins can be used to focus attention, serve as a resting place for the eye, or act as an area for subordinate information.

Flowlines are alignments that break the space into horizontal bands. Flowlines help guide the eye across the format and can be used to impose additional stopping and starting points for text or images. There may one flowline or several.

If there are numerous flowlines at regular intervals, breaking the page top to bottom in a repeated proportion, a system of **rows** is created that intersects the vertical columns.

Modules are individual units of space separated by regular intervals that, when repeated across the page format, create columns and rows.

Spatial zones are groups of modules that form distinct fields. Each field can be assigned a specific role for displaying information; for example, one horizontal field might be reserved for images, and the field below it might be reserved for a series of text columns.

Markers are placement indicators for subordinate or consistently appearing text, such as running heads, section titles, folios, or any other element that occupies only one location in any layout.

Columns are vertical alignments of type that create horizontal divisions between the margins. There can be any number of columns; sometimes they are all the same width, and sometimes they are different widths, corresponding to specific information. The page diagrammed here shows four columns of even width.

Column Grid Information that is discontinuous benefits from being organized into an arrangement of vertical columns. Because the columns can be dependent on each other for running text, independent for small blocks of text, or crossed over to make wider columns, the column grid is very flexible. For example, some columns might be reserved for running text and large images, while captions might be placed in an adjacent column.

This arrangement clearly separates the captions from the primary material but maintains them in a direct relationship. The width of the columns depends, as noted, on the size of the running text type. If the column is too narrow, excessive hyphenation is likely and a uniform rag will be difficult to achieve. At the other extreme, a column that is too wide will make it difficult for the reader to find the beginnings of sequential lines. By studying the effects of changing

the type size, leading, and spacing, the designer will be able to find a comfortable column width. Traditionally, the gutter between columns is given a measure, x, and the margins are usually assigned a width of twice the gutter measure, or $2x$. Margins wider than the column gutters focus the eye inward, easing tension between the column edge and the edge of the format. This is simply a guide, however, and designers are free to adjust the column-to-margin

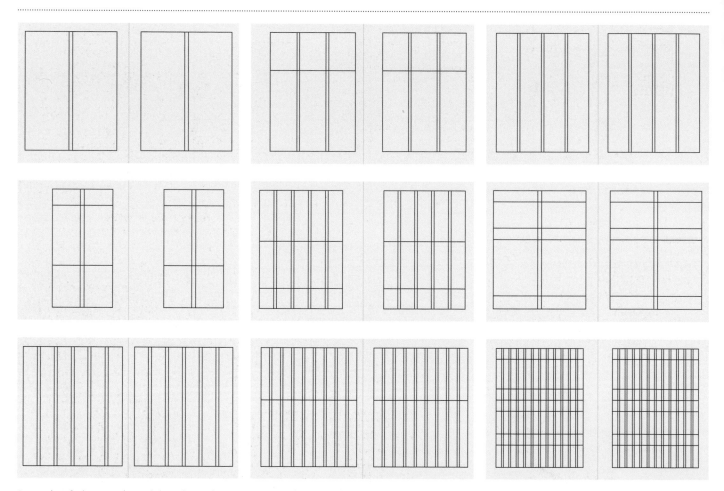

Any number of columns can be used, depending on the format size and the complexity of the content; even two- and three-column grids, among the most common used in designing publications, provide a tremendous number of layout options. Flowlines define horizontal alignments in increments from the top of the page. Regardless of the number of columns, the body and margins may be related asymmetrically or symmetrically (mirrored).

SEVEN GIFTS FOR GEEKY KIDS

COLOR-CODED ANTS REVEAL EFFICIENCY

ROCKING EMISSIONS

First, for the uninitiated, an explanation of the lighter salute: You´re at a concert. The music slows, the first guitar wails of a power ballad begin, and hundreds of disposable lighters illuminate the audience like so many sequins on a vest. Three or four minutes later, the song ends, and you pocket the Bic and get back to headbanging.

FOUND BALDNESS CURE

EARLY SWIM LESSONS MAY REDUCE DROWNING

TEACH BACTERIA

Iron-oxidizing microbes give fresh meaning and provide fresh. Iron-oxidizing microbes give fresh meaning and provide fresh. Iron-oxidizing microbes give fresh meaning and provide fresh. Iron-oxidizing microbes give fresh meaning and provide fresh.

POP VIDEO ⊕

CHEMICAL VAPOR DEPOSITION

Russell Hemley of the Physical Laboratory of the Carnegie Institution of Washington and researchers at Apollo Diamond, Inc. in Boston, have produced the largest and some of the most flawless diamonds so far. And Europe´s Carbon Power Electronics consortium, led by Dutch diamond maker Element Six, has created a synthetic diamond diode, the first step toward working diamond semiconductors. During the past year, scientists have mastered the ability to grow 10-carat single crystals.

WATCH PARROT-SIZED ROBOT CARS

TO SWING ON A STAR

FRECKLES AND FLAB MAKE BETTER STEM CELLS

PLAYSTATION'S PITCH: FORGET THE OLD GRAPHICS

---

ratio as they see fit. In a column grid, there is also a subordinate structure. These are the flowlines: vertical intervals that allow the designer to accommodate unusual breaks in text or images on the page and create horizontal bands across the format. The hangline is one kind of flowline: it defines the vertical distance from the top of the format at which column text will always start. A flowline near the top of the page might establish a position for running headers, pagination, or section dividers. Additional flowlines might designate areas for images (specifically) or different kinds of concurrent running text, such as a timeline, a sidebar, or a callout.

This full-scroll view of a website design shows the rigid use of a five-column grid, with some minor deviations from the structure that help add spatial contrast. The uneven number of columns allows for both symmetrical and asymmetrical organization of material to be integrated seamlessly.
YOUJIN CHOI/SCHOOL OF VISUAL ARTS UNITED STATES

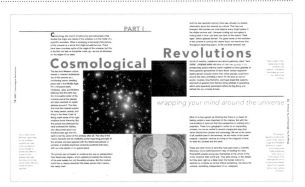

A six-column grid provides ample opportunity for variations in text shaping and image proportion.
YONG CHOI/SCHOOL OF VISUAL ARTS UNITED STATES

An apparently four-column grid reveals itself to be structured on nine columns, accounting for the different text widths at the bottom of the left-hand page. BACHGARDE DESIGN SWEDEN

Modular Grid Extremely complex projects require even more precise control, and, in this situation, a modular grid might be the most useful choice. A modular grid is essentially a column grid with a large number of horizontal flowlines that subdivide the columns into rows, creating a matrix of cells called "modules." Each module defines a small chunk of informational space. Grouped together, these modules define areas called spatial zones to which specific roles can be assigned. The degree of control within the grid depends on the size of the modules. Smaller modules provide more flexibility and greater precision, but too many subdivisions can become confusing or redundant. A modular grid also lends itself to the design of tabular information. The rigorous repetition of the module helps to standardize tables or forms and integrate them with the text and image material. Aside from its practical uses, the modular grid accords a conceptual aesthetic. Between the 1950s and 1980s, the modular grid became associated with ideal social or political order. These ideals have their roots in the rationalist thinking of both the Bauhaus and Swiss International Style, which celebrates objectivity, order, and clarity. Designers who embrace these ideals sometimes use modular grids to convey this additional meaning.

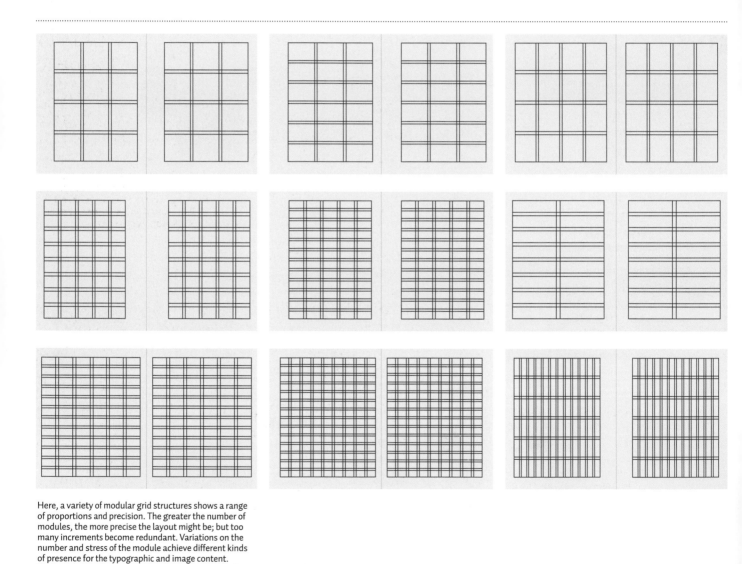

Here, a variety of modular grid structures shows a range of proportions and precision. The greater the number of modules, the more precise the layout might be; but too many increments become redundant. Variations on the number and stress of the module achieve different kinds of presence for the typographic and image content.
The increased potential for arranging and proportioning content in a modular grid is seen here. Combining modules into zones for images (the gray areas) ensures variety as well as a unified relationship with text.

How does a designer determine the module's proportions? The module could be the width and depth of one average paragraph of the primary text at a given size. Modules can be vertical or horizontal in proportion, and this decision can be related to the kinds of images being organized or to the desired stress the designer feels is appropriate. The margin proportions must be considered simultaneously in relation to the modules and the gutters that separate them.

Modular grids are often used to coordinate extensive publication systems. If the designer has the opportunity to consider all the materials that are to be produced within a system, the formats can become an outgrowth of the module or vice versa. By regulating the proportions of the formats and the module in relation to each other, the designer might simultaneously be able to harmonize the formats and ensure they are produced most economically.

Detailed modular grids are a hallmark of newspaper design, permitting rapid and varied layout changes. Here, the module's depth is defined by the height of the masthead; its width is to be found in the small section markers just below that. E-TYPES DENMARK

A grid that is only five columns wide is enough to accommodate the needs of running text, callouts, and images in this annual report's front section; but twelve rows are required to deal with not only editorial content but financial material that follows. TRISH ERNE UNITED STATES

The six-column, square-module grid that structures this website defines the navigation area within the top row; because the content is dynamic, there is no limit to the number of rows. They can be added on as needed. NAROSKA DESIGN GERMANY

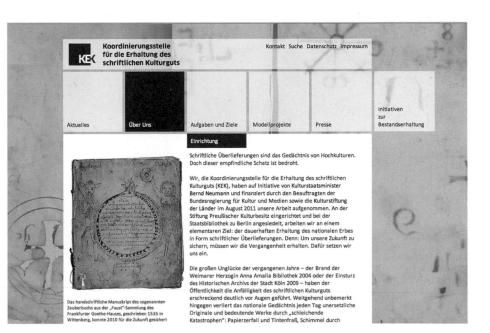

Grid Hybrids and Combinations Depending on the complexity of the publication, a designer might find that multiple grids are needed to organize the content, within sections or even a single page spread. Working with several grids together can take several directions. First, a grid with a large number of precise intervals might be developed as a basis for a variety of grids used for particular information. For example, a grid with twenty columns to a page might be used to order a five-column, four-column, two-column, and three-column grid with a larger margin for captions in a specific section. In this kind of approach, all the column widths will share a proportional relationship that will also be noticeable in how images relate to text set in these various widths. Another option is simply to use two, three, or more different grids that share outer margins, allowing them to be relatively arbitrary in their relationship to each other. In this approach, the alternation of the grids will be pronounced, since their internal proportions are unrelated; the differences in visual logic between layouts using different grids can make very clear distinctions between sections or types of content. A third option is to combine grids on a single page but to separate them into different areas. For example, primary text or images might occupy a three-column grid

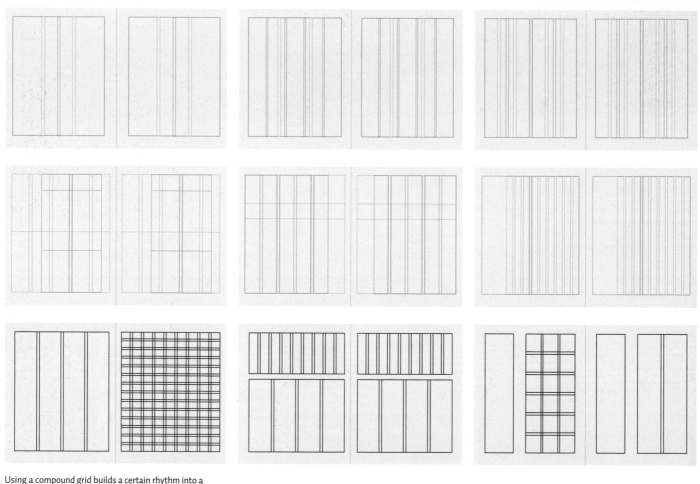

Using a compound grid builds a certain rhythm into a publication. As the grid changes to accommodate different information, the rhythm of each grid's occurrence becomes an integral part of the pacing and style of the work. Shown here are a number of compound structures: some superimpose two grids within the boundaries of the margins; others superimpose grids that establish independent margins; and still others apply different grids to opposing pages or to different parts of the same page.

in the upper two thirds of the page, but a five-column grid might hold captions or other secondary content in the lower third of the page.

Two opposing grids are combined in this book to create conflict between text and image areas. The overlap of text and the pushing and pulling of image proportions create a collage-like atmosphere that is edgy and intuitive. **COMA** NETHERLANDS

A simple hierarchic grid defines a wide column for running text, a narrow one for callouts, and two flowlines for markers. **STUDIO ASTRID STAVRO** SPAIN

This website combines multiple column grids, each used in specific areas to organize specific content and navigation, rather than attempting to accommodate all the material on one overly complex grid. **STUDIO BLUE** UNITED STATES

Grid Development Building an appropriate grid for a publication involves assessing the shape and volume of the content, rather than trying to assign grid spaces arbitrarily. The shape of the content, whether text or image, is particularly important—its proportions become the source for defining the grid spaces. When considering text as the essential building block, the designer must look at variations in the text setting. Considering image as a source for the grid spaces is another option. If the publication is driven by its image content, this might be a more appropriate direction. The proportions of the images, if they are known, can be used to determine the proportions of columns and modules. The result of both approaches is that the structure of the page develops naturally from the needs of the content, presenting an overall organic, unified sense of space.

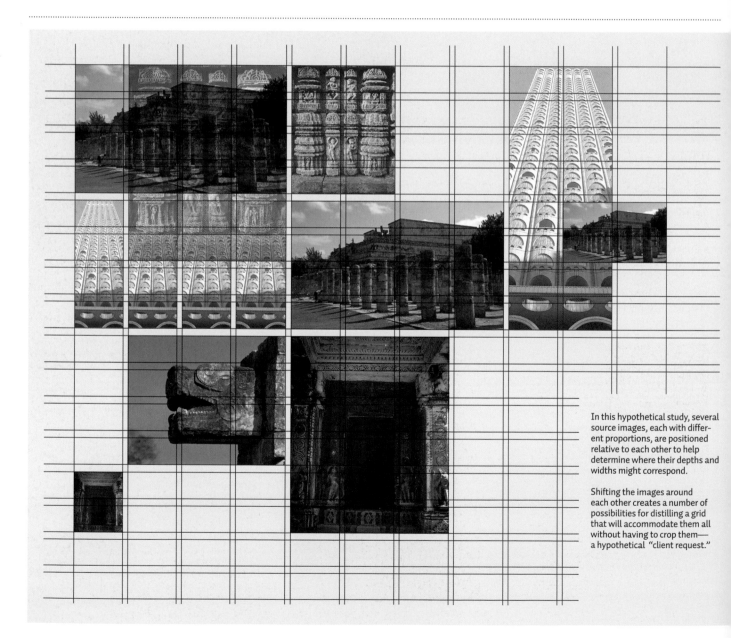

In this hypothetical study, several source images, each with different proportions, are positioned relative to each other to help determine where their depths and widths might correspond.

Shifting the images around each other creates a number of possibilities for distilling a grid that will accommodate them all without having to crop them— a hypothetical "client request."

Grid by Image A grid might be defined by image content through comparison of its proportions. Beginning with a universal height or depth for the images, and a consistent alignment among them, will allow the designer to assess how varied they are in format—squares, verticals, and horizontals. The designer must then decide how the images are to be displayed in terms of their size relationship to each other: Will the images be shown in sizes that are relative to each other or will they be allowed to appear at any size? If all the images hang from a particular flowline, their depth varying, the designer will need to address the images with both the shortest and deepest depths to determine what is possible for text or other elements below these variations. From these major divisions in space and the logic that the designer uses to govern them, a series of intervals might be structured for the images and for text areas surrounding them. It is also possible to structure the grid based on how images will be sized in succession. Perhaps the designer envisions sequencing the images in a particular way: first bleeding full off one page, then a half-page vertical, then inset, and then a three-quarter bleed. In this case, the proportions of the images as they relate to the format will define a series of intervals.

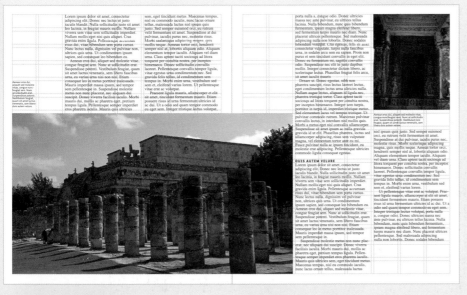

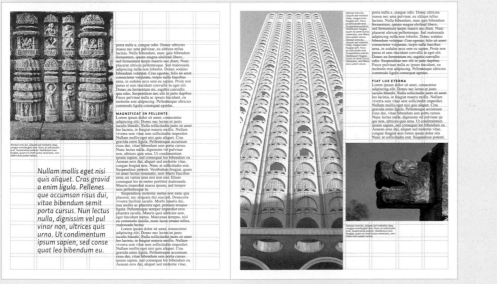

The module proportion discovered through the image study (opposite) gives rise to a grid that permits the designer to scale any of the images as he or she sees fit without cropping them: The module's proportion accommodates all of the images' varied aspect ratios—the relationship of each image's height to its width. As a result, the designer retains the same desired flexibility for layouts that a modular grid provides, without having to compromise the client's interest in maintaining the various images' integrity. Shown here are two hypothetical page-spread layouts that demonstrate this flexibility with dramatic changes among the images' sizes and positions, in concert with text.

Grid by Text Alternatively, the designer might approach the grid from the perspective of the text shape and volume. The sheer amount of text that the publication must accommodate is an important consideration; if each page spread must carry a particular word count to fit a prescribed number of pages, the designer will have some sense of how many lines of type must appear on each page. This variable might eventually affect the column width or depth, but the optimal setting is a good starting point. Achieving an optimal setting for text at a given size and in a given face will indicate a width for columns, and, from there, the designer can explore how many columns will fit side by side on a single page. Adjusting the size of the text, its internal spacing, and the gutters between columns will allow the designer to create a preliminary structure that ensures optimal text setting throughout. From this point, the designer must evaluate the resulting margins—head, sides, and foot—and determine whether there is enough space surrounding the body to keep it away from the edges of the format. Since optimal width can vary a little with the same text setting, the designer has some leeway in forcing the columns to be wider or more narrow, closer or further away from each other, until the structure sits comfortably on the page.

Optimal setting attributes for a selection of text styles—running text, caption, callout, and deck—reveals closely related width proportions that, with a little adjustment, may point toward a universal column measure that will support each. A designer's second consideration is the number of columns (and gutters between them) that will fit the page width; the remaining spaces will determine outside and gutter margins.

Donec quis elitquis erat blandit placerat at dapibus velit. In acumsan lacus id sapien scelrisque non sagittis diam ornare. Cras pretium sagittis lectus. Pellentesque at dolor nisi, nec scelerique tellus. Vivamus at justo eget elit ferentum dap ibus. Suspendisse ac nibh massa, et imperditero. In hac habitasse platea dictumst. Cras non tellu vel turpis auctor tristique. In hac habitasse platea dictumst. Morbi sit amepurus urna. Aenean accumsan interdu massa, eu hendrerit est sodales quis. Praesent sagittis fringilla

The leading of the body text, decks, callouts, and captions might have some proportional relationship based on their sizes.

For example, the body text might be 10 points, set on a leading of 12; captions might be 6 points, set solid on a leading of 6; callouts might be 15 points, set on a leading of 18. The numeric relationship between these leading measurements is 6 points; a certain number of lines of each text component will, at some depth interval, share the same top and lower baseline, and this depth interval might very well indicate the depth of a row.

After defining the row depth, and that of the gutters between them, the designer will determine how many rows can fit comfortably within the height of the page; the remaining spaces above and below will become the head and foot margins.

The grid in this brochure was developed based on the proportions of the type sizes given to each level of information in the hierarchy and the resulting mathematical relationship between the baselines of their leading. Comparing the baselines of larger text elements with those of smaller text elements reveals that they correspond on a regular basis, hinting that the grid is modular as well as columnar. **LOEWY**
UNITED KINGDOM

Similar to the design of the publication above, the grid's proportions are based on the optimal attributes of point size, character count, and leading for the running text. Because this resulted in a symmetrical structure, the designer chose to violate the columns with images to improve the layouts' fluidity of movement.
MARIELLE VAN GENDEREN + ADRIAAN MELLEGERS
NETHERLANDS

Column Logic and Rhythm on a Grid

The way in which columns of text interact with negative space is an important aspect of how a grid is articulated. The spaces above and below columns play an active part in giving the columns a rhythm as they relate to each other across pages and spreads. The options available to a designer are endless but can be described as fitting into three basic categories: columns that justify top and bottom; columns that align vertically at top or bottom and rag at the other end; and columns that rag top and bottom. Each kind of logic has a dramatic impact on the overall rhythm of the pages within a publication, ranging from austere and geometric to wildly organic in feeling—all the while ordered by the underlying grid. Changing the column logic from section to section provides yet another method of differentiating informational areas. The designer, however, must carefully consider the rhythm of that change. Some regularity or system must clearly exist in the alternation of column logic to be meaningful; otherwise, the audience simply recognizes the change but not its significance. When columns begin to separate vertically, shifting up and down past one another—or dropping to different depths while adhering to a single hangline above—consider the relationship between lines of text across the gutter

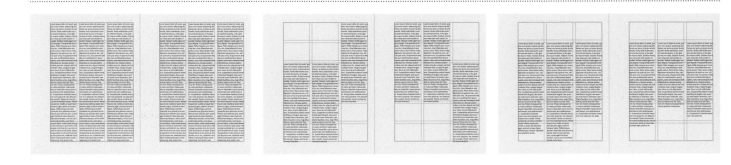

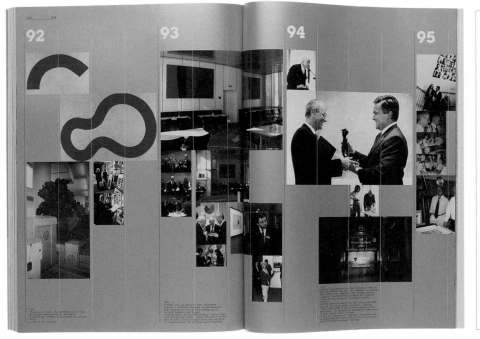

In this page spread, regularity is established by repeated vertical lines, evenly spaced to define the column structure. Images and text counter this regularity by forming dynamic clusters that show off the modules.
SPIN UNITED KINGDOM

A six-column modular grid helps integrate text and images of various sizes to provide contrast and variation but without sacrificing the harmonic proportional unity of the panels. CLEMENS THÉOBERT SCHEDLER
AUSTRIA

separating the columns. In a grouping of columns set justified, with no line breaks (or a hard return of the same leading) between paragraphs, the baselines between columns will align. Any other situation, and the baselines between columns will not align. In hanging columns, text will align between columns until a paragraph change. Because the depth of the hanging columns changes, this might feel appropriate. A problem will occur in a page spread set with columns justifying top and bottom, however, if the paragraph space introduces an uneven line: the lines of text at the foot margin will be noticeably off.

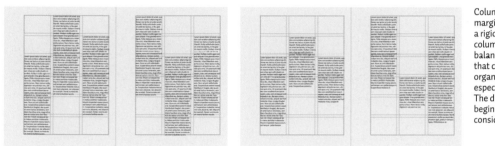

Columns justified to the head and foot margins, or to a specific module depth, create a rigidly geometric band of text. Hanging columns provide a measure of consistency, balanced by their changing depth. Columns that change hangline and depth offer the most organic and flexible option for arranging text, especially in terms of integrating images. The differences in interval between column beginnings and endings must be decisive and considered for their rhythm.

Relating Images to a Grid As a compositional structure that emphasizes the orthogonal relationship between images and text, a grid is exceptionally useful for creating formal congruence between the two kinds of material. No less so for images than for text elements, a grid's systematic nature rigorously enforces harmonic proportional relationships while providing the designer incredible flexibility in layouts. Even though using a grid to organize images might seem to stifle their visual potential, remember that a grid has a kind of built-in, organic flexibility to it. A simple column grid has consistent width intervals that pictures can traverse—the more columns, the more possible widths for images—but it also allows a variety of depths for the images. Images might be allowed to meet a system of flowlines if they are established as part of the column grid. Modular grids, which at first appear to limit possibilities for images, actually provide enormous flexibility for how images might interact on a page. Each module can contain an image, and groupings of modules in any combination may also contain images—2 x 3, 1 x 6, 3 x 5, and so on, all the way up to full-bleed images and large divisions of the overall spread. Furthermore, images may expand outward from the structure to bleed across the page gutter or any edge of the page. As images increase

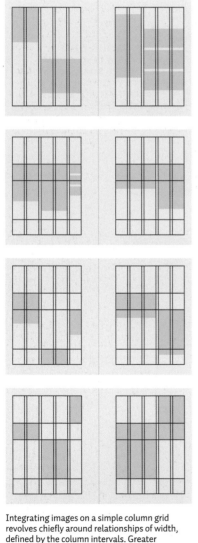

Integrating images on a simple column grid revolves chiefly around relationships of width, defined by the column intervals. Greater complexity occurs when there are flowlines—whether the images hang from one; hang from several; or stretch between flowlines in a more rigid approach.

A modular grid—even a very simple one, as shown here—will provide an almost endless number of possibilities for arranging images. Clearly, less can do more.

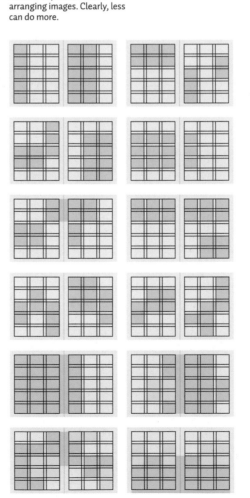

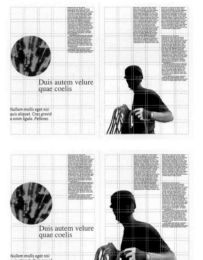

Although silhouetted images and those cropped into non-orthogonal forms are irregular in shape, the designer must ensure that they "feel" as though they're proportioned and situated like grid-structured images, yet retain their inherent organic quality without feeling stiff or awkward. This usually means adjusting such images' edges to extend past grid lines (remember that curved forms appear to contract or shrink) and positioning their internal elements to correspond with other aligned elements around them. Note how the silhouetted figure's contours violate the actual boundaries of columns (as do the contours of the dotlike form), as well as how heavily weighted material appears to sit within, or on, rows.

in size, based on the widths of columns or modules, their internal visual qualities become more pronounced, and the structural quality of the type begins to contrast the image. As images shrink, relative to the grid, their internal visual qualities become less pronounced and their shapes as geometric objects within the text structure become more important.

The images one chooses to include within a grid-based project need not be rectangular: images cropped into circles or non-orthogonal polygons, as well as silhouetted images that are irregular in shape, are all valid options. Such images, however, demand special care with regard to their sizes and the positioning of their outer edges so they will seem to correspond to the grid's columns and rows. A designer also should consider the visual material within these

kinds of images as sources for alignment and fit. Analyzing the internal composition of full-bleed images is important, too, for the same reason. A full-bleed image shouldn't be thought of simply as a window where anything can happen—the way the designer chooses to scale and position any image material within the bleed area should result in the image's form elements coming to rest in some alignment and proportional relationship with the grid.

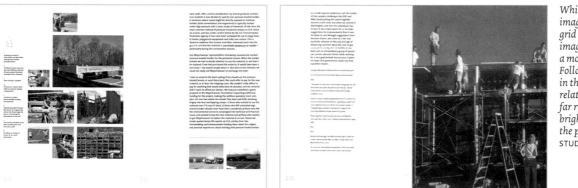

While a cluster of small inset images directly articulates the grid beneath it, the full-bleed image on the near spread shows a more subtle relationship: Follow the major horizontals in this image to see how they relate to the row gutters in the far right spread; also note the bright elements ordered along the page's diagonal axis.
STUDIO WORKS UNITED STATES

Silhouetted images with irregular contours bring tremendous contrast and life to layouts that are geometrically ordered by a grid. This organic quality creates a need to establish clear visual relationships between such images' shaping and internal syntax so that they will integrate with the regimented quality of the structure. In this brochure spread, the images are scaled and positioned to align major compositional axes within them to the columns and rows of the modular grid with which they interact: test this notion by following the horizontal line defined by the top edge of the arm on the left page all the way across to the right-hand page.
FROST DESIGN AUSTRALIA

Variation and Violation A grid is truly successful only if the designer rises above the uniformity implied by its structure and uses it to create a dynamic visual narrative of parts that will sustain interest page after page. The greatest danger in using a grid is to succumb to its regularity. Remember that the grid is an invisible guide existing on the bottommost level of the layout; the content happens on the surface, either constrained or sometimes free. Grids do not make dull layouts—designers do. Once a grid is in place, it is a good idea to sort all the project's material spread by spread, using a storyboard, to see how much will be appearing in each. Here, the designer can test layout variations on the grid and see the result in terms of pacing—the rhythm of the layouts. What visual logic might there be to how elements interact with the grid from page to page? Do pictorial elements alternate in position from one spread to another? Perhaps the sizes of images, or the ratio of text to image vary from spread to spread. Even simply placing images toward the top of the pages in one spread and then toward the bottom of the pages in the next achieves a powerful sense of difference while still ensuring overall visual unity. Violating the grid is a necessity of designing, sometimes because circumstance dictates it—content that must occupy a specific spread won't quite

A simple trick to achieving layout variation is to alternately cluster images toward the top or bottom from spread to spread; another is to force a small, medium, and large image onto a spread—and then use the same sizes, but placed in different locations, on the next spread.

Articulating material across several column structures within the same project—but using similar positioning logic throughout—creates a tremendous difference in the overall rhythm of the layouts while retaining a certain unity.

Occasionally ignoring a rigorous grid has a dramatic effect on pacing and hierarchy. In this study, just such an instance stands out among a series of layouts that are heavily structured. The resulting surprise breathes life into the sequence and highlights featured content.

fit—or because it is visually necessary to emphasize some feature of the content or to create some surprise for the reader. Within a rigorous grid structure, violations must be relatively infrequent or relatively small or they begin to undermine the reader's sense of the grid's consistency. Any specific item or general layout that violates the grid will be very dramatic. Not only will it be instantly noticeable, but it also will become the element of greatest hierarchic focus—simply by virtue of its difference. Designing a two-page spread that ignores the grid established for the remaining pages of a publication ensures that spread will be memorable. The problem then facing the designer is that of integrating the layout so that it clearly belongs to the same publication. Using typefaces and colors that are used elsewhere will do so, but these alone will not be enough. The designer must create some reference to the established structure even as he or she violates it—perhaps a typographic element from the previous spread continues onto the unique spread. In addition, the designer must consider the transition back into the grid-structured pages following the violation; if the pages following this particular spread are a continuation of its content, the designer might add smaller violating elements that recall the major violation while restating the regular structure.

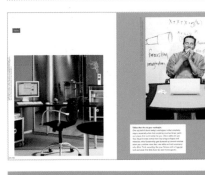

These pages, selected from several related brochures, use a relatively tight column structure as a means of radically altering margin, image, and text proportions from page to page. The greater number of columns means that simple blocks of content can shift around dramatically, but the proportions of the negative spaces and content objects remain unified in feeling.
PEOPLE DESIGN UNITED STATES

Images in this publication continually change size and shift position from spread to spread, an ideal, simple way to avoid monotony. In addition, graphical lines circulate around the margins, responding to the column gutters but changing color on a regular basis.
MARIELLE VAN GENDEREN + ADRIAAN MELLEGERS
NETHERLANDS

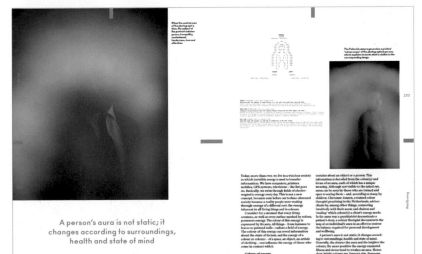

Exploring Other Options: Nonstructural Design Approaches Grid structure in typography and design has become part of the status quo of designing, but, as recent history has shown, there are numerous ways to organize information and images. The decision whether to use a grid always comes down to the nature of the content in a given project. Sometimes, that content has its own internal structure that a grid won't necessarily clarify; sometimes, the content needs to ignore structure altogether to create specific kinds of emotional reactions in the intended audience; and sometimes, a designer simply envisions a more complex intellectual involvement on the part of the audience as part of their experience of the piece. Our ability to apprehend and digest information has become more sophisticated over time as well; constant bombardment of information from television, film, and interactive digital media has created a certain kind of expectation for information to behave in particular ways. One has only to look at television news broadcast-ing or reality-based programming, where several kinds of presentation—oral delivery, video, still images and icons, and moving typography—overlap or succeed each other in rapid succession to understand that people have become accustomed to more complex, designed experiences.

Compare the location of spatial breaks from left to right across this page spread with the grid diagram; although the majority of typographic and image content responds to the column structure, several items noticeably shift off the structure to introduce visual surprise and focus attention. **COBRA** NORWAY

This spread from a theatrical season brochure responds to a 3 x 3 module structure as a base, but the module alignments appear to shift, forcing the type into new alignments. **RESEARCH STUDIOS** UNITED KINGDOM

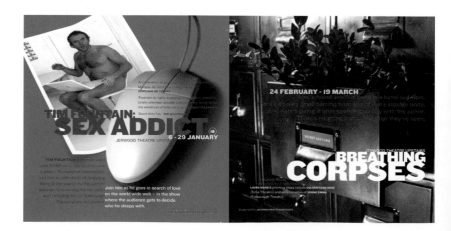

In an effort to create a meaningful impression that competes with—and distinguishes itself within—this visual environment, designers have pursued various new ways of organizing visual experience.

The material in both of these posters is organized intuitively and spontaneously in an almost collage-like or painterly fashion, considering the visual qualities of the components in a more organic way. In the poster at top, this spontaneity is tempered by the influence of an illusory cube that helps create dimensional breaks in space; in the poster at right, the composition is dramatically looser.

LUDOVIC BALLAND [ABOVE]
NIKLAUS TROXLER DESIGN [RIGHT]
SWITZERLAND

Grid Deconstruction The first option is splitting apart a conventional grid, even a very simple one. A structure can be altered in any number of ways. A designer might "cut apart" major zones and shift them horizontally or vertically. It's important to watch what happens when information that would normally appear in an expected place—marking a structural juncture in the grid—is moved to another place, perhaps aligned with some other kind of information in a way that creates a new verbal connection that didn't exist before. The shifted information might end up behind or on top of some other information if a change in size or density accompanies the shift in placement. The optical confusion this causes might be perceived as a surreal kind of space where foreground and background swap places. A conventional grid structure repeated in different orientations could be used to explore a more dynamic architectural space by creating different axes of alignment. Similarly, overlapping grids with modules of different proportions, or that run at different angles in relation to each other, can introduce a kind of order to the spatial and directional ambiguity that layering creates, especially if some elements are oriented on both layers simultaneously.

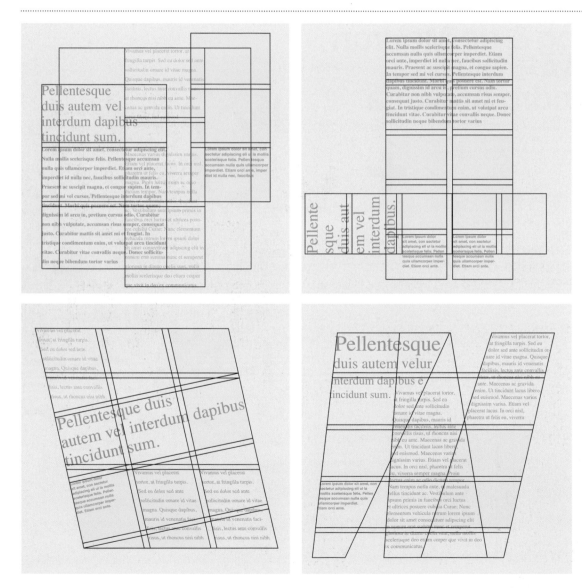

Shifting or breaking apart grid modules or columns so that they begin to overlap, even while they carry sequential information (like running text), creates a perception of layers within the compositional space. The textures of different columns interacting as they run over each other establishes a perception of transparency in which text, or other elements, appear to float in front of each other. Shown here are a few of the nearly unlimited possibilities for deconstructing a grid, and how text and image elements might respond to them.

In a remarkably funny twist, typographic elements are deconstructed off the grid of the walls in hotel rooms to create an amusing spatial environment for guests.
E-TYPES DENMARK

Shifting columns and exaggerated textural qualities harmonize the type with the images. **HYOSOOK KANG/ SCHOOL OF VISUAL ARTS** UNITED STATES

Slight overlaps in columns, changing column widths, and column rotation create movement and geometric spaces reminiscent of the design work and historical context of the poster's subject without copying his style or showing any of his own projects.
LEONARDO SONNOLI ITALY

Groupings of modules for content areas are separated from the understructure to float in a less rigidly defined space. **TIMOTHY SAMARA** UNITED STATES

Spontaneous Optical Composition

Far from being random, this compositional method can be described as purposeful intuitive placement of material based on its formal aspects: seeing the inherent visual relationships and contrasts within the material and making connections for the viewer based on those relationships. Sometimes, designers will use this method as a step in the process of building a grid, but its use as an organizational idea on its

This poster organizes typographic material loosely and organically, showing evidence of the designer's attention to tension and contrast relationships in proximity, clustering, overlap, edge-to-format spacing, and angular versus curvilinear logic. CALLY KEO/THE ART INSTITUTE, ORANGE COUNTY UNITED STATES

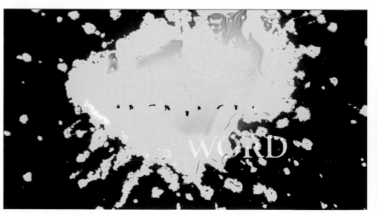

Nearly uncontrolled (or so it seems) spatters and washes of ink hide and reveal text in this motion sequence. DAEUN KO/SCHOOL OF VISUAL ARTS UNITED STATES

own is just as valid. This approach starts fast and loose: The designer works with the material much like a painter does, making quick decisions as the material is put together and the relationships are first seen. As the different optical qualities of the elements begin to interact, the designer can determine which qualities are affected by those initial decisions and make adjustments to enhance or negate the qualities in whatever way is most appropriate for the communication. The method's inherent liveliness has an affinity with collage; its sense of immediacy and directness can be inviting to viewers, providing them with a simple and gratifying experience that is very accessible. The result is a structure that is dependent on the optical tensions of the composition and their connection to the information hierarchy within the space.

The designer of this poster responds to the figure's position with irregularly shaped, colored forms and an energetic spattering of glitch texture. Typographic elements play off these rhythms through scale and weight change, interaction with diagonal lines, and rotation.
VIKTOR MATIC ITALY

In this poster, the boldness of an arrangement of massive forms is countered by internal alignments between tonal boundaries and small details of text, contour, and texture.
OHYESCOOLGREAT NETHERLANDS

Conceptual or Pictorial Allusion Another interesting way of creating compositions is to derive a visual idea from the content and impose it on the page format as a kind of arbitrary structure. The structure can be an illusory representation of a subject, like waves or the surface of water, or can be based on a concept, like a childhood memory, a historical event, or a diagram. Whatever the source of the idea, the designer can organize material to refer to it. For example, text and images might sink underwater or float around like objects caught in a flood. Even though no grid is present, sequential compositions are given a kind of unity because of the governing idea. Margins, intervals between images and text, and relative depth on the page might constantly change, but this change has recognizable features that relate to the overall idea; these might even be called allusive structures. In projects of a sequen-

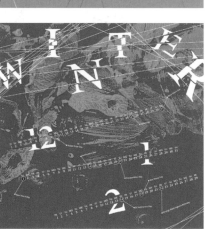

Little explanation is needed to clarify the image that is being created by the configuration of justified text blocks in this foldout brochure. LSD SPAIN

The designer of these seasonal calendar panels expresses the feeling and energy of each season through abstract images. The typography responds not just formally but conceptually, alluding in different instances to falling rain, leaves, and snow. HAE JIN LEE/SCHOOL OF VISUAL ARTS UNITED STATES

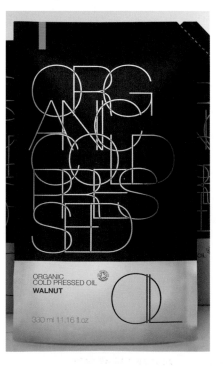

The overlap of the type refers to the action of "pressing" without invoking the literal. **SABOTAGE PKG** UNITED KINGDOM

tial nature, like books or walls in an exhibit, visual elements relate to each other in time, as though in frames of a film. Images might move across a format or otherwise be changed from page to page, affecting other images or text that appear later. A simple example of this visual kinesis might be a sequence of pages where text appears to advance forward in space because its scale changes incrementally every time the page is turned. Using sensory experiences of space and time as organizing principles can be a powerful tool for evoking a visceral, emotional response from viewers.

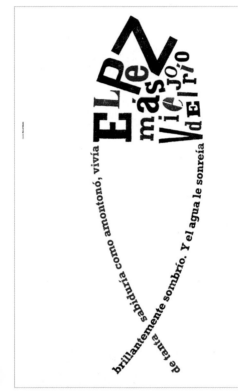

In this poster, the primary type is pictorialized to represent a fish. Even the small, informational text near the lower right edge of the format plays into this strategy—spaced rhythmically to suggest the flow of water, despite the poster's format being vertical. MANUEL ESTRADA SPAIN

Veils of colored texture and transparent type—running in two directions—evoke the veil of Arabic culture and reference that language's reading direction in contrast to that of Western reading. LEONARDO SONNOLI ITALY

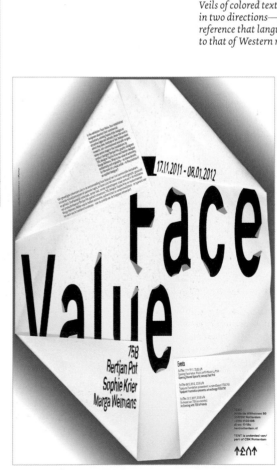

This poster alludes—almost literally—to the folding of the sheet on which it is printed, bringing up the question of whether the poster's "face" has value. The planar shapes and irregular diagonal axes provide interesting results for the positioning of text elements. OHYESCOOLGREAT NETHERLANDS

Thinking Systematically The vast majority of designed works—printed, interactive, and environmental—are systematic in nature; the existence of a single-format, one-off design piece is exceedingly rare. A website, for example, consists of multiple pages that interact; consider, too, the pages of a book in sequence, all of which must relate to each other, as well as to the exterior of the book as an object itself. Most publications are produced serially (as with magazines or newsletters) or sequentially, meaning that they are either a family of related items produced all together or individual items produced at different times, such as a series of brochures. Advertising campaigns, too, are systematic: a single format might be used serially, placed in sequential issues of a magazine, or the ads within a campaign might appear simultaneously in multiple publications, but in different formats—single page, double-page spread, half-page vertical or horizontal, and so on. Even environmental design work is systematic in that it addresses the integration of information and visual experience among multiple spaces: for example, the exterior and entry lobby of a building, a set of exhibit spaces, or public areas such as shopping centers or mass transit stations.

These two systems are rigid, or programmatic, meaning the rules that define the system are applied consistently to every part in a particular order or position, with limited variation present.

In the website, a four-column grid anticipates different conditions that might arise for content, whether there may be a single image with complex text support or mutliple images in a gallery formation. Text is styled consistently with respect to its hierarchic function. STUDIO DIEGO FEIJOO SPAIN

In the packaging, the same kinds of text elements are listed top to bottom, in the same order and treatment; an inset photograph accompanies the text and may be positioned below it—or, if the available space demands, embedded within the text's justified area. Limited color changes in the typography are a restrained variation. P&W DESIGN CONSULTANTS UNITED KINGDOM

Because of this aspect, a designer's understanding of the visual language he or she is creating for such work is critical: The language itself must remain unquestionably unified, but also must accommodate changes in format, viewing conditions, informational complexity, and methods of production. The project's visual logic must be managed such that its elements are of a distinct kind; that their compositional relationships are equally distinct; and that when changes occur in the nature of individual elements, as well as among their relationships, that these changes are speaking the same language. Alongside such needed adaptation, being able to introduce variations within a system also prevents the experience from becoming monotonous for the audience.

Systems often are extremely programmatic and rigorously consistent—but they also may be remarkably organic, almost to the point of seeming random. The characteristics of the system depend on the content: how it is ordered or sequenced, how many different kinds of parts it may have, and how such organizational qualities must be expressed to convey an appropriate tone or concept that will continually engage and refresh the audience.

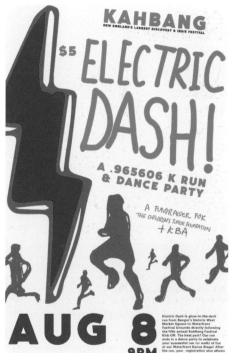

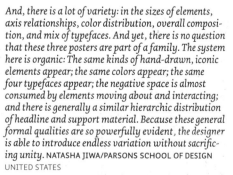

This project—a series of posters promoting a city's cultural festival—present few, if any, of the complex requirements of the projects on the opposite page. The formats are large, yet the volume of information is relatively small. This condition frees the designer to explore greater variety in position and scale relationships as part of the visual language.

And, there is a lot of variety: in the sizes of elements, axis relationships, color distribution, overall composition, and mix of typefaces. And yet, there is no question that these three posters are part of a family. The system here is organic: The same kinds of hand-drawn, iconic elements appear; the same colors appear; the same four typefaces appear; the negative space is almost consumed by elements moving about and interacting; and there is generally a similar hierarchic distribution of headline and support material. Because these general formal qualities are so powerfully evident, the designer is able to introduce endless variation without sacrificing unity. NATASHA JIWA/PARSONS SCHOOL OF DESIGN
UNITED STATES

Ordering Content Figuring out what goes where, in what order, and how it should be arranged from an informational or experiential standpoint is the first task at hand, and it demands a lot from a designer. A client might supply some content in a particular order, but the designer really has to understand the content and, potentially, reorder it when necessary to improve its clarity or enhance its conceptual aspects. Further, the content may not be presented all at one time, in one place, or all in the same format. A brand identity program, for example, is a system whose ordering must be considered not only sequentially, but among a multitude of items. It may integrate such components as stationery, website, brochures, ad campaigns, posters, environmental signage, and vehicle livery with each of these necessitating unique requirements for ordering. Some components of this complex system come with obvious roles, of course. And, again, the client may impose certain criteria for the ordering of others. Breaking content down within an individual part or sequence in the system will likely involve dialogue between client and designer. On a visual level, how much appears at any given time and the actual arrangement are decisions a designer alone must make.

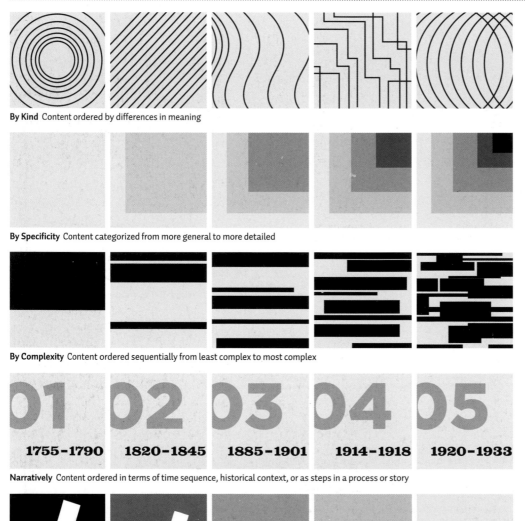

By Kind Content ordered by differences in meaning

By Specificity Content categorized from more general to more detailed

By Complexity Content ordered sequentially from least complex to most complex

01 02 03 04 05

1755–1790 1820–1845 1885–1901 1914–1918 1920–1933

Narratively Content ordered in terms of time sequence, historical context, or as steps in a process or story

By Relevance Content ordered according to which information is most important

Strategies for organizing content involve sorting the material into manageable parts that may relate to each other in different ways, as seen at left. Some strategies are often applied to particular kinds of projects to address audience expectations. Newspapers, for example, organize information based on local relevance and timeliness; packaging divides information among its sides based relevance and complexity.

This kind of thinking corresponds directly to projects of a clearly sequential nature: websites, books, motion sequences, and environmental wayfinding. But it also is applicable to projects that are serial, or those made up of many independent parts, such as a branding program, in that one may consider a viewer's interaction with a brand as a sequential activity. That is, a viewer may encounter each instance of a brand—"touch-points," or "applications," such as an ad, a business card, a web-site, the product package, and so on—in a kind of sequence. From launch ads that direct a viewer to a website, where the viewer buys a product that is packaged a certain way and includes an invoice form, branding agencies often consider, and attempt to impose, a particular order in which consumers will traverse a brand's individual communications as a kind of program.

In its raw form, the amount of information—both visual and verbal—that the designer discovers *must* appear in each component provides him or her with a first glimpse of compositional possibilities and limitations, meaning: even before exploring whether the images are photographs or illustrations, whether the typeface is this sans serif or that, the designer will be able to see how much material exists—and what kinds are present—in each component.

These facts become the basis for the compositional approach that will underpin the system; it grows from factual givens and necessities, not the other way around—trying to fit stuff into a preconceived compositional structure. This by no means downplays the role of intuiton: Designers are visual thinkers, so naturally the ordering of the content will happen in dialogue with the designer's visual imagination (which it should be). But the bare fact that

only three lines of text and a picture will be present in one instance, for example, and 2,000 words will be accompanied by four pictures in another instance, is going to drive the designer's compositional ideas as he or she tries to resolve this disparity so that such wildly different conditions can play by the same rules—and so become unified throughout.

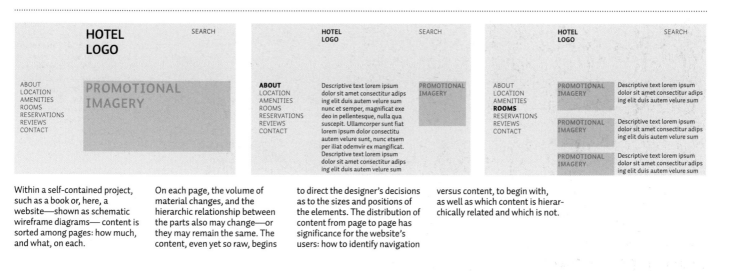

Within a self-contained project, such as a book or, here, a website—shown as schematic wireframe diagrams— content is sorted among pages: how much, and what, on each.

On each page, the volume of material changes, and the hierarchic relationship between the parts also may change—or they may remain the same. The content, even yet so raw, begins

to direct the designer's decisions as to the sizes and positions of the elements. The distribution of content from page to page has significance for the website's users: how to identify navigation

versus content, to begin with, as well as which content is hierarchically related and which is not.

On a single page of the site (the home page, in this case) sorting the same content in different ways might call attention to specific parts over others and

thereby affect the emphasis of these specific parts. Convention generally dictates that material that comes first should be assumed to have greater

significance. Adjusting the order to create a narrative flow that enhances focus on specific content changes the experience.

System Function into System Form As the content's distribution reveals conditions of necessity and possibility, the designer now must begin to identify specific visual attributes and their particular interaction. What kinds of image material are needed to communicate clearly? How are the images and the text visually and conceptually related? How does the text's hierarchy affect its size and positioning, as well as its style? These questions have to do with concept—first, what information is expository, or literally needed for understanding ("These are a set of available health care services"); and second, what narrative, if any, will frame the information ("These health care services provide peace of mind" or "These health care services build a healthy community"). The base of the system's visual language will address the content's exposition—what and how—through the choice of image subject matter and the composition of text and image elements; form language—shapes, media, color, iconography, and typfaces—will address the narrative aspects. From the expository standpoint, if the designer sees that every part of the system involves three kinds of text, but images appear only occasionally, the designer then knows that the typography will be a more pronounced component of the visual language: that it is likely to need two or three columns, and

Every part of this system performs the same function and presents the same volumes and kinds of information. Its primary goal is to deliver a consistent (branded) experience. A language of painterly marks, in a fresh, cool palette, creates a changing backdrop for centered text, set all caps in a sans serif and foil stamped in gold. **ANAGRAMA** MEXICO

possibly three font styles, and that it will often require more dramatic use of space—when, for example, no image is present. From the narrative standpoint, a designer's visualization of the project's subject matter may offer a direction: If the subject is life sciences, for example, the designer may focus on a use of dots to suggest molecules, which may then mean that images will be cropped into circular forms, and that one of the three fonts will have ball serifs. If a

logo is part of the system (as it often is), its own visual language may further help the designer identify the form language—a very linear logo may suggest that lines are used throughout the system—as well as its exposition, indicating the proportions of spatial breaks, or opportunities for the alignments of type elements, as a way of integrating the logo.

Answering these questions involves switching between analytical and intuitive study of the content—messing around with the material to see what's possible, analyzing the visual and conceptual clarity of the results, and then returning to freer exploration to test whether the analysis is accurate or useful. The designer's conclusions—this kind of image, these fonts and shapes—define the first rules that will contribute to the system's consistency.

Although the typography throughout this identity program is rigidly styled on a consistent grid, the designer has introduced flexibility in form at every level: variations in the visual shape of the logotype lockup; a series of abstract linear illustrations that can be used in a number of ways; and a strong color palette of analogous hues with varying levels of intensity.
CLEMENS THÉOBERT SCHEDLER AUSTRIA

Rules and Variables: Enforcing Consistency and Creating Flexibility The nature of a system is one of reliability and deviation held in dynamic tension; establishing this tension is a difficult task. At one extreme, lies the risk of disintegrating the visual coherence that is needed for a unified and memorable experience in an effort to continually refresh the viewer. At the other extreme, treating material too consistently will kill the project's energy; it might even do the material a disservice, decreasing the clarity of either the concept or informational relationships by not allowing these to flex as they must. The renowned designer, Massimo Vignelli—known chiefly for his rigorous use of grid structures—put it this way: "A [structure] is like a cage with a lion in it, and the designer is the lion-tamer; playing with the lion is entertaining . . . but the lion-tamer has to know when to get out so he doesn't get eaten."

A designer's understanding of the internal logic of the visual language he or she is creating is paramount. Form identities, media, and compositional approaches, derived from the narrative concept and the most useful way of distributing the content, as noted, are the primary rules that every part of the system must follow in some way. It's the "in some way" part that leads to a set of secondary rules—reinterpretation of the primary rules themselves,

RIGID   ORGANIC

Series of promotional posters for an experimental dance event
KIYOKO SHIROMASA/PARSONS SCHOOL OF DESIGN
UNITED STATES

Form Organic, figural shapes are spliced along alternating diagonal axes.

Color Three ink colors of similar intensity are distributed randomly among images and text.

Typography One sans-serif face, in a single weight, styles spliced headlines that change size; text responds to the splice angles.

Imagery Soft-focus, monotone photographs of silhouetted figures, spliced along diagonals of changing axis

Composition Asymmetrical distribution of material across triangular spatial breaks or formal variation. Every form element or relationship may be varied, but these variations must be intrinsically related to the element or relationship they vary. The fact of dots, ordered in a grid, for example, might be a primary rule; the number of dots, their sizes, the spaces between them, and the proportions of the grid in which they're ordered may be changed without impairing the reliability of recognition. At the same time, just these few variables on only one rule can result in thousands of variations—flexibility. The first step is to consider what the components of that visual logic are, and, if necessary, make a written list of them. Asking simple questions of oneself is a great way to begin the evaluation process—and answering such questions as simply as possible is equally important. "What are the visual components of this project?" "What kind of images am I using?" "Is geometry important in the shapes or relationship?" "Is there spatial depth, and, if so, what creates it—transparency, scale change, overlap?" "Do I sense movement, and, if so, is it lateral, vertical, frenzied, calm and repeated?" Once the designer has answers to these questions, focusing on one or two of the variables for each rule will create a visual system that may be continually updated without ever losing its fundamental visual consistency.

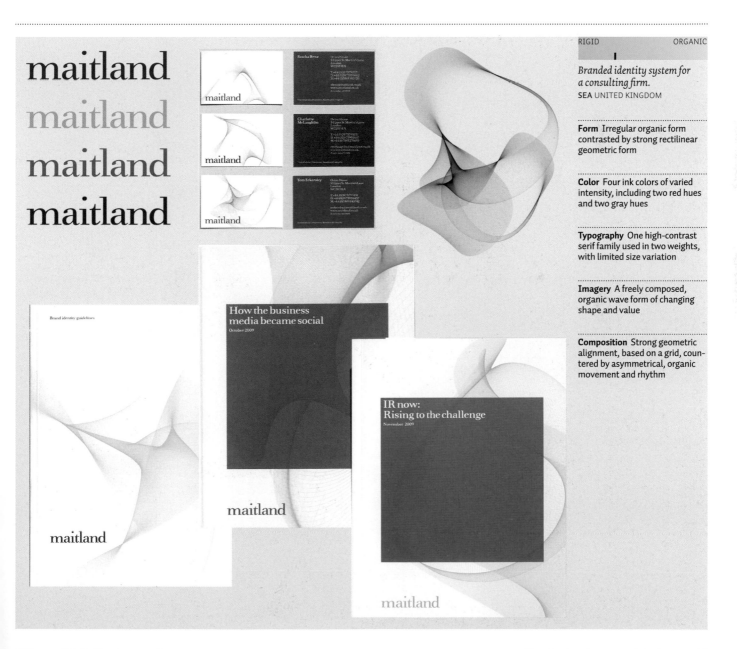

RIGID   ORGANIC

Branded identity system for a consulting firm.
SEA UNITED KINGDOM

Form Irregular organic form contrasted by strong rectilinear geometric form

Color Four ink colors of varied intensity, including two red hues and two gray hues

Typography One high-contrast serif family used in two weights, with limited size variation

Imagery A freely composed, organic wave form of changing shape and value

Composition Strong geometric alignment, based on a grid, countered by asymmetrical, organic movement and rhythm

RIGID   **ORGANIC**

Packaging design for high-end chocolates
TEMPLIN BRINK DESIGN
UNITED STATES

Form Horizontal rectangle of consistent proportion, contrasted by patterns of irregular rhythm

Color A universal deep, cool brown hue, contrasted by three intense pure hues

Typography Hand-drawn script face combined with geometric sans-serif face

Imagery Hand-drawn, linear patterns that change in shaping and rhythm

Composition Vertical pattern emphasis

RIGID   **ORGANIC**

Branded collateral system for an architecture firm
DESIGN RANCH UNITED STATES

Form Geometric planes and line patterns created by grids and typography, and logo dot

Color A warm gray, applied to imagery, contrasts an intense red-orange hue, applied to type.

Typography One condensed, relatively square-shouldered sans-serif family—set mostly all uppercase; alternately conforming to a grid and violating it

Imagery Low-contrast, black-and-white photography

Composition Rigid grid structure countered by random cropping of typographic elements

Identity, packaging, and advertising for a sporting goods manufacturer DEBRA OHAYON/ PARSONS SCHOOL OF DESIGN UNITED STATES

Form Primarily a contrast of line weights and rectilinear fields that contain information

Color Black and a warm neutral, accented by an intense red that is applied in differing proportions, depending on use: as line in type, as heavy line in packaging, and as rectangle in advertising

Typography One monospace sans serif, set all uppercase in flush-left alignment throughout

Imagery Linear iconography contrasted by monochrome black-and-white photography

Composition Geometric spatial breaks of varied proportion

I RATHER FANCY A BITER.

BITER:
A STONE THAT JUST TOUCHES THE OUTER EDGE OF THE 12' CIRCLE, THUS REMAINING IN PLAY.

ROCK HARD, ROCK ON.

stone's throw

It's worth noting that the more rules, the greater the number of variables for each, and the more extreme the expression of each variable, the more organic the system will be—and so greater the potential for the system to fall apart. Limit the rules to two or three, total, as well as the numbers, kinds, and degrees of, their variations: the result will be a more easily controllable, and unified, system. Lest this suggestion of restraint seem overly limiting, remember

the example of the dots in a grid, described previously on page 279: the simplest rule may instigate a profusion of variations. Further, the rules and their individual variations must be applied consistently among the respective parts to which they correspond. If certain colors have been assigned to specific levels of the typographic hierarchy, don't suddenly decide in some instance to switch it up. Instead, where discrepancies arise—either out of need

or desire—consider these as incentive to reinvestigate the entire color system to see what changes need to be implemented. The discrepancy may be edited out or, perhaps, it may give rise to a new rule that must be resolved among existing elements.

RIGID   ORGANIC

Series of book covers for a limited-edition imprint
CORALIE BICKFORD-SMITH
UNITED KINGDOM

Form Dense, intricate patterns

Color A variety of two-color combinations, either analogous or complementary

Typography One transitional serif face, in one weight, centered

Imagery Patterns made of pictorial elements

Composition Symmetrical

RIGID   ORGANIC

Series of book covers for a limited-edition imprint
PARALLAX AUSTRALIA

Form Linear patterns defined by square, triangle, and circle

Color Solid black and white

Typography One high-contrast, bold-weight serif and one sans-serif face used in bold and regular weights

Imagery A universal pattern composition, cropped differently within each format

Composition Asymmetrical, grid-based

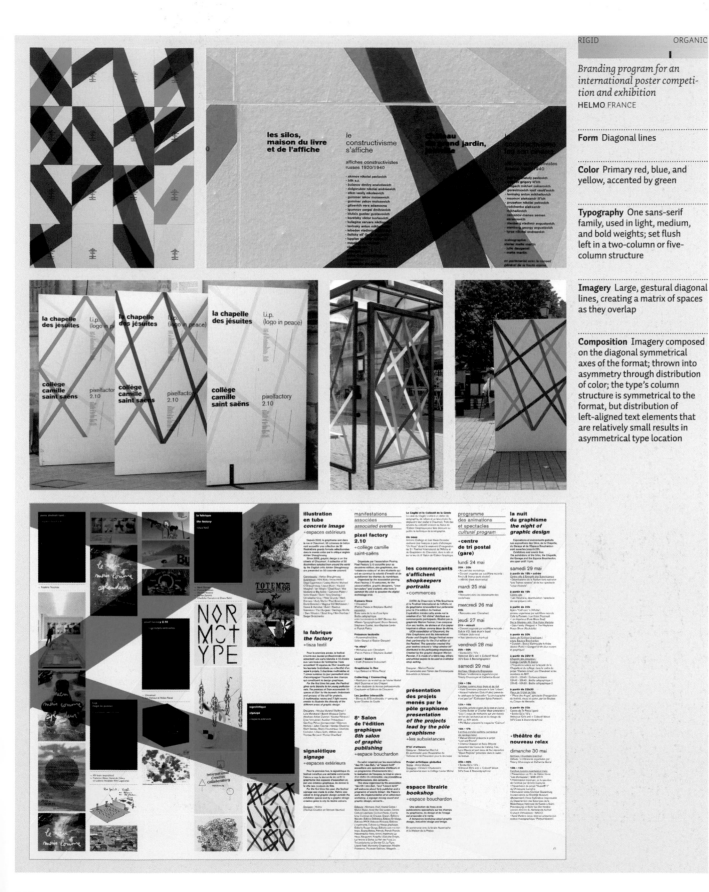

Branding program for an international poster competition and exhibition
HELMO FRANCE

Form Diagonal lines

Color Primary red, blue, and yellow, accented by green

Typography One sans-serif family, used in light, medium, and bold weights; set flush left in a two-column or five-column structure

Imagery Large, gestural diagonal lines, creating a matrix of spaces as they overlap

Composition Imagery composed on the diagonal symmetrical axes of the format; thrown into asymmetry through distribution of color; the type's column structure is symmetrical to the format, but distribution of left-aligned text elements that are relatively small results in asymmetrical type location

Visual Pacing Building off the idea of variation, the rhythmic pacing of visual presentation from part to part in a system within a sequence-based format—a publication, a website, a physical environment, or a motion sequence—can be a powerful means of keeping a system lively. Pacing can be understood as a kind of cadence or "timing" a viewer will apprehend from one part to another, as well as the degree of dynamism or activity they perceive.

By varying this rhythm from slow to fast, or from quiet to dynamic, the designer can accomplish several goals. One of these is strictly visual: Each turn of a page engages the reader in a new way by varying the presentation. Another result might be that the reader is cued to a significant content change, thereby clarifying informational function. To some degree, the pacing of material relates directly to its ordering, or distribution (see page 274). The ordering process accounts for location and actual sequence of raw content, whereas pacing is concerned with the formal variation that has been imposed upon it—that is, its varying levels of contrast, as defined by the form language, in the particular sequence in which it has been distributed. Ordering is about function; pacing is about feeling. Indeed, such organization may be an intrinsic part of the concept that governs the visual presentation of the content.

The designer of this book focused on value progressions as a way to create distinction between, and flow within, various sections. The above thumbnail overview of all the book's spreads shows a pronounced cadence of dark-to-light change from beginning to end—in the first section versus the remainder, and within each section. L2M3 GERMANY

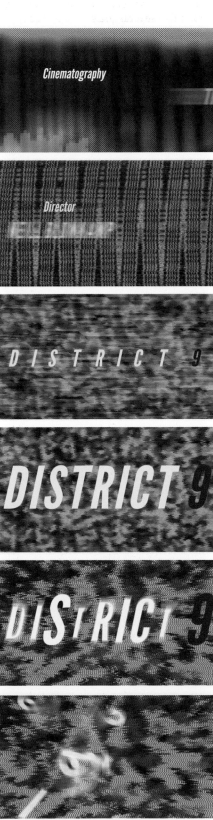

Content organization often derives directly from generally accepted (even legally required) conventions as to how particular content ought to be delivered. For example, the general public assumes that the upper levels of a website's content will be more general, each directing them toward more specific content as they delve further into the site. Conventions also abound for publications such as books or periodicals, where the average reader assumes a certain

After the film's conceptual slogan is introduced through a rapid, jarring series of transitions, the majority of this opening title sequence builds suspense through a slower pacing strategy. Production credits are introduced by sliding them laterally across the screen while they dissolve in and out of view, and the background texture begins slowly to morph in a reference to a character's alien transformation. In a startling shift, the pattern rapidly distorts and the film's title emerges from deep space to explode out of the frame. The pacing in the sequence mirrors that of the film's events.

KIYOTAKA SUMIOSHI/PARSONS SCHOOL OF DESIGN
UNITED STATES

kind of introductory sequence, followed by sections or chapters that group related or sequential content. The designer may get some sense of a project's potential pacing while ordering its content, but it ultimately depends on the message he or she is trying to convey with the system's rules. Throughout a sequence of page spreads in a publication, for example, application of the system's rules for the sizes, weights, and styles of various text elements will automatically create a recognizable rhythm that will likely support the informational hierarchy. However, this intrinsic pacing may seem, at the designer's discretion, too even, or quietly paced, in the context of his or her concept; or, the designer may decide that this quietness generally is appropriate, but notices that some content elements could benefit from a pacing change that employs another of the system's formal rules to help emphasize or feature them. Subsequently, he or she may respond with additional pacing changes create tension and enhance the viewer's experience.

It could be argued that a project's pacing should derive naturally from its content's hierarchy, but it is up to the designer to balance this need with that of invigorating the viewer. Although pacing is somewhat intuitive, being methodical may initially allow the designer to see, in broad strokes, how a pacing strategy will unfold over a

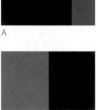

A

B

C

D

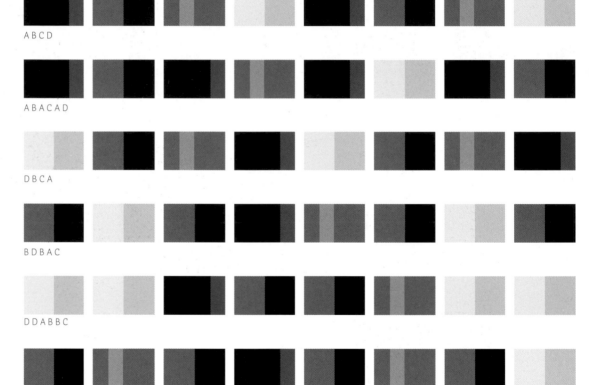

ABCD

ABACAD

DBCA

BDBAC

DDABBC

BCBABCBD

Abstractly representing different states of visual activity in a simplified form gives the designer a means of rapidly testing alternative approaches to a pacing strategy. For a hypothetical sequence of page spreads, a designer has first defined a category of change—that of value, relative to spatial break—and several possible variations, arranged from darkest to lightest, overall, and labeled accordingly.

As a second step, the designer explores different sequences of these basic variations: cycling through them in order, reversing that order, alternating between two or three, repeating some and not others, and so on.

The labels help the designer identify the nature of the rhythm in a method that is common to musical composers: A B C D, for example, or A B A C A D. Repeating a state (A B B B C D) slows the pacing in some areas, while rapid changes from state to state speed it up.

Following this study, the designer will compare the visual rhythms to the project's actual distribution of content and, in consideration of its effect on hierarchy, choose a pacing strategy to pursue, or continue looking for other strategies that more closely correspond with the content's hierarchic requirements, if it appears necessary to do so.

given sequence of material. By conceiving, in simplest terms, of visual states to be achieved—dark/light, vertical/horizontal, rapid/slow, quiet/dynamic—and creating for each an abstract or iconic sketch, a designer may quickly rough out a storyboard for a pacing strategy. It will then be necessary to compare the storyboard to the actual conditions imposed by the content to see how they may correspond—or not. With regard to this latter possibility, the designer has some leeway for imposing a pacing strategy if, in his or her estimation, it will improve the quality of the pacing without sacrificing the hierarchy—downplaying the importance of content that is actually in need of emphasis or, conversely, emphasizing that which ought to be made less important. Alternative sequencing may reveal more varied and engaging experiences for the viewer.

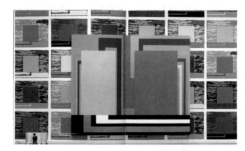 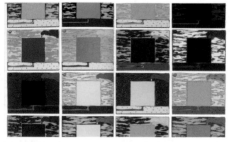

Full-bleed photographs of a gallery environment lead viewers experientially through an exhibit, moving them from room to room and then close up to artwork on individual walls. Content traveling horizontally through a spatial zone at the bottoms of the pages provides commentary and supporting photographic images. **COMA** NETHERLANDS

 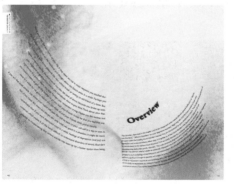 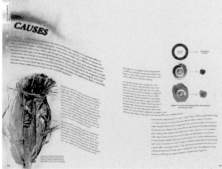

The spreads in each chapter of this book on abnormal psychology progress from arrangements of image and type that communicate the quality of a given disorder to a state of grid-based resolution that *describes various treatment options and successful case studies.* HAE JIN LEE/SCHOOL OF VISUAL ARTS UNITED STATES

Concept Development Every designer works differently, and every project is unique. Regardless, the process of designing ultimately starts with ideation, or developing concepts. Designers approach concept development from myriad directions. The very notion of *what a concept is* differs among designers: some see the content itself as the concept, while others see it as a raw thing, to benefit from embellishment, visual metaphor, allusion, or a kind of storytelling. And some designers weigh these philosophies and choose one or the other approach as appropriate at a given time. The process of ideation involves research. To craft a visual form for an idea that supports all its richness, a designer must first fully understand that idea. There are many means of researching material: Comparing existing projects of a similar nature; making brainstorming lists and mind-maps; collecting images or objects by association; and simply sketching intuitively. Many designers follow a staged process learned from early formal training, even if they are very experienced: researching, and then brainstorming as many different ideas as possible; comparing these to find aspects that are potentially useful, or which, if any, may be combined to mutually enhance each other; focusing on the result of this comparison to construct the necessary parts of the

Comparative Research
One important method of research is collecting samples of design work that is related to the project one is conceptualizing—potentially for inspiration but, more importantly, to establish a sense of the context in which one's project will ultimately find itself. Seeing how other designers have communicated a given idea helps understand not only the expectations of the project's intended audience but also of what conceptual directions to beware in favor of those that will help differentiate the work being undertaken for the project at hand.

List-Base Brainstorming and Mind-Mapping
Most people are familiar with brainstorming in the form of a written list. A mind-map is a form of diagrammatic brainstorming that allows a designer to track the paths from association to association and—even better—to see when particular associations appear along different paths, suggesting rich narrative interconnections between seemingly unrelated ideas.

Making Mood Boards
Another method of research is to collect visual material that seems somehow relevant—either literally or metaphorically, by way of association. Such material might include images of people, found objects, fabric swatches, chips of paint, and even text like poems or excerpts from literature. The materials are then assembled onto boards to create a kind of library of feelings and ideas (hence, "mood boards").

Visual Exploration
The designer examines a range of different approaches to understand their respective potentials in the given context: visual brainstorming to discover possibilities. The goal of this phase is not to arrive at any conclusions—and never to preconceive the outcome—but, rather, to roughly and rapidly generate as many ideas as can be.

project; and then refining the parts at increasingly detailed levels. In some sense, every stage of the design process is one of exploration, so it's important to really understand what that means: investigating, without preconception. To envision an end result usually results in a formulaic response or cliché; it blinds one to potentially more inventive solutions. At every step, the designer must accept the exploration's results, whether potentially successful or not: The point is to discover what is effective and discard that which isn't. Being open to rethinking is critical. Try not to like anything in advance: Find what works and then like it because it does. Once the designer identifies the best concept, then builds and evolves it, he or she will follow a final process of clarifying the message and refining its formal aspects to achieve a state of resolution, a condition in which the project's visual attributes have become somewhat singular: indisputably embodying particular qualities that seem considered, well-crafted, decisive and, in the context of its eventual environment, will seem the one best way for it to be.

The general rule of this investigative process is "The more, and the more different, the better." There's no point in getting caught up in refining any single idea until a multitude exist from which to make comparisons and, eventually, a selection of one or several that seem most viable.

The visual development stages shown here as a typical example of the design process are from the author's own work in creating a visual identity for Streamline Healthcare Services, a medical billing consultancy.

Focus and Testing
Comparing the results of the exploration, the designer evaluates which possibility—or combinations thereof—may yield the most interesting and clearest direction for the visualization of the subject.

Refinement
As the project takes shape, the designer experiments with variations—in scale, rhythm, position, and so on—to determine how these options confuse, clarify, or augment the communication on both conceptual and formal levels. Not to be confused with "clean-up" or mere simplification, this stage concerns editing the form to clarify relationships—to bring them to a state in which they appear purposeful and somehow complete.

Design Process and Workflow In a practical or business context the approach to workflow usually follows a process similar to that of concept development: research and strategic planning; creating visual form; refining the design through a process of revisions; and, finally, implementing the project by the appropriate means—printing, coding, fabricating, and so on. Every project, being different, oftentimes will alter this process as unique contingencies arise, but the work process outlined here is representative of the majority of situations. A designer or studio usually will show a prospective client a portfolio of completed projects to demonstrate their expertise; the client will describe the goals to be achieved, including time frame; and client and designer will agree on a contract for services and appropriate fees.

Research and Strategy

The designer or studio engages in an audit of competitors' materials to determine how best to position the project's communication, relative to the client's stated goals. The audit considers existing visual languages, as well as the audience's cultural expectations, to form a framework for determining what approaches may be useful to consider. Based on their findings and, in conjunction with more conventional library and online research, mind-mapping, collection of marketing data, testing with focus groups, buidling mood boards, and so on—the designer or studio will formulate a written strategy, or creative brief, that outlines their intended creative process for the client.

Competitive Audit

Conceptual Research

Data Collection

Audience/Cultural Analysis

Focus Testing

Marketing Research

Brainstorming and Mind-Mapping

Mood Boards

Formulation of Strategy

Creative Brief

Visual Design Development

Armed with the creative brief, the designer (or design team) embarks on visualizing the communication in alternative ways that will achieve the client's goals. To be considered are the project's format, the ordering of content, how and where it will be encountered by its audience—as well as, of course, possibilities for its visual language. Preliminary concept studies will be reviewed internally to focus on specific directions, and these will then be evolved to a somewhat refined level so that the client can understand how they work. Typically, three to five concepts in the form of rough prototypes, or "comps" (short for "comprehensive rough") are presented to the client.

Revisions and Refinement

Upon the client's review and, hopefully, approval of one of the concepts presented, the designer or team will then build out the remainder of the project and address any concerns the client has raised. During this stage, there are likely to be several phases of back-and-forth review of the project between the designer(s) and the client. In addition to revising and possibly correcting hierarchic or functionality problems, the designer(s) also will be steadily refining the visual language of the project's parts, clarifying image and color use, details of weight, spacing, and structure in its typography, and so on. After a previously agreed-upon number of rounds of revisions, by which point the designer(s) have achieved resolution, the client will approve the project for production.

Implementation

With the project's visual design finally approved, the designer(s) focus attention on its production or fabrication—whether this entails printing, coding, fabricating and installing objects, and so on. For whatever production process is required, the designer(s) create the artwork or digital files as requested by a specialist engaged to perform the production work. Generally, designer(s) will seek cost estimates from several specialists for whatever production services are needed, selecting the most appropriate provider based on their expertise, and in consideration of the client's budget. The designer(s) will see prototypes or proofs of the work to check its quality and often may personally oversee the production process.

Concept Exploration

Internal Review and Critique

Investigation of Media for Production

Concept Selections

Constructing and Testing

Problem Solving

Creation of Rough Prototypes

Presentation to Client

Creation of Additional Components

Addressing Client Concerns

More Specific Problem Solving

Clarifying Hierarchy

Fine-Tuning Color and Image Logic

Subcontracting Photography/Illustration

Detailed Typesetting and Styling

Exploring Relevant Media in Depth

Proofreading and Visual Corrections

Submission to Client for Final Approval

Formulation of Production Specifications

Requesting Cost Estimates for Production

Contracting Production Specialists

Creating Relevant Artwork or Files

Reviewing Proofs or Prototypes

Correcting Files to Improve Quality

Overseeing Production or Fabrication

Delivery of Realized Project

Good Natured Cooking, Inc. Brand Identity

A REAL-WORLD CASE STUDY

TIMOTHY SAMARA UNITED STATES

For a certified macrobiotic chef's new business venture that included a mix of services—nutrition coaching and menu planning, personal chef engagements, public speaking and educational workshops, and food writing—the designer developed a visual brand that would crystallize the client's innovative approach to enjoyable, healthy eating grounded in educated choices over fads, organic and seasonally available foods, and flavor.

The project encompassed naming the company, strategic planning and, ultimately, the creation of an identifier, or logo, and a system of print and digital applications. Comprehensive research and a competitive audit segued into visual exploration for the company's logo. The resulting mark was a clean, contemporary, linear icon combining messages about cooking, farming, and a nod to the Asian influence on macrobiotic cooking. With the logo approved,

Research began with a review of existing similar brands to define market context and audience, exploiting the Internet, in-store product analysis, and the designer's library of brand-identity literature. Together with exploration of macrobiotic culture and healing arts, this research created a foundation for the designer's visual ideation of a logo.

From more than thirty options that tested nonpictorial symbols, icons, letter/image combinations, and purely typographic ideas, six were presented to the client—and two were chosen for refinement. The final mark, together with its typography, appears immediately above—an icon that depicts a fork growing from roots in the earth. Its language and proportion refers obliquely to Asian "chop" signatures found on scrolls.

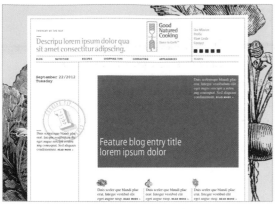

the designer could address color and typography that would accompany the symbol, paving the way for a second extensive investigation of visual languages that would create an overall system for application to stationery, a blog and website, advertising and, eventually, packaging for a line of cooking products. The designer presented the client with two concepts for the system's brand language; together, he and the client selected one for refinement.

AGNRHaefg&?!12
AGNRHaefg&?!12
AGNRHaefg&?!12
Primary Typography

AGNRHaefg&?!12
AGNRHaefg&?!12
Secondary Typography

AGNCaefg&?!123
AGNRHaefg&?!
Accent Faces

Primary Color Palette

Secondary Color Palette

While still refining the logo, the designer explored several possibiltiies for evolving a brand language for applications, but was drawn to two in particular: one focused on engravings that evoked seasonality and natural, Old-World cooking ideas; and one focused on clean, silhouetted photography with a family of graphical patterns that carried a more professionally culinary quality. The client immediately chose the engraving direction. The subject of a farm in that study, initially

appealing, seemed off-message and so was replaced by images of fruits and vegetables. Color studies and comparisons of the symbol and images with various typefaces led to a palette of a rich violet and green, supported by secondary colors for particular applications.

The designer formatted a single, large-scale composition of engraved images in a dense pattern to be used throughout print and online applications; it may be cropped in a variety of ways.

The logo itself gave rise to a grid structure to organize material. The width of the symbol is multiplied by three to form supercolumns that may be subdivided or grouped for larger text applications.

The selected brand language that focused on nineteenth-century engravings of vegetables as a backdrop underwent a series of revisions for composition. Initially, individual images were to be loosely composed, but the complexity and detail of the images, when used as separate elements, competed with simpler planar areas where product information would go. Instead, a dense pattern of the images was developed, to be cropped as needed; fields for information were divided into a column grid based on the width of the logo icon, and the business stationery and web architecture were designed around this structure. Rule lines were introduced as part of the language to separate text hierarchies and bring greater detail to the materials. The form language was extended to a modular system of advertising formats designed to incorporate varied image styles for different messaging.

At the time of this writing, the stationery was complete, the first ads published, and the website was nearing its projected launch date.

The final website templates at left show the engraving pattern used as a backdrop for a flat plane that contains branding and informational content, including photography. The color-band solution to a legibility and contrast problem created by reversing type out from an image contributed a new graphical element that was later incorporated into the print advertising system shown above and to the right.

A full-size print of the engraving art is inserted into the folder as a flysheet; it appears behind the letterhead as a physical backdrop. The flysheet is held in place by a sticker that wraps the folder's foredge.

Headline lorem
ipsum dolor
sitat duis autem.

Good
Natured
Cooking

Chef Services
Nutrition Coaching
Educational
Workshops and
Presentations

GOODNATUREDCOOKING.COM

Chef Services
Nutrition Coaching
Educational Workshops and
Presentations

Headline
lorem ipsum
dolor sitat
duis autem
semper.

Good
Natured
Cooking

GOODNATUREDCOOKING.COM

down to Earth

Headline lorem
ipsum dolor
sitat duis autem.

Good
Natured
Cooking

GOODNATUREDCOOKING.COM

Chef Services
Nutrition Coaching
Educational
Workshops and
Presentations

down to Earth

Headline lorem
ipsum dolor sitat
duis autem nuc
et semper.

Good
Natured
Cooking

Chef Services
Nutrition Coaching
Educational
Workshops and
Presentations

GOODNATUREDCOOKING.COM

down to Earth

No, you don't have
to eat like a rabbit.
Although I've noticed
the incidence of
diabetes is really low
among rabbits.

GOODNATUREDCOOKING.COM

Good
Natured
Cooking

down to Earth

lindag@
goodnatured
cooking.com

407.947.9988

PO Box 502
Norfolk, CT 06058

down to Earth

goodnaturedcooking.com

Good
Natured
Cooking

Linda Garrettson

Chef/Owner
Nutrition Coach
Food Writer

The stationery is printed in three spot ink colors on a muted ivory paper stock that adds warmth to the presentation. The inks are overprinted to achieve specific interplay of the violet and green hues. Supporting elements, whether an engraving or the company's tag line, "Down to Earth," are printed in a slightly desaturated, medium-light value yellow-green ink as a way of enhancing spatial depth, adding texture, and creating a chromatic transition between the logo and the paper. This color system, together with a hotter pink hue, is used interchangeably in the advertising system. The ads themselves are modular and may be built to any proportion using the logo-based grid so as to fit the formats of different publications. The image area is designed to accept a variety of image types so that campaigns produced at various times may be conceived of with flexibility.

CAUSIN' SOME TROUBLE:

WHEN AND WHY TO BREAK EVERY RULE IN THIS BOOK

Don't expect theory to determine how things look.

MICHAEL ROCK/DESIGNER AND EDUCATOR / *Principal, 2x4, New York*

Rules in graphic design exist as guidelines that provide context for evaluating work and serve to help designers avoid problems that interfere with communication. It is often said, however, that rules are made to be broken, and this is never truer than in design. No two projects are alike: Every project comes with different requirements, different ideas to be expressed and, often-times, audiences with very particular needs. No design approach is ever out of bounds or "illegal"—thou shalt not, on pain of death. In breaking rules, it is important for designers to understand what a rule means and, most importantly, what will happen when the rule is broken. Some rules are less flexible than others, and there is likely to be a trade-off in breaking any rule—something will be gained, and something lost. The designer must decide whether the sacrifice is acceptable and ultimately be prepared to accept the consequence of the decision. Once a designer feels confident that he or she understands how the rules work and what the effects of breaking them will be, a designer must decide why, when, and how. Some of the greatest innovations in graphic design will happen when the designer knowingly—and intelligently—throws the rule book away.

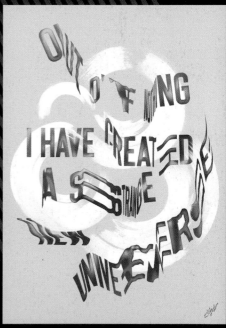

SAWDUST UNITED KINGDOM

HAVE A CONCEPT. BREAKING IT:

Sometimes, the content needs to speak with as little interference as possible. This is true in the case of pure information design—in forms, for example, where the content's only requirement is to be understood very easily—but might also be true for other project types, as well. Being neutral and having no concept—presenting content very directly and efficiently, refining legibility and hierarchy, and using color and material to craft a refined artifact—is a concept unto itself. This approach can result in a quickly accessible, informative, and functionally user-centric experience, which is not without its appeal.

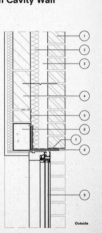
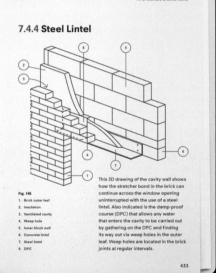

The design of this trade book approaches its subject as information to be delivered in a clear, concise, and neutral way—letting the content speak for itself. It is, after all, an instructional volume. The restrained presentation allows the book's readers to access the content without interference.
CONOR & DAVID IRELAND

7.4.3 Steel Lintel in Cavity Wall

In cavity wall construction, it is necessary to provide a lintel to both the internal and external walls. This can be done in a number of ways.

In Fig. 144, the internal wall is carried by a precast concrete lintel. The external wall of brick is supported by a steel angle fixed back to the inner leaf. The steel angle runs beyond the length of the opening and bears on the wall on either end. Its main benefit is that it allows brick coursing to continue uninterrupted on the external leaf, as can be seen in Fig. 145.

Fig. 144
1. Brick outer leaf
2. Insulation
3. Ventilated cavity
4. Inner block wall
5. Stepped DPC
6. Concrete lintel
7. Weep holes
8. Steel lintel
9. Window

Inside   Outside

7.4.4 Steel Lintel

Fig. 145
1. Brick outer leaf
2. Insulation
3. Ventilated cavity
4. Weep hole
5. Inner block wall
6. Concrete lintel
7. Steel lintel
8. DPC

This 3D drawing of the cavity wall shows how the stretcher bond in the brick can continue across the window opening uninterrupted with the use of a steel lintel. Also indicated is the damp-proof course (DPC) that allows any water that enters the cavity to be carried out by gathering on the DPC and finding its way out via weep holes in the outer leaf. Weep holes are located in the brick joints at regular intervals.

PRINCIPLES OF CONSTRUCTION

7.4 OPENINGS & JUNCTIONS

432   433

3

Drawing Techniques

There is no distinction between a drawing of construction and a thought of construction. This correlation turns drawings into the most sophisticated expressions of architectural theory.
—Marco Frascari

As you get used to the tools and principles of architectural representation, it is important to know the conventions of architectural drawing. Architectural conventions – such as representing materials, understanding scale, how and when to add dimensions and notes to your drawings, and how to indicate elements such as windows, doors and stairs – allow your drawings to be understood by others. They also allow you to 'read' the drawings of other architects.

The conventions of architectural drawing have developed over centuries and constitute a language in their own right. A clear understanding and application of these conventions allows your design intentions to be legible and clearly understood – whether by a tutor in college or a builder on site.

Like any language, it takes practice to achieve fluency. As a student of architecture, you should get into the habit of using these conventions from the outset. They will soon become second nature to you and give clarity to your own designs.

Studio Craft & Technique

by
Miriam Delaney
& Anne Gorman

COMMUNICATE— DON'T DECORATE.
BREAKING IT:

When the message warrants it, use form willy-nilly, without regard for its meaning. This, in itself, might be interpreted as a message and—on rare occasions—that message is appropriate as part of a design solution. A project concerning Baroque or Victorian aesthetics, for example, might very well benefit from extremely decorative treatments that would otherwise constitute a crime against nature.

A kaleidoscopic collage of varied form languages and image elements capture the experimental energy of a hip cultural event. Rather than attempt to parse the visual langauge for meaningful content, viewers will absorb the imagery's exuberant color and movement to interpret an appropriate feeling. VIKTOR MATIC ITALY

BE UNIVERSAL.
BREAKING IT:

Always tailor the message to the audience. For a subculture whose expectations of visual messaging are very specific—a hip-hop website, as opposed to a large-scale, general-public branding campaign—using visual metaphor, idiosyncratic stylistic treatments of type or image, and color that references their shared context will resonate more powerfully than images and color that are designed to speak to the world at large.

The audience targeted by this poster is young and interested in messages that speak to them obliquely, pose questions rather than answer them, or suggest ideas that may be anti-establishment, or discussed only within small segments of the population. While the formal manipulation of the type suggests some relationship to electronica, the image of the wild boar is a conceptual message inserted to provoke a reaction. SUPERSCRIPT FRANCE

04

SPEAK WITH ONE VISUAL VOICE.
BREAKING IT:

The quickest way to draw attention to a particular element is to make it different from everything else around it, and this can be highly effective as a communication strategy. Disharmony among visual elements, whether stylistic, compositional, or chromatic, is also a message unto itself.

Unified by their shape and bold, black exteriors, these packages of coffee are each given a radically different style of illustration to more clearly differentiate each roast. In one sense, the consistent change of the visual language in each package becomes a kind of system unto itself.

A-SIDE UNITED KINGDOM

05

IF YOU CAN DO IT WITH LESS, THEN DO IT.
BREAKING IT:

By all means, add extra stuff if it helps the message. Intricate, complicated, maze-like arrangements of form, even though somewhat daunting at first, will appeal to specific audiences. Including apparently unrelated forms or images, or creating an overload of form or texture, may add an important subtext that, in the end, helps support the project's intent.

This poster trades on the vernacular of nineteenth-century circus posters and Hatch Show prints, invoking the busy, "undesigned" aesthetic of those predecessors to create a metaphorical context for a cultural event. The addition of multiple clusters of text information at different sizes, in different styles, together with overlapping images and surreal details captures the romance of the circus and its carnival-like multitasking quality of entertainment.

THE NATIONAL GRID [JONTY VALENTINE, MAX LOZACH, AND LUKE WOOD] NEW ZEALAND

CREATE SPACE— DON'T FILL IT.

BREAKING IT:

OK, there's no good way to break this rule. An absence of negative space is a disaster and always will be. That said, allowing visual material in particular segments of a project to overwhelm the compositional space—on occasion, in response to other segments in which negative space is used liberally—can be an excellent strategy for introducing dramatic rhythm and helping focus attention on special material.

Similar to other examples presented in this section, this poster promotes its subject— alternative music perfor- mances, in this case—to a very specific, subcultural audience. The explosive rhythm of yel- low, black, and white type and blocks of color that just about fills the poster's format edge- to-edge conveys the visceral quality of the experience to be had and the wall of sound that attendees will expect.
HI: MEGI ZUMSTEIN+CLAUDIO BARANDUN GERMANY

GIVE 'EM THE ONE-TWO PUNCH.
BREAKING IT:

Presenting a multitude of items for simultaneous consideration gets the information out front quickly, leaving the viewers to decide what is most interesting or important at a particular moment—making them participate in getting the information, rather than handing it to them on a plate. If they have to work for it, they might enjoy it and remember it more easily later.

As a metaphor for a particular season's fashion collection that celebrates repurposing of design gestures and materials, this advertising poster delivers multiple levels of information simultaneously—in essence, the scattering of image and text elements takes on the quality of detritus to be picked through as a source for ideas and style.
RÉGIS TOSETTI UNITED KINGDOM

BEWARE OF SYMMETRY.
BREAKING IT:

Symmetry evokes a set of classical, Old-World, elitist messages; it can, therefore, be powerfully exploited for formal, historical, and serious material—and as a foil to more dynamic content. Tension between spatial intervals, density and openness, and light and dark becomes critical in maintaining visual activity so that the symmetry becomes elegant, lively, and austere, rather than heavy handed, stiff, and dull.

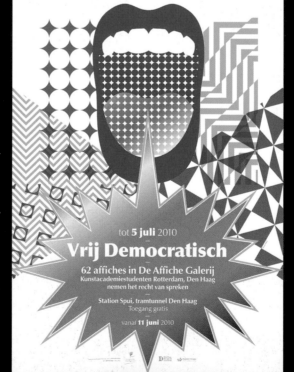

The designer of this poster very skillfully navigates its symmetry and counters any potential static presentation with pattern and icon elements that are confrontationally large and introduce compositional tension; further, the patterns are distributed to the left and right of the central axis in alternating hues of different value and temperature, drawing the eye inward and outward from the axis with different degrees of emphasis.
DENNIS KOOT NETHERLANDS

FIGHT THE FLATNESS.
BREAKING IT:

Proceed with caution. The primary danger here is causing viewers to disengage, because it is the illusion of depth and movement that creates wonderment and makes them forget that they're looking at a designed communication. Static arrangements of material, however, can be very focused and restful, an alternative to dramatic movement and deep spatial illusion, and in that sense can be useful at times.

Optically flat arrangements can provide visual punctuation to aggressive presentation, and contrasting moments of focus and introspection. A pronounced lack of spatial experience creates an altogether different feeling in a project and, when it makes sense for the message, is quite appropriate.

Brasilia
50th Anniversary

Design by Sawdust

"It is not the right angle that attracts me, nor the straight line, hard and inflexible, created by man. What attracts me is the free and sensual curve - the curve that I find in the mountains of my country, in the sinuous course of its rivers, in the body of the beloved woman."

— Oscar Niemeyer

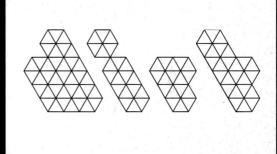

The linearity of this logo for a landscape designer, which optically flattens it out, cleverly plays with the suggestion of dimensional, cubic forms. The line structure is also reminiscent of landscape design plans.
PARALLAX AUSTRALIA

Gigantic, flat semicircles and rectangles of white and black carve out a dramatic shape cluster in this poster that carves out the title and punches the illusory depth into an almost singular plane—and punches the viewer in the proverbial gut with its unapologetic and

BREAKING IT:

Being more or less random—choosing colors whose usual association purposely conflicts with expectation—is a viable method that can achieve some surprising results. After a time, choosing color using familiar methods yields combinations that may be somewhat expected or, worse, completely uninteresting. Purposely selecting color combinations that feel awkward or disharmonious often presents unexpected options that somehow retain chromatic relationships. Additionally, a random color choice might sometimes aid in communication, depending on the nature of the project. Seeming randomness, like other messages, can be valid given the concept the designer intends to convey.

FRANÇAIS 9ᵉ

FRANÇAIS 7ᴱ

RÉPUBLIQUE ET CANTON DE NEUCHÂTEL DÉPARTEMENT DE L'ÉDUCATION, DE LA CULTURE ET DES SPORTS

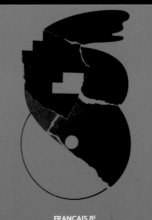

FRANÇAIS 8ᴱ

RÉPUBLIQUE ET CANTON DE NEUCHÂTEL DÉPARTEMENT DE L'ÉDUCATION, DE LA CULTURE ET DES SPORTS

The designers of this publication—part of a European city's branding program—chose color not so much at random, but in terms of defaults: the process colors magenta and yellow, combined with two tones of black. The overlap of the red ink on the yellow ink— which has been slightly adjusted toward a greener hue—creates a jarring, randomlike chromatic jumble, in concert with the middle-value neutral gray.
ONLAB GERMANY

This project follows a similar approach to color, relying on the bold primary qualities of the base process colors to emphasize the drama in the rich tones and shaping of the collaged numerals. While each of these book cover's own color is as different from the others as is possible (with regard to the color wheel), this in itself is a recognizable logic that helps unify the set.
THIBAUD TISSOT GERMANY

LESS COLOR IS MORE.

BREAKING IT:

As with all the rules, be careful and considerate when breaking this one—and always for a reason of communication. A firestorm of thousands of hues, of differing values and intensities, may not yield a specific color idea that viewers can commit to memory, but the experience of being overwhelmed by uncontrolled extravagance is surely not easily forgotten.

Rich, vibrant hues that transition through every part of the spectrum work to create a vividly sensuous support for the surreal illustration in this poster. One effect of the candy-like saturation and multiplicity of hues is that the image becomes possibly less threatening than it might if it were rendered in a limited palette.
LA BOCA UNITED KINGDOM

MASTER THE DARK AND THE LIGHT.

BREAKING IT:

A tonally quiet, soft presentation in which contrast between light and dark (or temperature and intensity) is minimized can be very effective in garnering attention, helping to separate viewers from surrounding, more active, visual activity. Low-contrast images and typography are perceived as more contemplative and elegant, rather than urgent or aggressive.

An extremely low-contrast range of dark-value tones creates a smoky, dreamlike nocturnal experience that reflects a theme of the fashion event that this poster promotes: "noir," or blackness. Although the poster's typography is reversed out to white, it is of such small scale that it nearly is absorbed into the surrounding fields of gray, darker gray, and black texture. Adding a taste of luxury—as well as exacerbating the low-contrast near invisibility of the imagery—the poster is printed on a highly reflective metallic paper stock. TSTO FINLAND

TYPE IS ONLY TYPE WHEN IT'S FRIENDLY.
BREAKING IT:

As you might guess, the relative accessibility of type greatly depends on the message being conveyed. Making portions of type illegible, overbearing, aggressive, sharp and dangerous, nerve-wracking, or fragile is perfectly acceptable—indeed, preferable—when the job calls for it. There is no excuse for typography that doesn't viscerally communicate in an appropriate way, even if this means frightening, frustrating, or confusing viewers in service of the right concept.

And—all of these attributes are present in this poster, which promotes a film festival that gives special attention to the work of directors who explore dark and disturbing themes. The typography may, in fact, be read by focusing on the boundaries where the individual lines of text meet, to find a kind of anchoring point; or, by viewing the poster from extreme angles so that the perspective renders the type more regular in appearance (much like crosswalk warnings printed in the street). The notion of "extreme viewing angle," however, as well as the film-striplike flicker, both communicate more about the poster's subject than does the text itself.
RAF VANCAMPENHOUDT + JORIS VAN AKEN NETHERLANDS

USE TWO TYPEFACE FAMILIES MAXIMUM.
BREAKING IT:

Complex text, with a great many parts, will be clarified by strong, varied changes in type style. Sometimes, you'll need many different typefaces working together to create a kind of busy texture that conveys something really important. Thinking outside the type box can be difficult, especially if you're comfortable with a select set of typefaces: So take a deep breath, close your eyes, and click the font list at random.

This stylishly elegant magazine spread derives much of its beauty from the contrasts in width, weight, structural changes, and detailing within an astutely considered mix of some ten typefaces.
VRUCHTVLEES NETHERLANDS

TREAT TYPE AS YOU WOULD IMAGE.
BREAKING IT:

There are always times when typography needs to shut up and get out of the way—especially when the type accompanies cataloged artwork or is acting in support of images that are carrying the brunt of the communication burden. In such instances, treat the type as quietly and as neutrally as possible. Even so, carefully consider its size, spacing, and stylistic presentation.

To prevent this book cover's titling type from overpowering the fire image—which is presented quietly in a dithered texture and with relatively diminished contrast—the designers chose a light-weight sans serif and low-reflection metallic foil that would cause it to sink elegeantly into the surface. The type's elegantly restrained quality is enhanced by a simple, flush left arrangement .
FINEST MAGMA GERMANY

AVOID REDUNDANT REDUNDANCIES.
BREAKING IT:

The breaking of this rule is more of a practical issue, driven by the content of a given project: If you're designing a magazine about travel, clearly the images will show what the text describes. Still, repetition of text content by image and, vice-versa, can be useful for making a point crystal clear. Subtle differences in the same subject or idea, presented verbally and visually, will add depth and richness.

Food packaging is one of those types of project that almost requires visual/verbal redundancy: Consumers want to see the food and understand its freshness or tastiness, even though the label tells them what's inside the box. This packaging system explodes the images of the contents around the edges of the format in almost surreal supersaturation of color. KREZIMIR MILOLOSA CROATIA

CREATE IMAGES— DON'T SCAVENGE.

BREAKING IT:

True, finding an image to stick into a layout tends to be quicker; sometimes, however, purposely using banal, almost meaningless or kitsch images from stock sources can be great fun, especially if the project calls for a vernacular approach or conceptually refers to the ubiquity of image content and the influence of day-to-day pop culture. But the real benefit of scavenging is acquiring pieces and parts that can be used to create custom images.

Even more intriguing is the possibility of revitalizing the understanding of very familiar, or time-worn, content by creating an unexpected relationship with imagery that has been repurposed or pulled out of its expected context.

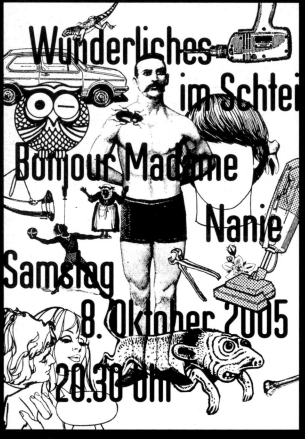

In this design of a cover for a master of highbrow literature, the designer appropriates low-culture comic book imagery to convey the disturbing political and emotional turmoil of Franz Kafka's story. BEN GRANDGENETT/SCHOOL OF VISUAL ARTS UNITED STATES

A collage of clip art from various generations delivers ambiguous messages to intrigue viewers of this poster that promotes a conceptual art exhibition. MIXER SWITZERLAND

The design of this book that explores the musical work of DJ Spooky alludes to the practice of sampling and the ubiquity of branded messages in a current context. COMA NETHERLANDS

LOOK TO HISTORY, BUT DON'T REPEAT IT.

BREAKING IT:

Don't get me wrong: history is a treasure trove for designer and public, alike. Books or exhibitions that focus on historical subjects, or invitations to period-themed events, for example, are perfect vehicles for exhuming visual style from the vaults of antiquity. The potential fun here is not so much copying the style, outright, as sampling portions thereof, adjusting them so they become new again.

This CD cover revels in its appropriation of period design style without succumbing to the wholly derivative— a difficult line to walk. The typography evokes the design sensibility of Blue Note jazz albums from the 1950s and 1960s in its use of slab-serif typefaces and black/blue/ yellow color scheme. The confrontational, close-up image is a decidedly contemporary gesture, making the layout fresh and inventive while still honoring a general style of photography from the period.
STEREOTYPE DESIGN
UNITED STATES

IGNORE FASHION. SERIOUSLY.

BREAKING IT:

Riding the current stylistic trend has occasional benefits. In choosing to do so, a designer may opt to speak directly to an audience whose subcultural zeitgeist makes them likely to bypass visual material that doesn't appear to speak to them. This is especially true when communicating to adolescents, who identify with very specific visual styles at any given moment and will ignore anything else.

Because the fashion industry, in particular, is characterized by the shifting of trends, the fact that this runway show invitation is up to the minute in its trendy, retro 1980s style Swiss Punk aesthetic is quite appropriate. And, it's visually engaging, showing a dynamic use of space and beautiful textural contrasts between type, flat geometry, and spray-painted stipple gradations.
STUDIO NEWWORK
UNITED STATES

BREAKING IT:

Ambiguity can be a good thing. While clear visual and conceptual relationships are usually favored for the sake of quick, accessible communication, introducing mixed states of being among elements—elements that appear to be in the foreground, as well as in the background, as a simple example—can create an impulse on the part of the viewer to question and investigate more thoroughly. The gap between the concrete idea and the ambiguously presented image that refers to it can provide more complex avenues of interpretation and a rich, engaging experience that yields deeper, more complex understanding.

A caveat to start: The design of this poster is remarkably confident in its contrasts, scale relationships, and conceptual deconstruction of a flag image by planes that are both flat and three dimensional at the same time. What might normally be perceived as indecision—misalignments between text and image forms that appear to be very close to aligning, deep indents in text that begin to compromise the integrity of the text's flush edges, and so on—here come off as the spontaneous results of intuitive image making. Discrepancies in these details fail to overshadow the more important aspects of a rich, ambiguous interplay between flat and spatial, solid and outline, and foreground and background.
2XGOLDSTEIN GERMANY

CONTRIBUTORS

2 FRESH
www.2fresh.com
216, 228

2XGOLDSTEIN
www.2xgoldstein.de
133, 310

344 DESIGN, LLC
www.344design.com
51

A-SIDE STUDIO
www.a-sidestudio.co.uk
300

A10 DESIGN
www.a10.com.br
18, 120, 197

ADAMSMORIOKA
www.adamsmorioka.com
13, 59, 65, 106, 145, 149, 229

AMES BROS.
www.amesbros.com
91, 207, 208

ANAGRAMA
www.anagrama.com
276

AND PARTNERS
www.andpartnersny.com
135, 195

APELOIG DESIGN
www.apeloig.com
33, 55, 123, 142, 200

ARIANE SPANIER DESIGN
www.arianespanier.com
102

ART:TECAJI
www.art-tecaji.com
198

ATIPUS S.L.
www.atipus.com
56

BACHGÄRDE A.B.
www.bachgarde.com
170, 249

**LUDOVIC BALLAND
[TYPOGRAPHY CABINET]**
www.ludovic-balland.ch
265

JONATHAN BARNBROOK
www.barnbrook.net
83, 163

BEETROOT DESIGN GROUP
www.beetroot.gr
96

MARIS BELLACK
www.marismaris.com
86, 230

CORALIE BICKFORD-SMITH
coralie@cb-smith.com
23, 54, 193, 282

BIG ACTIVE
www.bigactive.com
187, 217

BILLY BEN+ANNA HAAS
www.billyben.ch
27

BILLIE JEAN
www.billiejean.co.uk
209

SARAH BIRMINGHAM
c/o University of the Arts
www.uarts.edu
211

BRUKETA+ZINIC
www.bruketa-zinic.com
39, 126, 215, 223

BUREAU MIRKO BORSCHE
www.mirkoborsche.com
79

C+G PARTNERS, LLC
www.cgpartnersllc.com
21, 42, 57, 149, 156, 215

C. HARVEY GRAPHIC DESIGN
www.charvey.com
47, 71, 145

CAROLYN CALLES
c/o The Art Institute,
Orange County
cncalles@yahoo.com
88-89

CATHERINE CASALINO DESIGN
www.catherinecasalino.com
82, 193, 215

MYUNG HA CHANG
c/o School of Visual Arts
mchang4@sva.edu
185

TAMMY CHANG
c/o Carnegie Mellon
University
www.design.cmu.edu
166

CHENG DESIGN
www.cheng-design.com
74, 151

KELLY CHEW
kelly.chew@gmail.com
198

CHK DESIGN
www.chkdesign.com
72, 136, 148

YONG CHOI
c/o School of Visual Arts
www.sva.edu
249

YOUJIN CHOI
c/o School of Visual Arts
www.sva.edu
33, 249

CHRISTINE CHUO
c/o Carnegie Mellon
University
www.cmu.edu
166

COBRA
www.cobra.no
09, 31, 107, 163, 172, 226, 264

COMA
www.comalive.com
229, 253, 287, 308

CONOR & DAVID
www.conoranddavid.com
20, 69, 99, 298

THOMAS CSANO
www.thomascsano.com
12, 31, 51, 60, 109, 125, 199, 229,
240

CYR STUDIO
www.cyrstudio.com
201, 208

DAS BURO BRAND IDENTITY
www.dasburo.nl
27

DESIGN RANCH
www.design-ranch.com
280

DESIGN RUDI MEYER
design.rudi-meyer@
easyconnect.fr
16, 74, 185

DESIGNERS UNITED
www.designersunited.com
36

DETAIL DESIGN STUDIO
www.detail.ie
100, 126

DISTURBANCE
www.disturbance.co.za
12

DOCH DESIGN
www.dochdesign.de
188

JELENA DROBAC
www.d-ideashop.com
104, 107, 142, 215

DROTZ DESIGN
www.drotzdesign.com
105, 206

E-TYPES
www.e-types.com
46, 131, 251, 267

EARSAY
www.earsay.org
154, 167

TRISH ERNE
www.trisherne.com
251

MANUEL ESTRADA
www.manuelestrada.com
20, 22, 35, 142, 189, 192, 204,
215, 271

ESTUDIO DIEGO FEIJOO
www.dfeijoo.com
83, 170, 272

GREG FALCONI
c/o University of the Arts
www.uarts.edu
211

FINEST MAGMA
www.finestmagma.com
38, 158, 215, 227, 241, 307

FOLCH STUDIO
www.folchstudio.com
245

FORM
www.form.uk.com
48, 57

KIM FOSTER
c/o School of Visual Arts
www.sva.edu
177

FROST DESIGN
www.frostdesign.com.au
34, 124, 169, 242, 261

JESSIE GANG
c/o School of Visual Arts
www.sva.edu
82

GLASHAUS DESIGN
www.glashaus-design.com
209

GOLDEN COSMOS
www.golden-cosmos.com
14

VERA GORBUNOVA
c/o School of Visual Arts
www.sva.edu
143

ANDREW GORKOVENKO
www.gorkovenko.ru
188, 202

BEN GRANDGENETT
c/o School of Visual Arts
www.sva.edu
308

GRAPEFRUIT
www.grapefruit.ro
142

DEBORAH GRUBER
www.deborahgruber.com
215

JIL GUYON
www.jilguyon.com
244

MACIEJ HAJNRICH
www.nietylko.net
206

HAEEUN HAN
c/o School of Visual Arts
www.sva.edu
83

HELMO
www.helmo.fr
219, 283

HELMUT SCHMID DESIGN
www4.famille.ne.jp/~hsdesign
142, 171

SOOIM HEO
c/o School of Visual Arts
www.sva.edu
215

**HI: MEGI ZUMSTEIN +
CLAUDIO BARANDUN**
www.hi-web.ch
301

GERILYN HISIGER
www.gerilynbethdesigns.com
92

KATE HOOVER
khoover131@gmail.com
241